MAKING INVISIBLE LATINO ADOLESCENTS VISIBLE

MICHIGAN STATE UNIVERSITY SERIES ON CHILDREN, YOUTH, AND FAMILIES
VOLUME 7
GARLAND REFERENCE LIBRARY OF SOCIAL SCIENCE
VOLUME 1103

Michigan State University Series on Children, Youth, and Families

John Paul McKinney, *Senior Editor*
Lawrence B. Schiamberg, Amy B. Slonim, Linda Spence, Vincent J. Hoffman, and Francisco A. Villarruel, *Associate Editors*

CHILD MALTREATMENT
AND OPTIMAL CAREGIVING
IN SOCIAL CONTENTS
By Diana Baumrind

ADOLESCENT PARENTHOOD
AND EDUCATION
Exploring Alternative Programs
by Mary Pilat

UNIVERSITY-COMMUNITY
COLLABORATIONS FOR
THE TWENTY-FIRST CENTURY
*Outreach Scholarship
for Youth and Families*
edited by Richard M. Lerner
and Lou Anna K. Simon

ADOLESCENTS, CULTURES,
AND CONFLICTS
Growing Up in Contemporary Europe
edited by Jari-Erik Nurmi

TEACHING ABOUT ADOLESCENCE
An Ecological Approach
edited by John Paul McKinney
Lawrence B. Schiamberg
and Lawrence G. Shelton

AFRICAN-AMERICAN WOMEN
An Ecological Perspective
edited by Norma J. Burgess and
Eurnestine Brown

MAKING INVISIBLE LATINO
ADOLESCENTS VISIBLE
A Critical Approach to Diversity
edited by Martha Montero-Sieburth
and Francisco A. Villarruel

Making Invisible Latino Adolescents Visible
A Critical Approach to Latino Diversity

Edited by
Martha Montero-Sieburth and
Francisco A. Villarruel

Falmer Press
a member of the Taylor & Francis Group
New York & London
2000

Published in 2000 by
Falmer Press
A member of the Taylor & Francis Group
19 Union Square West
New York, NY 10003

Copyright © 2000 by Martha Montero-Sieburth and Francisco A. Villarruel

All rights reserved. No part of this book may be reprinted or reproduced or utilized in any form or by any electronic, mechanical, or other means, now known or hereafter invented, including photocopying and recording, or in any information storage or retrieval system, without permission in writing from the publisher.

10 9 8 7 6 5 4 3 2 1

Library of Congress Cataloging-in-Publication Data

Making invisible Latino adolescents visible : a critical approach
  to Latino diversity / edited by Martha Montero-Sieburth
  and Francisco Villarruel
    p. cm.—(MSU series on children, youth, and families ; v.7)
  Includes bibliographical references and index.
  ISBN 0-8153-2344-1 (alk. paper)
  1. Hispanic American teenagers—Social conditions. 2. Hispanic American teenagers—Ethnic identity 3. Multiculturalism—United States 4. United States—Ethnic relations. I. Montero-Sieburth, Martha. II. Villarruel, Francisco. III. Series: Michigan State University series on children, youth, and families ; v.7
E184.S75 M36 1999
305.235—dc21   99–35516
                                                                                                     CIP

Printed on acid-free, 250-year-life paper
Manufactured in the United States of America

This book is dedicated to my children, Barbi Kelleher, Michael Batt, Aisha Sieburth, and Derek Sieburth; to my grandchildren, Brian Russell and Caitlin Sunshine; and to future generations of Latino children and adolescents, whose lives, I hope, we may touch.

Martha Montero-Sieburth

Many people have contributed to the completion of this volume. We acknowledge the support and encouragement of Richard M. Lerner, who was a catalyst for this volume. Linda Chapel Jackson of the Institute for Children, Youth, and Families was a constant support and invaluable resource. My wife, Gail, has allowed me to devote time to this and other endeavors. Finally, I with to dedicate this volume to my daughters, Staci and Amalia, who have helped me understand issues of adolescence just a little more.

Francisco A. Villarruel

Contents

Series Editor's Preface   vii
Introduction: Latino Youth and America: Time for a Change   xi
    Francisco A. Villarruel and
    Martha Montero-Sieburth

Chapter 1: Latino Youth: Converting Challenges to Opportunities   1
    Rudy Hernández, Marcelo Siles, and Refugio I. Rochin

Chapter 2: The Impact of Growing Up Poor or Welfare-Dependent
    on the Economic Status of Young Adults   29
    Anna M. Santiago

Chapter 3: Sexual Behaviors of Latina Adolescents   61
    Antonia M. Villarruel

Chapter 4: An Ecological, Risk-Factor Examination of Latino
    Adolescents' Engagement in Sexual Activity   83
    Daniel F. Perkins and Francisco A. Villarruel

Chapter 5: The Contrast between the Pathological Attributes and
    the Status/Aspirations of Mexican American Youth   107
    Jaime Chahín

Chapter 6: The Multicultural Literacies of Precollege Latino
    Students   131
    Raimundo Mora

Chapter 7: Demystifying the Images of Latinos: Boston-Based
　　　　　Case Studies　　　　　　　　　　　　　　　　　155
　　　　　Martha Montero-Sieburth

Chapter 8: The Development of Coping Strategies among
　　　　　Urban Latino Youth: A Focus on Help-Seeking
　　　　　Orientation and Network-Related Behavior　　　203
　　　　　Ricardo D. Stanton-Salazar

Chapter 9: Family Values of Latino Adolescents　　　　　239
　　　　　*Heidie A. Vázquez García, Cynthia García Coll,
　　　　　Sumru Erkut, Odette Alarcón, and Linda R. Tropp*

Chapter 10: Authority Plus Affection: Latino Parenting during
　　　　　Adolescence　　　　　　　　　　　　　　　　265
　　　　　Maribel Vargas and Nancy A. Busch-Rossnagel

Chapter 11: Migrant Adolescents: Barriers and Opportunities
　　　　　for Creating a Promising Future　　　　　　　289
　　　　　Bertha López, Lucila Nerenberg, and Marina Valdez

Chapter 12: Child Welfare and Latino Adolescents　　　　309
　　　　　Robert M. Ortega

Afterword: *Pensamientos*　　　　　　　　　　　　　　333
　　　　　*Martha Montero-Sieburth and
　　　　　Francisco A. Villarruel*

Contributors　　　　　　　　　　　　　　　　　　　　339
Index　　　　　　　　　　　　　　　　　　　　　　　347

SERIES EDITOR'S PREFACE
Outreach Scholarship for Children, Youth, and Families
A Foreword to the Michigan State University Series on Children, Youth, and Families

The publication of Martha Montero-Sieburth and Francisco A. Villarruel's volume, *Making Invisible Latino Adolescents Visible: A Critical Approach to Latino Diversity*, signals the continued prominence and success of the Michigan State University Series on Children, Youth, and Families as a resource for scholars, researchers and practitioners whose concern is families and children in communities. The scholarly work of Montero-Sieburth and Villarruel in organizing a book which focuses on the ecology of development of Latino youth is a prime example of the creative emphasis on cutting-edge scholarship addressing the needs of a diversity of children, youth, families, and communities which the MSU Series represents. In particular, this book promises to be a seminal and landmark volume in providing a framework for understanding the experiences of Latino youth in context as well as for the development of effective interventions and programs which, in turn, derive from a contextually sensitive approach to human development. The rich and diverse array of chapters on such timely and relevant topics as sexual behavior, coping strategies, demystifying the images of Latinos, family values, migrant status, and child welfare provide insight into the rich life trajectory of Latino youth.

Furthermore, this volume is a clear illustration of the goals of the Institute for Children, Youth, and Families (ICYF), as an example of the relationship of outreach scholarship to essential issues of policy and program development which, in turn, has the potential for enhancing the lives of children, youth and families in the diverse communities which the Institute serves. Likewise the publication of this challenging and most impressive volume provides evidence that the MSU Series serves as a compendium of scholarly work reflecting the very best scholarship aimed at enhancing the life experiences of a diversity of children, youth, and families. As such, both this volume and the MSU Series provide evidence for the importance and feasibility of the mission of ICYF in integrating research and outreach.

The mission of the Institute for Children, Youth, and Families at MSU is based on a vision of the nature of a land-grant university as an academic institution with a responsibility for addressing the welfare of children, youth, and families in communities. More specifically, the mission of ICYF is shaped by an ecological perspective to human development which places the life span development of human beings in the context of the significant settings of human experience, including community, family, work and peer networks (Lerner, et al., 1994; Schiamberg, 1985, 1988). Historically, the ecological perspective has both been associated with, and a guiding frame for, colleges of home economics or, as they are more recently termed, colleges of human development, human ecology, or family and consumer sciences (Miller & Lerner, 1994). Using the ecology of human development as a conceptual framework, the Institute for Children, Youth, and Families continues to develop programs that integrate the critical notion of development in context with the attempt, indeed the necessity, of creating connections between such scholarship and social policy, program design, delivery, and evaluation.

The MSU Series is a unique collection of books, designed to provide a vehicle for the publication and transmission of research/outreach efforts characterized by the collaborative relationship (and potential relationship) between university expertise and the community. The Montero-Sieburth and Villarruel book represents the careful thinking of authors who have both worked in, and have knowledge about, the rich and broad variety of contexts for the support and enhancement of Latino youth and, as well, with the power and potential of a contextual or ecological perspective for the development of "best practice" efforts for enriching their life prospects. As universities begin to respond to continuing social pressures to apply their resources to address a variety of critical social problems, there is a compelling need for such careful thinking and best practice in helping universities and communities to frame joint programs addressing the needs of the diverse children and families that both serve. The Michigan State University Series on Children, Youth, and Families is, itself, an example of the outreach scholarship which reflects the contextual and practical policy focus of the ICYF research program. The MSU

Series Editor's Preface xi

Series publishes reference and professional books, including monographs and edited volumes, which appeal to a wide audience in communities as well as in universities, including such constituencies as scholars, practitioners, service deliverers, child and family advocates, business leaders, and policymakers. The MSU Series has substantial import and appeal to these constituencies primarily because of its focus on the integration of research and outreach and, as well, an emphasis on collaborative relationships between universities and communities.

The unique role and perspective of both ICYF and the MSU Series can be further appreciated in light of the ongoing and persisting trends for both university accountability and social contribution. In particular, the various university stakeholders, including business, government, and community leadership, are increasingly urging universities to use their research and scholarly resources to address problems of social, political, and technological relevance (Boyer, 1990; Votruba, 1992). Thus, communities are seeking a greater involvement in outreach on the part of their universities. Both ICYF and Michigan State University are committed to integrating outreach into the full fabric of university responsibility (Provost's Committee on University Outreach, 1993).

The Montero-Sieburth and Villarruel volume represents an outstanding contribution to this emerging outreach/research focus. The MSU Series board of editors, including John Paul McKinney, Vincent J. Hoffman, Lawrence B. Schiamberg, Linda Spence, and Francisco A. Villarruel, as well as the staff editor of the Institute for Children, Youth, and Families at MSU, Linda Chapel Jackson, are proud and grateful to have this path breaking book as part of the MSU Series—a book on the emerging issues and developmental patterns of Latino youth, as an example of the improving understanding of diverse communities of America.

Lawrence B. Schiamberg
Senior Editor, MSU Series

REFERENCES

Boyer, E. L. (1990). *Scholarship reconsidered: Priorities of the professoriate.* Princeton, NJ: The Carnegie Foundation for the Advancement of Teaching.

Lerner, R. M., Miller, J. R., Knott, J. H., Corey, K. E., Bynum, T. S., Hoopfer, L. C., McKinney, M. H., Abrams, L. A., Hula, R. C., & Terry, P. A. (1994). Integrating scholarship and outreach in human development research, policy, and service: A developmental contextual perspective. In D. L. Feather-

man, R. M. Lerner, & M. Perlmutter (Eds.), *Life-span development and behavior, 12* (pp. 249–273). Hillsdale, NJ: Erlbaum.
Miller, J. R., & Lerner, R. M. (1994). Integrating research and outreach: Developmental contextualism and the human ecological perspective. *Home Economics Forum, 7,* 21–28.
Provost's Committee on University Outreach. (1993). *University outreach at Michigan State University: Extending knowledge to serve society.* East Lansing: Michigan State University.
Schiamberg, L. B. (1985). *Human development* (2nd ed.). New York: MacMillan.
Schiamberg, L. B. (1988). *Child and adolescent development* (2nd ed.). New York: MacMillan.
Votruba, J. C. (1992). Promoting the extension of knowledge in service to society. *Metropolitan Universities, 3*(3), 72–80.

INTRODUCTION
Latino Youth and America
Time for a Change

FRANCISCO A. VILLARRUEL
AND MARTHA MONTERO-SIEBURTH

According to the U.S. Census Bureau, a significant event in the history of the United States was largely unnoticed. In October 1996, for the first time in the history of this nation, there were more youth of Latino origin than any other ethnic or racial group except non-Hispanic white youth. This event marks the beginning of a transition that demographers have long predicted: that Latinos will soon be the majority of the population base in the United States.

Unfortunately, non-Latino scholars have overlooked the challenges to positive healthy development among Latino youth—traditionally at the national level through ineffective policies, within educational institutions through outdated practices, and at the community level by encouraging Latino youth to abandon cultural practices that contribute to their sense of self and family.

However, the need to develop a critical area of Latino scholarship has not gone unnoticed. Several prominent adolescence scholars (e.g., Lerner, 1995), educators (Darder, Torres, & Gutiérrez, 1997; García, 1992; García & Hurtado, 1995; Suárez-Orozco & Suárez-Orozco, 1997), and demographers (Hayes-Bautista, Schink, & Chapa, 1988) have brought attention to issues that confront Latino youth and also challenged scholars to address the paucity of research that deals directly with the lives, conditions, and situations of Latino youth. Moreover, these scholars underscore the need to develop new paradigms of research: first, to move away from explanations of cultural and genetic deficit to explanations that capitalize on Latino assets and resilience; second, to break down the monolithic generalizations that have been made of Latinos as one culture to demonstrate the complexities *between* Latino cultures (e.g., Dominican as opposed to Puerto Rican) as well as *within* same cultures (e.g., multiple generations of Mexicans; differences among geographies where Latino cultures reside); third, to establish contextually and culturally relevant research which identifies the unique aspects of Latino youth and communities (e.g., Luis Moll's 1992 Community Funds of Knowledge research); and finally, to utilize this information to establish and redefine practices that will provide the foundation of structural supports for Latino youth. Without this refocused scholarship, policy, programs, and practices that can be developed to address the array of issues that must be overcome by Latino youth will be less than adequate. In other words, any effort that falls short of building upon the unique contributions of Latino youth and families, in essence, can, and perhaps will, lead to the continued failure and underachievement of Latino youth and communities throughout the United States.

The challenges to working with Latino youth and communities may seem daunting for a variety of reasons, among them lack of personal knowledge, language, stereotypes, discriminatory practices, and color blindness. The situation is further exacerbated by research that has inadequately described research samples (Fisher, Jackson, & Villarruel, 1997), utilized measures and techniques that do not match Latino cultures (Marín & Marín, 1991), as well as national studies that have failed to disaggregate data for Latino cultures, and the limited data sets that have focused only on Latino cultures; e.g., Hispanic Health and Nutrition Examination Survey, 1982–1984 [HHANES] (National Center for Health Statistics, 1995), and the Latino National Political Survey [LNPS] (De la Garza, DeSipio, García, García, & Falcón, 1992)—the first and only national survey to focus on Latino political life. Moreover, even these data sets are limited to a narrow focus (e.g., health, political participation), which results in an incomplete picture of the state of Latinos in the United States.

Research and practice are further complicated by geographical differences and density shifts of Latino populations. Prior to the 1990s, Latinos had been concentrated in primarily seven states. Now, they have become one of the fastest-growing segments of the population in areas such as Minnesota, North Dakota, North Carolina, and Massachusetts. Unlike some of the border states, which have fed Latino populations into the Southwest, the newer patterns of migration are secondary. In other words, these Latino migrants established themselves first in more densely populated states, and are now moving to other states in search of economic and educational opportunities.

Introduction

The complexity of understanding and working with Latino communities is further related to regional differences, some of which have long existed and some of which are just beginning to emerge. In the Southwest, for example, issues of immigration (e.g., undocumented status, access to health and education, migration patterns) and the complex national and local responses to immigration (e.g., retaliation, fear of being perceived as sympathetic to Latino issues, language dominance of English and Spanish, and even loss of funding by local, state, and federal agencies for serving undocumented Latinos) obfuscate the challenges of working with Latino youth. In contrast, other regions of the country (e.g., the Midwest and the South) do not have to be as concerned with the aforementioned issues. While these regions of the country are experiencing rapid growth among Latino cultures, Latinos still comprise a relatively small segment of the population in general. Most of the youth and families who reside in these regions of the country have lived in the United States for relatively longer periods of time, and as such, have a general understanding of life in the United States. Other areas of the nation, such as the Northeastern part of the United States, which has served as a corridor of immigration for Caribbeans and Central Americans since the 1940s, are now becoming communities where newfound population groups (e.g., Poblanos from the state of Puebla in Mexico) are locating and establishing businesses. In greater metropolitan Boston, for example, Dominicans and Puerto Ricans have been the established Latino population group. With recent immigration patterns bringing more Central Americans and Mexicans to this region of the country, not only is the political base shifting, but so too are the business and educational issues and opportunities within these communities. Hence, the entire nation is confronted with the challenge of working with and understanding the heterogeneity of the Latino population.

This volume first gives an overview of Latino youth in the United States, which sets the stage for the issues to be addressed. Next we discuss the sustaining promises of health, education, and economic well-being for Latino youth. In these chapters, the authors present an array of issues that confront Latino youth. At the same time, they provide recommendations on ways to effectively respond to these issues in a culturally relevant manner. The final chapters link family and community contributions to resilient development in Latino youth. The opportunities to develop networking strategies and community interventions, and to build upon the collective support that families provide, are reinforced.

While the authors are well aware of the majority Latino cultural groups that are often cited in research of Latinos in the United States

(Mexican, Puerto Rican, and Cuban), in this volume Mexicans, Puerto Ricans, and Central Americans are the focus for two main reasons. First, in comparison to other Latino cultures, the Cuban population is relatively geographically isolated, concentrated in Florida. Moreover, the Cuban population, in contrast to other Latino cultural groups, is relatively older. This does not in any way imply that Cuban adolescents do not have unique challenges that have to be confronted and assets that can be built upon. To the contrary, the Cuban community reflects a Latino culture that has been relatively successful in the United States. By the same token, the Cuban population growth is based primarily on fertility rates in subsequent generations. Until the U.S. policy toward Cuba changes, the influx of new Cubans into our nation will be minimal at best, with population increases related to fertility. On the other hand, other Latino cultures are dynamic and rapidly growing in relation to both fertility and patterns of migration and immigration; hence, the challenges and issues are continually evolving. Finally, since the intent of the volume has been to establish a foundation for future research, this volume cannot be, nor should it be, viewed as a comprehensive and authoritative analysis of Latino youth. Rather, this is a preliminary step in the unfolding research that is warranted and needed both for individual Latino cultures and for the collective Latino issues that our nation currently faces and will need to address in the future. It is expected that in future research, communities such as Costa Ricans, Peruvians, Brazilians, Uruguayans, Panamanians, and Ecuadoreans—to name just a few—will demand attention.

WHAT WE ALREADY THINK WE KNOW

From a national perspective, numerous challenges must be overcome if our nation is truly committed to developing policies and practices that ultimately will contribute to the well-being of Latino cultural communities, families, and individuals. Foremost is the need to extend our collective understanding of Latinos in the United States. Numerous volumes have documented the challenges that confront Latino communities and families (e.g., Abalos, 1986; Hayes-Bautista, Schink, & Chapa, 1998; Sotomayor, 1991; Zambrana, 1995). Collectively, these volumes underscore the challenges that families must overcome (e.g., the lack of culturally relevant and sensitive medical, human service, and educational practices) in order to live healthy lives. Concurrently, they draw attention to the unique resources that exist within Latino families, such as the respect and guidance that is offered by elders, the significance of cultural identity and pride, and health practices that are tied to the balance between self and Mother Earth.

A second, albeit just as significant, issue that is highlighted in the aforementioned volumes is the unique dimensions of Latino ethnicity. In many ways, the utilization of panethnic terms such as *Latino* or *Hispanic* serve only to confound the challenges of truly understanding the contextual and ethnic strengths that exist among individuals of Latino descent (Giménez, 1989; Hayes-Bautista & Chapa, 1987; Murguía, 1991). Thus, if our national leaders, educators, and/or practitioners are committed to building upon the unique capacities that exist among Latino youth, then it is essential to focus attention on a segment of the Latino population that will sustain and contribute a significant facet of our nation's growth: Latino youth.

WHERE WE NEED TO GO

The aforementioned challenges notwithstanding, the complexities that confront Latino youth are multifaceted and interrelated. While it is difficult to isolate any single condition or context as undermining the well-being of Latino youth, or providing structures and supports that contribute to the resiliency of Latino youth, this volume explores four specific areas which reflect the most serious Latino issues, needs, and opportunities: employment and economic opportunities, health, education, and family and community.

The interrelations among the various dimensions of Latino life are clearly noted within educational institutions. Throughout the history of the United States, educational institutions have been deemed an environment that is critical to the successful transition of adolescents into productive and contributing members of society. Education has been closely tied to opportunities for economic development, serving as an equalizer for "integration" of society, and as the major institution that supports the transition of adolescents to adulthood. While this "pipeline" has served other ethnic minority groups fairly well, it has failed for many Latino youth because of the price that Latino youth must "pay"—they must abandon their language, culture, and certain values for transition to be deemed "successful." In an effort to illustrate this interrelationship, the context of education follows. The purpose of this discussion is to underscore how institutional practices, often considered to be "state of the art," result in less than optimal environments for Latino youth.

EDUCATION: AN INSTITUTIONAL CORNERSTONE OF ADOLESCENT DEVELOPMENT— BUT NOT FOR LATINO YOUTH

Despite the fact that Latinos have the highest dropout rate (i.e., two times greater than the dropout rate of non-Hispanic whites [U.S. Department of Education, 1992]), many Latino youth do successfully graduate from high school. Overcoming the odds is a challenge that many Latino youth confront within our educational institutions (Romo & Falbo, 1996). While national educational reform efforts have enhanced the success of African-American and non-Hispanic white youth, the proportion of Latino youth earning high school diplomas has increased at a dramatically smaller rate (U.S. Bureau of the Census, 1992).

Even as the current wave of nationwide as well as state and local educational reform efforts are under way, evidence of how schooling has miserably failed underserved populations in general, but more specifically Latinos, is quite apparent in urban areas (cf. Darder & Upshur, 1993; Rivera & Nieto, 1993; Wheelock, 1990). Wheelock (1990), for example, identified several factors that contributed to the tracking of Latinos in Boston. Low-level math and science classes, a watered-down curriculum, inadequate support programs beset with ineffective classes and teachers, as well as poor administration confronted with external underfunding were identified as factors that have led to the underachievement of Latino youth. These are but a few of the circumstance and conditions that challenge Latino students in Boston and other communities throughout the United States.

Mired within this system, the image of Latinos persists as academic underachievers, illiterates, dropouts, incompetents in reading, writing, and numeracy—in other words, as failures in their own right. That image, we assert, continues to be fostered because the underlying assumptions for these students, while based on well-intentioned notions of helping them compete within schools, are totally dissociated from understanding the cultural and educational contexts of Latino students and families. Moreover, underlying many of these assumptions are outmoded, traditional perspectives that need to be questioned.

Throughout the country, the majority of school administrators, teachers, and staff tend to be ethnically white, with careers spanning well over twenty-five years, and with a seniority which has been earned through years of coping and surviving a highly political system. The prevailing assumption is that keeping students in line with policies and prac-

Introduction

tices that are universal to schools will engender the kinds of adjustment for all students to directly focus on learning. Undetected within these assumptions are the underlying facts that not all students arrive at school with the same upbringing, language, cultural backgrounds, or knowledge and skills, and that many of these new students have immigrant histories and experiences unknown to the administrators, teachers, and staff. Moreover, the notion that all kids should be treated in the same manner represents a color-blind position which disallows for the differences which students bring to the school doorstep.

Today administrators, teachers, and staff are dealing with unprecedented numbers of very different types of students, with very different learning opportunities and styles, different readiness for school, and different language preparation in their native, let alone second language than the students they began teaching years ago. Strategies that seemed to work then, with homogeneous groups and basic neighborhood schools using one single language of instruction and basic monocultural curriculum texts and teaching modalities, are not those which operate for Latino families and link Latino students and their families to schools today.[1]

This negative image of Latinos continues to be held in schools, because as these authors argue, it becomes diversionary to blame students rather than to define the *cultural* contexts which increase student's disengagement from learning, and the *educational* contexts which could inhibit such disengagement (Fine, 1990). Such an undertaking would demand delving into deeper and more controversial solution-oriented practices than educators or policymakers are willing to make. It would also require the unlearning of the internalized failure to which Latino students readily succumb in school.

VARIABLE DEFINITIONS OF SUCCESS

If we analyze "success" as a variable used in high schools, we find first that success is measured from the results of academic testing and comparative scores across and between ethnic groups. Such rationality is competitively driven, in that underserved students are matched against the norm of mainstream white, Anglo students and are also compared in terms of their own ethnic counterparts. Asians are compared with Latinos, African Americans, and Native Americans; this comparison is normed and value-laden in favor of mainstream criteria of success, which in this case refers to being English-speaking, compliant with standards of appropriateness determined by school administrators or teachers, maintaining behavioral standards which are based on interpretation of certain values, and having the cultural background to learn in specific ways. Frederick Erickson (1987, p. 8) provides the following example of such cultural expectation:

> In educational institutions the mean is a ubiquitous measure of what happened. Yet statisticians know that measures of central tendency obscure certain interesting kinds of variation. The school board may ask for a ten year tabulation of mean scores for the Scholastic Aptitude Test as a measure of the effectiveness of instruction in the high school. Looking at the year by year variance in test scores rather than looking at the mean might yield much more information. Yet it does not occur to the board members, to central administrators, to principals or to teachers to consider the variance.

Second, McDermott (1989, p. 363) defines success as "a culturally necessary part of the American school scene." In a sense, the successes of some are a result of isolating and explaining the failures of others. Thus, McDermott emphasizes that "those who fail in school, by their presence, by their being explained, by their failures, make our successes possible" (p. 362). The very fact that all of the measures of achievement are cognitive and do not include noncognitive, social adaptive behaviors and knowledge dismisses what may be for Latinos local "community funds of knowledge," that is, ways in which Latinos learn which may not be represented within the context of schools.

The negative image of Latinos in terms of failure is also compounded by the single use of national aggregate data sets which do not untangle within-group variations, or provide indications of how Latinos might fare using multiple data sources and analysis of variation. We know far more about the failure of Latino students than the success stories of outliers, and those variations within groups may prove to be unique patterns of success which have strong social and cultural implications. Ethnographic research such as Mehan's (1992) is contributing to such fine-line descriptions (see also Mehan, Villaneuva, Hubbard, & Lintz, 1996).

Third, unlike their privileged white counterparts, Latinos do not have the opportunities to acquire the same cultural capital, habitus, and social capital to succeed if they happen to be poor, illiterate, and non-English-speaking. If we consider Pierre Bourdieu's (1977) notions of habitus (the conditions acquired early on from one's life and family environment which predispose one to acquire specific knowledge and power) and cultural capital (the social beliefs, patterns of behavior, and thinking which sustain one's ability to use such knowledge and power), Latino students may not have the currency to exchange their knowledge for such status and power.

With regard to schooling, cultural capital simply translates to mean that Latinos may not be as well prepared to face the demands of the dominant mainstream schooling culture. More recently, James Coleman's (1987, p. 36) notion of social capital, as the "norms, social networks and the relationships, between adults and children that are of value for the child's growing up" and which serve "to reinforce the family and community's role in education and achievement," illustrates that "where such social capital is diminished, the kinds of attitudes, effort and conception of self that children and youth need to succeed in school and as adults" must be fostered (p. 38). This becomes an exceedingly difficult task where the relationship of Latino parents to schooling is disparate and where Latino parents basically mistrust schools.

Finally, success in schooling has also been differently defined by the policies of cultural dominance. Such policies have identified differential status for diverse ethnic groups during different historical educational periods. Each period has an underlying rationale for what is considered success.

Prior to the 1950s, studies of comparative intelligence among groups and particularly underserved students proffered genetically driven explanations of the superiority of one group over another. Thus, the rates of success were always against standards which had not been analyzed for their embedded cultural dominance. Distinctions among different learning styles or contextual approaches to learning were not readily introduced into the literature of academic achievement. Instead, the assumption was that with perseverance any student, except one with a low IQ, should be able to succeed particularly due to the greater access to secondary education provided through universal expansion of high schools. This assumption persisted until Gunnar Myrdal's (1964) analysis of the status of African Americans in America made it compellingly clear that there was differential treatment of blacks and whites in America and that the haves and have-nots coexisted side by side without each knowing much about the other.

By the 1960s, the notion of cultural deprivation and disadvantage compelled educators to seek solutions in the form of compensatory educational programs. The idea behind such programs was that by compensating for the lack of reading, writing, and thinking skills in underprivileged students, they would gain the knowledge to level the playing field. The pendulum swung in favor of developing programs which would enhance the learning of such students through programs like Head Start and Follow Through. The question remains, when did such compensation achieve its goal?

Certainly, by the 1970s the theory of cultural deprivation and disadvantage was cast in another mold, shifting from families and groups to a focus on individual students. Under the standard of a quality education for all, underserved students would be able to profit from the outcomes of effective schooling. *Quality* remained an amorphous term which was interpreted not only by a mix of inputs and outputs, but with added values given to direct teaching, time on task, and mastery learning.

Programs emphasizing aspects of quality, from pedagogy to curriculum and assessment, proliferated, and time on task was particularly advanced as one of the real breakthroughs in measuring learning as a function of time needed compared with time spent on completing tasks. This was followed by analysis of standards of excellence during the 1980s as *A Nation at Risk* (National Commission on Excellence in Education, 1984) gave educators and policymakers a call to action about the dire state of American education. High expectations for achievement were revisited again. Underserved students came under attack for "lowering the standards," and under the rubric of maintaining excellence, testing and assessment became even more pronounced measures of achievement.

Since the early 1990s, massive school reform efforts throughout the country have indicated that the success of students is contingent upon multiple factors, which include, at least, changes in the traditional curriculum and, at best, delegation of authority to school-based management. School site councils have replaced the hierarchical structure of schooling. Within such reform, it is clear that systemic changes are needed, requiring multiple interventions and redefinitions of roles and authority as well as what might be differential success strategies for students. This has brought into the foreground discussions of multiple ways of knowing, thinking, and learning, along with different applications of intelligences and restructuring programs. These include Theodore Sizer's (1984, 1992, 1996) Coalition of Essential Schools, James Comer's (1987) New Haven Program, Henry Levin's (Hopfenberg et al., 1993) Accelerated Program, and Robert Slavin's (1989) studies of risk factors at Johns Hopkins University at the Center for Research on Education of Students Placed at Risk (CRESPAR).

INVISIBLE STATUS OF LATINOS

How do Latinos fare in the midst of these restructuring and platform initiatives by different ethnic/racial groups? Latinos are the crux of the matter. Their *invisible* status between African Americans and whites hides many of the conditions that elicit experiences of success instead of the more often publicized failure. Determinants of success that have had little to do with the life experiences and sociocultural adaptations of Latino high school students have become operant explanations of failure. Instead of focusing on how Latinos create countercultures, or act in oppositional ways to "succeed" on their own terms, they are relegated to the framework of criticism of other racial and ethnic groups, that is, to close scrutiny about why they fail rather than under what conditions and circumstances they succeed.

Latinos have once again been cast in terms of negative images through a series of recent events. The publication of *The Bell Curve* (Hernstein & Murray, 1996) has reignited the genetic deficit theories, changes in immigration laws have played upon xenophobia, bilingual education funding has elicited stronger reactions from the English Only movement, and welfare reform has all but indicted those who are poor, non-English-speaking, and noncitizens.

Further complicating this negativism are current educational restructuring policies, which do not take into account the diversity of students and their families, particularly immigrants, migrants, and refugees. These policies are not targeted at the linguistically and culturally diverse student but are concerned with larger management outputs. As federal funding for educational programs continues to decrease, tensions between ethnic and racial groups will be blatantly felt. The "divide and conquer" scenario of pitting groups against each other will become more evident as each group struggles for limited resources. How such ethnic and racial groups play out conflicts, create coalitions, or compromise will be a decisive test of educational parity into the twenty-first century.

In summation, it appears that more reasons to perpetuate images of failure than of success for Latino students seem to be sustained. To deconstruct such images would require understanding the rationality and assumptions under which failure has been explained, and in most cases the predominant models have explained failure in terms of pathology, class, or ethnicity. To analyze Latino students' successes would require an examination of how success has been historically and is presently conceptualized, from whose perspective and to what ends. More importantly, to understand the conditions that contribute to Latino youth success, other domains external to educational environments need to be explored in greater depth, with particular emphasis on the context of economic and employment opportunities, health, and family and community.

From a Latino paradigm, a response to a "problem" does not exist in isolation. Rather, the "problem" is tied to, and influenced by, economic, social, cultural, and linguistic factors in order to comprehend an issue in depth. This "problematization" allows scholars to examine given situations from an array of perspectives, yielding multiple "solutions" and levels of understanding. To that end, we have attempted in this volume to address these domains succinctly and begin to deconstruct the negative images sustained for Latino youth, and to reconstruct from primary data images of what is positive and may contribute to the healthy development of Latino youth in the United States.

CHAPTERS IN THIS VOLUME

In chapter 1, Rudy Hernández, Marcelo Siles, and Refugio Rochín provide an overview of Latino youth in terms of demographic shifts that underscore the necessity of examining and redefining research on and about Latino youth. Specifically, the authors address the growing role of Latino youth in the changing national context, identity issues in relation to Hispanicity, and an examination of Latino diversity and unity. In addition, the authors provide an overview of the relationship of immigration to fertility, historic origins, and the race and *mestizaje* among Latinos. Of particular importance related to the conditions that unify Latinos are issues of language preferences (Spanish versus English only), family values and structures, interests in immigration rights, socioeconomic indicators, work ethics, and labor force participation patterns. Throughout this chapter, the authors demonstrate the importance of utilizing a "Latino paradigm." By framing the consequences of Latino demographic shifts in multiple domains, the authors demonstrate a multifaceted approach to investing in the future of Latinos in the United States. They advocate for the development of "progressive programs that address issues of identity, education, income, growth, purchasing power, and deviant and criminal behavior" (p. 60), embedded within a bicultural approach.

In chapter 2, Anna Santiago utilizes the National Longitudinal Survey of Youth (NLSY) to examine the impact of growing up poor and welfare-dependent—specifically, how parental AFDC receipt and other family background characteristics affect subsequent dependency on

Introduction xxv

AFDC. In addition, Santiago examines how attitudes about welfare and state AFDC levels affect dependency. Finally, Santiago examines how patterns and factors associated with AFDC dependency vary across racial and ethnic lines. Comparing Latino households with African American and white households, Santiago notes that black and Latina women were more likely than Anglo women to be dependent upon welfare during the 1980s. Given the differences that were noted across groups, Santiago recommends a reassessment of the impact of family background characteristics, economic contexts, and welfare policies for minority women.

In chapter 3, Antonia Villarruel undertakes an integrated review of health behavior research on the sexual behavior of Latina adolescents. In addition to providing an overview of Latina sexual behaviors, the biological, social, and cultural factors that influence sexual behaviors of Latina adolescents (including both health risk and protective behaviors) are explored. Villarruel notes that research concerned with the sexual behavior of Latina adolescents is critically limited both in scope and amount, and offers several recommendations for future scholarship. Among the recommendations that are put forth, Villarruel underscores the importance of focusing upon both inter- and intragroup variability among Latinas as well as an increased focus upon the cultural values that are ascribed to Latino populations (e.g., familism, gender role differentiation, and religion). Villarruel concludes her chapter by presenting six areas for future research and theoretical development and a brief discussion of the implications for practice.

Like Antonia Villarruel, in chapter 4 Daniel Perkins and Francisco Villarruel challenge models that have been developed for "minorities" which, in actuality, have been developed with white or African American populations. In an effort to underscore the significance of unique cultural models, Perkins and Villarruel examine the risk and resiliency factors associated with Latino adolescent engagement drawn from the Community-Based Profile of Michigan Youth Study (Keith & Perkins, 1995). The authors note that the risk factors examined in the present study, which were previously noted as predictors of sexual activity among African American and Anglo youth, did not predict sexual activity among Latino adolescents. They suggest that further studies should examine cultural values and norms (e.g., religious norms) that may be associated with risk factors and sexual activities among Latino youth.

In chapter 5, Jaime Chahín undertakes a historical analysis of the research literature pertaining to the status and aspirations of Mexican American youth. He begins by examining the value orientations of Mexican

Americans in the Southwest. Through this cumulative analysis, Chahín indicates that even though the research related to the educational status aspirations of Mexican Americans is limited, the existing literature does provide evidence that Mexican American youth, regardless of migrant background or gender, have high educational and occupational aspirations and expectations. Chahín puts forth several recommendations that might support and advance the aspirations of Mexican American youth, including the development of programs that are culturally relevant, career counseling that explores the breadth of alternatives available to Latino youth, the engagement of parents at all levels of educational programming, and a continuous assessment and evaluation of policies at the local, state, and federal levels which would have a realistic impact on the educational opportunities of isolated communities.

In chapter 6, Raimundo Mora bridges student literacy with the requirements of a science program in higher education. Mora presents case studies of students who are acquiring academic literacy in a science foundation course to enable them to enter college-level courses. Through their accounts, the obstacles they face and the responses of college faculty are highlighted. Policy implications derived from these case studies identify the need to bridge the language realities of students with those of the university context. Mora offers several recommendations for bridging these realities. In his conclusion, Mora proposes a type of literacy that goes beyond a skills-oriented focus, one that is comprehensive in including the economic, cultural, and social dimensions as the context for literacy development.

In chapter 7, Martha Montero-Sieburth attempts to demystify the images of Latino students by presenting case studies from Boston schools. In her case studies of the teachers and two students in a mainstream civics classroom and in a bilingual mathematics classroom, Montero-Sieburth frames an analysis of language, culture, and gender in terms of DeVos and Súarez-Orozco's (1990) notion of affective dissonance. This study suggests that teachers may enhance the learning of Latino students by using language to establish a social context. Yet, within the educational environment, students must abandon the linguistic skills with which they feel most comfortable and with which they can, and often do, succeed. As a consequence, Latino students, lacking the leverage of skills in English, give up on themselves or leave school altogether. What is recommended is the creation of socially constructed environments that permit Latino students to use their native language, the maintenance of core values, and opportunities to desist.

Introduction   xxvii

In chapter 8, Ricardo Stanton-Salazar examines variations in network orientation, defined as perceptions, attitudes, and beliefs, and the correspondent behaviors that either motivate or inhibit Latino youth from actively seeking help and support available from resourceful adults in the community, school, and other institutions. Stanton-Salazar argues that a considerable change in the institutional culture of school is warranted—one that facilitates intergroup relations between community members and professionals based on principles of trust and reciprocity as opposed to hierarchy and exclusion.

In chapter 9, Heidi Vázquez García, Cynthia García Coll, Sumru Erkut, Odette Alarcón, and Linda Tropp focus on the family values of Latino adolescents. The chapter begins with a conceptualization of family values and functioning and then moves to adaptation and diversity of Latino family values. The influences of migration, acculturation, and gender on family values are also examined. The authors find that adolescents' adherence to family values changes as a result of contextual and developmental demands including migration, acculturation, and gender role expectations and behaviors. The authors note that Hispanic adolescents are able to negotiate various contextual and cultural demands to successfully complete developmental and culturally defined tasks. Moreover, while some dimensions of traditional Hispanic values and functioning (i.e., familism) are adhered to, other traditional values (e.g., *respeto*) are not maintained. The authors conclude that future research is needed on the relation of socioeconomic status, nutrition, health care, and education to Hispanic adolescent family values. The authors assert that the maintenance of some family values indicates a fusion of traditional and modern family values within a different cultural context.

Chapter 10, by Maribel Vargas and Nancy Busch-Rossnagel, discusses how the family unit for Latino adolescents is critical to positive and healthy development. The authors assert that the Latino family unit is critical for youth, who have to balance the demands of two divergent cultural systems as they develop their own sense of identity. In addressing parenting qualities that Latino cultures have in common, most specifically, through the examination of three salient attributes (familism, *respeto*, and machismo) that are embedded within Latino cultures, Vargas and Busch-Rossnagel demonstrate that the traditional models of parenting which have been integrated into mainstream literature do not fit Latino cultures. As such, the authors conclude that the study of Latino cultures should not be embedded in between-group comparisons (i.e., with non-Latino cultures). Instead, Vargas and Busch-Rossnagel recommend that efforts not be undertaken to identify a "modal type" of Latino parenting. They assert that a differential approach *within* Latino populations should be employed to identify clusters of parenting qualities that emerge in Latinos and how these clusters, along with national background and other sociodemographic characteristics, contribute to educational outcomes.

In chapter 11, Bertha López, Lucila Nerenberg, and Marina Valdéz discuss the barriers and opportunities that migrant Latino adolescents and their families must confront. While they specifically focus on Michigan, their discussion has implications for Latino migrants throughout the United States. Gathering data from a comprehensive literature review, information from migrant families, and their own experiences, they identify issues confronting migrant youth, and present approaches that have contributed to their positive and healthy development.

In chapter 12, Robert Ortega notes that child welfare has historically led to individual-based policies and practices which consistently threaten Latino familistic values. These clashes, he asserts, have served as a barrier between programs and families. Toward this end, Ortega recommends additional research on child maltreatment among Latino adolescents that more closely examines both causes and types of Latino adolescent maltreatment.

SUMMARY

From all of these chapters, it is clear that the portrayal of Latino adolescents as assets rather than liabilities is a conviction shared by most of the authors. The concerns raised cannot be resolved in a linear or sequential manner, "quick fixes," or solutions based on lessons learned with non-Latino youth, given the unique aspects that exist within Latino cultures. In an effort to address these issues, the authors in this volume underscore the importance of developing new paradigms of understanding—the understanding of Latino cultures from their own perspectives and contexts. It is imperative that we move the discourse of Latino adolescents away from the traditional (pejorative and deficit-oriented) explanations of failure to pointing out their successes as determined by the unique cultural values and experiences.

Into the twenty-first century, more concentrated research of this type must evolve. In this regard, analysis of the "traditionally successful" (e.g., Cuban) adolescents as well as Central Americans and South Americans must be a focus of attention that equals the concentration of research that has traditionally been done with Mexican and Puerto Rican youth. More importantly, this research must be intergenerational in scope, examining the impact and experiences of first, second, and third generations related to the issues that are addressed within this volume. Additional emphasis should also explore issues that have not been addressed in this volume, such as violence, gangs, and language loss (with youth still self-identifying as being members of a specific Latino culture). Given the often tenuous pressures that are placed upon youth by society and peers in general, additional research should focus on the struggles of cultural and political identity, and the contribution of these dimensions to the positive and healthy development of Latino youth. Included in the challenge of future research within and between Latino cultures is an analysis of the variability that exists between and within "high-acculturation" and "low-acculturation" families and youth. This intergroup analysis will, undoubtedly, underscore the variability that exists within and between Latino cultures. Moreover, the impact of circular migration patterns, the reemergence of cultural identity and maintenance, and the underlying reasons that contributed to the migration of Latinos to the United States (e.g., economic and social advancement or political refuge) should also be integrated into these endeavors.

The authors of this volume share the same conviction expressed in a quotation attributed to the Mexican revolutionist Emiliano Zapata: "Es mejor morir de pie que vivir de rodillas" (It is better to die standing up than to live on one's knees). In other words, the self-determination of Latino cultures will provide the *empuje* (drive or motivation) for the future success of *la raza cósmica*.

NOTES

[1]The notion of the melting pot which is so prevalent may have functioned for previous immigrant groups insofar as some of the early generations *made it* through high school if they were lucky enough to have simply completed the common school. Many dropped out of the common school into the workforce after three grades. In fact, the number of dropouts from school was as great as it is today, yet the difference is in the fact that immigrants were able to procure jobs, once they left school with the skills they had gained. The process of Americanization which was put into practice during the early part of the century had as its underlying premise the notion that by raising the economic and educational standards of the immigrants they would reap the benefits of their new homeland. Thus, learning English, leaving cultural ways behind, and forging a new nation-

alism which was based on democratic ideals were considered the way to success. However, it should be noted that while the emphasis has historically been on the immigrants who succeeded, there are more cases of immigrants who did not succeed. Their stories have only recently been recognized by historians and social scientists reconceptualizing U.S. immigrant history.

REFERENCES

Abalos, D. T. (1986). *Latinos in the United States: The sacred and the political.* Notre Dame, IN: University of Notre Dame Press.

Bourdieu, P. (1977). Cultural reproduction and social reproduction. In J. Karabel & A. H. Halsey (Eds.), *Power and ideology in education* (pp. 487–510). New York: Oxford University Press.

Coleman, J. S. (1987). Families and schools. *Educational Researcher, 16,* 32–38.

Comer, J. C. (1987). New Haven's school-based community connection. *Educational Leadership, 44,* 13–16.

Darder, A., Torres, R. D., & Gutiérrez, H. (1997). *Latinos and education: A critical reader.* New York: Routledge.

Darder, A., & Upshur, C. C. (1993). What do Latino children need to succeed in school? A study of four Boston public schools. In R. Rivera & S. Nieto (Eds.), *The education of Latino students in Massachusetts: Issues, research, and policy implications* (pp. 127–146). Boston: University of Massachusetts, Mauricio Gastón Institute for Latino Community Development and Public Policy.

De la Garza, R. O., DeSipio, L., García, F. C., García, J., & Falcon, A. (1992). *Latino voices: Mexican, Puerto Rican, and Cuban perspectives on American politics.* Boulder, CO: Westview.

DeVos, G. A., & Suárez-Orozco, M. (1990). *Status inequality: The self in culture.* Newbury Park, CA: Sage.

Erickson, F. (1987). Transformation and school success: The politics and culture of educational achievement. *Anthropology and Education Quarterly, 18,* 335–356.

Fine, M. (1990). Making controversy: Who's at risk. *Journal of Urban and Cultural Studies, 1,* 55–68.

Fisher, C. B., Jackson, J. J., & Villarruel, F. A. (1997). The study of ethnic minority children and youth in the United States. In R. M. Lerner (Ed.), *Handbook of child psychology: Vol. 1. Theoretical models of human development* (5th ed., pp. 1145–1207). New York: Wiley.

Garcia, E. E. (1992). "Hispanic" children: Theoretical, empirical, and related policy issues. *Educational Psychology Review, 4,* 69–93.

García, E. E., & Hurtado, A. (1995). Becoming American: A review of current research on the development of racial and ethnic identity in children. In W. D. Hawley & A. W. Jackson (Eds.), *Toward a common destiny: Improving race and ethnic relations in America* (pp. 163–184). San Francisco: Jossey Bass.

Gimenéz, M. E. (1989). Latino/Hispanic—who needs a name? The case against a standardized terminology. *International Journal of Healthy Services, 19,* 557–571.

Hayes-Bautista, D., & Chapa, J. (1987). Latino terminology: Conceptual bases for standardized terminology. *American Journal of Public Health, 77,* 61–68.

Hayes-Bautista, D. E., Schink, W. O., & Chapa, J. (1988). *The burden of support: Young Latinos in an aging society.* Stanford, CA: Stanford University Press.

Hernstein, R. J., & Murray, C. (1996). *The bell curve: Intelligence and class structure in American life.* New York: Free Press.

Hopfenberg, W. S., Levin, H. M., Chase, C., Christensen, S. G., Moore, M., Soler, P., Burnner, I., Keller, B., & Rodriguez, G. (1993). *The accelerated schools resource guide.* San Francisco: Jossey Bass.

Keith, J., & Perkins, D. F. (1995). *13,000 adolescents speak: A profile of Michigan youth.* East Lansing: Michigan State University, Institute for Children, Youth, and Families.

Lerner, R. M. (1995). *America's youth in crisis: Challenges and options for programs and policies.* Thousand Oaks, CA: Sage.

Marín, G., & Marín, B. (1991). *Research with Hispanic populations.* Newbury Park, CA: Sage.

McDermott, R. (1989). Making dropouts. In H. Trueba, G. Spindler, & L. Spindler (Eds.), *What do anthropologists have to say about dropouts?* (pp. 16–26). New York: Falmer.

Mehan, H. (1992). Understanding inequality in schools: The contribution of interpretive studies. *Sociology of Education, 65,* 1–20.

Mehan, H., Villanueva, I., Hubbard, L., & Lintz, A. (1996). *Constructing school success: The consequences of untracking low-achieving students.* New York: Cambridge University Press.

Moll, L. C. (1992). Funds of knowledge for teaching: Using a qualitative approach to connect homes and classrooms. *Theory into Practice, 31,* 132–141.

Morales, R., & Bonilla, F. (1993). *Latinos in a changing U.S. economy: Comparative perspectives on growing inequality.* Newbury Park, CA: Sage.

Murguía, E. (1991). On Latino/Hispanic ethnic identity. *Latino Studies Journal, 2,* 8–17.

Myrdal, G. (1964). *An American dilemma*. New York: McGraw-Hill.
National Center for Health Statistics. (1995, September). *Plan and operation of the Hispanic Health and Nutrition Examination Survey, 1982–84*. Vital Health Statistics, Series 1, No. 19 (DHHS Pub. No. (PHS) 85–1321). Washington, DC: U. S. Government Printing Office.
National Commission on Excellence in Education (1984). *A nation at risk: The full account*. Cambridge, MA: USA Research.
Rivera, R., & Nieto, S. (Eds.). (1993). *The education of Latino students in Massachusetts: Issues, research, and policy implications*. Boston, MA: Mauricio Gastón Institute for Latino Community Development and Public Policy.
Romo, H. D., & Falbo, T. (1996). *Latino high school graduation: Defying the odds*. Austin, TX: University of Texas Press.
Seizer, T. R. (1984). *Horace's compromise: The dilemma of American high school*. Boston, MA: Houghton Mifflin.
Seizer, T. R. (1992). *Horace's school: Redesigning the American school*. Boston, MA: Houghton Mifflin.
Seizer, T. R. (1996). *Horace's hope: What works for the American high school*. Boston, MA: Houghton Mifflin.
Slavin, R. E. (1989). *School and classroom organization*. Hillsdale, NJ: Lawrence Erlbaum.
Sotomayor, M. (1991). *Empowering Hispanic families: Issues for the 90's*. Milwaukee, WI: Family Service of America.
Suárez-Orozco, C., & Suárez-Orozco, M. (1997). *Transformations: Migration, family life, and achievement motivation among Latino adolescents*. Stanford, CA: Stanford University Press.
U.S. Bureau of the Census (1992). *School-enrollment: Social and economic characteristics of students*. Current Population Reports, October, 1990 Series (p-20, No. 460). Washington, DC: U.S. Government Printing Office.
U.S. Department of Education. (1992). *Dropout rates in the United States, 1991*. Washington, DC: U.S. Government Printing Office.
Wheelock, A. (1990). The status of Latino students in Massachusetts public schools. In R. Rivera & S. Nieto (Eds.), *The education of Latino students in Massachusetts: Issues, research, and policy implications* (pp. 11–32). Boston, MA: Mauricio Gastón Institute for Latino Community Development and Public Policy.
Zambrana, R. E. (1995). *Understanding Latino families: Scholarship, policy, and practice*. Thousand Oaks, CA: Sage.

Making Invisible Latino Adolescents Visible

CHAPTER 1
Latino Youth
Converting Challenges to Opportunities
RUDY HERNÁNDEZ, MARCELO SILES,
AND REFUGIO I. ROCHÍN

INTRODUCTION AND OVERVIEW

Latino youth face challenges which have heretofore been ignored. Their issues transcend the usual minority problems of adolescence, family crisis, education, poverty, promiscuity, drugs, and staying out of trouble. Their challenges extend to being part of an increasingly diverse, fast-growing population that is expanding across the United States. Their challenges emanate in part from being perceived and treated as foreign-born immigrants in a society with growing xenophobia, exacerbated by widespread ignorance about who they are, and general confusion with identity in terms of labels that are prescribed and utilized: Hispanic, Latino, Chicano, *Boricua, raza,* etc. These forms of identity are also interspersed with stereotypical depictions of Latino youth as gang-bangers, graffiti artists, and oddly enough, migrant children who work the fields of agriculture. To a degree these labels describe the predicament of Latino youth. They are heterogeneous with many identities. They are covered in the media in various ways, but mostly under the rubric of "Hispanic." Their population is growing so quickly that Latinos themselves are oftentimes not connected to each other by common themes and issues.

Yet, Latino youth are being challenged in new and important ways. They are at a major crossroads of mainstream society, facing new roles as future leaders and workers (Duany & Pittman, 1990). Latino youth are entering a new century where they will be expected to convert their challenges into opportunities. With these concerns at stake, it is increasingly imperative to deepen our understanding of Latino youth. In this chapter, we focus on the following:

1. An assessment of the demographic transformation that is giving importance to studying the Latino population in general
2. An examination of the growing role of Latino youth in the changing national context
3. An overview of Latino youth in terms of the official definition of who they are and a discussion of the growing debate over Latino identity and Hispanicity
4. An examination of Latino diversity and unity

We also discuss the reasons why national immigration and welfare reform policies heighten awareness of Latinos. In addition, we examine some troubling socioeconomic indicators—low income, education, unemployment, deviance, and juvenile crime—that challenge Latinos as a whole.

These facts reveal serious challenges ahead for Latino youth. Foremost, Latino youth are not achieving the type of education that will prepare them for better-paying, high-skill, professional jobs. They are facing problems of poverty, family dysfunction, and deviant behavior, at least on par with other groups but maybe to a greater degree. Nonetheless, our intent is not to ignore the positive facts that are shared by the majority of Latino youth. They represent a critical part of this nation's future leaders and workers. They will be needed by an aging population in a global world of more trade and international competition. Despite these concerns, most Latino youth possess the skills ideally suited for a global world, namely, the skills of being bilingual, multicultural, and acutely aware of social changes within local communities.

THE CHANGING DEMOGRAPHY

Several reports have identified the "changing demography" in the United States as the most important reason for studying Latinos. According to Chapa and Valencia (1993, p. 167), "Latino population growth is the future." Similarly, Aponte and Siles (1994, p. 1) note that "few societal changes in sight match the coming demographic shift, commonly known as 'the browning of America.'" And more recently, del Pinal and Singer (1997, p. 14) wrote: "Next to diversity, rapid growth is the most extraordinary aspect of the U.S. Hispanic population."

Between 1980 and 1990 the total U.S. population grew by 9 percent to about 249 million people, while the Hispanic population grew by 53 percent, from 14.6 million in 1980 to 22.4 million in 1990. In 1980, the Hispanic population was a little less than 5 percent of the U.S. population. By 1990, it had risen to 9 percent. Latest figures from the Census Bureau place the Hispanic population at about 28 million, roughly 11 percent of the nation's population (U.S. Bureau of the Census, 1995). In less than five years, domestic Latinos increased by over 5 million, a rate of 27 percent in five years (del Pinal & Singer, 1997). If Latinos continue to increase at this rate, the number of Latinos will equal or surpass the number of African Americans by 2010, becoming the United States' largest minority population (Aponte & Siles, 1994; Hodgkinson & Outtz, 1996).

By the year 2050, Latinos could reach 130 million in number, constituting 22 to 24 percent of the total U.S. population (del Pinal & Singer, 1997). Between now and then, according to del Pinal and Singer (p. 15), Hispanics "are projected to furnish more than one-half of the national population growth." Thus, within two generations, non-Hispanic whites will no longer be a majority population in America and Hispanics will command a more critical role.

Of the 27 million estimated for 1994, Mexican Americans accounted for the overwhelming majority, numbering over 17 million (64 percent). South and Central Americans were counted as 14 percent (3.7 million), Puerto Ricans (not including islanders) as 2.8 million (10 percent), other Hispanics as 1.9 million (7 percent), and Cuban Americans as 1.1 million (4 percent) (National Association of Hispanic Publications, 1995).

DRIVING FORCES: IMMIGRATION AND FERTILITY

Immigration and relatively high fertility rates have fueled the rapid growth in the American Hispanic population. Between 1980 and 1990, approximately half of the Latino population growth was due to births to Latinos in the United States and half to foreign immigration. Right now, immigration contributes the lion's share of Hispanic increase. According to del Pinal and Singer (1997, p. 2), "In the 1990s, about two-thirds of the U.S. residents who identify themselves as Hispanics or Latinos are immigrants or the children of immigrants."

Rumbaut (1996) notes that Latin America and the Caribbean alone accounted for nearly 43 percent of the foreign-born persons in the United

States in 1990 (8.4 million), and that fully half of them came during the 1980s. Rumbaut (1996) also notes that only Mexico, Argentina, and Colombia have larger Spanish-origin populations than the United States. Mexico, because of its history and proximity to the United States, is the most significant contributor of foreign-born Latinos in the United States, and there are few signs to suggest that the influx will slow in the next decade.

California receives about half of the immigrants from Latin America and the Caribbean, followed by Texas, New York, Florida, and Illinois. These are also the states with the nation's largest concentrations of Hispanics. In 1990, California had 7.7 million Hispanics (26 percent of the state's population); Texas, 4.3 million Hispanics (26 percent); New York, 2.2 million (12 percent); Florida, 1.6 million (12 percent); and Illinois, almost 1 million (8 percent). Altogether, these five states held nearly 75 percent of the nation's total Latino population (see Rumbaut, 1996, Table 1).

HISTORIC ORIGINS

Another force behind the current pattern of immigration and settlement of Latinos is their historic origin. Latinos have been a part of the American fabric for centuries, preceding the explorers from England, France, and other parts of Europe by many decades. One should not forget that Christopher Columbus was sponsored by Spanish royalty and what followed him were waves of Spanish explorers who ventured into many parts of the United States, opening the regions of Florida, Louisiana, Kansas, New Mexico, and California. Thus, the history and precedent of the early *españoles* have given cause for Latinos to make parts of the United States their permanent homes.

But recent history has also affected new patterns of Latino settlement and growth along the Eastern seaboard and into the middle states, where Latinos have come in droves to work in agriculture, services, and construction. There are very few states where Latinos have not significantly increased their presence, and very few states where they have not found jobs and settled.

As a result of more recent histories, Hispanics have laid claims to land that was once Spanish. Their historical connections to the United States include, for example, the Treaty of Guadalupe Hidalgo of 1848; the Spanish-American War and the Treaty of 1898, when Spain ceded Puerto Rico and other countries to the United States; the Mexican Revolution and the invasion of American troops into Mexico; the bracero period (roughly 1942–1964); Fidel Castro, the Bay of Pigs, and the subsequent influx of Cuban *Marielitos* and *balseros* (boat people). There is much more to discern from the histories of different Latino groups; suffice it to say that the backgrounds of Latinos are varied and unique to each. Puerto Ricans, for example, are U.S. citizens, as part of the treaty of the Spanish-American War of 1898. Today, Puerto Ricans encounter no legal barriers to migration to the mainland. Their perceptions of themselves as Americans are different from the perceptions of other Latinos in the United States.

Mexicans have had a long-standing history with the United States. Before the Treaty of Guadalupe Hidalgo of 1848, Mexico owned nearly one-third the territory of the United States. That territory today is called the Southwest, where Latinos have settled in large numbers. Today, however, the Mexican immigrant faces many barriers to entering the United States, much greater than at the turn of the twentieth century when the border was almost an open frontier. For Mexicans who entered the United States from 1901 to 1965, legal impediments to entry were rudimentary. Mexicans (so-called braceros) were actually recruited to work the farm fields of America between 1942 and 1965. After 1965 U.S. barriers to Mexican immigration rose much higher and changed the status of Mexicans in the United States to that of "illegal aliens." Thus, Mexicans who entered the United States after 1965 have tended to experience more of a reaction against total assimilation than a desire to become Americanized.

RACE AND *MESTIZAJE* AMONG LATINOS

A distinctive and interesting trait of Hispanics is in fact related to their historic origins. They are for the most part a mixture of bloods between Native Americans and immigrants from Europe, especially from Spain. Latinos include mixed-blood African descendants whose ancestors were slaves on the sugar plantations of Mexico, Puerto Rico, Cuba, and the Dominican Republic; descendants of Spaniards whose families intermarried with American Indians; Chinese descendants whose forebears went to Cuba and Central America as contract laborers; and full-blooded "Native American" Latinos, such as the Mixtecs of Mexico who speak Spanish as a second language. Such ethnic differences can affect the receptiveness of distinct groups of Latinos to programs for Asians or blacks, for example.

While race has been used as a way to study populations in the United States, Latinos seldom use race as a group identifier. Instead, they may identify themselves by the term *mestizo*, referring to persons of "mixed blood or ancestry." To call oneself a mestizo is to say that one is a mixture of some combination of white, black, Asian, Native American, and so on. Recent research has found that Latinos tend to marry within their own national origin group, but intermarriage is increasing. According to del Pinal and Singer (1997, p. 28):

> Two features of the intermarriage of Hispanics are important to their place in U.S. society. First, they are much more likely than African Americans to marry outside their race/ethnic group, suggesting that Hispanics are more assimilated into U.S. mainstream society than African Americans. Second, Hispanics are more likely to marry a non-Hispanic than someone from another Latino group. This underscores the distinct identity of each Hispanic ethnic group.

Being mestizo does not mean that a Latino ignores the question of race or racism. But being mestizo suggests that race is rarely dichotomized. Rather, race exists on a continuum. Thus, non-Latinos should not expect Hispanics and Latinos to willingly categorize themselves by race, that is, black, white, or Asian, as expected in the United States where color and race are used to identify ethnic groups.

On the other hand, Latinos may refer to themselves and others by color or physical features, such as *güero* or *blanco* (terms for light skin), or *moreno, prieto,* or *negro* (terms for dark skin). Among Mexican-origin Latinos, you hear people called by nicknames such as *flaco* (skinny), *gordo* (fat), *chato* (plugged nose), *peludo* (hairy), or *barbudo* (bearded). These are usually terms of endearment rather than of denigration, and are frequently used as interpersonal identifiers.

In addition, given the intermarriage of Latinos, they can have a variety of last names which come from many parts of the world. Latinos may be named Hernández or Martínez. But they can also be named Rosenberg or Wong. Names are not as critical an issue either among Latinos. Instead, a Latino develops a sense of himself or herself according to other traits or interests which we discuss later in this chapter.

Of the multiple generations of Latinos in America, not all speak Spanish and not all are Catholic or even religious for that matter. Not all are fully assimilated or even acculturated to the degree that they all speak English well and prefer to be called "American." Nonetheless, their diversity is often lost in the popular images of Latinos and consequently, Latinos are mistakenly treated as a monolithic group.

TAKING STOCK OF LATINO YOUTH

Beyond changing demographics, there are several challenges that Latino youth struggle to overcome. Today's Latino youth, for example, will be most affected by the aging of the non-Latino population. In the year 2000, Latino youth will have to face the so-called "burden of support" in America. Consider the following example. In 1990, 30 million people were elderly (65 or over). By 2000, that number will have increased to 35 million and by 2010 it will be 40 million, more or less. Looking further out to 2030, when today's Latino youth will be in their forties and fifties, they will likely be the majority of the labor force and all of the retired will be made up primarily of white, non-Hispanic, and black senior citizens, amounting to about 65 million persons over the age of 65. In short, the burden of support relates to who will work and who will support the retired workers. Also consider the following: In 1950, 17 people were at work for every retired person. Today the number has dropped to roughly 3 active workers for every retired person. By 2000 or a little later, we could be looking at only 2.5 workers per retiree. By 2030, we could easily expect 2 workers per retiree, and at least one of those workers will be a Latino.

The burden of supporting these future generations may rest primarily on a "minority-status" Latino population, which will certainly be smaller in relation to the white population it supports. It is very conceivable that today's Latino youth will be expected to carry a burden of support of one Latino worker for every two retired folk. For some time, the white (non-Hispanic) birthrate has been falling, to a point where it is now below the zero population growth level. In 1990, non-Hispanic whites had a fertility rate (live births per 1,000 women) of 12.9, which was less than half that of the fertility rate for Hispanics (26.0). The African American birthrate has gone down, too, and appears to be approaching the white birthrate. The Asian American birthrate is in between the rates for African Americans and Latinos. Because of these differences, the white (non-Latino) and African American fractions of the population are shrinking relative to the Latinos (and Asian Americans) who are growing in absolute terms.

The different age structures are also apparent in the population pyramids of del Pinal and Singer (1997). Each of the two pyramids (Figures

1.1 and 1.2) is graphed the same way. On the horizontal axis is the percentage of "male" and "female" of the populations in question. On the vertical axis is the number of males and females of particular age groups. The pyramid for the non-Hispanic group has a relatively narrow base, tapered inward at the bottom for the population less than 40 years of age. This shape shows that non-Hispanics are not sustaining their numbers by maintaining previous rates of fertility. It is also evident that the bulk of the non-Hispanic group is over 40 years of age and increasing its share of the aged population much more quickly than the Hispanic group. In comparison, the pyramid for the Hispanic group widens at the base, showing that Latinos have more children in their pipeline for future generations, relative to the aging groups of Latinos.

It is reasonable to predict that the pyramids for Hispanics and non-Hispanics will project in different ways. Latino youth will grow disproportionately larger over time and non-Hispanic youth (except for Asian American youth) will shrink steadily in number.

A closer look at the base of the pyramid shows the potential stock of "human capital." In 1990, approximately 8.5 million Latinos were under the age of 20. More importantly, there has been a clear-cut increase in the rise of Latino youth as indicated in Table 1–1. Notice, for example, how the group of Latinos under 5 years of age is much larger than the older groups, going up in age. If this growing number of Latinos is educated and prepared for the new types of employment of the market, then America will be in a strong economic position. These data suggest that Latino youth may be as important to the future of the majority population as they are to the future of Latinos themselves.

Table 1.1 Hispanic Youth, by Sex and Age, 1990

Age	Males	Females	Total
Under 5 years	1,187,526	1,142,826	2,330,352
5 to 9 years	1,109,396	1,065,067	2,174,463
10 to 14 years	1,020,192	967,764	1,987,956
15 to 19 years	1,044,635	937,263	1,981,898
Total	4,361,749	4,112,920	8,474,669

Source: From U.S. Bureau of the Census. *1990 Census of Population* [On-line]. Available: http://www.census.gov/main/www/cen1990.html (April 20, 1999).

Figure 1.1 Demographic Pyramid for Hispanics, 1990

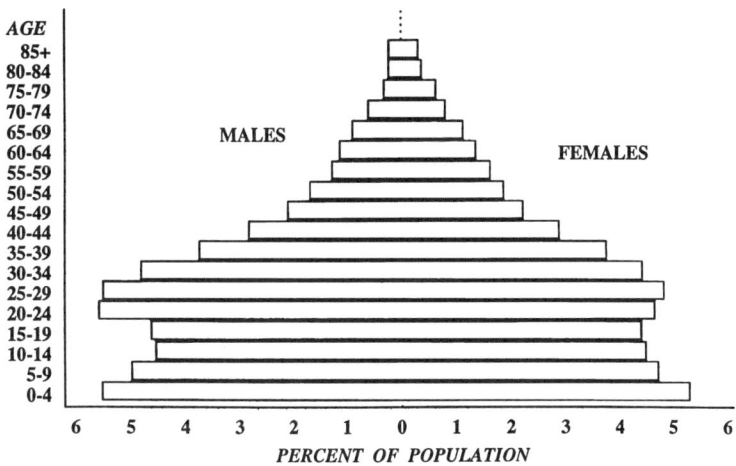

Source: U.S. Bureau of the Census. (On-line) at http:/www.census.gov/ population/estimates/nation/e90s/e9696rmp.zip (March 7, 1997)

Figure 1.2 Demographic Pyramid for Non-Hispanics, 1990

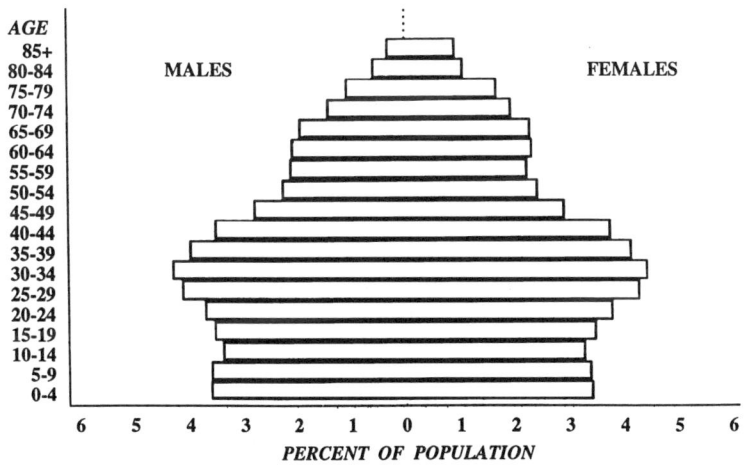

Source: U.S. Bureau of the Census. (On-line) at http:/www.census.gov/ population/estimates/nation/e90s/e9696rmp.zip (March 7, 1997)

LATINO CONCENTRATION

On the basis of fertility rates alone, Latino youth will assuredly become the majority population in certain states like California, Texas, and Illinois. Latinos will constitute the larger share of school-age children in many schools. In California, the state's leaders of education already refer to the next decade of Latinos as "Tidal Wave II." Furthermore, Latino youth will be entering the labor market at increasing rates and it is not certain if they will have a preferred place in better-paying occupations.

Where Latino concentration rises, however, studies have shown more problems than opportunities exist for them. On the one hand, Latino youth are caught in situations of more social conflict and tensions. On the other hand, Latino youth can also be in a position to take more active roles as leaders and workers. Changing demographics will certainly produce a social revolution wherein secular traditions of doing business, forming alliances, defining family and community, and generating public choices and policies will be transformed. Thus, the new millennium poses a critical juncture for Latino youth to convert the current challenges into future opportunities.

Given these challenges, should society in general want to know if Latino youth will be prepared for the opportunities emerging with such demographic changes? Will Latino youth be satisfied members of communities and be able to do the kinds of jobs the United States needs most? Will their social and political relationships with non-Hispanics be harmonious and productive? If Latino youth, for example, become the nation's largest minority population in the United States, will the balance of attention shift primarily to them and with what status?

DEFINING AND MEASURING LATINO YOUTH

Several studies of Latinos all conclude that Hispanic Americans are extremely difficult to define. Most academics concur that Hispanic Americans are so diverse that they cannot be categorized into a homogeneous group. They all point to the profusion of many different labels to identify and account for Latinos. How then do we count and assess the ethnic identity status of Latinos?

Since 1980, the term *Hispanic* has been used frequently in census counts and government programs and projects. But the term is not uniformly accepted by all Latinos. The vast majority of Latinos generally identify themselves in relation to the country from which they or their ancestors came, such as Chicano (U.S. Southwest), Cuban American, Mexican American, *Dominicano, Boricua* (the indigenous name of Puerto Rico), and so on. According to some researchers, including the authors of this chapter, the term *Latino* or *Chicano* has been more commonly expressed in California, but is growing in popularity in the Midwest as migration across the States has grown. In the Southwestern and Midwestern states, in general, the term *la raza* is used among Latinos as a way to refer to themselves as people related by blood ties or strong bonds, particularly among Mexican Americans. According to Anzaldúa (1997, p. 240), the term *raza* is attributable to José Vasconselos, the Mexican philosopher who conceived *"una Raza mestiza, una mezcla de razas afines, una raza de color—la primera raza sintesis del globo"*[1] (p. 240): the cosmic race. The term *Latino* appears to be more popular in areas with the greatest concentrations of Mexican Americans and Mexicans. In addition, according to del Pinal and Singer (1997), persons who identify themselves as Latinos tend to be more involved than self-identified Hispanics in enhancing the political rights and opportunities of their group, but the term is not preferred by most Hispanics. In 1997 del Pinal and Singer reported (p. 5) "A 1995 survey by the Census Bureau that found that 58 percent of persons of Hispanic/Latino background preferred the term Hispanic; only 12 percent favored Latino."

THE MEANING OF *HISPANIC* AND ISSUES OF HISPANIC IDENTITY

In 1980 and 1990 the U.S. Census counted respondents of any race as Hispanics if they identified themselves as part of any of the following groups: Mexican, Mexican American, Chicano, Puerto Rican, *Nuyurican* (of New York), Hispano (of Colorado and New Mexico), *Tejano* (of Texas), Cuban, South and/or Central American. In other words, individuals who self-identified as being of Latin American origin, including persons from Spanish-speaking countries of the Caribbean or from Spain, would be counted as Hispanic. In contrast, unless Americans self-identified as being of Spanish origin from the aforementioned groups, they would not be considered Hispanic by the Census Bureau.

There are several problems with the concept and measure of "Hispanics" in the United States. For example, Earl Shorris (1992, p. xiii), in the first line of his magnus opus *Latinos: A Biography of the People,* notes that "Latinos, who will soon be the largest group of minorities in the United States, are not one nationality, one culture, but many." Shorris goes on with several biographical sketches to prove the point of great diversity and great divisions between Latinos.

Also, as noted by Geoffrey Fox (1996, p. 3):

> "Hispanics" don't have a common biological descent. "Hispanics," the Census Bureau reminds us . . . can also be of any religion and any citizenship status, from undocumented to U.S. citizen by birth, and may have any of over twenty distinct national histories . . . they do not even all share the first language . . . Others whose ancestors may never have really mastered Spanish but who had Spanish surnames imposed on them by their conquerors—Mayans, Quechuas, Filipinos, and so on—are often given, and sometimes willingly assume, the label "Hispanic."

Also, according to Massey (1993, p. 453):

> In theory, Hispanics include all those who trace their origins to a region originally colonized by Spain. It subsumes Argentines whose grandparents migrated from Italy to Buenos Aires at the turn of the century, Chinese whose forebearers were brought to Cuba as contract laborers, Amerindians whose progenitors entered the Amazon 30,000 years ago, Africans whose ancestors were imported to work as slaves on the sugar plantations of Puerto Rico, Spaniards whose families colonized Mexico, and mestizos who trace their lineage to the coerced union of Amerindian women and Spanish men.

But Fox (1996), on the other hand, suggests that all these issues of identity may not dissuade Latinos from adopting the concept of "Hispanic." He argues (p. 239) that more and more Latinos relate to the idea of Hispanicity, partially due to discrimination:

> The Hispanic nation is American not only because the ancestors of many of its members were established here before there was a United States. It is American because the whole idea of "Hispanicness" or of a "Latino community" is a home-grown response to problems of discrimination. It is not an ethnic identity that Spanish-speaking people bring with them when they arrive but something they create in response to conditions here in this country and is shaped by U.S. institutions ranging from the structure of the telecommunications industry to the practices of art galleries and museums.

Latino Youth 13

According to Bean and Tienda (1987), Hispanic identity is and will always be a personal matter, formulated by local conditions where ethnicity is "socially produced." Specifically, Bean and Tienda (p. 11) assert that:

> We believe that ethnicity is predominantly a social phenomenon organized around outwardly visible physical and cultural differences between two or more groups... That many Hispanic immigrants and their descendants have yet to assimilate culturally or socially and occupy lower socio-economic positions raises the possibility that a greater congruence of ethnic distinctiveness and socio-economic position may characterize their experience.

THE CONDITIONS THAT UNIFY LATINOS

According to Fox (1996) Hispanic Americans are unifying in distinct and discernible ways because of the growth of Latino culture. To wit (quoting from book jacket):

> Only in recent years have great numbers of Hispanics begun to consider themselves as related within a single culture. Hispanics are redefining their own images and agendas, shaping a population, and paving wider pathways to power. In the process, they are changing both themselves and the culture, government, and urban habits of the communities around them.

Of course, Fox's assertion still begs the question, What draws Latinos together? What are the conditions under which Latinos unify? And, for Latino youth, are they even interested in ultimately choosing one label that becomes a marker of panethnic self-identity?

Although Latinos are not all alike and do not comprise a single, monolithic community in the United States, there are many situations when Latinos rally together. In the decade of the 1990s alone, Hispanics were brought to the forefront of national interest with ballot initiatives in California, Texas, and other states against bilingual (English-Spanish) education; affirmative action; changing street names to recognize Hispanic leaders such as César Chávez; noncitizens; and border crossers from Mexico, whether legal or undocumented. The availability of more written works on Latinos by Latino authors, Spanish-language materials, bilingual programs, and Spanish heritage music, arts, and so on has begun to generate a Latino call to a common cause. Other factors for unification are issues of family (*familia*), immigration, work ethic, and community (*la comunidad*).

Few studies address the unifying issues of Latinos. But to us there is something to be said about recent issues being discussed by the popular press, especially in the 1990s. Our thoughts to date include the following causes for unity among Latinos.

Spanish Language versus English Only

The Spanish language is a common interest of the Latino population. Attacks against bilingual education have tended to harness Latinos together to defend Spanish teaching and Spanish materials in public places. This is supported by the fact that about 80 percent of Hispanics (age 5 and older) speak Spanish rather than English at home. In 1990 nearly 40 percent reported that they did not speak English well or at all. But the remaining 60 percent spoke English, of whom approximately 10 percent spoke only English at home (U.S. Bureau of the Census, available online). Thus, the Spanish language plays an important role in mediating the diversity among Hispanics.

This adherence to Spanish does not include resistance to learning English or working hard in the American economy. As highlighted in *Latino Voices,* a recent book by Latino scholars (De la Garza, DeSipio, García, García, & Falcón, 1992), Latinos prefer reading and watching news in the English media, although persons who speak no English still need Spanish news.

Nearly all studies about language show that Latinos vow to learn English. They see English as the primary way to get ahead in the United States today. Unlike proponents for English only, Latinos discard the supposition that English acquisition should constitute a rejection of Spanish language and Latino culture. English and Spanish are not treated as mutually exclusive alternatives among Latinos as a whole. Moreover, the experience of most Latinos is that a lack of English does not necessarily reduce employability. Research groups (e.g., Massey, 1993) have found that English language ability is not related to the likelihood of employment among Hispanics of all national origins.

Family Values and Structures

Another common theme among Latinos pertains to the values they attach to family, or *la familia*. The subject of recent movies, the notion of a common interest in *la familia* is not always seen in a positive light. While strong Hispanic family values lead to what is perhaps the world's most humane treatment of the aged by subsequent generations, according to Harrison (1992, p. 34), "The radius of trust and confidence ends with the family, and that means that the sense of community ends with the family. It leads to nepotism, corruption."

We do not agree with this blanket description of Latino families. Our understanding of Latino heterogeneity alone should lead readers to discount Harrison's general depiction of Latinos.

Nonetheless, psychologists, social scientists, and some anthropologists describe Latinos as imparting certain family values with various shades of adherence. The most commonly ascribed traits of Latinos, as compared to non-Latino whites, are that Latinos are relatively *(a)* more allocentric and group-oriented, and less individualistic and competitive than non-Latino whites; *(b)* more sympathetic, congenial, and relatively respectful of the needs and behaviors of others; *(c)* more familistic, showing a relatively strong solidarity and attachment to extended families; and *(d)* more socially close, liking personal associations and close distance in conversation.

In addition to these traits, we also add that Latinos have in common a unique form of "trust," or *confianza*, between each other and with regard to non-Latinos. To a certain degree Latinos are "cooperative soldiers," joining common causes such as marches for the United Farmworkers or protests against discrimination. Latinos tend to build *confianza* over several incidences of cooperation and trust. Within the Latino community, building and maintaining relationships is not only paramount, but a source of individual and familial support, trust, and cooperation. This sense of trust or cooperation, however, is not always understood or appreciated by non-Latino whites. So when a thin line of trust is broken between Latinos and non-Latinos, a concomitant rise in suspicion and noncooperation may result. All it takes is one lie or a sense of distrust to lose commitment and interest among Latinos to work with non-Latino groups. Although the degree of such cooperation, or *confianza*, may vary widely among Hispanics themselves, the knowledge that such feelings exist in general should be factored into the work of antipoverty agents who work with Latino poor.

Common Interests in Immigrant Rights

Immigrant status and questions of immigration are sensitive matters among Latinos. Immigrant rights also connect Latinos to common causes concerning police actions and protective labor laws. Let us highlight some particular facts about immigrants that draw a common interest among Latinos. Despite the fact that immigration has loomed large in importance in this decade, only a small percentage of Latinos, albeit a significant fraction, are directly affected by immigrant status. That is, only 36 percent of all Latinos (as of the 1990 Census) were born outside the United States or its territories. This means that the majority of Latinos are native-born or U.S. citizens by right of birth. So of the 29 million Hispanics in the United States today, only about 9 million are foreign-born. Of these, approximately 30 percent of the foreign-born Latinos are naturalized U.S. citizens. So altogether, when we talk about Latinos as an immigrant population, we should not lose sight of the fact that about 75 percent of the total of 28 million are U.S. citizens. Moreover, of the foreign-born population of Latinos who are not yet naturalized citizens, the overwhelming majority are legal residents, living and working in the United States as legitimate taxpayers. Of the largest group of Latinos, Mexican Americans, who currently bear the brunt of anti-immigrant bashing in California, only about 33 percent (of 14 million) were born in Mexico; the rest, or 67 percent, were born in the United States or elsewhere.

Nonetheless, almost all Latinos have relatives in Latin America. They are connected to Latin America by language, culture, and family ties. Such connections have grown in recent years with the opening of trade (e.g., the North American Free Trade Agreement) and travel between nations. Such connections have strengthened because of music, literature, art, and global communication networks which allow Latin American programs to be seen readily in the United States. Hence, for Latinos, actions against Latino immigrants are taken as actions against Latinos.

No wonder that attacks by non-Latinos on Mexican immigrants, for example, and related measures for English-only documents, are rallying cries for most Latinos. Instead of backing down in the face of anti-immigrant issues—in particular, California's Proposition 187—Latinos are registering to vote in record numbers, applying for U.S. citizenship, and reinforcing their interests in bilingual education, multiculturalism, reform of school curricula, and so on. Thus, the attempts of non-Latinos to force Latinos to assimilate the Anglo way are being met with resistance (see García, 1996).

Common Socioeconomic Indicators

The poverty rate among Latinos is high, approximating the poverty rate among African Americans. The poverty rate among female-headed

Latino households is critical: almost 50 percent are poor. More alarming, the number of female heads of households in poverty is growing more among Latinos than among non-Latinos. However, the largest share of the increase in Latino poverty can be attributed to married couples. Although the poverty rate of Latino married-couple families was 18.5 percent in 1992, this was 6 percentage points higher than in 1979. Moreover, Latino married couples accounted for 49 percent of the total growth in the number of poor Latino families during the 1980s, growing in number from 298,000 impoverished couples in 1979 to 680,000 in 1992.

There are relatively higher incidences of Latino youth living in poverty. In 1979, 21.3 percent of Hispanic families were living in poverty. When considering only families with children under the age of 18, the poverty rate for Hispanic families increased to 25.2 percent, compared to 9.4 percent for white families with children under the age of 18. Most discouraging is that 56.3 percent of Hispanic female-headed families with children under the age of 18 lived in poverty. This figure compares to 32.1 percent for whites and 52.7 percent for blacks.

In this decade, Latino poverty cannot be separated from immigrant status because many foreign-born Latinos are recent arrivals who carry the burden of under- and unemployment as well as limited education and English language fluency. Newly arrived immigrants from Mexico, Puerto Rico, and the Dominican Republic are invariably poor and less educated. They bring with them a big heart for work but a difficult set of socioeconomic traits that limit their occupations.

Work Ethic and Labor Force Participation

A fundamental trait of Latinos has to do with the work ethic. With few exceptions, Latinos are the most active participants in the American labor market, beginning employment at an early age and working well into the usual years of retirement. While studies of labor force participation show a general trend toward declining rates of people at work or looking for work, Latino men, especially Mexican men, consistently present a higher rate of labor force participation than the non-Latino population in general.

Among Latinos, a work ethic is passed down from generation to generation, immigrant or not. In 1980, Hispanic males age 16 to 19 participated in America's workforce at a rate of 48.3 percent, which trailed the national average (for this age group) by 1.6 percent. White, black, and Asian American males of the same age group participated at 53.2 percent, 33.0 percent, and 38.4 percent, respectively. The same year, 38.7

percent of Hispanic females age 16 to 19 were in the workforce, compared to 48.8 percent of white females, 29.8 percent of black females, and 39.0 percent of Asian American females. Ten years later, the rate of employment for this same age group of Hispanic males (16 to 19) rose to 50.1 percent, surpassing the national average of 49.5 percent. They were second, in terms of participation, only slightly to white males, whose percentage was recorded as 52.6 percent, but by far exceeded black males (36.7 percent) and Asian American males (35.6 percent). The year 1990 also saw a rise in the labor force participation rate for Hispanic females 16 to 19 years of age. Although their rate measured in at 42.1 percent, it was still lagging behind the rate reported for white females (52.5 percent), but surpassed that of black females (38.3 percent) and Asian American females (36.0 percent).

Unfortunately, as indicated above, foreign-born Latinos also spend a great deal of time unemployed and looking for work. That is due in part to the precarious nature of their employment in industries that provide few worker protections or fringe benefits of employment and health insurance. Latino males continue to work mainly as laborers, fabricators, and operators. Latino females continue to work mainly in sales, secretarial, and clerical jobs. Unemployment rates remain consistently higher for Latinos than for non-Latinos, usually 1.5 times higher. With such occupational conditions, it is no wonder that the median earnings for year-round, full-time Latino males were about 63 percent those of non-Latino white males in 1992 ($20,054 to $31,765), while the median earnings of Hispanic females were about 78 percent those of non-Latino white females ($17,124 to $21,930). Two segments of the American workforce which are largely disregarded but oftentimes play an integral economic role in Latino communities are the unlicensed vendor and the unskilled pieceworker.

All combined, these factors relate to two conflicting characteristics of Latinos. One is that Latinos work hard but do not earn enough to escape poverty. They are concentrated in low-wage jobs with few fringe benefits or opportunities for employment security and upward mobility. In either case, Latino workers do not receive much recognition for the work they do or adequate attention to their work-related poverty; thus, they are deprived of programs and policies to relieve the poor.

The growing Latino presence underscores the need to address the "working poor." While Latino males have one of the highest rates of labor force participation (referring to the fact that over 80 percent of working-age Latinos are in the labor force, most of the time), their low wages and seasonal employment (often without fringe benefits and long-term security) relegate them to the ranks of the poor. Their poverty is persistent and increasing, characterized by low levels of education and low participation in public assistance programs.

HOW LATINO YOUTH SEE THE FUTURE

What are the chances that Latinos will overcome poverty and benefit from their growing numbers? One answer depends on their sense of identity and willingness to align themselves with common issues and concerns.

Recently, while delivering a stirring university graduation speech, a Chicano student activist proudly proclaimed that he owed all his academic success to his *jefe* (literally meaning "boss" or "chief," but commonly used by Chicanos as a term of endearment for their father). This young man proudly boasted that his father didn't finish high school and could barely read English. He never helped him with his homework and he never went to school with him to intercede when there was a problem. But he said that he owed everything to him for teaching him how to get up in the morning. He owed his father for teaching him a work ethic. He went on to describe how his father told him that education is the key to upward mobility in this country, and the best way to understand this concept is to be uneducated.

In a society where the pool of jobs which require little or no postsecondary education continues to evaporate, this young man's father's advice is wise, indeed. The Rand report on Latino education (Sorenson, Brewer, Carroll, & Bryton, 1995) estimates that Hispanic men with a bachelor's degree enjoyed a $500,000 lifetime premium over Hispanic men with a high school diploma ($400,000 for Hispanic women). Furthermore, Hispanics with professional degrees increase their life earnings by over 200 percent or $1.7 million (Sorensen et al., 1995). These impressive projections notwithstanding, towering high school dropout rates coupled with very low postsecondary participation rates guarantee that the fastest-growing segment of our population will also be the fastest-growing pool of low-skilled laborers. The most interesting characteristic exhibited by these figures is not that they show signs of sporadic disparity drawn along racial/ethnic lines; rather, they reveal a noticeable gap between the rates shown for Hispanic males and females.

Latest figures show that at the national level Latino purchasing power is equal to $350 billion per year and growing at an annual rate close to 8 percent. The big Latino markets are located in the states with high concentrations of Latinos; thus, California, Texas, Florida, New York, and Illinois grasp a high percentage of the transactions made by Latinos. Most of the purchases made by the Latino community are oriented toward consumer goods and durable products. As might be expected, young Latinos purchase mostly consumer goods (food items, clothing, and cosmetics).

It is interesting to note that the purchasing characteristics of the Latino community differ based on the population's national origin, educational level, and wealth status. For example, Mexican-origin Latinos prefer to purchase traditional food products, which differ from the products demanded by the other communities (Puerto Ricans, Cubans, and others). Currently, all the communities are slowly adopting the food and clothing habits of mainstream America, demanding the same types of products that the majority of Americans consume.

We assume that the demand for consumer goods will increase considerably in the next decade in spite of the low income levels for most of the Latino households and their income inelasticity. Higher levels of purchasing power need to be correlated with the demand for high-quality products. All these issues have already been recognized by large and small companies trying to sell their products to Latinos. Large amounts of money are currently spent for the design and implementation of advertising campaigns directed to the community.

From the supply side, we can observe that Latinos are very good entrepreneurs. According to the 1990 Census (U.S. Bureau of the Census, available on-line), in the last decade the number of Latino companies nationwide has doubled. Currently there are more than 10,000 Hispanic-owned firms in the United States. These companies created 500,000 new jobs. The level of businesses generated by these new companies has been steadily increasing. New markets have continually been opened. Some of these companies are competing in the international markets with high-quality products, and trying to expand their business activities at home and abroad. Most of the new entrepreneurs are young people looking for new business possibilities.

SOME NEGATIVE SIGNS: POTENTIALLY SERIOUS ISSUES

The youthfulness of the Latino population and its burgeoning size have been identified as key factors behind the nation's future supply of labor. Employers will only gain by investing more of their resources and activity in partnering with higher education to ensure the employability of this growing population of Latino workers. If educational alliances work, then we could expect Latinos to comprise one of the most valuable components of the labor market by the year 2000. But Latino youth have options and problems to contend with. They are not all oriented toward mainstream society. As Latino youth are the fastest-growing segment of our society, it is of paramount importance that we become more familiar with the serious issues that they face. A quick review of the national statistics gives glaring evidence that middle and high school dropout rates, low rates of postsecondary educational participation, gang membership, substance abuse, teen pregnancy, and HIV/AIDS-related health problems are issues which merit serious concern. Although these issues are potentially devastating for all youth, regardless of race/ethnicity, researchers suggest that they may be more prevalent for this community than for the overall population of the United States (Ramos, 1991; Solis, 1995). Furthermore, the racial, ethnic, and socioeconomic diversity of this community requires that researchers approach it with an acute sensitivity to the cultural and socioeconomic underpinnings associated with these phenomena and not confuse them with the stereotypes being popularized by the mass media.

Deviant and Criminal Acts

There is little literature on Hispanic youth and delinquency from the last decade. Even in the decade of the 1990s this lack of information is not expected to improve, as the FBI has stopped compiling crime and delinquency data by ethnicity (Río, Santisteban, & Szapocznik, 1991). However, Hispanic youth are increasingly overrepresented in juvenile facilities. In 1991, Hispanic youth comprised 13.8 percent of the population in detention centers, 13.6 percent in recreational (detention) centers, and 8.5 percent of training schools (U.S. Bureau of the Census, available on-line). Nevertheless, incarceration rates are no reliable measure of delinquency, especially since Hispanic youth tend to have relatively higher rates of incarceration and receive harsher sentences than are warranted by the type and frequency of their offenses (Kristber, Schwartz, Fishman, Eisikovits, & Guttman, 1986; Morales, Fergusen, & Mumford, 1983: both as cited in Río, Santisteban, & Szapocznik, 1991). Most disturbing is that incarceration rates for Hispanic youth are quickly gaining on the rates at which this population is represented within the nation's educational system, which underscores our need for educational programs designed to recruit and retain this population rather than lose them to the penal system.

Culturally Relevant and Responsive Education Needed

As Hispanics as a whole struggle with mainstream issues to defy popular stereotypes, it is becoming increasingly clear that they need more education for survival. Educational attainment is at the top of their list of integrating strategies, becoming a common rallying cry of Hispanic communities across the nation. Nevertheless, Latino education has become a double-edged sword. On one side, it is highly regarded by this community as a means by which it can gain access to diminishing resources. On the other, the flourishing Hispanic presence has been at odds with other minority groups that perceive their own resources as being threatened by immigrant newcomers.

Between 1983 and 1993, the percentage of adult Latinos (age 25 and older) who reported graduation from high school increased from 46 percent to 53 percent. Meanwhile, about 9 percent have now attended at least four years of college, slightly more than a decade ago. But even as America's fastest-growing ethnic group, Latinos lag behind all others in education. Non-Latinos show graduation rates of 80 percent for high school and 22 percent for college. So there is a widening gap between Latinos and non-Latinos that cannot be ignored.

Being perceived as newcomers is a point of great contention for this community. Some community activists maintain that this is precisely the stereotype that the educational system fosters by its reluctance to include material that gives a more accurate portrayal of U.S. history and a less xenophobic approach to minority communities in its curricula. However, if assimilation has been a major goal of the U.S. society, it has seemingly used education as the fire that heats the melting pot. This melting pot mentality has been a great driving force throughout U.S. history, and it is largely responsible for the American way of life. However, certain minority groups (e.g., Latinos, blacks, Native Americans, and Asian Americans) have greatly suffered discrimination and have never been encouraged to join the American mainstream (Curiel, 1991).

Opponents of multiculturally based education seem to be following two paths in constructing their arguments. Both arguments, however, imply that Latino (minority) culture is inherently inferior, and is the reason for such poor educational and economic showing (Lambourne & Baca Zinn, 1993). Some boldly argue that poor educational achievement and low intelligence testing among Hispanics may be genetically linked (Curiel, 1991). However, there appears to be an emergence of a "new and improved" version of the "underclass model," which makes a cultural instead of genetic link, and is framed within an assimilationist perspective (Hurtado, 1995). This model seems to be an extension of the "culture of poverty" thesis, which contends that the reason for poverty is rooted in ethnic communities' cultural deviance from the Anglo mainstream. Hispanic children have long been assumed to be more affiliative and cooperative, whereas white children are more individualistic, competitive, and feel a need for achievement (Lucas & Stone, 1994). This concept promotes the notion that the lack of Latino economic and educational advancement is easily explained by such cultural transgressions as lack of parental interest in education (Lambourne & Baca Zinn, 1993), excessive masculinity, a strong sense of familism, and low aspirations (Baca Zinn, 1989, as cited in Hurtado, 1995). Therefore, success, educational or otherwise, will come with assimilation.

Ample evidence exists to support the correlation between the stratification of educational attainment along racial/ethnic lines and the processes of education itself (i.e., inequitable resources available to schools, differing teacher expectations, and tracking systems advantageous to those already benefiting from the educational system [Lambourne & Baca Zinn, 1993]). Nevertheless, conservative politicians and educators still argue against programs that are perceived to stall the assimilation process (e.g., bilingual education, culturally relevant curricula, affirmative action programs designed to increase the number of Latino students in higher education, and sorely needed Latino educators). However, as Latino scholars, politicians, community activists, and students themselves gain greater numbers, they can be proof positive that educational success is not tantamount to assimilation. Moreover, an emergence of young Latinos asserting the retention of their ethnic identity as a means, rather than a hindrance, to gaining success, seems to be gaining prominence.

The questions of identity are being played out in high schools and college campuses across the nation. Student and young community activists are pushing for the resurgence of the Chicano movement in the Mid- and Southwest, and the *Boricua* (Puerto Rican) movement in the East. Students originally chartered these two indigenously rooted movements during the Civil Rights unrest of the 1960s. However, they are now being commandeered by student activists across the nation who are advocating for institutional equity for Latinos through education; and appropriately so, given that 37.8 percent of all Hispanics (in 1990) were under the age of 19, and are the fastest-growing segment of the population. Even so, the 1990 Census (U.S. Bureau of the Census, available on-line) reported that only 52.1 percent of Hispanics between the ages of 18 and 24 had completed high school, compared to 81.7 percent of whites and 75.1 percent of blacks for the same age group. The same year counted 32.4 percent of the Hispanics between the ages of 16 and 24 as high school dropouts, more than triple the rate for whites (9.0 percent) and almost triple the rate for blacks (13.2 percent) in the same age group. Such dismal high school completion rates for Hispanics have gravely diminished the pool of admissible candidates for college, leaving them one of the most critically underrepresented groups in higher education. Fortunately, this rate is on an upward trend as the overall participation rate of Latinos in postsecondary education increased from 14.2 percent in 1980 to 22.9 percent in 1990. Despite this, Latino youth are still lagging behind their white (35.9 percent, 1990), black (27.1 percent, 1990), and Asian American (55.1 percent, 1990) counterparts. Additionally, only 12 percent of Hispanic 22-year-olds attain a bachelor's degree, compared to 15 percent of blacks and 25 percent of whites the same age (Sorensen et al., 1995).

CONCLUSIONS

Much more research and thought will be needed to identify opportunities for Latino youth and perhaps to develop strategies to incorporate Latino youth in more positive roles as leaders, academics, and workers. Indeed, we would argue that we need a full-scale blueprint for investing in Latino youth and their futures. We envision a need for progressive programs that address issues of identity, education, income, growth, purchasing power, and deviant and criminal behavior. This is a complex set of challenges requiring an acute sensitivity to the cultural and socioeconomic underpinnings associated with these phenomena.

We assert that Latino youth must be examined within the context of one of the most powerful institutions that exists in their community: *la familia*. Immigration, recency of arrival, racial/ethnic diversity within the Latino community, racial definitions, and religiously rooted customs within the Latino community all play an integral part in the formation of diverse familial structures, attitudes, and trends. However, the traditional strength and cohesion of *la familia* remains universal. *La familia* sets this community apart as a unique entity, which necessitates the creation of new models of study. If nothing else, *la familia* compels youth and family scholars to broaden their understanding of how this community has weathered over 150 years of subjugation, discrimination, segregation, and marginalization, but has still managed to retain its strength and cohesion.

Assimilationists would have us believe that Latinos will eventually acculturate—adopting values, beliefs, and normative behaviors of the dominant culture and departing from their traditional (inferior) cultural traits (Montalvo, 1991). However, this idea implies that all Latinos are relatively recent immigrants. It further implies that new and prolonged contact with Anglos will eventually cause the erosion of the Latino family function and structure. But it does not consider the fact that some Latino subgroups and their families have been in contact with Anglos for over 150 years and have retained many of their unique characteristics (Griswold del Castillo, 1984). This is not to say that the Latino family is a static institution. Instead, it may be that assimilationists make no room for biculturalism. Bicultural people are unique in their ability to interact with their own people on their own cultural terms as well as the ability with which they negotiate through the dominant society (Blea, 1988).

Latinos are a vastly understudied group, but one that merits serious consideration when approaching the Latino youth and their persistent familial traits. We believe that biculturalism significantly mitigates some of the conflicts that researchers assume arise from the ideals and norms that are perceived to be counter to the Latino youth's cognitive beliefs and norms (i.e., race, gender, familism versus individualism). We also believe that this phenomenon merits more consideration in ways that would add considerably to our understanding of this community, its youth, and the structure and function of its families. Perhaps biculturalism offers a better explanation for the persistence of some trends, and variation of others, within the Latino community than the popular but simplistic cultural arguments offered now.

Finally, we would like to help foster greater incorporation of Latino youth in the economy as private entrepreneurs and public officials. Such efforts will have to involve leaders of the educational system, the private sector, and philanthropy, in order to sponsor policies and programs which will address needed changes in our population.

Despite the immensity of the challenges, we feel confident that opportunities are within reach for Latino youth. What it will take is supporters with desire, courage, and personal dedication to facing challenges as opportunities for Latino youth.

NOTES

[1]Translation: "a mixed race, a mix of all races, a race of color, the first synthetic, global race."

REFERENCES

Anzaldúa, G. (1997). *La conciencia da la Latina: Towards a new consciousness.* In M. Baca Zinn, P. Hondagneu-Sotelo, & M. Messner (eds.), *Through the prism of difference: Readings on sex and gender* (pp. 240–248). Needham Heights, MA: Allyn & Bacon.

Aponte, R., & Siles, M. (1994). *Latinos in the heartland: The browning of the Midwest.* (Research Report No. 5). East Lansing: Michigan State University, Julian Samora Research Institute.

Bean, F., & Tienda, M. (1987). *The Hispanic population in the United States.* New York: Russell Sage.

Blea, I. I. (1988). *Toward a Chicano social science.* New York: Prager.

Chapa, J., & Valencia, R. (1993). Latino population growth, demographic characteristics, and education stagnation: An examination of recent trends. *Hispanic Journal of Behavioral Sciences, 15*(2), 165–186.

Curiel, H. (1991). Strengthening family and school bonds in promoting Hispanic children's school performance. In M. Sotomayor (Ed.), *Empowering Hispanic families: A critical issue for the nineties* (pp. 75–95). Milwaukee, WI: Family Service America.

De la Garza, R. O., DeSipio, L., Garcia, F. C., Garcia, J., & Falcon, A. (1992). *Latino voices: Mexican, Puerto Rican, and Cuban perspectives on American politics.* Boulder, CO: Westview.

del Pinal, J., & Singer, A. (1997, October). *Generations of diversity: Latinos in the United States* (Population Bulletin, Vol. 52, No. 3). Washington, DC: Population Reference Bureau.

Duany, L., & Pittman, K. (1990). *Latino youth at a crossroads.* Washington, DC: Children's Defense Fund.

Fox, J. (1996). *Hispanic nation.* New York: Carol Publishing Group.

García, V. (1996). All was not lost: The political victories of Mexican immigrants in Guadalupe, California. In R. Rochin (Ed.), *Immigration and ethnic communities: A focus on Latinos* (pp. 109–115). East Lansing: Michigan State University, Julian Samora Research Institute.

Griswold del Castillo, R. (1984). *La familia: Chicano families in the urban Southwest.* Notre Dame, IN: University of Notre Dame Press.

Harrison, L. E. (1992). *Who prospers: How cultural values shape economic and political success.* New York: Basic Books.

Hodgkinson, H. L., & Outtz, J. H. (1996). *Hispanic Americans: A look back, a look ahead.* Washington, DC: Institute for Educational Leadership, Center for Demographic Policy.

Hurtado, A. (1995). Variations, combinations, and evolutions: Latino families in the United States. In R. Zambrana (Ed.), *Understanding Latino families* (pp. 40–60). Thousand Oaks, CA: Sage.

Lambourne, K., & Baca Zinn, M. (1993). *Education, race, and family: Issues for the 1990s* (Working Paper Series, No. 16). East Lansing: Michigan State University, Julian Samora Research Institute.

Lucas, J. R., & Stone, G. L. (1994). Acculturation and competition among Mexican Americans: A reconceptualization. *Hispanic Journal of Behavioral Sciences, 16*(2), 129–142.

Massey, D. (1993). Latinos, poverty, and the underclass: A new agenda for research. *Hispanic Journal of Behavioral Sciences, 15*(4), 449–475.

Montalvo, F. F. (1991). Phenotyping, acculturation, and biracial assimilation of Mexican Americans. In M. Sotomayor (Ed.), *Empowering Hispanic families: A critical issue for the nineties* (pp. 97–119). Milwaukee, WI: Family Service America.

National Association of Hispanic Publications. (1995). *Hispanics ó Latinos: Diverse people in a Multicultural Society* (Current Population Reports). Washington, DC: Author.

Ramos, J. (1991). Foreword. In M. Sotomayor (Ed.), *Empowering Hispanic families: A critical issue for the nineties.* Milwaukee, WI: Family Service America.

Río, A. T., Santisteban, D. A., & Szapocznik, J. (1991). Juvenile delinquency among Hispanics. In M. Sotomayor (Ed.), *Empowering Hispanic families: A critical issue for the nineties* (pp. 191–214). Milwaukee, WI: Family Service America.

Rumbaut, R. (1996). Immigrants from Latin America and the Caribbean: A socio-economic profile. In R. Rochin (Ed.), *Immigration and ethnic communities: A focus on Latinos* (pp. 1–9). East Lansing: Michigan State University, Julian Samora Research Institute.

Shorris, E. (1992). *Latinos: A biography of the people,* New York: Norton.

Short, J. F., Jr. (1996). Foreword: Diversity and change in U.S. gangs. In C. R. Huff (Ed.), *Gangs in America.* Thousand Oaks, CA: Sage.

Solís, J. (1995). The status of Latino children and youth: Challenges and prospects. In R. Zambrana (Ed.), *Understanding Latino Families* (pp. 62–80). Thousand Oaks, CA: Sage.

Sorensen, S., Brewer, D. J., Carroll, S. J., & Bryton, E. (1995). *Increasing Hispanic participation in higher education: A desirable public investment.* http://www.rand.org.

U.S. Bureau of the Census. *1990 Census of Population* [On-line]. Available: http://www.census.gov/main/www/cen1990.html (April 20, 1999).

U.S. Bureau of the Census. (1995). *Current Population Statistics.* P25–1130. Washington, DC: U.S. Government Printing Office.

U.S. Bureau of the Census. Available: http://www.census.gov/population/estimates/nation/e90s/e9696rmp.zip (March 7, 1997).

CHAPTER 2
The Impact of Growing Up Poor or Welfare-Dependent on the Economic Status of Young Adults
ANNA M. SANTIAGO

> *I grew up in a family that would be euphemistically characterized as the "working poor." The phrase implies that there is some dignity to living in poverty if you work hard. As a teenager and later as a young adult, I found no dignity in living in our tiny, three-room basement apartment with the rotting wood floors and raw sewage that routinely overflowed into our bathroom. Nor was poverty particularly comforting when sheets of ice formed on the inside of the unheated walls of my bedroom during the wintertime. In retrospect, I sometimes wonder if we would have been better off living in one of the public housing projects. I also wonder about the dignity attached to work—thinking about my mother who had a master's degree but never earned more than $5.50 an hour for her labor. Nevertheless, I still bought into the dream that getting an education would be the ticket out of poverty. I was one of the lucky ones to escape, unlike many of my peers.*
>
> AUTHOR'S DESCRIPTION OF GROWING UP
> IN THE WALKER'S POINT NEIGHBORHOOD

INTRODUCTION

Concern about the long-term effects of growing up poor or in welfare-dependent families resurged in the 1980s as poverty rates in the United

States climbed to 15 percent, public assistance expenditures soared to $69 billion, and the number of Aid to Families with Dependent Children (AFDC) recipients grew to approximately 11 million (U.S. Bureau of the Census, 1990). This concern was reinforced by empirical studies (e.g., Congress of the United States, 1990; Danziger & Gottschalk, 1993; Ellwood, 1988; Tienda & Jensen, 1988) which reported continued high poverty rates (U.S. Bureau of the Census, 1991a), increased numbers of workers with low earnings (U.S. Bureau of the Census, 1991b), increased income inequality, particularly between minorities and Anglos (Danziger & Gottschalk, 1993), and a growing concentration of poor blacks and Latinos in inner-city poverty neighborhoods (Massey & Denton, 1993; Santiago & Wilder, 1991; Wilson, 1987).

Particularly alarming was the sharp rise in child poverty rates during the 1980s. By 1989, approximately 20 percent of the nation's children were poor, giving the United States the dubious honor of ranking first among advanced industrialized nations in the proportion of children living in poverty (Danziger & Danziger, 1993; Duncan, 1991). This increase in child poverty was disproportionately shouldered by minority children: approximately one-half of the additional 2.2 million children who became poor in the 1980s were Latino and another one-quarter were black (Johnson, Miranda, Sherman, & Weill, 1991). Stemming from the increased impoverishment of minority families, nearly 45 percent of black and 40 percent of Latino children were poor in 1989 (Center on Budget and Policy Priorities, 1989; Danziger & Danziger, 1993; Johnson et al., 1991). Not surprisingly, changes in the composition of the welfare population during the 1980s reflected the rise in child poverty: approximately one-half of the nation's welfare recipients in 1989 were children (Danziger & Danziger, 1993; Duncan, 1991).

Recent studies (e.g., Crooks, 1995; Duncan, 1991; Huston, 1991; Danziger & Danziger, 1993) have reoriented the current poverty and welfare debate to more closely examine the impact of chronic poverty and welfare dependency on children. These studies suggest that poor children have limited opportunities for success. The negative impact of poverty on cognitive skills and academic achievement has been well documented (see reviews in Crooks, 1995; Huston, 1991). Edelman and Ladner (1991) reported that poor adolescents were more likely to be behind in grade level than nonpoor adolescents. Further, studies using longitudinal data have documented the long-term consequences of poverty status and welfare dependency. Relative to nonpoor children, Hill and Ponza (1983) found that three times as many children who grew up in poverty were poor as adults. Corcoran, Gordon, Laren, and Solon (1992) found that men growing up in poverty or in welfare families had lower earnings as adults. Similarly, Santiago and Padilla (1995) found that black and Latino men and women were more likely to have poverty-level earnings as young adults than their nonpoor counterparts. A number of studies also document higher rates of welfare dependency for women with welfare backgrounds (Antel, 1992; Duncan, 1991; Duncan, Hill, & Hoffman, 1988; Gottschalk, 1990, 1992). Finally, numerous studies have underscored the deleterious effect of poverty on children's health (see Crooks, 1995; Johnson et al., 1991). These studies suggest that poor children, particularly black and Latino children, have higher prevalence rates of low birth weight, chronic illness, lead poisoning, low health status, poor nutrition, and cognitive deficits.

The objective of this chapter is to examine the impact of growing up poor or in welfare-dependent families on the economic status of young adults. Specifically, three questions are addressed: (1) How do existing patterns of poverty and welfare dependency vary along ethnic lines or across the life course? (2) How does growing up poor or living in a welfare household during childhood affect the economic status of young adults? and (3) To what extent is chronic poverty or welfare dependency reflective of the intergenerational transmission of subcultural values propelling some individuals into a state of chronic deprivation? Or are these conditions the result of massive economic, demographic, and social change?

The chapter begins with a description of recent trends and patterns in poverty and welfare dependency in the United States. This is followed with a review of current explanations for the rise in poverty and welfare dependency. Next, the study methodology is described and the results of the empirical analyses are presented. The chapter concludes with a discussion of the policy implications of the findings.

TRENDS IN POVERTY AND WELFARE DEPENDENCY IN THE 1980s

Poverty Status

In 1989, slightly more than 10 percent of the population in the United States was poor. However, the risk of being poor varied considerably along ethnic lines and across the life course. For example, individual poverty rates for Latinos and blacks were approximately two to three times higher than the rates for Anglos (see Table 2.1). Among children, the differential in poverty rates between Anglos, blacks, and Latinos was even more dramatic. Latino child poverty rates were approximately three times higher than Anglo rates; black child poverty rates were about three and a half times higher. In addition, child poverty rates in 1989 were nearly twice the rate for the population as a whole (19.6 percent). Among young adults, the poverty rate for 18 to 24-year-olds was nearly 50 percent higher (15.3 percent) than the rate for the entire population. However, poverty rates for 25 to 34-year-olds were only slightly higher than overall poverty rates (11.1 percent).

During the 1980s, individual poverty rates in the United States rose slightly, from 10.1 percent to 10.6 percent. Overall, black poverty rates

Table 2.1 Recent Trends in Child and Young Adult Poverty Rates

	1979	1989
Child Poverty Status (0–18)		
All children	17.1	19.6
Anglo children	11.7	12.4
Black children	36.1	43.7
Latino children	28.3	36.2
Young Adult Poverty Status (18–24)		
All 18–24-year-olds	11.6	15.3
Anglo 18–24-year-olds	8.8	12.5
Black 18–24-year-olds	29.5	29.3
Latino 18–24-year-olds	19.6	25.7
Young Adult Poverty Status (25–34)		
All 25–34-year-olds	8.4	11.1
Anglo 25–34-year-olds	6.5	9.0
Black 25–34-year-olds	21.4	24.5
Latino 25–34-year-olds	16.9	20.9
All Persons		
Total	10.1	10.6
Anglo	8.0	8.6
Black	26.6	24.9
Latino	18.0	21.4

Source: Adapted from Danziger and Danziger, 1993; Johnson et al., 1991; U.S. Bureau of the Census, 1991b.

declined from 27 percent to 25 percent, Latino poverty rates rose from 18 percent to 21 percent, and Anglo poverty rates remained less than 9 percent. Moreover, poverty rates increased sharply during the decade in each of the age categories, and most dramatically among 18 to 24-year-olds.

The most significant changes in poverty rates during the 1980s were the dramatic increases in black and Latino child poverty. By 1989, approximately 44 percent of all black children were living in poverty—up from 36 percent in 1979. Latino child poverty rates rose from 28 percent in 1979 to 36 percent in 1989, matching the black child poverty rate of the previous decade.

Another significant change involved the sharp increase in the fraction of Latino young adults who had fallen into poverty during the 1980s. Approximately 26 percent of 18 to 24-year- old and 21 percent of 25 to 34-year-old Latinos were poor—rapidly approaching the poverty rates experienced by the black young adult population. Although the poverty rate rose among 25 to 34-year-old blacks during the 1980s (from 21 percent to 25 percent), the poverty rate for 18 to 24-year-old blacks declined slightly (29 percent). Of interest, although poverty rates for Anglo young adults also rose sharply in the 1980s, they still remained two to two and a half times lower than the rates for Latinos and blacks.

How persistent was poverty? As shown in Table 2–2, 57 percent of Latino and 60 percent of black adolescents age 14 to 17 resided in families that were poor at least one year during the period from 1978 to 1980, as compared to 12 percent of Anglo adolescents. Further, more than one of five black and one of six Latino teens lived in poverty during all three years. In contrast, only 2 percent of Anglo teens lived in poor families for that length of time. What happened to these teens as they reached young adulthood in the 1980s? While 68 percent of Anglos were not poor during the period from 1984 to 1989, only 42 percent of blacks and 51 percent of Latinos did not fall into poverty in any year. Moreover, growing up in poverty during adolescence was associated with a higher risk of being poor in young adulthood. Approximately 47 percent of Anglos, 60 percent of Latinos, and 69 percent of blacks who lived in poor households as teenagers were themselves living in poverty as young adults. In addition, blacks and Latinos from nonpoor families had a higher risk of falling into poverty in young adulthood. Nearly 40 percent of blacks and 35 percent of Latinos who grew up in nonpoor families were poor at some point during the mid to late 1980s. In contrast, 29 percent of Anglos from nonpoor families were themselves poor as young adults.

Table 2.2 Adolescent and Young Adult Poverty Status for Anglos, Blacks, and Latinos Age 14–17 in 1979[a]

Predictors	Entire Cohort %	Anglos %	Blacks %	Latinos %
Years in Poverty during Adolescence (Period 1978–1980)				
None	73.1	81.6	38.9	43.8
1 year	14.0	11.7	21.1	24.4
2 years	7.5	4.8	18.9	16.7
3 years	5.4	2.0	21.1	15.1
Years in Poverty during Early Adulthood (Period 1984–1989)				
None	63.6	67.9	42.2	51.1
1 year	17.9	17.3	20.7	21.2
2 years	8.1	7.2	13.0	11.5
3–4 years	7.7	6.0	15.9	12.0
5–6 years	2.7	1.6	8.2	4.2
Intergenerational Transmission of Poverty Status				
Poor in adolescence, poor in young adulthood	55.3	47.1	69.2	60.1
Nonpoor in adolescence, poor in young adulthood	29.4	28.6	39.9	34.8
Unweighted N	5442	2948	1432	788

[a]Data for adolescent poverty are weighted by 1980 sample weight. Data for poverty in young adulthood are weighted by 1989 sample weight.
Source: Tabulations by author for 14–17-year-old baseline (1979) cohort from the National Longitudinal Survey of Youth.

What accounted for the increase in poverty, particularly among children? These increases are linked in part to economic downturns in the national economy during the 1979–1983 period and the subsequent failure of the economic recovery to reach workers and their families displaced in the recessions. A second factor has been the erosion in real wages, especially for younger workers and workers with limited schooling or job skills. Particularly hard hit have been Latino workers. The median annual earnings of Latino family heads under age 30 and without

The Impact of Growing Up Poor or Welfare-Dependent

high school degrees fell by 41 percent between 1973 and 1986. For young family heads with high school degrees, median earnings fell by 27 percent (Center for Budget and Policy Priorities, 1989). In addition, the increase in mother-only families during the 1980s accounts for part of the rise in child poverty. Mother-only families are more likely to receive lower wages, have fewer full-time earners, and be less affected by periods of economic growth and recovery (Johnson et al., 1991). In the 1980s, child poverty rates in mother-only families hovered around 41 percent for Anglo families, and increased to 65 percent in black families and 69 percent in Latino families. As a result, individuals and families that remained on the fringes of the economy were more at risk of becoming dependent on government income support programs.

Welfare Dependency

To what extent are recent trends in welfare dependency similar to those noted for poverty? As shown in Figure 2–1, there were considerable racial and ethnic differences in patterns of welfare dependency. Although these differences were small at the onset of the period, they grew sharply during the early 1980s and again during the late 1980s. Blacks and Lati-

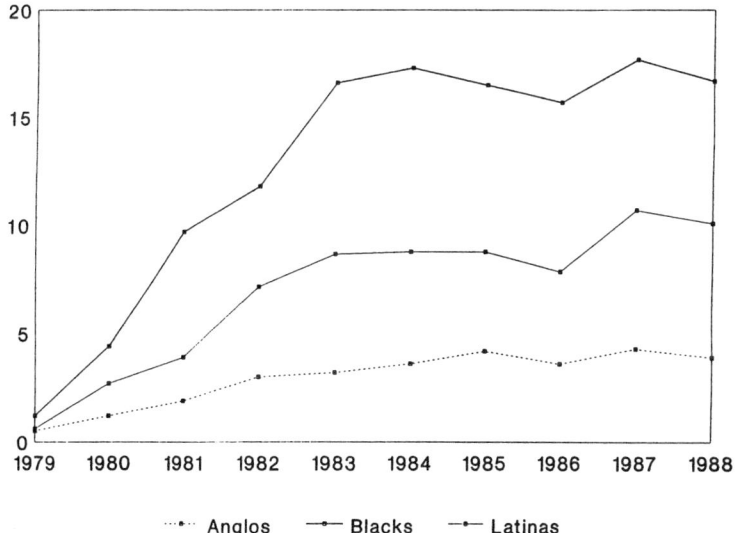

FIGURE 2.1 Percentage of Anglo, black, and Latina women dependent on AFDC, 1979–1988.

nas were two to three times more likely to be dependent on AFDC than Anglos. Since 1983, approximately one of six black and one of ten Latina women were dependent on AFDC for more than half of their annual income. In contrast, less than 5 percent of Anglo women were dependent on AFDC during the 1980s.[1]

Although it is clear that black and Latina women had higher AFDC dependency rates, it is important to note that when the focus was solely on AFDC recipients, the patterns of dependency were similar (see Figure 2.2). Thus, once women were receiving AFDC, the racial differences in terms of dependency were greatly reduced. Regardless of race or ethnicity, the majority (more than 80 percent) of AFDC recipients were dependent on AFDC as the primary source of income. The evidence suggests that Latinas were less likely than blacks or Anglos to combine periods of work with spells of AFDC. From a policy perspective, it is imperative to isolate the factors which dramatically increase the risk of welfare dependency among minority women since it is at that point where the greatest differences occur.

While the preceding discussion reveals an increase in the proportion of individuals dependent on AFDC over the course of the 1980s, these

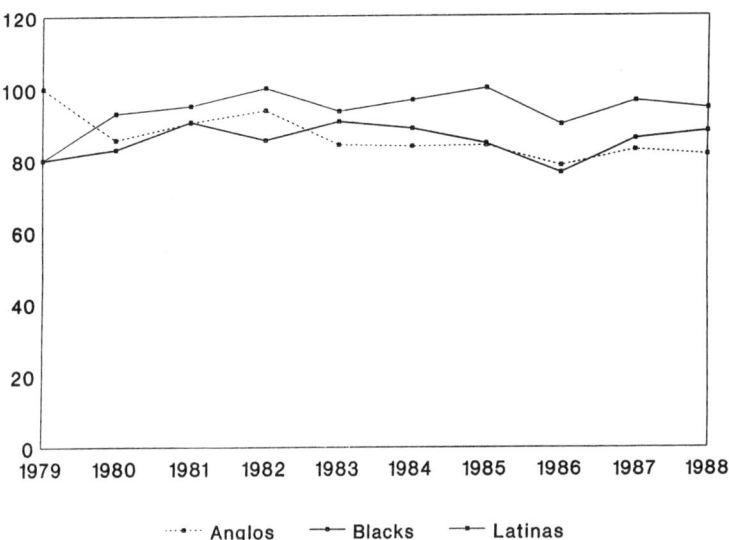

FIGURE 2.2 Percentage of Anglo, black, and Latina recipients dependent on AFDC, 1979–1988.

The Impact of Growing Up Poor or Welfare-Dependent 37

data did not reveal the dynamics of welfare use by individual recipients. In Figure 2.3, temporal patterns of welfare dependency are described. Among this cohort of women, who were 14 to 17 years old in 1979, approximately 91 percent had not been dependent on AFDC at any time during the 1980s. Although one of ten women was dependent on AFDC for at least one of the years, only one of one hundred women would have been characterized as being persistently dependent on AFDC (Santiago, 1995). These patterns of dependency were not uniform across subpopulations, however. Although 21 percent of black women and 14 percent of Latinas were dependent on welfare for one or more years, the comparable proportion was 7 percent for Anglo women.

To what extent do these differences in welfare dependency reflect differences in the social origins of the respondents? Contemporary discussions on the intergenerational effects of welfare (see Jencks, 1992; McLanahan, Astone, & Marks, 1991; Mead, 1992; Moffitt, 1992) have attempted theoretically and empirically to examine the purported effects of growing up in mother-only families or in families that are impoverished or have received AFDC benefits. Because these background conditions were measured when the respondent was an adolescent, it is

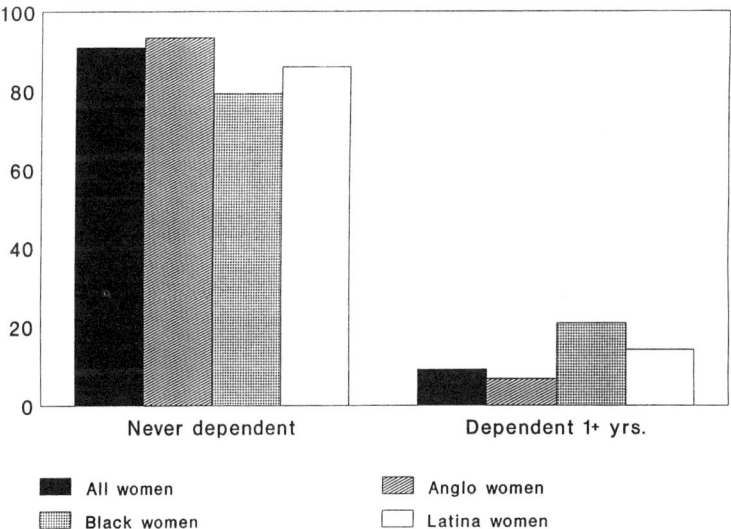

FIGURE 2.3 Incidence of AFDC dependency among young women by number of years dependent, 1979–1988.

assumed that these parental attributes or behaviors (i.e., being on welfare) will affect subsequent AFDC dependency by the respondent. Approximately 13 percent of the respondents grew up in households that received welfare at some point during the 1978–1980 period. This percentage varied along racial and ethnic lines: approximately 8 percent of Anglo women grew up in households that received welfare, and about 24 percent of Latinas and 39 percent of blacks grew up in similar households (see Table 2.3).

Nonetheless, regardless of social origins, most women did not become dependent on AFDC as young adults (see Figure 2.4). Three of four women who grew up in households that received welfare in 1978–1980 were not dependent on AFDC themselves in young adulthood, but women who grew up in such households were more likely to be dependent on AFDC as young adults than women from households that did not receive welfare. Among women who grew up in households receiving welfare, 18.7 percent of Anglos, 27.1 percent of Latinas, and 29.3 percent of blacks were dependent on AFDC for at least one year in the 1980s—two to three times higher than the rate for women from

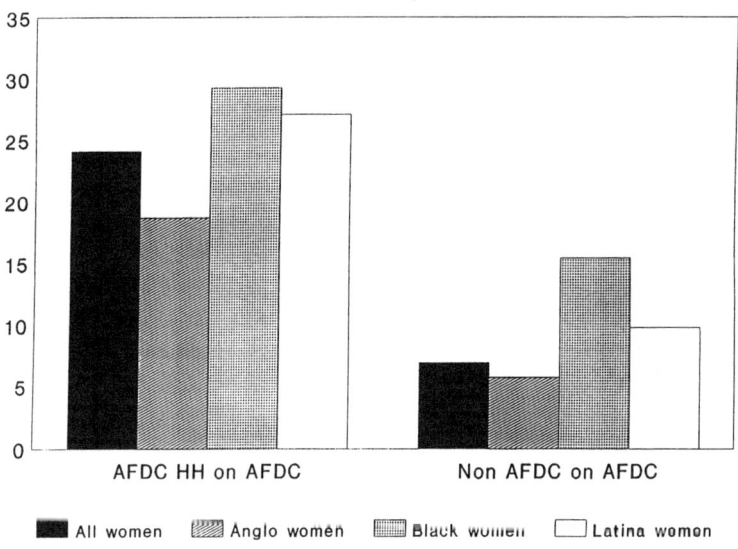

FIGURE 2.4 Incidence of AFDC dependency among young women by AFDC receipt in parental household during adolescence.

Table 2–3. Measures of Variables and Weighted Descriptive Statistics at Onset of Period (1979)[a]

Variables	Anglos Avr. or Proportion	S.D.	Blacks Avr. or Proportion	S.D.	Latinas Avr. or Proportion	S.D.
Background Characteristics						
Mother-only family at age 14	.10	.30	.37	.48	.20	.40
Parental household on welfare in 1978–1980	.08	.27	.39	.49	.24	.43
Average family income in 1978–1980	20446.46	12519.89	10692.33	9370.33	13794.75	9383.49
Welfare/Work Attitudes and Behaviors						
Willingness to do low-wage work	.74	.44	.68	.47	.74	.44
Willingness to go on welfare	.23	.42	.33	.47	.31	.47
Dependent on AFDC in 1979	<.01	.03	<.01	.04	<.01	.04
AFDC Benefits						
AFDC maximum (constant dollars)	442.41	150.45	359.91	159.76	438.32	184.71
Unemployed Parent Program (in state with program = 1)	.70	.46	.44	.50	.59	.49
Demographic Characteristics						
Proportion immigrant	.04	.19	.03	.17	.19	.40
Proportion Mexican descent[b]	—	—	—	—	.56	.50
Proportion Puerto Rican[b]	—	—	—	—	.11	.32
Average age of respondent	15.61	1.07	15.57	1.04	15.46	1.08

(*continued*)

Table 2–3. (continued)

Variables	Anglos Avr. or Proportion	S.D.	Blacks Avr. or Proportion	S.D.	Latinas Avr. or Proportion	S.D.
Employment/Family Changes						
Job loss	<.01	.01	.02	.01	<.01	.01
Birth of child	.01	.11	.05	.23	.02	.15
Marriage	.01	.08	<.01	.06	.01	.07
Divorce	<.01	.01	<.01	.03	.01	.07
Metropolitan Characteristics						
Average area unemployment rate	6.18	1.83	5.86	1.50	6.37	2.39
Average manufacturing wage (constant dollars)	356.63	54.36	327.92	54.39	344.30	32.78
Human Capital Attributes						
Years of schooling completed	9.21	1.19	8.96	1.32	8.74	1.33
Disability status	.04	.20	.04	.19	.04	.19
Years of work experience	.28	.36	.13	.27	.18	.30
Percentage of group in cohort	79.80		14.00		6.30	
Unweighted *n*	1,452		700		472	

[a]Data for women age 14–17 in 1979, follows cohort through 1988. *N* in person years.
[b]These variables were included only in the Latina models.

households that did not receive welfare. Of interest, among women who grew up in households that did not receive welfare, the risk of AFDC dependency in young adulthood was nearly twice as high for Latinas and three times as high for blacks as for Anglos.

Thus, as we entered the 1990s, more Latino and black children were living in poverty and had higher risks of living in welfare-dependent families. Many were living in families where the head of household was unable to fully support the family despite engaging in full-time work. Others were living in mother-only families particularly vulnerable to falling through the holes in the social safety net. Also, more Latino and black young adults were living in poverty by the end of the 1980s. Thus, it is not surprising that the number of young minority families dependent on welfare also rose during the 1980s. In the following section, explanations for the observed increase in child and young adult poverty are more fully explored.

CHRONIC POVERTY AND WELFARE DEPENDENCY: INTERGENERATIONAL TRANSMISSION OR STRUCTURAL CONDITIONING?

The trends described in the preceding section propelled scholars (see reviews in Moffitt, 1992; Patterson, 1986) to reexamine the extent to which poverty and welfare dependency had become intractable (Devine, Plunkett, & Wright, 1992; Duncan, 1984; Sawhill, 1988; Wilson, 1987). Moreover, it led scholars and policymakers to assess the extent to which government transfer programs fostered chronic poverty and welfare dependency (Bane & Ellwood, 1983; Ellwood, 1988; Mead, 1992; Murray, 1984).[2] Within this arena, debate focused on identifying the underlying causes of persistent poverty and welfare dependency. On one side of this debate, Wilson (1987) and others have argued that changing economic and demographic characteristics of urban areas transformed former working-class neighborhoods into areas of rising and concentrated poverty, limited employment opportunities, and high rates of dependency on government income support programs. Further, Harrington (1984) suggests that the dismantling of federal antipoverty programs during the 1980s led to the sharp rise in poverty.

On the other side of the debate, Mead (1992) contends that it is not the lack of jobs that has resulted in increased poverty and welfare dependency; rather it is the result of increased numbers of low-skill individuals who have chosen not to work. Murray (1984) argues that the decision not to work is encouraged by the inherent structure of the welfare system, particularly eligibility guidelines that discourage poor people from leaving the system and seeking gainful employment. At the forefront of this debate is an assessment of the deleterious effects of growing up in a poor or welfare-dependent household (see discussion in Huston, 1991). A key assumption underlying discussions of chronic poverty and welfare dependency is the notion that these statuses are transmitted intergenerationally. Attention is thus drawn to examining how the social origins of individuals contribute to the formation of a subculture that discourages economic self-sufficiency and achievement. Moreover, it is assumed that the subculture of the poor reproduces deficiencies in values and aspirations which will trap individuals into poverty and dependency (see Duncan, Hill, & Hoffman, 1988; Mead, 1992; Murray, 1984; Wilson, 1987). Implicit in this research is the notion that poor or welfare-dependent parents socialize their children to survive within the confines of poverty or dependency, thereby perpetuating these statuses across generations.

To date, findings regarding the effects of parental poverty status or welfare receipt on second-generation poverty or welfare use have been mixed (Antel, 1992; Duncan et al., 1988; Gottschalk, 1992; Hill & Ponza, 1983; Tienda & Stier, 1990). Indeed, these studies have shown a considerable degree of intergenerational mobility in and out of poverty and welfare. Hill and Ponza (1983) found that 57 percent of young adults who were impoverished as children did not fall into poverty after leaving home. Corcoran, Duncan, Gurin, and Gurin (1985) reported that 80 percent of poor children moved out of poverty as adults. Sawhill (1988) noted that parental attitudes and values had no effect on children's later economic outcomes.

Moreover, studies of welfare dependency have found the majority of welfare spells lasted two years or less (Duncan & Hoffman, 1988; Ellwood, 1986), and that less than 10 percent of the population was dependent on welfare for more than half of total family income. In addition, most young women growing up in homes receiving AFDC were unlikely to be on welfare themselves (e.g., Corcoran, Duncan, & Hill, 1986; Hill & Ponza, 1983). Instead, Corcoran et al. (1986) reported that parental economic status was a more powerful determinant of children's welfare use than parental welfare participation. Further, scattered evidence from survey data has not supported the notion that welfare dependency is linked to parental attitudes and values (Duncan et al., 1988; Hill & Ponza, 1983).

However, these studies underscore the increased risk experienced by individuals growing up in poverty or in welfare-dependent households. Poor children are three times as likely to be poor as adults as compared with nonpoor children (Hill & Ponza, 1983). Studies by Duncan (1984), Ellwood (1986), and others found that black families were at greater risk of receiving welfare and were more likely to remain on welfare than Anglos.[3] Hill and Ponza (1983) reported that blacks were eight times more likely to be raised in welfare-dependent homes than Anglos. Further, black families accounted for approximately one-half of the long-term welfare population (Coder & Ruggles, 1988; Coe, 1981). At the end of the 1980s, twice as many Latino families received welfare as Anglo families (U.S. Bureau of the Census, 1990).

Yet, others have argued that long-term poverty and welfare dependency, particularly among minority populations, reflected structural conditions such as poor education and job discrimination rather than personal deficiencies (see Sawhill, 1988). Wilson (1987), Tienda and Stier (1990), and others suggest that during the 1980s, structural factors such as the loss of manufacturing jobs assumed a more significant role in limiting the opportunities available to individuals with low levels of human capital. Santiago and Wilder (1991) and Massey and Denton (1993) argue that the increased concentration of poverty in minority communities was linked to the continued persistence of high levels of racial residential segregation.

In the next section, we test the assumptions made by proponents of both the intergenerational and structural explanations for persistent poverty and welfare dependency. Given the recent policy debates concerning the effects of growing up on welfare, the discussion that follows will focus on examining the factors that increase the risk of welfare dependency. For the purpose of this assessment, the analysis is restricted to examining dependency in one of the social welfare programs, the Aid to Families with Dependent Children (AFDC) program.

METHODOLOGY

Data for this study were obtained from the National Longitudinal Survey of Youth (NLSY) for the period 1979–1988. The NLSY is a nationally representative longitudinal survey of 12,686 young men and women between the ages of 14 and 22 as of January 1, 1979, who were 23 to 31 years old in 1988. Blacks, Latinos, and economically disadvantaged Anglos were overrepresented in the sample. Since 1979, respondents have been interviewed annually with a set of core questions focusing on marital history, schooling, labor force status, jobs and employer information, training, work experience and attitudes, military service, health limitations, fertility, income and assets, and geographic residence. In addition, information about the local community (e.g., unemployment rates and dropout rates) has been appended to individual records in a supplemental file available from the NLSY.

This study used a subset of the sample from the NLSY. Data were extracted for all females in the nonmilitary sample who were between the ages of 14 and 17 in 1979 and living at home at the onset of the period. The sample was further restricted to those women who had not received AFDC prior to 1979. This yielded a sample of 2,624 women (1,452 Anglos, 700 blacks, and 472 Latinas).[4] Persons receiving AFDC immediately before the onset of the survey were excluded because information regarding their early welfare spells was not available.[5]

The explanatory model tested in this study focused primarily on examining the effects of family background characteristics, welfare/work attitudes and behaviors, and state AFDC benefit levels on first AFDC dependency. In addition, the effects of respondents' demographic characteristics, employment and family compositional changes, metropolitan area context, and human capital attributes were also assessed. Each of these sets of factors is described below, and variable estimates for Anglo, black, and Latina women at the onset of the survey are presented in Table 2–3.

The transition to first AFDC dependency, the dependent variable, was estimated with an intensity of use measure described in Santiago (1995). If AFDC payments accounted for more than 50 percent of the total income in a given year, a code of 1 was given to represent the first transition to AFDC dependency.

To test the assumption that welfare dependency is conditioned by the social origins of the women recipients, three indicators of family background were included in the model: growing up in a household that received welfare, family structure, and family economic status. Because exposure to welfare during adolescence was hypothesized to increase the likelihood of AFDC dependency in adulthood, a dummy variable indicating welfare use by someone else in the parental family was constructed using the NLSY question, "Has any household member received public assistance or welfare in the past calendar year?" A household was coded as receiving welfare if a member of that household other than the respondent received welfare during the period 1978–1980. These women were living at home during this period, so the assumption is made that the parents are the recipients.[6]

Two additional measures of family characteristics were also included: a family structure measure indicating whether an individual lived in a mother-only family (code = 1) or in another family arrangement (code = 0), and an economic background measure, indicating the average family income during the period 1978–1980.

Murray (1984) and Mead (1992) have argued that the rise in welfare participation and dependency on government transfer programs stems from the unwillingness of young people to perform low-wage work—a direct result of the greater acceptance and availability of welfare benefits. Two measures were used to examine respondents' attitudes and behaviors regarding welfare. The first measures respondents' willingness to perform low-wage work. In 1979, respondents were presented with a set of hypothetical job offers which reflect their willingness to accept low-skill work.[7] All respondents were asked whether they would accept jobs such as washing dishes, factory work, janitorial work, neighborhood cleanup, working in parks, and working at fast-food restaurants. Respondents were asked if they were willing to work at these tasks for three different hourly wages ($2.50, $3.50, and $5.00 per hour). A measure was constructed to reflect the respondents' willingness to work at any of these occupations at the $3.50 hourly wage rate, which approximated the U.S. minimum wage in 1979. Individuals who were willing to perform one or more of these jobs at $3.50 an hour were coded as being willing to do low-wage work. It was expected that women who were willing to perform low-wage work were less likely to be dependent on AFDC.

A second variable measured respondents' attitudes toward welfare. At the onset of the survey, respondents were asked to indicate whether they would go on welfare in the event that they could not support their family. In this analysis, respondents who indicated that they would go on welfare were given a code of 1, and all others were coded 0. It was expected that persons who expressed more favorable attitudes toward welfare would be more likely to choose not to perform low-wage work and be dependent on AFDC.

Work by economists (e.g., Duncan, 1984; Moffitt, 1992) and others (e.g., Murray, 1984; Mead, 1992; Jencks, 1992) suggests that more liberal welfare policies diminish the return to work and increase the likelihood of dependency. Thus, if welfare benefits are high, it is argued that women would prefer welfare to work. Also, along this same line, if families with a male present are able to receive AFDC benefits through the

Unemployed Parent program (AFDC-UP), there would be a disincentive for seeking employment. Two measures of welfare policy were employed to test the effects of welfare program criteria on welfare participation: maximum AFDC benefits and the presence of the AFDC-UP program. Maximum state AFDC benefits for a family of four (in constant dollars) and an indicator for the presence of the AFDC-UP were appended for the period 1979–1988.

Previous studies have documented significant racial and ethnic differences in welfare participation and dependency (e.g., Duncan, 1984; Gottschalk, 1992; Tienda & Stier, 1990). Therefore, three ethnic status variables were included in the models to examine the effects of race and ethnic origin on the likelihood of being dependent on AFDC. It was hypothesized that the odds of being dependent on AFDC were higher for black, Mexican, and Puerto Rican women than for their Anglo counterparts because of their greater economic insecurity. Additionally, to control for differences in eligibility for and knowledge about AFDC, a measure of immigrant status was included as well. Respondents who indicated that they were born outside the United States were coded as immigrants. Finally, age of respondent was included to control for the effect of age on welfare dependency.

Events such as childbirth, marital disruption, and employment changes were hypothesized to affect the likelihood of AFDC dependency (see Bane & Ellwood, 1983; Duncan et al., 1988; Huston, 1991). Four dummy variables indicating birth of a child, marriage, divorce, and loss of a job were constructed to capture events occurring in each year between 1979 and 1988. It was hypothesized that additional births, divorce, or job loss would increase the likelihood of AFDC dependency and that marriage would be a means of escaping dependency.

The odds of being dependent on AFDC should also be affected by local labor market conditions. The work of Wilson (1987) and others suggests that increased poverty and welfare dependency are linked to the loss of inner-city manufacturing jobs. Two indicators of metropolitan labor market conditions were used as contextual variables. The continuous area unemployment rates between 1979 and 1988 were used to examine the effect of availability of jobs on welfare dependency. In addition, the average manufacturing wage (in constant dollars) for each area was appended to the files using data obtained from the Bureau of Labor Statistics, *Employment and Earnings* (various years). It was hypothesized that higher unemployment rates would increase the risk of AFDC dependency while higher manufacturing wages would decrease welfare dependency.

Attributes such as years of schooling completed, disability status, and work experience were incorporated into the analysis as controls for differences in human capital. Educational attainment was measured by years of schooling completed, which is reported in each survey year. Disability status was measured by a dummy variable indicating respondent self-report of disability during each survey year. Work experience was measured in terms of the cumulative number of years worked since 1979. It was hypothesized that previous work experience and higher levels of schooling increased earnings capacity and decreased the risk of AFDC dependency. However, the presence of a disability was expected to increase the risk of AFDC dependency because it would restrict the ability to work.

PREDICTING WELFARE DEPENDENCY

To examine the effects of the above variables on AFDC dependency, logistic regression models were estimated using the event history data for all women in our sample. A summary of these analyses is presented in Table 2–4. In all of the following discussion, the results are described using the odds ratios, which reflect the percentage change in the odds that a woman would become dependent on AFDC given a change in each of the predictor variables.[8]

One of the key findings of this analysis was that after controlling for differences in demographic characteristics, local area context, and human capital, only two background measures, parental family income and growing up in a household that received welfare, and one program measure, state AFDC benefits, significantly increased the odds of becoming dependent on AFDC. The odds of becoming dependent on AFDC were 68 percent higher for women growing up in households which received welfare relative to their counterparts from nonwelfare households. However, each $100 increase in parental family income reduced the odds of becoming dependent on AFDC by about 1 percent. Also, consistent with arguments made by Mead (1992) and Jencks (1992), these analyses provide support for the notion that welfare policies may induce welfare dependency. A $100 increase in the state AFDC benefit rate increased the odds of becoming dependent on AFDC by 23 percent.

If the effects of attitudes on AFDC dependency are explored, the results suggest that, contrary to the assertion by Mead (1992) that the poor refuse to work at low-paying jobs, an overwhelming proportion of the NLSY respondents reported a willingness to perform low-wage work.

Table 2.4 Significant Predictors of First AFDC Dependency for Anglos, Blacks, and Latinas

Predictors	All Women % Change in Odds	Anglo Women % Change in Odds	Black Women % Change in Odds	Latina Women % Change in Odds
Background Characteristics				
Mother-only family at age 14	09	63[b]	-02	-15
Parental family on welfare in 1978–1980	68[a]	78[b]	99[a]	33
Family income (in $100s)	-01[a]	-01	-01	-01
Welfare/Work Attitudes and Behaviors				
Willingness to do low-wage work	14	-10	44[b]	-04
Willingness to go on welfare	09	14	05	-03
AFDC Benefits				
AFDC maximum payment (in $100s)	23[a]	41[a]	03	17
AFDC-UP Program (1 = yes)	13	-06	21	204
Demographic Characteristics				
Immigrant	-67[a]	-99[a]	99	-60[a]
Black	73[a]	—	—	—
Mexican descent	48[a]	—	—	123[a]
Puerto Rican	-28	—	—	-27
Age of respondent	29[a]	43[a]	21[a]	33[a]
Employment/Family Changes				
Birth of child	383[a]	419[a]	482[a]	285[a]
Divorce	323[a]	505[a]	68	323[a]
Marriage	-22	43	-01	04
Job loss	28	33	39	07
Metropolitan Area Characteristics				
Area unemployment rate	06[a]	07[a]	07[a]	02
Average manufacturing wage	-01	00	-01	-01[b]

(*continued*)

Table 2.4 (continued)

Predictors	All Women % Change in Odds	Anglo Women % Change in Odds	Black Women % Change in Odds	Latina Women % Change in Odds
Human capital attributes				
Years of schooling completed	-01	-13[a]	05	01
Disability status	212[a]	183[a]	218[a]	339[a]
Years of work experience	-44[a]	-41[a]	-46[a]	-54[a]

[a]Significant at $p < .01$ level
[b]Significant at $p < .05$ level
Source: Adapted from Santiago (1995). Intergenerational and Program-Induced Effects of Welfare Dependency: Evidence from the National Longitudinal Survey of Youth. *Journal of Family and Economic Issues,* 16(2/3), pp. 294–295, 298.

Nevertheless, these positive attitudes did not translate into significant reductions in the odds of becoming dependent on AFDC. Further, positive attitudes toward welfare also were found to be insignificant predictors of AFDC dependency.

What other factors were associated with AFDC dependency? Even after controlling for differences in background, attitudes, human capital, and metropolitan context, race and nativity status continued to have a significant effect on AFDC dependency. Mexican and black women, respectively, had 48 and 73 percent higher odds of becoming dependent on AFDC than Anglo women. As expected, immigrant women were less likely to be dependent on AFDC than native-born women (with a 67 percent reduction in the odds). When age and work experience are controlled in the same model, the results provide us with the impact of an additional year of not working. Thus, if a woman spends another year out of the labor force, the odds of her becoming dependent on AFDC increase by 29 percent.

Consistent with previous studies (Coe, 1981; Bane & Ellwood, 1983; Blank, 1986; Duncan et al., 1988), household compositional changes and local labor market conditions were significant predictors of AFDC dependency. The odds of becoming dependent on AFDC were 383 percent higher for women who experienced additional births. Also, women experiencing a marital disruption increased their risk of becoming dependent on AFDC by 323 percent. Further, women residing in communities with high unemployment rates were more likely to be dependent on AFDC. Each percentage point increase in area unemployment rates was associated with a 6 percent increase in the odds of becoming dependent on AFDC.

These results also provide support for previous studies that underscore the continued importance of human capital in mitigating welfare dependency. The model underscores the importance of increasing work experience for decreasing the likelihood of welfare dependency. For each additional year of work experience, the odds of becoming dependent on AFDC are reduced by 44 percent. One variable often omitted from welfare models, disability status, was a significant predictor of AFDC dependency. The risk of becoming dependent on AFDC increased by 212 percent for women with disabilities. While poor health may make women less likely to be self-sufficient, it is also important that because of less stable work histories as well as the eligibility requirements for participation in disability insurance programs that emphasize paid work, women with disabilities are more likely to receive benefits from means-tested income transfer programs such as AFDC.

Do the factors associated with AFDC dependency vary across racial and ethnic lines? The results presented in Table 2–4 suggest that they do. Although the results were mixed, we are better able to predict AFDC dependency for Anglo and black women than for Latinas. Moreover, several key variables in current debates on welfare dependency were found to be insignificant or only affected particular groups of women. Particularly noteworthy was the insignificance of background characteristics on Latina AFDC dependency and the limited effect of welfare/work attitudes and AFDC benefit levels on subsequent dependency. These findings are described in more detail below.

While growing up in a household that received welfare was associated with an increase in the odds of becoming dependent on AFDC by 78 percent for Anglo women and 99 percent for blacks, it had no effect on Latinas. The welfare/work attitude variables were generally insignificant, but it was interesting to note that despite positive attitudes toward low-wage work, black women who were willing to do this type of work had 44 percent higher odds of becoming dependent on AFDC. This seems to suggest two things: first, that low-wage work will not keep a person from becoming dependent; and second, that even these jobs may not be available. Although results suggested that state AFDC benefit levels were significant predictors of AFDC dependency, this seems to be so only for Anglo women.

Household compositional changes, most notably the birth of an additional child and marital disruption, were significant predictors of AFDC dependency across the groups. The odds of Latina, Anglo, and black women who experienced additional births were 285, 419, and 482 percent higher, respectively, to become dependent on AFDC than women who did not have additional births. Further, experiencing a marital disruption was significant for Anglo and Latina women. Latinas and Anglos who experienced a divorce had 323 and 505 percent higher odds, respectively, to become dependent on AFDC than their married counterparts.

Metropolitan area conditions, particularly unemployment rates, were significant predictors of AFDC dependency for Anglo and black women. For each percentage point increase in the area unemployment rate, the odds of becoming AFDC-dependent increased by 7 percent. For Latinas, however, reductions in the odds of becoming dependent on AFDC were associated with prevailing wage rates. A $1 increase in the average manufacturing wage was associated with a 1 percent reduction in the odds of becoming dependent on AFDC.

The effects of human capital on AFDC dependency also varied along racial and ethnic lines. Increases in educational attainment significantly reduced the odds of AFDC dependency by 13 percent for Anglo women, but the effects were insignificant for blacks and Latinas. Additional years of work experience were particularly important for minority women. Each additional year of work experience was associated with 46 percent lower odds of AFDC dependency for blacks. For Latinas, additional work experience reduced the odds of becoming dependent on AFDC by 55 percent. For Anglos, this reduction was 41 percent. Disability status proved to be an even greater source of difference across the groups. While the odds of Anglo and black women with disabilities becoming dependent on AFDC were 183 and 218 percent higher, respectively, the odds for Latinas with disabilities becoming dependent were 339 percent higher as compared to their nondisabled counterparts.

DISCUSSION AND POLICY IMPLICATIONS

As the United States entered the 1990s, higher fractions of children and young adults were living in poverty or were dependent on public welfare programs. The recessions in the early and late 1980s, the erosion of real wages, and the phenomenal growth of mother-only families are often cited as primary causes for the growth and persistence of poverty and welfare dependency. However, woven into the public discourse on poverty and welfare issues are deep-rooted assumptions regarding the permanency of being poor or dependent in contemporary American society. Central to the current debate is the degree to which individual life chances are hampered by subcultural values that devalue work and foster dependency vis-à-vis arguments that focus on blocked opportunity structures available to the poor.

The 1980s witnessed the sharp rise in poverty rates for Latino and black children and young adults. Welfare rates for young mothers increased as well. By the end of the decade, more than one-third of Latino children and nearly one-half of black children were living in poverty. In addition, approximately 15 percent of black women and 10 percent of Latinas were dependent on welfare. Relative to Anglos, blacks and Latinos also were more at risk of being poor or welfare-dependent as young adults. However, once individuals were dependent on welfare, ethnic differences ceased to be significant.

Who is most likely to be welfare-dependent? Women who are black or native-born are more likely to be dependent. Additionally, women who grew up in households which received welfare were two to three times more likely to become dependent than women from nonwelfare households. Women experiencing household compositional changes, such as the birth of additional children and marital disruptions, are also at greater risk of welfare dependency, as are women residing in areas of high unemployment. Finally, women with disabilities and women with lower levels of work experience are more at risk.

What is the impact of previous exposure to welfare? The multivariate analyses revealed that women have an increased risk of welfare dependency if they grew up in households that received welfare, thus lending support to arguments that suggest an intergenerational effect of welfare dependency. However, the question remains, Are women from these households simply more at risk of becoming dependent because the welfare system creates disincentives for self-sufficiency, or because extreme levels of economic vulnerability and deprivation are produced and reproduced in poor households? The policy responses are quite different based on the interpretation of what is the underlying cause for the dependency. If one adheres to the former interpretation, programs would be designed to break the chains of dependency in welfare families, particularly focusing on fostering the requisite skills that will increase human capital among welfare recipients and their children. If the latter interpretation is made, policies aimed at improving health care, housing, educational, and financial resources available to the poor would be implemented in order to stabilize as well as increase the income of poor families. Welfare reform efforts would need to expand their focus to move beyond plans aimed at integrating welfare mothers into the labor force to a holistic approach that supports the efforts of parents employed in low-wage jobs.

This analysis provides little support for Murray's (1984) hypothesis that attitudes favoring the acceptance of welfare benefits affect actual dependency. Nor does this analysis support Mead's (1992) contention that dependency on welfare is tied to an unwillingness to perform low-wage work. The majority of the young women in this study (67 to 74 percent) expressed a willingness to perform low-wage work and did not see going on welfare as the only means for supporting a family. Indeed, less than one-third of the respondents envisioned going on welfare in times of financial need. This would suggest that among young adults, work—even low-paid work—is still valued. Unfortunately, even under the "best" circumstances (i.e., full-time with benefits) low-wage work does not guarantee a living wage for individuals and their families.

The findings do, however, provide support for concerns regarding the impact of higher welfare benefits on dependency, but the analyses reveal that these effects are significant only for Anglo women. These results run contrary to the stereotypical images of black and Latino families moving to high welfare-benefit states in order to live on the dole. While I don't believe these data suggest that Anglo women flock to higher-benefit states, I do think that they reflect greater disincentives to work in these states (i.e., higher child care, health costs, higher penalties for being gainfully employed) in low-wage jobs. Clearly, policies aimed at providing support to low-wage workers (such as low-cost day care, health insurance, and earned income tax credits) would reduce if not eliminate the disincentives to work.

The analysis underscores the significance of local labor market conditions and the level of human capital as determinants of AFDC dependency. Consistent with the argument made by Wilson (1987), women residing in areas with high levels of unemployment are more likely to turn to welfare if jobs are unavailable. This is particularly relevant to Latinas, who may be more vulnerable to economic downturns in the economy by virtue of their occupational segregation in industries hard hit by economic restructuring. This suggests the need to focus on job creation in addition to improving the employability of welfare recipients, particularly women of color who face not only reduced opportunities as a result of lower levels of human capital but lower wages and ongoing discrimination in the workplace.

As the data reveal, recipients are more likely to be dependent on welfare if they have limited work experience or education. Thus, policies aimed at increasing human capital should foster reductions in welfare dependency by virtue of increasing the job opportunities available to recipients. This is particularly salient for young Latinas, who have higher rates of school noncompletion and unemployment relative to Anglos and blacks.

Further, this study provides evidence linking poor health status with welfare dependency. The odds of becoming dependent on AFDC are two to three times higher for women who are disabled than for their nondisabled counterparts. Women with disabilities often lack the requisite employment in jobs covered by government-sponsored disability programs, such as social security and workers' compensation. Therefore, means-tested income support programs, like AFDC, become primary sources of support for women who are either disabled themselves or are caring for children with disabilities. Previous studies of Latino welfare recipients (i.e., Office of Program Planning, Analysis, and Development, 1991) reveal that a sizable fraction of recipients are dependent on welfare because they lack adequate health insurance for their families. Current discussions on health and welfare reform must address the interrelationships between health status and welfare dependency, particularly the need for health insurance. Moreover, the current debate needs to include discussions that recognize that a sizable fraction of welfare recipients will be unable to meet training or work requirements because they are physically or emotionally unable to do so or because they are primary caregivers to children with medical problems.

Finally, these findings suggest the need to reassess the impact of family background characteristics, economic context, and welfare policies on dependency, particularly for minority women. Although some of these factors affect all of the groups in similar ways, the results highlight the need to examine these groups separately instead of devising a single model and using dummy variables to "account" for racial and ethnic differences in universal models. For example, while teenage childbearing has been cited as one of the major factors increasing childhood poverty rates and welfare dependency, we need to be cognizant of the differential impact within minority communities. For instance, although high rates of teen births occur in Mexican-origin and Puerto Rican communities, the effects on these mothers, their families, and the larger community are quite different. Within Mexican-origin communities, a high fraction of these teen births are occurring to women who are married and whose male partners are working. In contrast, a high fraction of births to Puerto Rican women are occurring outside of marriage but are mitigated by extended family support networks. In both cases, the policy response would be quite different from that for women who have children out of wedlock and have limited support from extended family networks.

Furthermore, if these differences are caused by specific sets of factors, we need to seriously reassess theoretical frameworks as well as policy guidelines which assume that processes such as welfare dependency are uniformly determined. As we continue to look at other populations, there will be a need to carefully assess how other factors, such as language, timing of migration, accessibility of services, information networks, and alternative sources of support affect participation in welfare programs and subsequent dependency on these programs. Clearly a "one size fits all" approach to eliminating welfare dependency and fostering self-sufficiency is inadequate given the diversity of the welfare population in the United States. Although current policy debates encourage "flexible" welfare plans (i.e., more state control over welfare programs and policies), they really do not reflect the flexibility that responds to these differences. A "flexible" welfare plan would be able to address the needs of the working poor who need support such as tax credits, health and child care, or the enhancement of job skills in addition to providing meaningful training opportunities to individuals with limited education and work experience.

Finally, more attention needs to be directed to policies that look at the particular needs and concerns of children. With significant fractions of black and Latino children living in poverty in this country, we need to look at programs that will improve their quality of life because ultimately, the economic viability of the country as a whole is reliant on the optimal use of the talents of all citizens. In order to achieve this, current welfare policies must shift toward providing adequate financial, educational, and medical support to children (see Huston, 1991). Financial policies which would positively impact the well-being of children include child allowances or tax credits, expansion of the Earned Income Tax Credit provision, and increasing the minimum wage for low-wage workers. Educational policies include the expansion of preschool opportunities such as Head Start, increased funding for school nutrition programs, and expanded after-school programs, especially for older children. Health policies include free or low-cost immunizations and preventative care, as well as expansion of nutrition programs like the Women, Infants, Children (WIC) program. Of particular concern for Latino children, these policies must be made available to all eligible children, including the children of immigrant parents. If they are not, we may see (and in some cases already see) a return to the virulent outbreaks of infectious diseases such as tuberculosis and increases in chronic illnesses. While these programs would significantly increase the current expenditures targeted to children, the costs to society as a whole for not providing adequate support to children are, and will be, far greater. As the country moves into the twenty-first century, the poor children and young adults that we fail to serve today will be the ill-prepared workforce of tomorrow. Our failure to respond to the needs of children or to eliminate the barriers that currently restrict the life chances of poor families will serve to perpetuate poverty and deprivation in the United States.

NOTES

Portions of this article were published in the *Journal of Family and Economic Issues* 16(2/3), 281–306 (Fall 1995) and are reprinted with permission. This research was partially funded by a postdoctoral fellowship from the SSRC Program on Urban Underclass, an NICHD postdoctoral fellowship at the Population Studies Center, and grants from the Rockefeller and Ford Foundation to the Research and Training Program on Poverty, the Underclass, and Public Policy, whose support is gratefully acknowledged. Special thanks to Mary Corcoran, Sheldon Danziger, Greg Duncan, Irwin Garfinkel, Martha Hill, and Robert Moffitt for comments on earlier versions of this manuscript.

[1]Data were weighted by 1988 person weight, and follow cohort of women who were age 14 to 17 in 1979. In work not reported here, I have found that patterns of AFDC participation among Latinas vary considerably by Latina national origin. As has been reported in the work of Tienda (1990) and Tienda and Stier (1990), Puerto Rican women in the NLSY sample had AFDC participation rates that resembled those for blacks. Mexican women had participation rates that were slightly higher but similar to those for Anglo women. These analyses need to be interpreted with a word of caution, however, because the sample sizes are relatively small.

[2]Most studies have tended to focus on the temporal dimension of welfare recipiency. Duration models are problematic since we generally lack information regarding the total duration of welfare receipt. In this study, welfare dependency is measured in terms of intensity of use. An individual woman is defined as being welfare-dependent if AFDC benefits provide more than one-half of her annual income. Further, the definition is restricted to assessing dependency on transfers from the AFDC program.

[3] In this chapter, persons who self-identified as racially white and of European ancestry (excluding Spaniards) are identified as Anglos.

[4] This sample selection process can be traced as follows. Beginning with the total sample of female respondents in 1979 ($n = 6,283$), selection of only those women who were age 14 to 17 in 1979 reduced the sample to 2,737. If the sample is restricted to only those women who did not receive AFDC in 1978, the sample decreases to 2,715. To examine the impact of family attributes during late adolescence, which can be done by reconstructing the family variables for the period 1978–1980, the sample was further restricted to those living at home with one or both parents ($n = 2,628$). Finally, because the NLSY dropped the military oversample in the mid-1980s, the focus is only on those respondents who were part of the nonmilitary sample. This yields a final sample of 2,624 individuals.

[5] Only 16 of the women in the 14-to-17 sample were excluded from the analysis because they had received AFDC prior to 1979.

[6] The questions in the NLSY enable only the distinction of welfare receipt for respondents, their spouses, and other family members.

[7] Because these measures were only asked in 1979, they do not capture any changes that might have occurred in the attitudes of the respondents as they grew older. But, if there is an intergenerational transmission of beliefs and values regarding work and welfare, it is assumed that women who have a taste for welfare and a distaste for low-wage work when young would tend to maintain these tastes into adulthood.

[8] The odds ratio represents the antilog of each regression coefficient X (X^*) and can be interpreted as the unit change in the odds of Y occurring given a unit change in X. When the change in the odds ratio is greater than 100, it is interpreted as the percentage increase in the odds. When the odds ratio is less than 100, the interpretation reflects a reduction in the odds. If we use several examples from Table 2–4, we see that the odds of a woman being dependent on AFDC increased by 6 percent with each additional percentage point increase in the area unemployment rate. They also increased by 383 percent with the birth of a child. However, the odds of becoming dependent on AFDC were reduced by 44 percent with each additional year of work experience, after controlling for differences in the social origins, demographic characteristics, metropolitan area characteristics, and changes in family structure and employment.

REFERENCES

Antel, J. J. (1992). The inter-generational transfer of welfare dependency: Some statistical evidence. *The Review of Economics and Statistics, 74,* 467–473.

Bane, M. J., & Ellwood, D. (1983). *The dynamics of dependence and the routes to self-sufficiency.* Final report to U.S. Department of Health and Human

Services. Cambridge, MA: Kennedy School of Government, Harvard University.
Bean, F., & Tienda, M. (Eds.). (1987). *The Hispanic population of the United States*. New York: Russell Sage.
Blank, R. M. (1986). *How important is welfare dependence?* (IRP Discussion Paper No. 821–86). Madison: University of Wisconsin, Institute for Research on Poverty.
Bureau of Labor Statistics. (various years). *Employment and earnings*. Washington, DC: U.S. Department of Labor.
Center on Budget and Policy Priorities. (1989). *Shortchanged: Recent developments in Hispanic poverty, income, and employment*. Washington, DC: Author.
Coder, J., & Ruggles, P. (1988). *Welfare recipiency as observed in the SIPP* (Survey of Income and Program Participation Working Paper Series No. 8818). Washington, DC: U.S. Bureau of the Census.
Coe, R. (1981). A preliminary empirical examination of the dynamics of welfare use. In M. S. Hill, D. H. Hill, & J. N. Morgan (Eds.), *Five thousand American families* (Vol. 9, pp. 121–168). Ann Arbor: University of Michigan, Institute for Social Research.
Congress of the United States (1990). *Sources of support for adolescent mothers*. Washington, DC: Congressional Budget Office.
Corcoran, M., Duncan, G. J., Gurin, G., & Gurin, J. (1985). Myth and reality: The causes and persistence of poverty. *Journal of Poverty Analysis and Management, 4*, 516–536.
Corcoran, M., Duncan, G. J., & Hill, M. S. (1986). The economic fortunes of women and children: Lessons from the Panel Study of Income Dynamics. In B. C. Gelpi, N. C. M. Hartsock, & M. H. Strober (Eds.), *Women and poverty* (pp. 7–24). Chicago: University of Chicago Press.
Corcoran, M., Gordon, R., Laren, D., & Solon, G. (1992). The association between men's economic status and their family and community origins. *Journal of Human Resources, 27*, 575–601.
Crooks, D. L. (1995). American children at risk: Poverty and its consequences for children's health, growth, and school achievement. *Yearbook of Physical Anthropology, 38*, 57–86.
Danziger, S., & Danziger, S. K. (1993). Child poverty and public policy: Toward a comprehensive antipoverty agenda. *Daedalus, 122*, 57–85.
Danziger, S., & Gottschalk, P. (1993). *Uneven tides*. New York: Russell Sage.
Devine, J. A., Plunkett, M., & Wright, J. D. (1992). The chronicity of poverty: Evidence from the PSID, 1968–1987. *Social Forces, 70*, 787–812.
Duncan, G. J. (1984). *Years of poverty, years of plenty*. Ann Arbor: University of Michigan, Institute for Social Research.

Duncan, G. J. (1991). The economic environment of childhood. In A. C. Huston (Ed.), *Children in poverty: Child development and public policy* (pp. 23–50). Cambridge, MA: Cambridge University Press.

Duncan, G. J., & Hoffman, S. D. (1988). The use and effects of welfare: A survey of recent evidence. *Social Service Review, 62*, 238–257.

Duncan, G. J., Hill, M. S., & Hoffman, S. D. (1988). Welfare dependence within and across generations. *Science, 239*, 467–471.

Edelman, P., & Ladner, J. (1991). *Adolescence and poverty: Challenge for the 1990s.* Washington, DC: Center for National Policy Press.

Ellwood, D. T. (1986). *Targeting "would-be" long term recipients of AFDC.* Princeton, NJ: Mathematica Policy Research, Inc.

Ellwood, D. T. (1987). *Understanding dependency: Choices, confidence, or culture?* Report prepared for the U.S. Department of Health and Human Services/ASPE. Waltham, MA: Brandeis University, Center for Human Resources.

Ellwood, D. T. (1988). *Poor support, poverty, and the American family.* New York: Basic Books.

Gottschalk, P. (1990). AFDC participation across generations. *American Economic Review, 80*, 367–371.

Gottschalk, P. (1992). The intergenerational transmission of welfare participation: Facts and possible causes. *Journal of Policy Analysis and Management, 11*, 254–272.

Harrington, M. (1984). *The new American poverty.* New York: Harper and Row.

Hill, M. S., & Ponza, M. (1983). Poverty and welfare dependence across generations. *Economic Outlook USA, 10*, 61–64.

Huston, A. C. (1991). *Children in poverty: Child development and public policy.* Cambridge, MA: Cambridge University Press.

Jencks, C. (1992). *Rethinking social policy.* Boston: Harvard University Press.

Johnson, C. M., Miranda, L., Sherman, A., & Weill, J. D. (1991). *Child poverty in America.* Washington, DC: Children's Defense Fund.

Massey, D. S., & Denton, N. A. (1993). *American apartheid: Segregation and the making of the underclass.* Boston: Harvard University Press.

McLanahan, S. S., Astone, N. M., & Marks, N. F. (1991). The role of mother-only families in reproducing poverty. In A. C. Huston (Ed.), *Children in poverty: Child development and public policy* (pp. 51–78). Cambridge, MA: Cambridge University Press.

Mead, L. M. (1992). *The new politics of poverty.* New York: Basic Books.

Moffitt, R. (1992). Incentive effects of the U.S. welfare system: A review. *Journal of Economic Literature, 30*, 1–61.

Murray, C. (1984). *Losing ground: American social policy, 1950–1980.* New York: Basic Books.

Office of Program Planning, Analysis, and Development. (1991). *Hispanic ADC recipients in New York City: Barriers to employment and self-sufficiency.* New York: New York State Department of Social Services.

Patterson, J. T. (1986). *America's struggle against poverty, 1900–1985.* Cambridge, MA: Harvard University Press.

Santiago, A. M. (1995). Intergenerational and program-induced welfare dependency: Evidence from the National Longitudinal Survey of Youth. *Journal of Family and Economic Issues, 16,* 281–306.

Santiago, A. M., & Padilla, Y. C. (1995). Persistence of poverty across generations: A comparison of Anglos, blacks, and Latinos. *New England Journal of Public Policy, 11,* 117–146.

Santiago, A. M., & Wilder, M. G. (1991). Residential segregation and links to minority poverty: The case of Latinos in the United States. *Social Problems, 38,* 492–515.

Sawhill, I. (1988). Poverty in the U.S.: Why is it so persistent? *Journal of Economic Literature, 26,* 1073–1119.

Tienda, M. (1990). Welfare and work in Chicago's inner city. *American Economic Review, 80,* 372–376.

Tienda, M., & Jensen, L. (1988). Poverty and minorities: A quarter century profile of color and socioeconomic disadvantage. In G. D. Sandefur & M. Tienda (Eds.), *Divided opportunities: Minorities, poverty, and social policy* (pp. 23–61). New York: Plenum Press.

Tienda, M., & Stier, H. (1990, July). *Intergenerational continuity of welfare dependence: Racial and ethnic comparisons.* Paper presented at the 12th World Congress of Sociology, Madrid, Spain.

U.S. Bureau of the Census. (1990). *Statistical abstract of the United States.* Washington, DC: U.S. Government Printing Office.

U.S. Bureau of the Census. (1991a). *Poverty in the United States: 1990* (Current Population Reports Series P-60, No. 175). Washington, DC: U.S. Government Printing Office.

U.S. Bureau of the Census. (1991b). *Workers with low earnings, 1964 to 1990* (Current Population Reports Series P-60, No. 178). Washington, DC: U.S. Government Printing Office.

U.S. House of Representatives, Committee on Ways and Means. (1994). *Impact of immigration on welfare programs: Hearing before the Subcommittee on Human Resources of the Committee on Ways and Means, House of Representatives, One-Hundred Third Congress, first session, November 15, 1993.* Washington, DC: U.S. Government Printing Office.

Wilson, W. J. (1987). *The truly disadvantaged: The inner city, the underclass, and public policy.* Chicago and London: University of Chicago Press.

CHAPTER 3
Sexual Behaviors of Latina Adolescents
ANTONIA M. VILLARRUEL

Unintended pregnancy, sexually transmitted diseases (STDs), human immunodeficiency virus (HIV), infertility, and cervical cancer are some of the short- and long-term adverse health consequences faced by young girls who engage in early sexual intercourse (i.e., before 17 years of age). Latina[1] adolescents are especially vulnerable to these adverse consequences because of the added burdens of poverty, discrimination, changing cultural norms, and barriers to culturally and linguistically appropriate quality health care (Centers for Disease Control, 1992; Darabi & Ortiz, 1987; Hein, 1989; National Center for Health Statistics [NCHS], 1990). Since health behaviors learned during adolescence persist in adulthood, the ability to influence positive values, attitudes, and behaviors related to health in general, and sexual behavior specifically, can contribute to a healthy and productive adulthood. Further, since health and health behavior cannot be addressed in isolation from daily threats of the environment, knowledge about Latina sexual behaviors and the biologic, social, and cultural factors that influence them is necessary to guide adolescents, parents, educators, health professionals, and policymakers to address this issue of major health and social significance to Latino populations.

This chapter presents an integrated review of health behavior research on the sexual behavior of Latina adolescents.[2] Existing research in this area will be synthesized in order to provide a knowledge base from which researchers and practitioners can draw to create strategies for improving adverse health outcomes associated with sexual behavior. First, an overview of Latina sexual behavior is presented. Second, the biologic, social, and cultural factors that influence sexual behavior of

Latina adolescents, including both health risk and protective behaviors, are examined. Issues related to health status and access to health care of Latino adolescents also are discussed. Throughout this chapter, the diversity among Latina adolescents, both in factors that influence sexual behaviors and health outcomes, is highlighted. Finally, recommendations for future research efforts and practice are suggested.

SIGNIFICANCE

Why the focus on Latina sexual behavior? First, while from a health perspective the early sexual activity of both Latino and Latina adolescents is of concern, Latinas in particular are at greater risk than their male counterparts for acquiring HIV/AIDS (acquired immunodeficiency syndrome) and other sexually transmitted diseases. In general, based on findings from regional studies, black and Hispanic women are at greater risk for contracting AIDS, and further, higher increases of AIDS are predicted among these women in the future (Capell et al., 1992; Gayle, Selik, & Chu, 1990; Sabogal, Faigeles, & Catania, 1993; Smith, McGraw, Crawford, Costa, & McKinlay, 1993). The primary mode for contracting AIDS among these groups is through heterosexual contact with an infected partner. In an analysis of AIDS cases diagnosed in the United States between 1983 and 1988, for example, the rate of AIDS cases attributed to heterosexual contact was reported to be more than eleven times higher for black and Hispanic women than for white women (Holmes, Karon, & Kreiss, 1990).

The increased risk of heterosexually transmitted HIV/AIDS among Latinas has been attributed to such factors as (1) the early onset of sexual intercourse; (2) increases in the transmission of other sexually transmitted diseases that facilitate the spread of HIV; (3) the more efficient transmission of HIV from males to females; (4) the high-risk sexual behavior of Latino men (i.e., multiple sex partners, homosexual partners); (5) the high incidence of intravenous drug use among Latino men; and (6) barriers to condom usage (Holmes et al., 1990; Sabogal et al., 1993; Smith et al., 1993). While the actual number of AIDS cases among all adolescents is low, this cannot be used as an accurate indicator of the extent of HIV infection among teenagers. The low rate of HIV testing among adolescents and the long incubation period of AIDS (approximately ten years) contribute to the underestimation of risk among this age group.

It is important to note that higher rates of HIV/AIDS exist among women in their twenties, and again, because of the incubation period of

AIDS, those who show AIDS symptoms in their early twenties are most likely to have contracted HIV during adolescence. The increased risk of acquiring HIV/AIDS through heterosexual contact and factors associated with this risk experienced by older Latinas (e.g., barriers to condom usage, high-risk behavior of Latino men) is similar to that among Latina adolescents. However, these factors may be of greater significance during adolescence as they are likely to be further compounded by peer influences, lack of parental communication about sexual practices, and lack of access to primary and secondary health care services.

Several researchers have examined the risk status of Latina adolescents. In one such study in which a random sample ($n = 578$) of primarily Puerto Rican adolescents from 15 to 19 years of age was utilized, HIV risk estimates were reported to be higher among Latina than Latino adolescents (Smith et al., 1993). In this study, HIV risk was estimated by calculating the frequency of exposure, condom usage rates, and number of sexual partners during the last six months. Of the sexually active adolescents, more than 76 percent of females in the sample had infection probabilities greater than 1/100,000 as compared with only 3 percent of males. Further, primarily females were represented in the 8 percent of the total sample that were determined to be in the high-risk group.

Similarly, in a study which examined HIV risk status among pregnant Hispanic adolescents seeking prenatal care ($n = 87$), one-third were determined to be at increased risk for acquiring HIV. The most frequently reported risk factors included having an STD alone and having an STD and a history of multiple sexual partners. Significant differences in risk status were not associated with age or onset of sexual activity; however, the nationality (Puerto Rican and other Hispanic) and birthplace (U.S.-born and non-U.S.-born) of adolescents were significantly associated with risk status. While adolescents born in Puerto Rico were at greater risk than non-U.S.-born Hispanics, birthplace was not significantly associated with risk status among Puerto Ricans. However, among the other Hispanic adolescents, those born in the United States were at increased risk as compared to those who were born outside the United States. While both the small size and nonrandom sample limit the generalizability of results, these studies illustrate the high-risk status of Latina adolescents for acquiring HIV/AIDS. In addition, the diversity among Latina adolescents in relation to health status and risk factors associated with HIV provides support for the inclusion of factors such as nationality and birthplace in future studies with Latino populations.

A second reason to focus on the sexual behavior of Latina adolescents is that Latinas are more likely to bear the social and economic burdens related to pregnancy, childbirth, or pregnancy termination. For Latina adolescents who choose to terminate their pregnancy, the cost of abortion services and the psychological impact associated with the decision fall primarily with the woman. For those Latina adolescents who choose to become mothers, difficulties in completing school, limited employment opportunities that result from low educational attainment, and the perpetuation of the poverty cycle for children of adolescent mothers are but a few examples of economic burdens which Latinas must confront. A more comprehensive discussion relating to issues of poverty, educational attainment, and employment has been presented earlier in this volume by Santiago.

In general, pregnancy rates among Latina adolescents (13 percent) are higher than for white adolescents (8 percent) (Alan Guttmacher Institute [AGI], 1994). Reasons for higher pregnancy rates among Latinas has been attributed to such factors as a lack of knowledge related to reproductive issues and contraceptive use (Padilla & Baird, 1991; Smith, McGill, & Wait, 1987); and the cultural imperative to be a mother in Latino cultures (De Anda, Becerra, & Fielder, 1988; Russell, Williams, Farr, Schwab, & Plattsmier, 1993). Latina adolescents are more likely than black or white adolescents to have wanted to get pregnant; however, this might in part be related to higher marriage rates among Latinas (AGI, 1994).

It is important, however, to recognize the diversity in pregnancy rates and birth outcomes among Latina adolescents. In general, among pregnancies that were unintended, few Hispanic adolescents as compared with white adolescents chose to terminate their pregnancy (AGI, 1994). From a secondary analysis of the Hispanic Health and Nutrition Examination Survey (HHANES) (National Center for Health Statistics [NCHS], 1985), pregnancy rates among Mexican American (14.1 percent) and Puerto Rican (14.6 percent) adolescents were similar; however, Mexican American adolescents had the highest number of live births. In contrast, Cuban Americans had the lowest reports of pregnancy (4.4 percent) and number of live births (37/1,000) among the three Hispanic subgroups.

While there is diversity in pregnancy rates and birth outcomes among Latina subgroups, there is also diversity within Latina subgroups. Factors such as acculturation and generational distance have been associated with some of this diversity, including the early initiation of sexual intercourse among Mexican American adolescents (Reynoso, Felice, &

Schragg, 1993) and, in general, the greater number of premarital births among Latino adolescents (Aneshensel, Becerra, Fielder, & Schuler, 1990; Darabi & Ortiz, 1987). However, further research is necessary to examine the nature of differences within and between Latino subgroups as it relates to both pregnancy rates and birth outcomes.

SEXUAL BEHAVIOR OF LATINA ADOLESCENTS

Sexual behavior as used in this discussion refers to patterns of heterosexual intimacy and includes intercourse (vaginal sex) and outercourse (i.e., kissing, petting, fondling). In general, much of the research and what is known about sexual behavior of adolescents is related to patterns of intercourse. Among female adolescents, approximately 45 percent have had sexual intercourse by age 15, while over 65 percent have had intercourse by the time they are 17 years of age (NCHS, 1992). From several national surveys, patterns of sexual intercourse reveal strong differences by age, gender, and ethnicity; however, fewer data exist on the sexual behavior of Hispanic adolescents, and even less is known about the sexual behavior of Hispanic subgroups (Newcomer & Baldwin, 1992).

However, several studies have examined sexual behaviors, specifically the initiation of intercourse among Latina adolescents. For example, in findings from a study in which sexual behaviors of a primarily Mexican American sample of sixth through eighth graders were examined, lower percentages of girls (2.6 to 4.42 percent) than boys (17.5 to 40 percent) had indicated ever engaging in intercourse (Christopher, Johnson, & Roosa, 1993). In an analysis of data from the National Survey of Family Growth [NSFG], the average age of Hispanics who had engaged in sexual intercourse (42 percent) was 15.3 + 1.8 years (Durant, Pendergrast, & Seymour, 1990). There were no statistically significant differences among Cuban, Puerto Rican, Mexican American, Central/ South American, and other Hispanic adolescents in average age or in the percentage of those who had engaged in intercourse. Finally, in a study which compared Hispanic and non-Hispanic white sexual activity, Mexican American female adolescents were found to delay sexual activity longer from the time of onset of dating than non-Hispanic white groups (De Anda et al., 1988).

The importance of understanding sexual behavior other than intercourse is derived from a body of work conducted by Udry and colleagues (Smith, Udry, & Morris, 1985; Udry & Billy, 1987; Udry, Talbert, & Morris, 1986), who have examined the relation between coital (intercourse) and noncoital behaviors of adolescents. In one such study (Smith et al., 1985), a predictable pattern of noncoital behaviors was found prior to first intercourse among white adolescents, while among black adolescents noncoital behaviors were not patterned and were less frequent. Further, while for white adolescents noncoital behaviors was a significant predictor of intercourse, engagement in noncoital behaviors was not a significant predictor of intercourse among black adolescents. Differences between black and white adolescents suggest that there are different normative behaviors for each group regarding sexual behavior. Knowledge of the nature, timing, and pattern of noncoital behaviors of Latino adolescents and the relation between these behaviors and the timing and initiation of intercourse becomes important in order to determine the nature and timing of interventions to promote safer sex practices.

Few studies exist in which the sexual behaviors of Latina adolescents have been explored. However, in one study both noncoital and coital behaviors of a predominantly Mexican American sample of adolescents ($n = 489$) were examined (Christopher et al., 1993). In general, across all grades, males had more sexual involvement, and further, higher percentages of males reported having intercourse (17.5 to 40 percent) than females (2.6 to 4.42 percent). Among females there was a more pronounced engagement in kissing behaviors between sixth and seventh grades and a more pronounced engagement in petting or fondling behaviors between seventh and eighth grades. The relation between noncoital and coital behaviors was not explored in this study. Clearly, further research is needed to describe the nature, onset, frequency, and context of sexual behaviors (both intercourse and outercourse) of Latina adolescents.

BIOLOGIC, SOCIAL, AND CULTURAL FACTORS ASSOCIATED WITH SEXUAL BEHAVIOR

Several biosocial models have been developed recently to understand sexual behavior of adolescents. A major assumption underlying these models is that hormonal secretion, pubertal development, and sexual behavior of adolescents are interactive biologic and social processes. While few of these models have been tested with Latina adolescents, the correlates and causal sequences which can be derived from these models may provide some direction for understanding correlates and sexual expressions of intimacy among Latina adolescents. In this section, existing research concerned with the relation between biologic (pubertal development, hormonal secretion), social (peer and parental influences), and cultural (familism, gender roles, and religion) factors and sexual behavior of Latina adolescents will be discussed within the context of two existing biosocial models.

Belsky, Steinberg, and Draper (1991) have proposed a model in which family context is viewed as affecting both child-rearing and subsequent psychological and behavioral development, which in turn affects somatic or pubertal development and reproductive strategies. A hypothesis derived from this model suggests that contextual stressors, including insecure parental attachments, single parenthood, and inadequate financial resources, foster insensitive child rearing, which leads to high levels of mistrust, impulsiveness, sadness, or social withdrawal. Within the model, these stressors are viewed as conditions which will accelerate pubertal development and sexual activity. Early maturation, early sexual activity, and short-term unstable pair bonds are viewed as components of a quantity-oriented reproductive strategy, an adaptive and evolutionary response to contextual stress.

Some empirical support for Belsky's model has been demonstrated in non-Latina samples. For example, girls from nonintact families and female-headed households were more likely to menstruate at earlier ages than those who were from intact families (Moffit, Caspi, Belsky, & Silva, 1992; Wierson, Long, & Forehand, 1993; Surbey, 1990). Similarly, a relation between nonintact families, father absence, and early engagement in sexual activity has also been reported (Flewelling & Bauman, 1990; Newcomer & Udry, 1987); however, it is important to note that the relation between early menstruation and early sexual activity was not addressed in these studies.

The high rates of poverty, the increasing rate of single-headed households, and experiences with discrimination experienced by Latinos can be considered elements of contextual stress. Thus, Belsky's model may be useful in the study of Latina sexual behavior. While no study was found in which Belsky's model was used in the study of Latina adolescents, support for the model is inconsistent based on research findings conducted with Latina adolescents. For example, in one study, Darabi and Ortiz (1987) reported premarital births of young Puerto Rican women to be inversely related to socioeconomic status, a relation consistent with that derived from Belsky's model. In contrast, however, among young women of Mexican origin a positive relation between socioeconomic status and premarital births was reported. It is of interest to note that these differences were eliminated when generational status was controlled. Similarly, in a study in which pregnancy outcomes of immigrant (n = 56) and acculturated (n = 60) Mexican adolescents were compared, no significant differences were found between mean age at menarche, gynecologic age, chronologic age at conception, or socioeconomic status (Reynoso et al., 1993). However, adolescents who were acculturated were significantly younger in age at first intercourse.

Findings contrary to relationships proposed in Belsky's model were reported in a study in which data from the NSFG (1984) (Durant et al., 1990) were analyzed. Young Hispanic women from five different Hispanic subgroups, who had ever engaged in intercourse, were significantly older (17.8 + 1.0), had an older age at menarche (12.7 + 1.6), and were from families with lower incomes than young women who had not yet engaged in intercourse. Despite differences in poverty, there were no significant differences in age of menarche for Puerto Rican and Mexican American adolescents. Similarly, from data analyzed from the HHANES (Pletsch, 1990), a higher mean person-months of fertility among Puerto Rican adolescents, followed by Cuban Americans and Mexican Americans, was reported. These differences did not correlate with poverty levels, however, as Puerto Rican adolescents were among the poorest, and Cuban Americans had the highest incomes among Hispanic subgroups.

From these studies conducted with Latina adolescents, despite the presence of contextual stressors, most notably poverty, the relations between poverty, early menarche, and early sexual activity as proposed by Belsky were not consistently supported. The presence of other contextual factors, specifically family and cultural values, may serve to modify the effects of contextual stressors and thus act as a protective factor in decisions related to early sexual behavior. Further investigation with Latina populations is necessary to test the model.

A contrasting biosocial model concerned with adolescent sexual behavior has been developed by Udry and colleagues (Udry et al., 1986; Udry & Billy, 1987). In this model, it is postulated that reproductive hormonal development exerts an independent influence on sexual motivation, or libido; however, cultural and social norms related to sexual behavior mediate the effects of reproductive hormones on sexual motivation and intercourse. Further, among females specific hormones (i.e., androgens) influence involvement in socially prescribed or acceptable, noncoital sexual behavior. This holds especially true for females who encounter a highly differentiated normative sexual environment (Udry et al., 1986). Further, in contrast to the model proposed by Belsky et al. (1991), in this model there is no relation between pubertal development and intercourse (Udry & Billy, 1987).

Elements of Udry's model, specifically the relation between sexual motivation and social norms, have been studied in non-Latina populations. From several studies in which parental influence or norms were examined, parental discussion of sexual matters among daughters with traditional family values (Moore, Peterson, & Furstenberg, 1986); the congruence of values between adolescents and parents (Hanson, Myers, & Ginsburg, 1987); careful and reasonable parental supervision of adolescents (Hogan & Kitiwaga, 1985; Miller, McCoy, Olson, & Wallace, 1986); and family closeness (Jessor & Jessor, 1975; Shah & Zelnik, 1981) were found to be associated with delays in and less frequent initiation of sexual activity, pregnancy, and nonmarital births. Similarly, the congruence between values of adolescents and parents as it relates to responsible behaviors, and the adolescents' perceptions of parental attitudes have been found to be predictors of adolescent sexual behaviors (Hanson et al., 1987; Jessor & Jessor, 1975; Newcomer & Udry, 1987; Shah & Zelnik, 1981). However, findings contrary to this study were reported in a study conducted with a primarily Mexican American sample (Christopher et al., 1993). In this study, adolescents' perception of parent-child communication and parental warmth was not correlated with level of sexual involvement. Given the importance of *familia* within Latino cultures and the cultural value of familism, further investigation as to parental influences on sexual behavior of Latinas is warranted.

The influence of peer norms on behavior has also been studied in various ethnic groups. Sexual behavior among Caucasian female adolescents was correlated with the sexual behavior, including intercourse and outercourse, of close and same-sex friends. However, this effect was contingent on the subjects' own pubertal development (Smith et al., 1985). In subsequent studies, this correlation was not significant for black females or white males (Udry & Billy, 1987).

Among Mexican American adolescents, perceived sexual behavior of peers was a predictor of sexual behavior for both males and females; however, this accounted for only a small percentage of variance in females (Christopher et al., 1993). The limited importance of peer approval in the decision to engage in sexual intercourse has also been reported (Padilla & Baird, 1991). In this study of a sample of primarily Mexican American ($n = 84$) adolescents, ranging from 14 to 19 years of age, only a small percentage (10 to 15 percent) indicated that having sex was "OK" because their friends "do it." These percentages were similar between genders, between older and younger adolescents, and between those who were and were not sexually active.

Several cultural tenets proposed to be common among Latino populations, specifically the importance of religion and gender role differentiation, have been linked with sexual behaviors of Latina adolescents. For example, the importance of religion as conceptualized by religious practice and belief, church attendance, and valuing religion has been associated with less permissive attitudes about sex and more limited sexual experience. In a national survey of Latina adolescents (Durant et al., 1990), religious affiliation and frequency of church attendance were significant predictors of not having intercourse. Frequency of church attendance has also been reported as a factor in predicting contraceptive use (Durant et al., 1990; Santelli & Beilenson, 1992; Thornton & Camburn, 1989).

Gender role expectations have also been associated with Latina sexual behavior. The differentiation of gender roles among Latinos is characterized by the cultural concepts of machismo and *marianismo*. Machismo is reflective of desired qualities for men such as virile, courageous, protective, and aggressive, while *marianismo* reflects ideal qualities for women such as chaste, pure, devoted to home, and submissive (Alvirez, Bean, & Williams, 1981; Rubel, 1966; Tamez, 1981). While these characterizations of Latino men and women by the social sciences have been criticized for their bias and inaccuracy (e.g., Amaro, 1988; Comas-Díaz, 1988; Vázquez-Nutall, Romero-García, & DeLeon, 1987), the descriptions persist. For example, the cultural imperative to be a mother, a component of gender role expectations for Latinas, has been associated with positive views of pregnancy and childbearing (De Anda et al., 1988; Smith et al., 1987; Russell et al., 1993), low contraceptive use (Hodges, Leavy, Swift, & Gold, 1992), and higher pregnancy, birth, and marriage rates (Smith et al., 1987). While these studies did not measure gender role expectations, their findings were consistent with existing conceptualizations of gender role expectations for Latinas.

One study did examine gender role expectations of Mexican American adolescents as a component of sexual attitudes and behaviors (Padilla & Baird, 1991). Consistent with existing conceptualizations of gender roles, there was strong agreement between male and female adolescents regarding the importance of having children and that women, but not men should be virgins when they marry. In contrast to existing conceptualizations, there was also strong agreement between male and female adolescents that it was important to control the number of children and in addition, that females are responsible for birth control. Further studies are needed to describe cultural patterns and beliefs including religion, gender roles, and familism and their relation to sexual behavior. Such knowledge is critical in the design of culturally competent strategies and programs to promote safer sexual behaviors among Latina adolescents.

ACCESS TO HEALTH CARE

The increased vulnerability of Latinas to the adverse health outcomes associated with sexual behavior and the biologic, social, and cultural factors that influence that behavior have been discussed. Because of the direct relation between early sexual behavior and adverse health outcomes, it becomes important to examine the accessibility of Latino adolescents to health care, specifically the prevention and treatment of conditions associated with sexual behavior.

In general, Latinos and Latino adolescents face a barrage of financial, structural, and institutional barriers to primary and preventive health care services. A major financial barrier to health care faced by a large portion of Latinos is lack of health insurance. For example, Latinos are more likely to be uninsured (32 percent) than whites (13 percent) or blacks (20 percent) (U.S. Bureau of the Census, 1991). Despite a high workforce participation, the overrepresentation of Latinos in low-paid, low-benefit occupations impacts the degree to which Latinos and their children are insured. Similarly, the rates of uninsured among adolescents is parallel to that of adults. One-third of Hispanic adolescents (32 percent) are uninsured as compared to non-Hispanic black (21 percent) and non-Hispanic white (12 percent) adolescents (American Medical Association, 1991). In addition to the lack of employer-based or private insurance, Latinos are less likely to receive public insurance, such as Medicaid. While in 1990, 28.1 percent of Latinos lived below the poverty level, only 18.2 percent received Medicaid benefits (U.S. Bureau of the Census, 1991). In part, this reflects the ineligibility of employed Latinos for Medicaid benefits. In addition, however, cultural and linguistic barriers, discrimination, and the fear of deportation are other factors which influence the lack of participation of Latinos in public insurance.

The lack of insurance as a financial barrier to health care for adolescents specifically is reflected in low physician utilization rates for primary care services. In a secondary analysis of data from the 1988 National Health Interview Survey, Lieu, Newacheck, and McManus (1993) examined insurance status, health status, and utilization of health services among 10- to 17-year-old white, black, and Hispanic children and adolescents. Similar to data from other national studies, a higher proportion of Hispanics (28 percent) than blacks (16 percent) and whites (11 percent) were uninsured ($p < .01$). Using the number of school loss days as an indicator of health status, Hispanics had the highest number of school loss days (6.6 days per year) compared to African American (3.8 days per year) and white (5.2 days per year) teens. However, despite a higher number of school loss days, there was a significant difference in physician contacts for both routine (i.e., preventive) and sick (i.e., primary) care between Hispanic (1.7 days) and white (2.6 days) teens. Further, Hispanic adolescents (19 percent) were significantly more likely to report that they had no usual source of sick care. It is of interest to note, however, that in an analysis of the effects of insurance on physician visits, insurance did increase by 21 percent the chances of Hispanic students having a usual source of care, but this increase was still less than for white or black adolescents.

Results from this study present a clear picture of how financial barriers affect access to health care. However, a finding from this study that has important policy implications is that insurance reform alone will not increase access to health care for Latinos. Because in this study insurance did not substantially increase access to care for Latino adolescents, the need to address structural and institutional barriers is underscored. Use of health care services is tied to both structural (e.g., culturally and linguistically appropriate health care services; availability of outreach services) and institutional (i.e., perceived level of discrimination; bilingual/bicultural providers; convenience of service hours; location of services and availability of transportation; waiting times) barriers.

It is important to recognize that while these barriers exist for health care in general, they are paramount in discussing preventive services for adolescents. First, although there has been growing attention to preventive health care, the emphasis on health care services remains primarily on the treatment of disease. Thus, necessary services for sexually active adolescents, including cervical cancer screening and family planning counseling, may not be reimbursable services. Second, while there has been a movement for the provision of school-based clinics as a means to make primary and preventive health care services more available to adolescents, many of these clinics are placed at the high school level. Given the both high and early dropout rate among Latino adolescents (National Council of La Raza [NCLR], 1992), these initiatives may not be adequate to address the primary and preventive health care needs of Latino adolescents in general, and those associated with sexual behavior in particular.

The lack of access to preventive services for Latina adolescents in both health and school settings has been deemed a factor in the consistently low levels of knowledge among Latina adolescents related to sexual issues and contraceptive use (Moore & Erickson, 1985; Padilla & Baird, 1991; Scott, Shifman, Orr, Owen, & Fawcett, 1988; Smith et al., 1987). Compounding the lack of access to health information related to sex is the limited communication between Latina parents and adolescents. De Anda et al. (1988) reported that Mexican American adolescents who were or had been pregnant indicated they had received no instruction from their mothers about sexual behavior or the use of birth control. Knowledge about birth control was reportedly learned during prenatal care visits from a health care provider and, further, after delivery nearly all respondents reported using a method of contraception. Similar results were reported in a study in which sex information given to pregnant and never-pregnant Latinas (predominantly of Mexican and Central American origin) by their parents was examined (Baumeister, Flores, & Marín, in press). Never-pregnant adolescents reported receiving significantly more information from parents about menstruation, sexual intercourse, and sexually transmitted diseases. It is of interest to note that information concerning birth control and body parts was similar between groups. In addition, greater adolescent-reported communication with parents about sex was associated with not being pregnant.

While the lack of parental communication about sex between Latina adolescents may be attributed to cultural beliefs and values about sex, these findings also present a challenge for teachers, health care, and other service providers. That is, parents of Latina preadolescents and adolescents must have access to the tools to talk effectively with children about choices they face in their adolescent years, including decisions about sexual behavior (National Coalition of Hispanic Health and Human Services Organization [COSSMHO], 1994). The design of culturally relevant and appropriate sex education and communication for Latina adolescents and their parents must be addressed in any preventive efforts.

These financial, structural, and institutional barriers affect health promotion and prevention efforts and associated health outcomes related to sexual behavior. For example, access to family planning and abortion services and the use of contraception have been associated with differences in teenage pregnancy and birthrates by race and ethnicity. In the period 1983–1988, 32 percent of Hispanic women, as compared with 58 percent of black women and 70 percent of white women, indicated they had used a method of contraception during their first reported premarital sexual intercourse (Mosher & McNally, 1991). Access to family planning services for Latino adolescents is tied to cultural and linguistic barriers, lack of physical availability of services, and lack of financial access to services (COSSMHO, 1994). Because of the multiple barriers that impede access to health care, the discussion and/or evaluation of both health risk and health protective behaviors of Latina adolescents in the context of access to primary and preventive health care services is warranted.

RECOMMENDATIONS FOR RESEARCH AND PRACTICE

From the review of existing research concerned with sexual behavior among Latina adolescents, it evident that research in the area is critically limited in both amount and scope. Gaps in knowledge and recommendations for further studies are summarized here. First, as was noted previously, the majority of studies concerned with Latina adolescents have been concerned with fertility patterns and contraceptive use. Conceptually it should be recognized that the initiation of sexual intercourse, while related, is different from decisions about pregnancy and birth and decisions to use contraception. Further, while more is known about the initiation and patterns of sexual intercourse, more research is needed about other sexual behaviors (i.e., to outercourse). Second, data about Latina adolescents have focused on the older adolescent (age 15 to 20). Because the initiation of sexual intercourse begins at an earlier age and is increasing in prevalence for all adolescents (AGI, 1994), information about the sexual behavior of preadolescents and young adolescents (10 through 15 years) is warranted. Third, baseline data related to onset of pubertal development and sexual maturation of Latina adolescents are almost nonexistent. These data are critical not only for obvious health-related issues, but also to examine the relation between pubertal development, hormonal secretion, and sexual behavior.

A fourth issue is that much of the research conducted concerning Latina sexual behavior is derived from nonprobability samples of Mexican Americans primarily in the West and Southwest. Thus, results from these studies cannot be generalized to other Latino populations. There is a critical lack of research concerned with the sexual behavior of other Latina subgroups. While several national data sets (e.g., National Longitudinal Survey of Youth [NLSY]; National Survey of Family Growth [NSFG]; Hispanic Health and Nutrition Examination Survey [HHANES]) are comprised of probability samples, there is not adequate representation of all Latino subgroups to allow for subgroup analysis. Thus, while differences in fertility patterns and contraceptive use between Latina and non-Latina adolescents and among Latina subgroups has been consistently reported, the nature of these differences has not been investigated. Further, both inter- and intragroup variability among Latinas has been difficult to discern because few studies have adequately included indicators of Latino ethnicity. Yet these indicators, including migration history, generational distance, and level of acculturation, are central in understanding the sexual behavior of Latina adolescents.

A fifth issue is that cultural values frequently ascribed to Latino populations including familism, gender role differentiation, and religion have been associated with differences in sexual behavior, fertility, and contraceptive use between Latina and non-Latina adolescents. However, the relation between cultural values and sexual behavior and the inter- and intragroup variation among Latino subgroups has not been examined.

Finally, existing theoretical models and empirical indicators that have been developed to understand the phenomena of adolescent sexual behavior have been based on the experiences of the majority group and/or only tested with white or African American populations. These models need to be tested with Latino populations and refined accordingly, or new models need to be developed exclusively for Latinas in order to guide both research and practice. Given the increased risks of young Latinas to the adverse health consequences associated with early sexual behavior, research in this area is critical.

Despite these existing gaps in research there are several practice recommendations that can be ascertained. The first, and most important, is that Latina adolescents are at risk for the adverse health consequences associated with early sexual behavior. Thus, health practitioners, teachers, community leaders, and parents must begin to dialogue with adolescents and preadolescents not only to discuss consequences of early sexual behavior, but also how to negotiate safer sex practices. These practices should include both primary (i.e., abstinence) and secondary (i.e., contraceptive use) prevention. Second, the design of primary and preventive health services for Latina adolescents must address the financial, structural, and institutional barriers to health care. The use of bilingual/bicultural providers, translators, and community outreach and peer educators is an important strategy in order to establish confidence and trust for both Latina adolescents and their parents. Flexible hours of service, including weekend and after-school hours, service schedules which can accommodate drop-ins, and convenient locations can also be useful in addressing access barriers. Latino community-based organizations have incorporated many of these strategies in the delivery of health and social services and as such have played a critical role in prevention efforts in Latino communities. Partnerships with these established agencies would be useful in promoting safer sexual behavior among Latinas.

A third recommendation is that cultural values must be incorporated in both individual and program strategies to promote safe sexual behavior. At a minimum, practitioners and educators should show respect for cultural values and practices held by Latino adolescents and parents. Respect can be communicated by making efforts to identify and understand values and beliefs of Latino adolescents and parents, acknowledging those beliefs and values as important, and attempting to problem-solve within the cultural framework of adolescents.

Further, while there is a lack of research that addresses the relation between cultural values and sexual behavior of Latinas, consideration should be given to the design of programs within the context of "Latino cultural values." For Latina adolescents this might include the negotiation of safer sexual practices given the role of women within Latina culture. Prevention efforts might also be directed toward parents and specific strategies might be to increase communication between parents and adolescents about sex, or to find an acceptable means whereby the adolescent might have access to that information (i.e., *comadre*, godmother, school, health clinic).

Representatives of the Latino community, including parents and adolescents, should be involved in the design of preventive efforts in order to ensure the cultural relevance of the program. A fourth and related recommendation is that prevention programs be developed to incorporate peer and family norms and expectations regarding sexual behavior. Because research is not conclusive as to the major influences in decisions related to sexual behavior of Latina adolescents, a multidimensional approach should be considered.

Finally, it is important to recognize that there are existing programs at both the national and community level which have been designed to address specific aspects related to Latina sexual behavior (i.e., pregnancy and AIDS prevention). While few of these programs have been evaluated on a systematic basis, they are invaluable resources for both the design and revision of similar preventive efforts. Sources are available that both identify and describe existing prevention programs (e.g., COSSMHO, 1993).

In conclusion, Latina adolescents are vulnerable to experiencing the adverse outcomes associated with early sexual behavior. Researchers, practitioners, educators, parents, and adolescents must work together to develop culturally relevant and effective strategies to address this critical issue.

NOTES

[1]*Latino/Latina* are the preferred terms of this author to refer to persons of Mexican, Puerto Rican, Cuban, and Central/South American descent. Efforts will be made when possible to distinguish among Latino subgroups. The term *Hispanic* will be used if it was the term used in research reported.

[2]*Adolescence* in this chapter refers to youth from 12 through 18 years of age. *Early adolescence* or *preadolescence* refers to youth from 10 through 12 years of age.

REFERENCES

Alan Guttmacher Institute. (1994). *Sex and America's teenagers.* Washington, DC: Author.

Alvirez, D., Bean, F. D., & Williams, D. (1981). The Mexican American family. In C. H. Mindel & R. W. Habenstein (Eds.), *Ethnic families in America: Patterns and variations,* 2nd ed. (pp. 269–292). New York: Elsevier.

Amaro, H. (1988). Women in the Mexican American community: Religion, culture, and reproductive attitudes and experiences. *Journal of Community Psychology, 16,* 620.

American Medical Association. (1991). *AMA profiles of adolescent health,* Vol. 2 (No. OPO 18091). Chicago: Author.

Aneshensel, C. S., Becerra, R. M., Fielder, E. P., & Schuler, R. H. (1990). Onset of fertility-related events during adolescence: A prospective comparison of Mexican American and non-Hispanic white females. *American Journal of Public Health, 80,* 959–963.

Baumeister, L. M., Flores, E., & Marín, B. V. (in press). Sex information given to Latina adolescents by parents. *Health Education Research.*

Belsky, J., Steinberg, L., & Draper, P. (1991). Childhood experience, interpersonal development, and reproductive strategy: An evolutionary theory of socialization. *Child Development, 62,* 647–670.

Capell, F. J., Vugia, D. J., Mordaung, V. L., Marelich, W. D., Ascher, M. S., Trachtenberg, A. I., Cunningham, G. C., Arnon, S. S., & Kizer, W. W. (1992). Distribution of HIV type 1 infection in childbearing women in California. *American Journal of Public Health, 82,* 254–256.

Centers for Disease Control. (1992). *Sexually transmitted disease surveillance: 1991.* Atlanta, GA: Author.

Christopher, F. S., Johnson, D. C., & Roosa, M. W. (1993). Family, individual, and social correlates of early Hispanic adolescent sexual expression. *Journal of Sex Research, 30,* 54–61.
Comas-Díaz, L. (1988). Mainland Puerto Rican women: A sociocultural approach. *Journal of Community Psychology, 16,* 21–31.
Darabi, K. F., & Ortiz, V. (1987). Childbearing among young Latino women in the United States. *American Journal of Public Health, 77,* 25–28.
De Anda, D., Becerra, R. M., & Fielder, P. (1988). Sexuality, pregnancy, and motherhood among Mexican American adolescents. *Journal of Adolescent Research, 3,* 403–411.
Durant, R. H., Pendergrast, R., & Seymore, C. (1990). Sexual behavior among Hispanic female adolescents in the United States. *Pediatrics, 85,* 1051–1058.
Flewelling, R. L., & Bauman, K. E. (1990). Family structure as a predictor of initial substance use and sexual intercourse in early adolescence. *Journal of Marriage and Family, 52,* 171–180.
Gayle, J., Selik, R., & Chu, S. (1990). Surveillance for AIDS and HIV infection among black and Hispanic children and women of childbearing age, 1981–1989. *Morbidity and Mortality Weekly Report, 40,* 41–44.
Hanson, S. L., Myers, D. E., & Ginsburg, A. L. (1987). The role of responsibility and knowledge in reducing teenage out-of-wedlock childbearing. *Journal of Marriage and the Family, 49,* 241–251.
Hein, K. (1989). Commentary on adolescent acquired immunodeficiency syndrome: The next wave of the human immunodeficiency virus epidemic. *Journal of Pediatrics, 114,* 144–149.
Hodges, B. C., Leavy, J., Swift, R., & Gold, R. S. (1992). Gender and ethnic differences in adolescents' attitudes toward condom use. *Journal of School Health, 62,* 103–106.
Hogan, D. P., & Kitawaga, E. M. (1985). The impact of social status, family structure, and neighborhood on the fertility of black adolescents. *American Journal of Sociology, 90,* 825–855.
Holmes, K. G., Karon, J. M., & Kreiss, J. (1990). The increasing frequency of heterosexually acquired AIDS in the United States, 1983–1988. *American Journal of Public Health, 80,* 858–863.
Jessor, S. L., & Jessor, R. (1975). Transition from virginity to non-virginity among youth: A study over time. *Developmental Psychology, 11,* 473–484.
Lieu, T. A., Newacheck, P. W., & McManus, M. A. (1993). Race, ethnicity, and access to ambulatory care among US adolescents. *American Journal of Public Health, 83,* 960–965.
Miller, B., McCoy, J., Olson, T., & Wallace, C. (1986). Parental discipline and control attempts in relation to adolescent sexual attitudes and behavior. *Journal of Marriage and the Family, 51,* 499–506.

Moffit, T. E., Caspi, A., Belsky, J., & Silva, P. A. (1992). Childhood experience and the onset of menarche: A test of a sociobiological model. *Child Development, 63,* 47–58.

Moore, D. S., & Erickson, P. I. (1985). Age, gender, and ethnic differences in sexual and contraceptive knowledge, attitudes, and behaviors. *Family and Community Health, 8,* 38–51.

Moore, K., Peterson, J., & Furstenberg, F. (1986). Parental attitudes and the occurrence of early sexual activity. *Journal of Marriage and the Family, 48,* 777–782.

Mosher, W. D., & McNally, J. W. (1991). Contraceptive use at first premarital intercourse: United States, 1965–1988. *Family Planning Perspectives, 23,* 108–116.

National Center for Health Statistics. (1984). *Public use data tape documentation: National Survey of Family Growth, Cycle III, 1982.* Hyattsville, MD: Department of Health and Human Services.

National Center for Health Statistics. (1985). *Plan and operation of the Hispanic Health and Nutrition Examination Survey, 1982–1984* (DHHS Publication No. PHS 851321). Washington, DC: U.S. Government Printing Office.

National Center for Health Statistics. (1990). *Health, United States, 1990.* Hyattsville, MD: Public Health Service.

National Center for Health Statistics. (1992). *Health, United States, 1992.* Hyattsville, MD: Public Health Service.

National Coalition of Hispanic Health and Human Services Organization [COSSMHO]. (1993). *Adolescent pregnancy prevention: Programs serving Hispanic communities.* Washington, DC: COSSMHO.

National Coalition of Hispanic Health and Human Services Organization [COSSMHO]. (1994). *Growing up Hispanic: A leadership report.* Washington, DC: COSSMHO.

National Council of La Raza & Labor Council for Latin American Advancement. (1992). *Hispanics and Health Insurance. Vol. 1: Status.* Washington, DC: Author.

Newcomer, S., & Baldwin, W. (1992). Demographics of adolescent sexual behavior, contraception, pregnancy, and STDs. *Journal of School Health, 62,* 265–270.

Newcomer, S., & Udry, J. (1987). Parental marital status effects on adolescent sexual behavior. *Journal of Marriage and the Family, 49,* 235–240.

Padilla, A. M., & Baird, T. L. (1991). Mexican American sexuality and sexual knowledge: An exploratory study. *Hispanic Journal of Behavioral Sciences, 13,* 95–104.

Pletsch, P. K. (1990). Hispanics: At risk for adolescent pregnancy? *Public Health Nursing, 7,* 105–110.

Reynoso, T. C., Felice, M. E., & Schragg, G. P. (1993). Does American acculturation affect outcome of Mexican American teenage pregnancy? *Journal of Adolescent Health, 14,* 257–261.

Rubel, A. (1966). *Across the tracks: Mexican Americans in a Texas City.* Austin, TX: University of Texas Press.

Russell, A. Y., Williams, M. S., Farr, P. A., Schwab, A. J., & Plattsmier, S. (1993). Patterns of contraceptive use and pregnancy among young Hispanic women on the Texas-Mexico border. *Journal of Adolescent Health, 14,* 373–379.

Sabogal, F., Faigeles, B., & Catania, J. A. (1993). Multiple sexual partners among Hispanics in high-risk cities. *Family Planning Perspectives, 25,* 257–262.

Santelli, J. S., & Beilenson, P. L. (1992). Risk factors for adolescent sexual behavior, fertility, and sexually transmitted diseases. *Journal of School Health, 62,* 271–279.

Scott, C. S., Shifman, L., Orr, L., Owen, R. G., & Fawcett, N. (1988). Hispanic and black American adolescents' beliefs relating to sexuality and contraception. *Adolescence, 23,* 667–687.

Shah, F. K., & Zelnik, M. (1981). Parent and peer influence on sexual behavior, contraceptive use, and pregnancy experience of young women. *Journal of Marriage and the Family, 43,* 339–348.

Smith, E. A., Udry, J. R., & Morris, N. M. (1985). Pubertal development and friends: A biosocial explanation of adolescent sexual behavior. *Journal of Health and Social Behavior, 26,* 183–192.

Smith, K. W., McGraw, S. A., Crawford, S. L., Costa, L. A., & McKinlay, J. B. (1993). HIV risk among Latino adolescents in two New England cities. *American Journal of Public Health, 83,* 1395–1399.

Smith, P. B., McGill, L., & Wait, R. B. (1987). Hispanic adolescent conception and contraception profiles: A comparison. *Journal of Adolescent Health Care, 8,* 352–355.

Surbey, M. (1990). Family composition, stress, and the timing of human menarche. In F. Bercovitch & T. Zeigler (Eds.), *The socioendocrinology of primate reproduction* (pp. 11–32). New York: Wiley-Liss.

Tamez, E. (1981). Familism, machismo, and child-rearing practices among Mexican Americans. *Journal of Psychosocial Nursing and Mental Health Services, 19,* 21–25.

Thornton, A., & Camburn, D. (1989). Religious participation and adolescent sexual behavior and attitudes. *Journal of Marriage and the Family, 51,* 641–652.

Udry, J. R., & Billy, J. O. G. (1987). Initiation of coitus in early adolescence. *American Sociological Review, 52,* 841–855.

Udry, J. R., Talbert, L. M., Morris, N. M. (1986). Biosocial foundations for adolescent female sexuality. *Demography, 23,* 217–227.
U.S. Bureau of the Census. (1991). *Marital status and living arrangements: March 1989* (Current Population Reports, Series P20, No. 445). Washington, DC: U.S. Government Printing Office.
Vázquez-Nutall, E., Romero-García, I., & DeLeón, B. (1987). Sex roles and perceptions of femininity and masculinity of Hispanic women. *Psychology of Women Quarterly, 11,* 409–425.
Wierson, M., Long, P. J., & Forehand, R. (1993). Toward a new understanding of early menarche: The role of environmental stress in pubertal timing. *Adolescence, 28,* 913–924.

CHAPTER 4

An Ecological, Risk-Factor Examination of Latino Adolescents' Engagement in Sexual Activity

DANIEL F. PERKINS AND
FRANCISCO A. VILLARRUEL

INTRODUCTION

Latinos represent the fastest-growing segment of the U.S. population under the age of 21. By 2030, the number of Latino children and youth will reach 9.6 million—more than double their number of 4.7 million in 1980 (Duany & Pittman, 1990). While Latino families appear to have adapted to their circumstances in ways that reflect sources of strength that need to be built upon rather than sources of weakness that need to be eliminated (Baca Zinn, 1990; Hayes-Bautista, Schink, & Chapa, 1988), Latino youth appear to be engaged in increasingly greater rates of risk behaviors that negatively impact their life chances (Johnson, Miranda, Sherman, & Weill, 1991).

Parents of many Latino youth have significantly low levels of education and income, and high levels of unemployment. With respect to education, only 42 percent of Latino adolescents have parents who are high school graduates, compared to 66 percent of African American and 80 percent of non-Hispanic white teenagers (U.S. Bureau of the Census, 1990). In terms of income, 54 percent of Latino youth live in families that earn less than $20,000 a year, compared to 60 percent of African American and 24 percent of non-Hispanic white youth (U.S. Bureau of the Census, 1990). In the area of unemployment, 31 percent of Latino teens live in households where parents are unemployed or looking for work, compared to 36 percent of African American teens and 14 percent of non-Hispanic white teens. The unemployment rates, however, for female-headed households are even more dramatic: 56 percent for Latina females, 47 percent for African American women, and 29 percent for non-Hispanic women, resulting in dramatic increases in welfare dependency (Danziger & Danziger, 1993; Duncan, 1991; Santiago, this volume). Clearly the effects of these factors appear to impact the resiliency of Latino youth toward engagement in risk behaviors (e.g., alcohol and drug use, early unprotected sex, delinquency, and school failure). Yet, previous research has documented that an important dimension of psychosocial development of Latino youth and children is the family. A number of studies have documented the high value that Latinos of various national origins place on family support (Sabogal, Marín, Otero-Sabogal, Marín, & Pérez-Stable, 1987). Given the grim data that suggest that Latino youth and adolescents are likely to live in poor social, environmental, and economic circumstances that have been noted to affect the growth and development of children, placing them at high risk for physical and developmental problems (Dryfoos, 1990; Hamburg, 1992; Hawkins, Catalano, & Miller, 1992; Hernández, 1993; Jessor, 1993; Luthar, 1991; Rutter, 1985, 1987; Werner & Smith, 1982, 1992), attention to risk and resiliency factors that may impact Latino children and adolescents is critical. This study is an initial attempt to understand the risk factors associated with Latino adolescents' engagement in one risk behavior in particular: sexual activity.

AN ECOLOGICAL MODEL FOR UNDERSTANDING EARLY SEXUAL ACTIVITY

This investigation proposes an ecological, risk-factor model for understanding why some Latino adolescents engage in sexual activity while others do not. Specifically, this investigation examines an ecological, risk factor model that had been employed in previous work (Luster & Small, 1994; Small & Luster, 1994) with predominantly European American samples of adolescents to assess whether it yielded similar or differential results in a sample of Latino adolescents.

Central to an ecological, risk factor model is the concept of cumulative risk; that is, as exposure to risk factors increases, the probability of becoming sexually active also increases. The model also proposes that the risks teens are exposed to can be organized into four levels of the adolescent's ecology: the individual; the family; extrafamilial contexts such as schools, neighborhoods, and peer groups; and the macrosystem (e.g., cultural values, the media, public policies [Bronfenbrenner, 1979, 1989; Small & Luster, 1994]).

Initial support for this model was found in a study with an ethnically diverse sample (51 percent Caucasian) from a community in the Southwestern United States (Small & Luster, 1994). Only 1 percent of female adolescents who were exposed to zero risk factors were sexually active, compared to 80 percent of those who were exposed to eight or more risk factors. Among male adolescents, 15 percent of those exposed to zero risk factors were sexually active, while 93 percent of those with scores of five or more risk factors were sexually active. A discriminant analysis showed that significant risk factors for sexual activity were found at all levels of the social ecology that were examined (i.e., individual, family, extrafamilial contexts) for both males and females. Very similar results were obtained with a Caucasian sample from Wisconsin (Small & Luster, 1990).

The risk factors for, and negative consequences of, sexual activity among European American adolescents have been well documented in the literature (Brooks-Gunn & Furstenberg, 1989; Dryfoos, 1990; Flick, 1986; Hayes, 1987; Irwin & Shafer, 1992; Jenkins & Westney, 1991; Jessor, 1993; Ketterlinus, Lamb, & Nitz, 1995; Luster & Small, 1994; Small & Luster, 1994). A few studies have examined the risk factors for sexual activity among African American adolescents (Day, 1992; Furstenberg, Morgan, Moore, & Peterson, 1987; Haurin & Mott, 1990; Hogan & Kitagawa, 1985; Jaccard, Dittus, & Gordon, 1996; Mott, Fondell, Hu, Kowaleski-Jones, & Menaghan, 1996; Stanton, Romer, Ricardo, Black, Feigelman, & Galbraith, 1993) and fewer still among Latino youth specifically (Christopher, Johnson, & Roosa, 1993; Costa, Jessor, Donovan, & Fortenberry, 1995; Day, 1992; Gibson & Kempf, 1990). The majority of studies that assessed Latino sexual activity did not examine within-group differences, such as Chicano, Cuban, or Puerto Rican.

Indeed, of the studies that examined sexual intercourse among Latino and Latina adolescents only Day (1992) has analyzed within-group differences for Latinos. He compared Chicano adolescents (Mexican-born or Mexican American) with other Latino adolescents (Cuban, Puerto Rican, and other Spanish) relative to age at first intercourse. Day (1992) found that Chicano men began sexual activity a full year later than the Latino group. For women, however, there was essentially no difference in age at initiation.

As Moore, Miller, Glei, and Morrison (1995) point out, more than half of Latino males have sex by age 17 on average. Similarly, 45 percent of Latina females are sexually experienced by age 17. Moreover, the birthrate for Latina females, age 15 to 19, is 107 per 1,000; the comparable rate for Caucasian adolescents is 40 per 1,000 (Moore, 1996). The increase in the birthrate that occurred among teens during the late 1980s was particularly large among Latina adolescents. From 1980 to 1993, the birthrate among 15- to 19-year-old Latinas increased from 82 per 1,000 to 107 per 1,000, whereas among Caucasian females, the birthrate decreased from 41 per 1,000 to 40 per 1,000 (Moore, 1996).

A search of recent literature yielded four studies focusing on predictors of sexual behavior among Latinos (Christopher et al., 1993; Costa et al., 1995; Day, 1992; Gibson & Kempf, 1990). These four studies looked at different predictor variables, age groups, and to some extent, outcomes (e.g., virgin versus nonvirgin status, level of sexual intimacy from kissing to intercourse). As noted previously, only Day (1992) examined within-group differences among various Latino groups. Given the amount of research that has been done, and the diverse findings from these studies, it is difficult to draw any conclusions at this point about factors related to early sexual activity among Latinos.

Understanding the issue of predictive factors that might lead to increased rates of sexual activity is further complicated by previous investigations that note that factors which predict sexual activity in one ethnic group do not necessarily predict sexual activity in another ethnic group (Costa et al., 1995; Day, 1992). In addition, those who have done research on Latino adolescents have reached different conclusions about whether the factors that predict sexual activity among Latinos are similar to factors that predict sexual activity in Caucasian samples (Christopher et al., 1993; Day, 1992). Clearly many questions remain regarding factors associated with sexual activity among Latino adolescents. The present study was conducted to add to our knowledge base in this area.

Although data were available on European American adolescents in the data set employed for this study, we decided not to include this subsample in the analysis. We were primarily interested in examining factors that were related to sexual activity *within* groups of Latino adolescents, and testing the usefulness of an ecological cumulative risk factor approach to predicting sexual activity within this group. We also had reservations about viewing the findings for members of the majority culture as the standard against which the results of other ethnic groups would be compared for this study.

This investigation attempts to identify and measure the group variables (or elements) that distinguish normative development within the Latino adolescent population. Once established, subsequent research can examine how these elements impact development across ethnic minority groups. As previous researchers have argued (e.g., Betancourt & Lopez, 1993; Fisher, Jackson, & Villarruel, 1998; Grahm, 1992; Lerner, 1995), such an approach will serve to enhance our understanding of both group-specific and group-general (universal) processes, as well as contribute to the integration of culture in theory development and practice. The basis for the application of the ecological, risk factor model has already been established in previous work (Luster & Small, 1994; Small & Luster, 1994). Thus, this study seeks to determine if the model is appropriate for samples of Latino youth.

RISK ELEMENTS OF THE ECOLOGY OF ADOLESCENTS

Individual Risk Factors

Although the survey instrument for this study was different from the one used by Small and Luster (1994), many of the same risk factors could be utilized because similar constructs were assessed. Risk factors at the individual level that were expected to be related to sexual experience included lack of school success (Billy, Brewster, & Grady, 1994; Furstenberg et al., 1987; Small & Luster, 1994), a tendency to engage in unconventional behaviors such as using alcohol (Costa et al., 1995; Small & Luster, 1994), and low religiosity (Billy et al., 1994; Day, 1992; Thornton & Camburn, 1989). A higher proportion of individuals who reported a history of physical abuse or sexual abuse were also expected to be sexually active (Boyer & Fine, 1992; Butler & Burton, 1990; Small & Luster, 1994). Age of the teen is also pertinent; the probability of being sexually experienced has been reported to increase throughout the teen years (Moore et al., 1995).

Familial Risk Factors

Family factors that were expected to distinguish between sexually active and nonsexually active teens included low levels of family support (Small & Luster, 1994, but see also Christopher et al., 1993, for contrary findings), and low levels of parental monitoring (Small & Luster, 1994). A concept related to parental monitoring that was also of interest was the amount of time the adolescents spent at home alone. Brewster and her colleagues (Billy et al., 1994; Brewster, 1994; Brewster, Billy, & Grady, 1993) reported that sexual activity rates tended to be higher among teens who lived in neighborhoods where a relatively high percentage of women worked full-time. Their explanation for this finding is that teens in these neighborhoods are likely to lack adequate adult supervision during working hours. In this study, we attempt to test this idea more directly by looking at the relation between adolescents' reports of how much time they spend at home without adult supervision and sexual experience.

Extrafamilial Risk Factors

Extrafamilial risk factors examined were involvement with peers who engage in unconventional behaviors (Christopher et al., 1993; Costa et al., 1995), and lack of positive experiences in school (Quinton & Rutter, 1988; Small & Luster, 1994). The employment of these risk factors provided a more comprehensive examination of the relationship of risk factors from multiple levels of the adolescents' ecology and the sexual activity for Latino adolescents than has been used in many earlier studies.

Cumulative Risk Factors

A single risk factor was not expected to adequately explain sexual activity for Latino adolescents. Instead, we propose that sexual activity is most likely to occur when adolescents are exposed to multiple risk factors. Although sexually active teens are likely to have many risk factors in common, there are also likely to be different risk factors that predispose various individuals toward sexual activity. Put another way, there are many different pathways to early sexual activity. For example, a combination of a lack of school success and residence in a neighborhood where economic prospects are bleak may push one individual toward sexual activity. Another individual with a history of abuse and poor family relationships may seek solace in relationships with peers, who may also have troubled histories. Because of these multiple pathways, the risk factors that are important may differ from individual to individual; thus, there is value in examining multiple risk factors in a single study.

In summary, this study examines the extent to which the ecological, risk factor approach, utilized by Small and Luster (1994) for studying sexual activity in samples in which Caucasians were the largest group, may be useful for explaining adolescent sexual activity in Latinos. We expected to find that as exposure to risk factors increased, so would the likelihood of sexual activity in Latino adolescents. Moreover, we expected to find that the risk factors that were related to sexual activity would be found at the level of the individual, the family, and extrafamilial contexts such as the school and peer groups. Research to date suggests that it would be unwise to assume that the same risk factors are important for both genders (Lauritsen, 1994; Small & Luster, 1994). However, past research is too limited to allow for any strong predictions about how the results may differ by gender.

METHOD

Participants

A sample of 438 Latino adolescents was drawn from the Community-Based Profile of Michigan Youth Study (Keith & Perkins, 1995). The sample employed here is all Latino adolescents who participated in the Community-Based Profile of Michigan Youth Study, which is an assessment of 16,375 adolescents, age 12 to 17 years old.

This study involved 43 middle and high schools in 36 communities throughout Michigan. Public school participation was solicited at the school or district level by one of three people: the county 4-H extension agent, the county extension home economist, or project staff. All students at each school participated unless they were absent or refused to participate in the study. The sample was representative of Michigan in terms of racial/ethnic participation and geographic location (e.g., urban, suburban, and rural; see Keith & Perkins, 1995, for a comprehensive description of the larger sample).

Data were collected via self-report surveys administered by classroom teachers, in either fall 1993 or winter 1994. The primary purpose of the surveys was to provide communities with information that could be used to influence policy and to educate school administrators, local policymakers, parents, youth, and other members of the community about the attitudes and behaviors of local youth.

The Latino sample consisted of slightly more female participants (51 percent) than male participants (49 percent). The mean age of the adolescents was 14.3 years (SD = 1.50). The sample included a diverse array of family structures (49.8 percent biologically intact, 34.1 percent single parent, 15.2 percent in a blended or step family, and .4 percent missing). A limitation of the data set is that questions of Latino ethnicity were not asked. Based on the 1990 census, however, it may be assumed that the majority of youth were of Mexican origin.

Measures

All participants in the Community-Based Profile of Michigan Youth Study were administered the Search Institute's *Profiles of Student Life: Attitude and Behavior Questionnaire* (ABQ), containing 152 items (Benson, 1990; Blyth, 1993). Cronbach alphas have been calculated to assess the reliability of variables that are comprised of multiple items (Perkins, Luster, Villarruel, & Small, 1998; Perkins, 1995).

Sexual Activity. Adolescents' sexual activity was assessed by one item on the ABQ which asked, "Have you ever had sexual intercourse ('gone all the way,' 'made love')?" The choices ranged from 1 (no) to 5 (4 or more times). In the present study, responses were transformed into a dichotomous variable, "sexually active versus not sexually active." All participants who reported having sexual intercourse at least once were coded as sexually active and scored a 1. Adolescents who reported that they had never had sexual intercourse were coded as not sexually active and scored 0.

Risk Factors. Using Small and Luster's ecological, risk factor approach, twelve risk factors were identified from the larger set of variables measured in the study. The risk factors were grouped into one of three levels of the social ecology: individual, family, and extrafamilial.

Individual Level
- *Age.* In this investigation, age was scored as a continuous variable. The range of ages in this sample was 12 through 17 years. As noted above, the mean age was 14.3 years (SD = 1.50).
- *Alcohol use.* Adolescents' alcohol use was measured by one item from the ABQ, which asked, "How many times, if any, have you had alcohol to drink, in the last 30 days?" The range of the scale was from 1 (zero drinks) to 7 (40 or more drinks).
- *Physical abuse.* Physical abuse was measured by one item, "Have you ever been physically abused by an adult (that is, where an adult caused you to have a scar, black and blue marks, welts, bleeding, or a broken bone)?" Participants reporting never having been abused by a parent or other adult were coded as 0. Conversely, adolescents who reported having been abused one or more times were coded as 1.
- *Sexual abuse.* Sexual abuse was measured by one item, "Have you ever been sexually abused?" Adolescents who reported they had

never been sexually abused scored a 0; those who reported being sexually abused one or more times scored a 1.
- *Grade point average (GPA).* Adolescents reported their GPA in terms of the letter grades they get in their courses at school. Letter grades were converted to their equivalent on a traditional 4-point grading scale.
- *Suicide ideation.* Suicide ideation was measured with one item. Adolescents were asked, "In the last year, how often, if at all, have you thought about killing yourself?" The range of responses was 1 (never) to 5 (6 or more times).
- *Religiosity.* Adolescents' religiosity was indexed by three items measuring their attendance of religious services and their views on the importance of religion in their lives. The first two items concerned actual involvement in church activities and services (e.g., "How often do you attend religious services at a church or synagogue?"). The range of choices was 1 (never) to 4 (about once a week). The third item asked the adolescents about their view of religion: "How important is religion in your life?" For this item, there were four possible responses ranging from 1 (not important) to 4 (very important). In this sample, the Cronbach alpha for religiosity was .72. The three items were standardized before being summed together.

Familial Level
- *Parental monitoring.* Parental monitoring was measured by one item, "How much of the time do your parents ask you where you are going or whom you will be with?" The range of possible responses was from 1 (practically never) to 5 (all of the time).
- *Family support.* Adolescents' reports of family support was derived from a five-item scale on the ABQ. These items were: "My family life is happy," "There is a lot of love in my family," "I get along well with my parents," "My parents help me and give me support when I need it," and "My parents often tell me they love me." All of the items from this scale were scored on a five-point Likert scale with responses ranging from 1 (strongly disagree) through 5 (strongly agree). The Cronbach alpha for this scale was .83.

Extrafamilial Level
- *Negative peer group.* Negative peer group membership was measured by a three-item scale that assessed the behavioral character-

istics of the participant's closest peers. Items from the scale included: "Among the people you consider to be your closest friends, how many would you say . . . drink alcohol once a week or more?" ". . . have used marijuana or cocaine?" and ". . . get into trouble at school?" The possible choices were based on a five-point Likert scale that ranged from 1 (none) to 5 (all). In this sample, the Cronbach alpha for the negative peer group scale was .72.

- *School climate*. Adolescents' perceptions of school climate were assessed with a seven-item scale. Examples of the items include: "My teachers really care about me," "My teachers don't pay much attention to me," and "I get a lot of encouragement at my school." For each item, possible responses ranged from 1 (strongly agree) to 5 (strongly disagree). Scores for five of the items were reversed and scored so that high scores on items were indicative of a more positive school climate. In this sample, the Cronbach alpha for the school climate scale was .67.
- *Home alone*. One item assessed how much time adolescents spent at home unsupervised by an adult. Adolescents were asked, "On an average school day, how many hours do you spend at home without an adult there with you?" The range of values was from 1 (none) to 5 (5 or more hours).

Procedure

Data collection involved group testing in each of the participating schools. Teachers administered the questionnaire by following a specific script and an instruction manual from the Search Institute. In a classroom setting, all of the participants, within their respective schools, were administered the questionnaire during one specific time during the school day.

The survey was administered to participants with the assurance of anonymity. Each school determined if written consent or passive consent of parents was required before students could participate in the survey. Passive consent of parents was employed by the schools from which this sample is drawn. Parents were notified about the survey. Their child could participate in the study unless parents indicated that the child was not allowed to participate. Moreover, verbal consent was received from each student, who was informed about the precise nature of the study. Students were told their responses were completely anonymous, that their participation was completely voluntary, and that they could withdraw from the study at any time without penalty. In addition, students were told that after all the questionnaires were completed, their teacher would seal the envelope which contained the questionnaires in front of the students; this procedure was intended to provide concrete assurance of anonymity.

Results

The analysis involved three steps. First, chi-square and t-tests were conducted to compare the average scores on the predictor variables of those who were sexually active and those who were not. Second, a logistic regression analysis was conducted with sexual activity (sexually active and not sexually active) as the dependent variable and the twelve risk factors as the predictors. In the third step, those variables that were found to be significant in the logistic regression analysis were examined in a cumulative risk analysis. For all analyses, males and females were examined separately.

Chi-Square and T-Tests: A Comparison of Sexually Active and Nonsexually Active Adolescents. A significantly higher percentage of Latino males were sexually active (54 percent) than Latina females (38 percent; $\chi^2 = 10.49$, $df = 1$, $p < .01$). There was no significant difference in the ages of Latino males and females. Thus, the significantly higher percentage of Latino males who were sexually active compared to their Latina female age-mates can not be attributed to age differences. Chi-square analyses were also employed to compare sexually active and nonactive adolescents on physical and sexual abuse because they were dichotomous variables. A significant association was found for Latino males between sexual activity and physical abuse but not between sexual activity and sexual abuse ($\chi^2 = 9.12$, $df = 1$, $p < .001$, and $\chi^2 = 2.25$, $df = 1$, $p > .05$, respectively). Thus, Latino males who had been physically abused were more likely to be sexually active than Latino males who were not physically abused. However, there were significant associations found in the chi-square analyses between sexual activity and physical abuse, and sexual activity and sexual abuse for Latina females ($\chi^2 = 6.87$, $df = 1$, $p < .001$, and $\chi^2 = 15.16$, $df = 1$, $p < .0001$, respectively) (see Table 4–1). Adolescent females were more likely to be sexually active if they had been physically abused or sexually abused.

As shown in Table 4.2, for both gender groups the sexually active groups significantly differed from the nonactive groups on the majority of risk factor variables. However, for Latino males, home alone and GPA

Table 4.1 Chi-Square Analyses between Sexual Activity and Physical Abuse or Sexual Abuse for Latino Males and Females

Variable	Latino Males			Latina Females		
	Not Sexually Active (n)	Sexually Active (n)	χ^2	Not Sexually Active (n)	Sexually Active (n)	χ^2
MALES						
Not physically abused	50.9% (87)	49.1% (84)	9.12[a]	66.9% (109)	33.1% (54)	6.87[b]
Physically abused	21.9% (7)	78.1% (25)		45.7% (21)	54.3% (25)	
Not sexually abused	47.7% (93)	52.3% (102)	2.25	69.6% (110)	30.4% (48)	15.16[a]
Sexually abused	16.7% (1)	83.3% (5)		39.2% (20)	60.8% (31)	

[a]Significant at $p < .0001$
[b]Significant at $p < .05$

Table 4.2 Comparisons of the Means between Nonsexually Active and Sexually Active Latino Males and Females

Variable	Means for Latino Males			Means for Latina Females		
	Nonsexually Active ($n = 94$)	Sexually Active ($n = 109$)	T-Score	Nonsexually Active ($n = 358$)	Sexually Active ($n = 1,320$)	T-Score
Age	13.84	14.58	-3.67[a]	13.92	15.03	-5.52[a]
Suicide ideation	1.45	1.86	-2.54[b]	1.54	1.95	-2.43[b]
GPA	2.61	2.39	1.70	2.81	2.42	3.51[b]
Alcohol use	.33	2.16	-5.00[a]	1.27	2.25	-5.82[a]
Home alone	2.84	3.23	-1.95	3.05	3.23	-1.38
Family support	19.34	18.04	2.22[b]	19.12	16.95	3.15[a]
Parental monitoring	1.70	1.43	2.65[b]	1.85	1.64	2.40[b]
Negative peer characteristics	5.42	6.93	-3.88[a]	4.98	6.92	-4.76[a]
Religiosity	.15	-.67	2.70[b]	.12	-.37	1.48
Positive school climate	25.10	23.54	2.62[b]	26.48	24.20	3.73[a]

[a]Significant at p < .001
[b]Significant at p < .05

scores were not significantly different for the two groups. For Latina females, home alone and religiosity scores did not differ significantly for the two groups. The direction of the group differences was as expected; that is, sexually active adolescents did worse on particular indices than the adolescents who were not sexually active.

Logistic Regression Analyses. Logistic regression was employed to identify factors that were related to sexual activity when other factors were controlled. Predictor variables were entered simultaneously and separate analyses were conducted by gender (see Table 4–3).

For Latino males, four variables predicted sexual activity: age, alcohol use, religiosity, and physical abuse (χ^2 =54.29, df = 12, p < .0001). Overall, 70 percent of the Latino males were correctly classified by the model. For the Latina females, four of the twelve variables were significant predictors of sexual activity: age, alcohol use, parental monitoring, and sexual abuse (χ^2 =87.1, df = 12, p < .0001). In the classification analysis, 79 percent of the cases were correctly classified for the Latina females.

Cumulative Risk Analysis. As the final step, a cumulative risk analysis was undertaken to determine what percentage of adolescents in each group were sexually active given exposure to varying numbers of risk factors. For Latino males, three variables were included in the cumulative risk index: alcohol use, religiosity, and physical abuse. For Latina females, three variables were also included in the cumulative risk index: alcohol use, parental monitoring, and sexual abuse. Moreover, following Small and Luster (1994), age was not included in the cumulative risk analysis because it was viewed as a risk factor that is shared by all adolescents and which is not amenable to intervention.

All risk factors were scored in the same manner for this analysis: 0 if the risk factor criterion was not met (i.e., the risk was not present), and 1 if the criterion was met (i.e., the risk was present). For each variable in the cumulative risk analysis a conceptually meaningful cutoff point was determined. The risk criteria for these variables were as follows: (1) alcohol use—using alcohol on a monthly or more frequent basis; (2) physical and sexual abuse—reporting ever having been physically or sexually abused; (3) religiosity—reporting "never" or "rarely" attending religious activities and reporting religion as "not important"; (4) parental monitoring—reporting that parents ask where they are going all the time.

A cumulative risk index was obtained by summing these individual

Table 4.3 Logistic Regression Analyses among Latino Males and Females

Variables	Ethnicity	β	SE	Wald	p	R	Exp (β)
Age	Males	.29	.12	6.06	.0139[a]	.1254	1.34
	Females	.57	.15	15.23	.0001[a]	.2216	1.77
Suicide ideation	Males	.26	.17	2.43	.1198	.0409	1.30
	Females	.27	.17	2.49	.1144	.0428	1.31
GPA	Males	-.03	.10	.10	.7487	.0000	.97
	Females	-.14	.13	1.14	.2847	.0000	.87
Alcohol use	Males	.36	.18	4.05	.0442[a]	.0891	1.44
	Females	1.01	.27	13.66	.0002[a]	.2080	2.74
Home alone	Males	.65	.44	2.16	.1416	.0249	1.92
	Females	.64	.43	2.16	.1413	.0247	1.89
Family support	Males	-.02	.05	0.19	.6612	.0000	1.02
	Females	-.02	.05	0.14	.7043	.0000	1.02
Parental monitoring	Males	-.47	.28	2.90	.0886	-.0591	.63
	Females	-.77	.36	4.44	.0351[a]	-.0952	.46
Negative peer group	Males	.10	.07	1.98	.1598	.0000	1.11
	Females	.05	.08	.33	.5644	.0000	1.05
Physical abuse	Males	1.18	.52	5.10	.0239[a]	.1097	3.27
	Females	.33	.47	.50	.4814	.0000	1.39
Religiosity	Males	-.18	.08	4.64	.0312[a]	-.1011	.84
	Females	-.01	.08	.01	.9372	.0000	.99
Climate	Males	-.03	.05	.37	.5408	.0000	.97
	Females	-.08	.06	1.82	.1771	.0000	.93
Sexual abuse	Males	1.79	1.34	1.79	.1812	.0000	6.02
	Females	1.00	.44	5.19	.0227[a]	.1089	2.71

[a] $p < .05$

risk factor scores. There were different ranges for the cumulative risk index depending upon gender and ethnicity. For Latino males, the cumulative risk index ranged from 0 to 2. The distribution of the cumulative risk index scores indicated that there were very few males with three risk factors; therefore, males with two or more risk factors were collapsed into a single category. The cumulative risk indexes ranged from 0 to 2 for

Latina females. The distribution of the cumulative risk index scores indicated that there were very few females with three risk factors. Thus, females with two or more risk factors were collapsed into a single category. The average number of risk factors for Latino males was 1.57. For Latina females, the average number of risk factors was 1.9. The relation between scores on the cumulative risk index and rates of sexual activity for Latino males and females are presented in Figure 4.1. As expected, as scores on the cumulative risk index increase, so does the probability of being sexually active. Thus, there appears to be a linear trend between the number of risks a person has and the likelihood for being sexually experienced. For Latino males and Latina females who were sexually active, the largest percentage increase occurred between those who were exposed to one risk factor and those who were exposed to two or more risk factors.

Latino males had the highest rates of sexual activity; over 20 percent of the Latino males in the zero risk category reported being sexually ac-

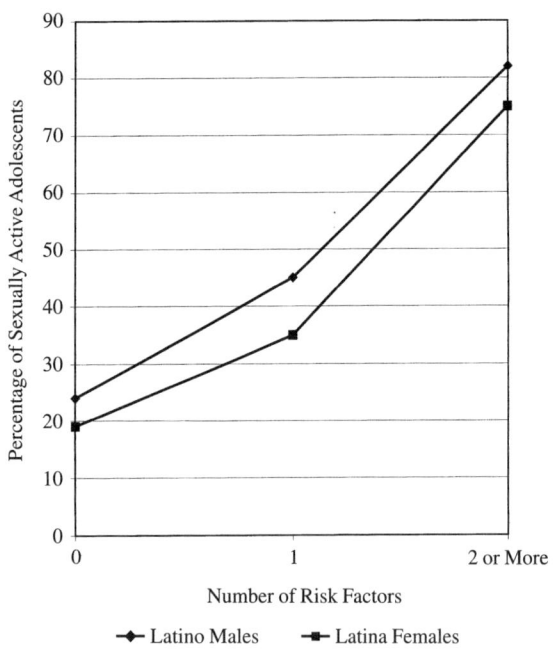

Figure 4.1 Percentage of sexually active Latino adolescents by number of risk factors

tive compared to 19 percent of the Latina females. The largest difference between those two groups occurred in the one risk category (35 percent for Latina females and 45 percent for Latino males). Overall, Latina females were less likely than Latino males to be sexually active regardless of risk category. Latino males and females with two or more risk factors were at much higher risk of being sexually active than those with fewer than two risk factors. In fact, for Latina females, going from zero to two or more risk factors increased the risk of sexual activity by approximately 55 percent. Nineteen percent of the Latina females who had zero risk factors present were sexually active, while 75 percent with two risk factors were sexually active.

DISCUSSION

Small and Luster (1994) demonstrated the usefulness of a cumulative risk approach for understanding the problem of heterosexual teenage sexual activity among a heterogenous group of American adolescents. The primary objectives of this study were (1) to examine what factors are related to sexual activity among Latino adolescents; (2) to examine whether the same risk factors are associated with sexual activity among males and females; and (3) to test the usefulness of Small and Luster's cumulative risk approach for predicting sexual activity in Latino adolescents.

Similar to Small and Luster's (1994) study, the risk factors in the logistic regression analyses found to be pertinent in this study were at two levels of the social ecology (i.e., individual and family). Contrary to other studies (Luster & Small, 1994; Perkins et al., 1998), in this study extrafamilial risk factors were not found to be significant for Latino adolescents' engagement in sexual activity. However, several of the risk factors linked to sexual activity in this study have been identified in previous studies (i.e., age, alcohol use, and religiosity). For example, Thornton and Camburn (1989) found that religiosity was related to teens' sexual activity. In this study low religiosity was found to be a significant predictor of sexual activity for Latino males but not for Latina females.

In addition, this study's results support Small and Luster's finding that physical and sexual abuse predicts sexual activity among some groups of adolescents. Physical abuse predicted sexual activity among Latino males and Latina females, while sexual abuse predicted sexual activity among Latina females but not Latino males. It is important to note that the relation to sexual abuse and sexual experience may be due to the fact that the sexual abuse experience involved intercourse. A survey of a national probability sample found that in cases where women reported a history of childhood sexual abuse, 49 percent of the cases involved actual or attempted intercourse (Finkelhor, Hotaling, Lewis, & Smith, 1990). For men in that national study, 62 percent of the cases involved actual or attempted intercourse. However, past research has established that one of the common symptoms associated with sexual abuse is sexualized behavior and precocious interest in sex (Briere & Runtz, 1993; Kendall-Tackett, Williams, & Finkelhor, 1993). Therefore, it seems likely that a history of sexual abuse also increases the risk that adolescents will become sexually active at an early age.

The extent to which peers influence sexual activity is unclear from past studies. However, research provides evidence of the association between perceived negative peer group behaviors and sexual activity (Christopher et al., 1993; Furstenberg et al., 1987; Stättin & Magnusson, 1990). In this study there was *not* a very clear association between level of negative peer group characteristics and sexual activity for Latino adolescents. This finding is contrary to results from a study by Christopher and colleagues (1993). In their study of 489 Latinos, they found perceived peer sexual activity to significantly predict sexual activity for males and females. The difference between the two studies may have to do with variation in the operationalization of the construct. The peer characteristics measure employed in this study did not measure perceived sexual activity of peers; rather, it measured peers' reported use of alcohol and drugs, and delinquency behavior.

Parental monitoring was found to be associated with sexual activity for Latina females and approached significance for Latino males. The lack of significance of parental monitoring among Latino males is contrary to Small and Luster's (1994) finding that parental monitoring was a significant predictor of sexual activity among mostly European American adolescents. However, similar to the explanation of the differences in peer group characteristics, this difference may be due to the measure of parental monitoring. For this study, parental monitoring was measured using a single item, while Small and Luster's measure of parental monitoring consisted of a multi-item scale. Another possible explanation is that extended kin play a greater role for Latina females, which decreases the importance of monitoring only by parents. The importance of kin may be explained in part by need; ethnic minority families have higher rates of dual household employment and higher rates of single-parent households and often must rely on a larger social network than European American families (A. Villarruel, this volume).

In this study, the same number of risk factors predicted sexual activity for females and for males. This finding is contrary with the results of earlier studies (Lauritsen, 1994; Small & Luster, 1994). In their studies, they found a greater number of predictors among females than males. Indeed, two risk factors (i.e., alcohol use and age) were significant in predicting sexual activity across Latino adolescents studied. Evidence for the relationship of alcohol use and age with sexual activity has been found in several studies (Christopher et al., 1993; Dryfoos, 1990; Ketterlinus et al., 1995; Luster & Small, 1994; Small & Luster, 1994).

The results of the cumulative risk analyses suggest that there is a relationship between the number of risk factors and involvement in sexual activity for Latino adolescents. Thus, an increase in scores on the cumulative risk index was associated with a higher percentage of sexually active adolescents. For example, only 19 percent of Latina females with zero risk factors were sexually active, while approximately three-quarters (75 percent) of the Latina females with two or more risk factors were sexually active. However, a notable proportion of Latina females (25 percent) possessing two or more risk factors were not sexually active. Protective factors not examined may explain why some of these adolescents are not sexually active. It would be useful, in future studies, to explore the reasons why some adolescents who are at high risk for sexual activity practice abstinence.

Future studies may want to examine cultural values/norms and their association with risk factors and sexual activity. Indeed, the influence of Catholicism on the Latino culture may actually lower Latino adolescents' engagement in sexual activity (A. Villarruel, this volume). Moreover, research is warranted to determine whether the risk factors related to sexual activity do vary as a function of ethnicity. However, Brewster (1994) suggests that the effect of race on sexual activity may be attenuated when the effects of neighborhood environment are held constant. Future research may also examine sexual activity among diverse ethnic groups matched on quality of neighborhood characteristics (e.g., rates of employment).

The determination of causal relations is not possible because the correlational analyses were conducted with cross-sectional data. In addition, because cross-sectional data were employed, often more than one interpretation of the data is possible. For example, teens who perceive that their parents are unsupportive may become sexually active searching for love and affirmation, or alternatively, their parents may seem to be less supportive if they know their teens are sexually active. In other cases, however, the likely direction of influence seems more clear-cut. It would be difficult to imagine that parents would monitor the behavior of their adolescents less or leave them at home alone more frequently because they know they are sexually active.

CONCLUSION

Given the results of the cumulative risk analyses, we believe that parents, programs, and communities should put their efforts and energies into a positive youth development approach to decrease sexual activity among *all* adolescents (Keith & Perkins, 1995; Lerner, 1995; Pittman & Cahill, 1991). That is, they should focus their efforts on decreasing the risk factors experienced by adolescents *and* provide opportunities for adolescents to build their competencies and skills to confront difficult situations. Indeed, recent research provides evidence that communities where the citizens and institutions focus their attention on increasing both the competencies of youth and the external supports at all levels of the ecology are most likely to succeed in building strong and resourceful youth (Benard, 1991; Blyth, 1993; Furstenberg & Hughes, 1995; Keith & Perkins, 1995).

NOTES

This study was supported by grants from the Lutheran Brotherhood Association and the Michigan Agricultural Experiment Station (Project No. 3306). In addition, the authors thank Dale A. Blyth, Director of Research and Evaluation, and Jean L. Wachs, Data Services Manager, from Search Institute for their assistance with the collection of the data used in this study.

REFERENCES

Baca Zinn, M. (1990). Family, feminism, and race in America. *Gender and Society, 14,* 62–86.

Benard, B. (1991). *Fostering resiliency in kids: Protective factors in the family, school, and community.* Portland, OR: Northwest Regional Educational Laboratory, Western Regional Center for Drug-Free Schools and Communities, Far West Laboratory.

Benson, P. L. (1990). *The troubled journey: A portrait of 6th-12th grade youth.* Minneapolis, MN: Search Institute.

Betancourt, H., & López, S. R. (1993). The study of culture, ethnicity, and race in American psychology. *American Psychologist, 48,* 629–637.

Billy, J. O. G., Brewster, K. L., & Grady, W. R. (1994). Contextual effects on sexual behavior of adolescent women. *Journal of Marriage and the Family, 56,* 387–404.

Blyth, D. A. (1993). *Healthy communities, healthy youth: How communities contribute to positive youth development.* Minneapolis, MN: Search Institute.

Boyer, D., & Fine, D. (1992). Sexual abuse as a factor in adolescent pregnancy and child maltreatment. *Family Planning Perspectives, 24,* 4–11.

Brewster, K. (1994). Race differences in sexual activity among adolescent women: The role of neighborhood characteristics. *American Sociological Review, 59,* 408–424.

Brewster, K. L., Billy, J. O. G., & Grady, W. R. (1993). Social context and adolescent behavior: The impact of community on the transition to sexual activity. *Social Forces, 71,* 713–740.

Briere, J., & Runtz, M. (1993). Childhood sexual abuse: Long term sequelae and implications for psychological assessment. *Journal of Interpersonal Violence, 8,* 312–330.

Bronfenbrenner, U. (1979). *The ecology of human development.* Cambridge, MA: Harvard University Press.

Bronfenbrenner, U. (1989). Ecological systems theory. In R. Vasta (Ed.), *Annals of Child Development* (Vol. 6, pp. 187–249). Greenwich, CT: JAI Press.

Brooks-Gunn, J., & Furstenberg, F., Jr. (1989). Adolescent sexual behavior. *American Psychologist, 44,* 249–257.

Butler, J., & Burton, L. (1990). Rethinking teenage childbearing: Is sexual abuse a missing link? *Family Relations, 39,* 73–80.

Christopher, F. S., Johnson, D., & Roosa, M. (1993). Family, individual, and social correlates of early Hispanic adolescent sexual expression. *Journal of Sex Research, 30,* 54–61.

Costa, F. M., Jessor, R., Donovan, J. E., & Fortenberry, J. D. (1995). Early initiation of sexual intercourse: The influence of psychosocial unconventionality. *Journal of Research on Adolescence, 5,* 93–121.

Danziger, S. K., & Danziger, S. (1993). Child poverty and public policy: Toward a comprehensive antipoverty agenda. *America's Childhood, 122,* 57–84.

Day, R. D. (1992). The transition to first intercourse among racially and culturally diverse youth. *Journal of Marriage and the Family, 54,* 749–762.

Dryfoos, J. G. (1990). *Adolescents at risk: Prevalence and prevention.* New York: Oxford University Press.

Duany, L., & Pittman, K. (1990). *Latino youths at a crossroads.* Washington, DC: Children's Defense Fund.

Duncan, G. J. (1991). The economic environment of children. In A. C. Huston (Ed.), *Children in poverty: Child development and public policy* (pp. 23–50). New York: Cambridge University Press.

Finkelhor, D., Hotaling, G., Lewis, I. A., & Smith, C. (1990). Sexual abuse in a national sample of adult men and women: Prevalence, characteristics, and risk factors. *Child Abuse and Neglect, 14,* 19–28.

Flick, L. H. (1986). Paths to adolescent parenthood: Implications for prevention. *Public Health Reports, 101,* 132–147.

Fisher, C. B., Jackson, J. F., & Villarruel, F. A. (1998). The study of African American and Latin American children and youth. In R. M. Lerner (Ed.), *Handbook of child psychology: Theoretical model of human development* (pp. 1145–1207). New York: Wiley.

Furstenberg, F., Jr., & Hughes, M. E. (1995). Social capital and successful development among at-risk youth. *Journal of Marriage and the Family, 57,* 580–592.

Furstenberg, F., Jr., Morgan, S. P., Moore, K. A., & Peterson, J. L. (1987). Race differences in the timing of adolescent intercourse. *American Sociological Review, 52,* 511–518.

Gibson, J. W., & Kempf, J. (1990). Attitudinal predictors of sexual activity in Hispanic adolescent females. *Journal of Adolescent Research, 5,* 414–430.

Grahm, S. (1992). "Most of the subjects were white and middle class": Trends in published research on African Americans in selected APA journals, 1970–1989. *American Psychologist, 47,* 629–639.

Hamburg, D. A. (1992). *Today's children: Creating a future for a generation in crisis.* New York: Times Books.

Haurin, R. J., & Mott, F. L. (1990). Adolescent sexual activity in family context: The impact of older siblings. *Demography, 27,* 537–557.

Hawkins, J. D., Catalano, R. F., & Miller, J. Y. (1992). Risk and protective factors for alcohol and other drug problems in adolescence and early adulthood: Implications for substance abuse prevention. *Psychological Bulletin, 112,* 64–105.

Hayes, C. D. (1987). *Risking the future: Adolescent sexuality, pregnancy, and childbearing.* Washington, DC: National Academy Press.

Hayes-Bautista, D., Schink, D., & Chapa, J. (1988). *The burden of support: Young Latinos in a changing society.* Stanford, CA: Stanford University Press.

Hernández, D. J. (1993). *America's children: Resources from family, government, and the economy.* New York: Russell Sage Foundation.

Hogan, D. P., & Kitagawa, E. M. (1985). The impact of social status, family structure, and neighborhood on the fertility of black adolescents. *American Journal of Sociology, 90,* 825–855.

Irwin, C. E., Jr., & Shafer, M. A. (1992). Adolescent sexuality: Negative outcomes of normative behaviors. In D. E. Rodgers & E. Ginzberg (Eds.), *Ado-*

lescents at risk: Medical and social perspectives (pp. 35–79). Boulder, CO: Westview Press.
Jaccard, J., Dittus, P. J., & Gordon, V. V. (1996). Maternal correlates of adolescent sexual and contraceptive behavior. *Family Planning Perspectives, 28,* 159–165.
Jenkins, R. R., & Westney, O. E. (1991). Sexual behavior in black adolescents, initiation of. In R. M. Lerner, A. C. Petersen, & J. Brooks-Gunn (Eds.), *Encyclopedia of adolescence* (pp. 1022–1027). New York: Garland.
Jessor, R. (1993). Successful adolescent development among youth in high-risk settings. *American Psychologist, 48,* 117–126.
Johnson, C. M., Miranda, L., Sherman, A., & Weill, J. D. (1991). *Child poverty in America.* Washington, DC: Children's Defense Fund.
Keith, J. G., & Perkins, D. F. (1995). *13,000 adolescents speak: A profile of Michigan youth.* East Lansing: Michigan State University, Institute for Children, Youth, and Families.
Kendall-Tackett, K. A., Williams, L. M., & Finkelhor, D. (1993). Impact of sexual abuse on children: A review and synthesis of recent empirical studies. *Psychological Bulletin, 113,* 164–180.
Ketterlinus, R. D., Lamb, M. E., & Nitz, K. A. (1995). Adolescent non-sexual and sex related problem behaviors: Their prevalence, consequences, and co-occurrence. In R. D. Ketterlinus & M. E. Lamb (Eds.), *Adolescent problem behaviors: Issues and research* (pp. 17–40). Hillsdale, NJ: Erlbaum.
Lauritsen, J. L. (1994). Explaining race and gender differences in adolescent sexual behavior. *Social Forces, 72,* 859–883.
Lerner, R. M. (1995). *America's youth in crisis: Challenges and options for programs and policies.* Thousand Oaks, CA: Sage.
Luster, T., & Small, S. A. (1994). Factors associated with sexual risk-taking behaviors among adolescents. *Journal of Marriage and the Family, 56,* 622–632.
Luthar, S. S. (1991). Vulnerability and resiliency: A study of high risk adolescents. *Child Development, 62,* 600–616.
Moore, K. A. (1996). *Facts at a glance.* Washington, DC: Child Trends.
Moore, K. A., Miller, B. C., Glei, D., & Morrison, D. R. (1995). *Adolescent sex, contraception, and childbearing: A review of recent research.* Washington, DC: Child Trends.
Mott, F. L., Fondell, M. M., Hu, P. N., Kowaleski-Jones, L., & Menaghan, E. G. (1996). The determinants of first sex by age 14 in a high-risk adolescent population. *Family Planning Perspectives, 28,* 13–18.
Perkins, D. F. (1995). *An examination of the organismic, behavioral, and contextual covariates of risk behaviors among diverse groups of adolescents.* Unpublished doctoral dissertation, Michigan State University.

Perkins, D. F., Luster, T., Villarruel, F. A., & Small, S. (1998). An ecological risk-factor examination of adolescents' sexual activity in three ethnic groups. *Journal of Marriage and the Family, 60,* 660–673.

Pittman, K. J., & Cahill, M. (1991). *A new vision: Promoting youth development* (Commission Paper No. 3 for the Center for Youth Development and Policy Research). Washington, DC: Academy for Educational Development.

Quinton, D., & Rutter, M. (1988). *Parenting breakdown: The making and breaking of inter-generational bonds.* Aldershot, UK: Averbury.

Rutter, M. (1985). Resilience in the face of adversity: Protective factors and resistance to psychiatric disorder. *British Journal of Psychiatry, 147,* 598–611.

Rutter, M. (1987). Psychosocial resilience and protective factors. *American Journal of Orthopsychiatry, 57,* 316–331.

Sabogal, R., Marín, G., Otero-Sabogal, R., Marín, B. V., & Pérez-Stable, E. J. (1987). Hispanic families and acculturation: What changes and what doesn't. *Hispanic Journal of Behavioral Sciences, 9,* 397–412.

Small, S. A., & Luster, T. (1990, November). *Understanding adolescent sexuality and pregnancy: An ecological perspective.* Paper presented at the Creating Caring Communities Conference, Michigan State University, East Lansing.

Small, S. A., & Luster, T. (1994). Adolescent sexual activity: An ecological risk-factor approach. *Journal of Marriage and the Family, 56,* 181–192.

Stanton, B., Romer, D., Ricardo, I., Black, M., Feigelman, S., & Galbraith, J. (1993). Early initiation of sex and its lack of association with risk behaviors among adolescent African Americans. *Pediatrics, 92,* 13–19.

Stättin, H., & Magnusson, D. (1990). *Pubertal maturation in female development.* Hillsdale, NJ: Erlbaum.

Thornton, A., & Camburn, D. (1989). Religious participation and adolescent sexual behavior and attitudes. *Journal of Marriage and the Family, 51,* 641–653.

U.S. Bureau of the Census. (1990). Household and family characteristics: March 1990 and 1989 (Current Population Reports Series P-20, No. 447). Washington, DC: U.S. Government Printing Office.

Werner, E., & Smith, R. (1982). *Vulnerable not invincible: A longitudinal study of resilient children and youth.* New York: McGraw-Hill.

Werner, E., & Smith, R. (1992). *Overcoming the odds: High risk children from birth to adulthood.* Ithaca, NY: Cornell University.

CHAPTER 5

The Contrast between the Pathological Attributes and the Status/Aspirations of Mexican American Youth

JAIME CHAHÍN

Institutions of education have long been acknowledged by society as a medium of social mobility, but within the Mexican American community, this has been more of a myth than a reality. The lack of educational attainment among Mexican Americans has been attributed to a lack of motivation and a deficient cultural environment (e.g., Johnson, 1970). Such stereotypical orientations have in essence justified the traditional public educational system's failure to meet the needs of Latino students. Stereotypes are exaggerated beliefs associated with a category which serves to justify the conduct of society in relation to that category (Allport, 1954). These stereotypes have served to create the educational neglect that has implicitly deprived Mexican American youth of equal opportunities as provided by the Fourteenth Amendment of the U.S. Constitution:

> No state shall make or enforce any law which shall abridge the privileges or immunities of citizens of the United States: nor shall any state deprive any person of life or prosperity without due process of law; nor deny to any person within the jurisdiction of the equal protection of the laws.

Educators have implemented programs and policies that have denied Mexican Americans equal protection under the law. As a result of these practices, the lower educational attainment of Mexican Americans has been justified and reflected by their lower participation in the endeavors of society at large.

To understand the past and current status of the Mexican American community, we must understand its historical developments, the analyses of social scientists, and more recent studies that examine the complexities of Mexican American youth. The first section of this study gives a historical account of the Mexican American presence in the Southwest. The second section examines literature pertinent to the development of a socially pathological view of Mexican Americans. The third section analyzes recent studies of Mexican American youth and how public institutions need to change to enhance opportunities for Mexican Americans. Thus, we examine how perceptions of Mexican American youth have evolved in terms of status and educational attainment and how institutional policies play a critical role in providing access and opportunities for them.

HISTORICAL PRESENCE OF MEXICAN AMERICANS

An understanding of the current social position of Mexican Americans in the Southwest requires a historical understanding of the setting. Standard history texts present a very distorted view of the Spanish-speaking people who have been settled in the Southwest for more than 300 years. As George I. Sánchez (1966, p. 46) writes,

> The villages north of Santa Fe, New Mexico, founded in 1598 are second only to St. Augustine, Florida, settled in 1565, as the oldest settlement of Europeans on the Mainland of the United States. The New Mexico settlements followed a century later by those in Texas and later by those in California represent a Spanish colonial effort that left an indelible imprint upon the history and culture of the Southwest and the United States. More important, that colonial endeavor left people from California to Texas whose descendants constitute a part of the group we now refer to very loosely as Spanish Speaking.

Thus, the historical setting from which the Mexican American community would evolve began to take its course of development prior to the settlement of Jamestown. The mestizo generation began creating a chain of settlements next to the Indians of the Southwest (Machado, 1978). The Southwest was slow in developing because of its geographical isolation; the inhabitants did not suspect that within a few decades their lives would be changed. First, in 1821 Mexico succeeded in gaining its independence from Spain, and thus the Southwest became part of the Republic of Mexico. Due to a lack of communication with the central government in Mexico City, Mexico at that time inherited many problems from Spain. During this same period, Anglo-Saxon settlers, under the leadership of Moses Austin, began to settle in Texas (Nava, 1969). By 1833, Mexico had issued land titles to 2,000 Anglo-Saxon families. Gradually, the influence of the Anglo-Saxon population began to increase. Though they were supposed to adhere to the clauses of their land titles, their autonomous ideology began to conflict with the Mexican government. This led to the War for Texas Independence in 1836, during which Texas became an independent nation (Montejano, 1989). Texas was annexed into the Union in 1845, and afterward the Mexican War broke out (Martínez, 1988). In 1848, after Mexico was defeated in the Mexican War, the Treaty of Guadalupe Hidalgo was signed. With the signing of this treaty, Mexicans in the Southwest were granted citizenship and equal protection under the law as stipulated in Article VIII (per Nava, 1973, p. 54):

> Those who shall prefer to remain in said territories may either retain the titles and rights of Mexican citizens, or require those of citizens of the United States. But they shall be under the obligation to make their election within one year from the date of the exchange of ratifications of this treaty; and those who shall remain in the said territories after the expiration of that year without having declared the intention to retain the character of Mexicans shall be considered to have elected to become citizens of the United States. In said territories property of every kind, now belonging to Mexicans not established there, shall be inviolably respected. The present owners, the heirs of these and all Mexicans who may hereafter acquire said property by contract, shall enjoy with respect to it, guarantee equally ample as if the same belonged to citizens of the United States.

In practice, the Treaty of Guadalupe Hidalgo and its protocol would soon be violated a thousand times over, and all the promises of protection broken. Many land grants and contracts belonging to Mexican Americans were nullified and not recognized by the American government (Blawis, 1971). Thus, the value orientations between the Anglo and Mexican American communities began to clash as their relations with each other began to conflict, since the treaty did not provide any explicit provisions to safeguard Mexican Americans' rights as a society. With its dominant philosophy of the "melting pot," perpetuated by cultural mapmakers, the United States failed to recognize the needs of the Mexican

Americans in the Southwest whose lifestyles and format of government was not congruent with the U.S. government (Horsman, 1981). As a consequence, the Spanish-speaking people became an isolated cultural group that had limited positive interactions with the dominant society (Montejano, 1989). The independence of Texas, the annexation of the Southwest, and the Treaty of Guadalupe Hidalgo are very significant historical events that laid the initial foundation for continuous conflict between Anglos and Mexicans as they attempted to integrate their institutions in the Southwest (Montejano, 1989). As a consequence of this limited accommodation by American social institutions, Mexican Americans were isolated, and they continued a way of life around the familiar social, economic, and political institutions of their own community (De León, 1982). Yet the conflict between Mexican Americans and public institutions continued, especially in public schools, because Mexican Americans continued to be excluded from and segregated in public schools in Texas (San Miguel, 1987). These historical violations have contributed to a sense of mistrust among Mexican Americans, who have experienced many situations of discrimination (Gibson & Ogbu, 1991).

ECONOMIC AND IMMIGRATION PATTERNS

The U.S. economy during the early 1900s was primarily dependent on agricultural and mining activities; however, labor was sparsely distributed throughout the Southwest. Much of the manufacturing activity in Colorado (as well as in Arizona and New Mexico) was tied to mining and was located in relatively isolated places near the resource base. Therefore, the apparent economic diversification in the Southwest may be deceptive in terms of its potential for interaction (Perloff, 1969), as during the early 1900s, the Southwest remained relatively isolated from the East. Most of the labor manpower was made up of immigrants from Mexico. Furthermore, the Mexican Revolution in 1910 provided a cheap labor market that was vital to the economic development of the Southwest. The rapid increase of Mexican immigrants along the border states after 1900 can be seen in Table 5.1 (McWilliams, 1948).

The continuous and steady population influx between 1900 and 1930, shown in Table 5.1, provides an adequate picture of the future heterogeneity of the population. However, the chart does not project other far-reaching issues and problems such as health, education, economics, and political orientation, which ultimately began to create depressing so-

Table 5.1 Mexican Immigration (Number in Thousands)

State	1900	1910	1920	1930
Arizona	14,171	29,987	61,580	114,173
California	8,086	33,694	88,881	368,013
New Mexico	6,649	11,918	20,272	59,340
Texas	71,062	125,016	251,827	683,681

Source: From McWilliams, C. (1948). *North from Mexico: The Spanish-speaking people of the United States.* Philadelphia: Lippincott.

cioeconomic conditions that eventually would become very costly (Sanchez, 1966).

During the early 1900s, the majority of the Mexican immigrants were engaged in farm labor, but by the 1920s, Mexicans were being lured into the United States by the expanding northern industrial manufacturing centers in Chicago, Detroit, and Milwaukee (Stoddard, 1973). There, as untrained factory employees, they had a chance at steady employment and income that was generous in comparison with farm wages. But they nevertheless continued to occupy the bottom rungs of the economic ladder.

After the Depression, America's involvement in World War II brought an economic boom as demands for industrial production increased. Some Mexican Americans began to migrate to the urban industrialized centers while others joined the military. Even though the war brought death and extreme suffering to many people, it had some beneficial results for Mexican Americans and other minorities, as more occupational and educational opportunities became available. Advocacy for veterans in essence began to provide minorities with some opportunities that were nonexistent before the war (Montejano, 1989).

Thus, the parameters of the Mexican American population's social integration have slowly been changing. By the mid-1960s the less transient and more stable Mexican American population had begun to demand the equal protection and opportunities which were bestowed to them as citizens of the United States. This came about as a result of the involvement of the Mexican American community in the Civil Rights movement of the 1960s.

The demographic shift in the Southwest clearly delineates a young Mexican American population that continues to grow but is underrepresented in institutions of higher education. It is imperative that institutions respond to its attributes and strengths in order to successfully resolve educational issues (Hayes Bautista & Chapa, 1988). The lack of response by institutions can be attributed to their lack of understanding, limited resources, and policies that take into account stereotypes that do not reflect the reality and strengths of the Mexican American community.

A CRITICAL ANALYSIS OF THE PATHOLOGICAL VIEW OF MEXICAN AMERICANS

The early social science literature is replete with references to Mexican American youth having certain pathological behaviors; this in essence serves to rationalize the poor social mobility of Mexican Americans (as well as other disadvantaged ethnic minorities). This "science" was primarily promoted by mainstream researchers with a stereotypical frame of reference, who were the only ones studying Mexicano communities at the time. Carter (1970, p. 26) states:

> Social scientists and others who have investigated orientations, usually concur that children of Mexican American sociocultural backgrounds are prone to do the following . . . (1) Devalue formal education, especially for girls, (2) See success more in terms of material acquisition, (3) See time as a gift of life to be enjoyed to the fullest, it must not be postponed. The Anglo concept of wasting time is not understood., (4) Be fatalistic, feeling they have little control over their natural or social environment, (5) See change as unappealing and not motivating, (6) Be submissive to the status quo, patient, conformist, and perhaps apathetic, (7) See work only to satisfy present needs, (8) Attach little importance to time schedules and the Anglo concept of punctuality, (9) Attach much importance to non-scientific explanation of natural phenomena (sickness and so forth).

The aforementioned configuration of orientations and values, when viewed as an integrated whole along with supporting social structures, is often used to label a subculture which has not been accepted by the dominant society. The rationalization of blaming the victim is designed to legitimize what is called the "pathological view" (Arciniega & Brishetto, 1973). This culturally deterministic view has often served as a basis for developing distorted generalizations that have explicitly attributed negative stereotypes to the Mexican American which serve to justify institutional actions.

In order to understand the negative connotations of the literature, it is imperative to examine the validity of the conclusions and inferences of past studies of Mexican Americans. One of the many to cultivate the theory of cultural determinism was Loaz Johnson, who stated that the Mexicans' desire to be among their own people, their carefree attitude, and their desire for unusually dramatic and even reckless action, sometimes at the expense of life, made the Spanish Americans' problems different from those of the Anglo-Saxons (Johnson, 1973). Linda Chávez (1991) further perpetuated this deterministic view when she argued that preserving language and culture is not a responsibility of government, as it sets Hispanics up for failure because they do not integrate.

Florence R. Kluckhohn's theory of variations of value orientations (Kluckhohn & Strodteck, 1961) was tested in a study which took place in New Mexico. While investigating the intra- and intervariations of value orientations of five cultures (Spanish American, Texan, Mormon, Navaho, and Zuñi Indian), Kluckhohn concluded that Spanish Americans had strong family ties and kinship in contrast to the individualistic principle, dominant in Anglo-American culture, where individual goals have primacy over the goals of lineal groups such as the family. Her study of this desolate village in New Mexico embraced many generalizations that would be fostered by other investigators.

Talcott Parsons (1951) theorized that Anglo society can be characterized as influenced predominately by ascriptive value orientation patterns. On the other end of the continuum, Spanish-speaking people are characterized by predominantly deterministic value orientation patterns. Parsons (p. 210) stated:

> There tends to be a certain lack of concern with the remoter framework of the society, unless it is threatened. Similarly, there is no inherent objection to authority so long as it does not interfere too much with expressive freedom; indeed, it may be welcome as a factor of stability. But there is also not the positive incentive to recognize authority as inherent that exists in the cases of positive authoritarianism. The tendency to indifference to larger social issues creates a situation in which authority can become established with relatively little opposition. Hence, a susceptibility to dictatorship is not uncommon in such a society. The Spanish American seems to be a good example of this social type.

This culturally deterministic theory, which portrayed Mexican Americans as very homogeneous, was further emphasized by Lyle Saunders (1954), who stated that Mexican Americans' cultural values were in direct opposition to the values of the dominant society. Knowlton (1962) wrote that the values contained in Mexican American culture would have to be exchanged for those positive ones contained in the Anglo culture. Simmons (1969) also stated that Mexican Americans have characteristics that are not congruent with the achievement patterns of the dominant society. Moreover, Madsen (1964) found that Latinos lack the future orientation of the Anglos and their passion for planning ahead. Thus, social scientists were portraying cultural differences as determining an orientation that an individual, whether Anglo or Mexican American, might have toward life.

THE DEVELOPMENT OF PROGRAMS AND POLICIES EMBEDDED IN THE DETERMINISTIC PERSPECTIVE

In the 1960s, the cultural deterministic viewpoint which portrayed Mexican Americans in a certain pathological continuum was further perpetuated by Celia Heller's (1966, 1969, 1971) sociological studies. Her studies clearly suggested that in order for children to succeed they have to exchange their set of cultural values for those of the dominant culture. Heller (1966) described the inadequacies of the home socialization of Mexican American youth by stating that the socialization process of Mexican American youth stresses values that are deficient and incongruent with the values of Anglo youth. Thus, only those youth that resemble their Anglo peers will be able to overcome the inhibiting environment of their Mexican American upbringing.

Moreover, in a later and more comprehensive study, Heller (1971) indicated that the development of the Chicano movement helped enhance the aspirations of Mexican American youth to the traditional conception of the American dream. However, her conclusions still appeared to favor the cultural deterministic viewpoint to explain their lack of social mobility. This orientation was further perpetuated in more recent studies conducted by the Mexican American Study Project at UCLA (Gordon, 1970). The findings of this report indicate that the highest achievers are those Mexican American pupils who have been most thoroughly socialized to the dominant American culture, both at home and in the school environment (Gordon, 1970). Thus, the culturally deterministic model for the Mexican American youth continues to be used to explain their educational attainment or lack of it.

Much of the literature thus portrays the socialization process of Mexican American youth as displaying values that obviously prohibit

The Contrast between the Pathological Attributes and the Status 115

upward social mobility. This deterministic analysis does not take into consideration the internal and external structures of our institutions and the discriminating practices of the dominant society, which inhibit economic and social development. George I. Sánchez (1966) was incredulous of the ostensible explanatory power of cultural determinism, and in his book *La Raza: Forgotten Americans*, he pointed out the interrelationships between Mexican American children and the failure of educational institutions in meeting their special needs, to be found in the nature and quality of the educational facilities and the resources available to them. Furthermore, it is imperative for educators to understand the needs of the student population. As documented in the study of Matute-Bianchi (1991), the Mexican American student population is very heterogeneous; educators must begin to change the school climate, structure, and practices to accommodate this diverse student clientele.

The most extensive research illustrating the unresponsiveness of educational institutions to Mexican Americans in the Southwest was first conducted by the United States Commission on Civil Rights Mexican American Educational Series. These comprehensive studies were conducted to assess the nature of the educational opportunities available to Mexican Americans in the Southwest. The findings of these studies were made public in six separate reports published between 1970 and 1974 by the U.S. Commission on Civil Rights (1970, 1972a, 1972b, 1972c, 1973, 1974).

The findings of the commission substantiated that Mexican Americans enrolled in public schools in the Southwest were severely isolated by school district and by school within individual districts. Furthermore, Mexican Americans were underrepresented on school district professional staffs and on boards of education (U.S. Commission on Civil Rights, 1970). The findings also indicated that without exception, minority students achieve at a lower rate than Anglos; their school holding power is lower; their reading achievement is poorer; their repetition of grade level is more frequent; their overageness is more prevalent; and they participate in extracurricular activities to a lesser degree than their Anglo counterparts (U.S. Commission on Civil Rights, 1971).

The findings further indicated that school systems of the Southwest have not recognized the culture and traditions of Mexican American students and have not adopted policies and programs which would enable those students to participate fully in the benefits of the educational process (U.S. Commission on Civil Rights, 1972b). The findings also substantiated that the system of school financing, devised by the state of

Texas based on property taxes, created fiscal inequities that are detrimental to school districts with high Mexican American concentrations (U.S. Commission on Civil Rights, 1972a).

In terms of teacher and student patterns, the findings clearly stated that schools in the Southwest were failing to involve Mexican American children as active participants in the classroom to the same extent as Anglo children. On most of the measures of verbal interaction between teacher and student, there were gross disparities in favor of Anglo students (U.S. Commission on Civil Rights, 1973).

This commission attempted to identify specific conditions and practices that bear on the failure of schools in the Southwest to provide equal educational opportunity to Mexican American students. The last report clearly documented the systemic failure of schools to meet the educational needs of Chicano students. Instead, the schools suppressed their culture and stifled their hopes and ambitions (U.S. Commission on Civil Rights, 1974).

As the aforementioned studies indicate, many other factors besides cultural determinism are detrimental to the opportunities available for Mexican American youth. Thus, the paradigm of cultural determinism that has been applied to numerous social problems to provide a causal explanation for the lack of achievement of Mexican Americans is in essence a distortion of reality. By viewing the causality of the social ills of Mexican Americans as stemming from within their culture, all institutions in American society are absolved of any complicity (Vaca, 1970).

Policymakers and educators, perhaps influenced by both the educational literature and popular stereotypes, may operate under the cultural deterministic model which depicts the Mexican American lifestyle as deficient and sees the school as the inculcator of the dominant society's values. Thus, the villain remains the Mexican American family, which produces all the "wrong" value orientations, ones not conducive to success in the dominant society.

A deficit philosophy, which attributes the poor school performance of minority children to growing up in a deficient environment, does not take into account their differences in culture, language, mobility, economic level, and social perceptions (Cárdenas & Cárdenas, 1972). If these variables are taken into consideration, institutions can develop a learning environment that will stimulate development in those areas that are critical to educational success in typical school situations. Moreover, James P. Cummins (DeVillar, Faltis, & Cummins, 1994) recommends that educators should strive to develop collaborative relations of power so that microinteractions between educators and teachers promote identity formation and knowledge generation that increases the success of minority students (DeVillar et al., 1994). Furthermore, Antonia Darder (1991) indicates that we need to develop a sensitivity to aspects of culture to be able to address the needs of bicultural students. A comprehensive analysis of the aforementioned variables could help ameliorate some of the generalizations that have deprived Mexican Americans and other minorities of opportunities available in our society. In addition, institutions that understand the needs of their students can provide opportunities to enhance their educational attainment.

Forty years ago Merton (1957) proposed that the "success ethic" has been inculcated by most youth of all social classes, and as a consequence they maintain high-level success goals (i.e., occupational and educational aspirations). Thus, having high aspirations is not unique to one group in society, but is a universal pattern that cuts across class and ethnic distinctions. This aspirational reference is composed of personal goals for status attainment that will serve to guide anticipatory socialization into adult roles. Turner (1964) further acknowledged that there is a youth culture; however, he pointed out that the youth culture has not obscured the differentiation of values and discrimination of social ties along the lines of either stratum of origin or stratum of aspiration. Students do not necessarily accept disparagement and social isolation as the cost of pursuing high academic success. Young people might be active participants in the youth culture, but this does not mean that they will not be formulating certain personal goals from their interactions with other role models. However, the relative differences in the goals of youth will be dependent upon the availability of educational opportunities, positive role models, and institutions that will compensate for socialization factors that impede the full human development of some youth.

The conceptual framework introduced by Merton conceived of only one frame of status projection, that involving aspirations (desires). However, Stephenson (1957) first noted that youth maintain a set of status expectations (anticipations) which often differ from their desires. This was also confirmed by De Hoyos (1961), who investigated the occupational and educational aspirations of Mexican American youth and found that the youth also had certain expectations. The distinction should be clear between the two types of status projections. While desire is aspiration, expectation is an anticipation of attainment (Kuvlesky & Bealer, 1966). Expectation is, then (p. 267), the individual's estimation of his probable attainment in reference to particular goal-area, i.e., what occupational position he expects to reach. Expectations should not be confused with aspirations, for the object involved with an expectation is an anticipated occurrence, and the individual's orientation toward the expected state may be favorable or unfavorable.

The divergence, if any, between the desired and the anticipated status within a particular area of potential status attainment is labeled "anticipatory goal deflection." This represents the degrees of modification that are anticipated by the individual (Kuvlesky & Ohlendorf, 1968). The goal deflections can be positive or negative and they can vary in degree. Yet Kuvlesky and Bealer (1966) call attention to another analytical dimension of status projections which they called the "orientation element." This, in essence, represents the strength of the orientation that a person maintains toward the status object involved in either aspiration or expectation. In reference to aspiration, this would be the strength of desire associated with obtaining the status goal specified, and is referred to as "intensity of aspiration." The comparable element involved in expectation is labeled as "certainty of expectation" (Merton, 1957). The scheme delineated above has been used in numerous studies by authorities in the area of youth status projections.

RELATED STUDIES

Prior to 1967, there were very few significant studies describing the nature of educational and occupational status projections of Mexican American youth in the Southwest. More recently a number of social scientists have begun to investigate the structural impediments of the dominant society which constrain the social mobility of Mexican Americans. Studies have indicated that issues such as school practices, teacher attitudes, and irrelevant curricula inhibit learning and promote a negative school experience that alienates the Mexican American youth (Carter, 1970). Many prevailing educational problems of Mexican American youth are thus caused by institutional practices and policies (Grebler, Moore, & Guzman, 1970). Other studies on Puerto Ricans (Walsh, 1987) continue to document how current educational practices fail to take into account the unique language and cultural needs of Latino students, which results in a negative effect on their achievement.

Since the impact of each of the numerous forces which contribute to deficient education for Mexican Americans cannot be assessed or isolated, it might be best to examine the ultimate results. Educational attainment can be viewed as one of the critical elements between human desires and their satisfaction in a society that is characterized by achievement and high standards (Kahl, 1957). In this regard, it seems that if you talk to the average Mexican American man on the street, at the tavern, in his home, at meetings, or in the migrant fields about the importance of an education, he will invariably speak regretfully of his lack of education and how it has kept him from getting a decent and steady job or how it has hindered any opportunity for advancement. He wants an education for his children, but in reality his lack of economic stability will determine the opportunities that he can provide for his children. This lack of effective institutional responses to the educational needs of Mexican Americans is reflected in the 1990 census data (Kominski & Adams, 1994), which indicates that 50 percent of Hispanics who are 18 years or older have less than a high school education (as shown in Table 5.2).

The stigma of the lack of educational attainment can have a great effect on related but peripheral characteristics such as income, employment or unemployment, housing, and occupation. Jorge Chapa's (1992)

Table 5.2 Educational Attainment for Persons Age 18 and Older of Hispanic Origin, March 1990

Years of School Completed	Total Population in Millions	Percentages
Less than 4 years of high school	7,950	50.0%
High school graduate	4,027	25.3%
Some college	2,147	13.5%
Associate's degree	629	4.0%
Bachelor's degree	833	5.2%
Master's degree	213	1.3%
Professional	66	0.4%
Doctorate degree	35	0.2%
Total	15,900	100%

Source: From Kominski, R., & Adams, A. (1994). *Educational attainment in the United States: March 1993 and 1992* (U.S. Bureau of the Census, Current Population Reports, P20–476). Washington, DC: U.S. Government Printing Office.

analysis of the 1990 census materials shows that a high concentration (50 percent) of Spanish-speaking people fall under the indicator of "under four years" of education which in turn is described by some educators as being functionally illiterate. However, the continued low educational performance of Mexican Americans cannot be explained without taking into account the conflict between the incongruent expectations of schools and youth.

Even though the empirical literature on educational aspirations is substantial, there is limited research indicating status projections for Mexican American youth. One of the first relevant studies was conducted by Irene Guerra in Laredo, Texas, in 1959. Guerra's primary objective was to compare the occupational and educational aspirations of the youth to the aspirations of their fathers. In reference to educational aspirations, she found that regardless of socioeconomic class, a substantial proportion (94 percent upper-class and 67 percent lower-class) of fathers wanted a college education for their sons. A comparison of father's and son's educational aspirations indicated considerable agreement (Guerra, 1959).

In 1961, De Hoyos studied ninety-one Mexican Americans, age 15 to 18 in grades 8–12 from Lansing, Michigan. He defined aspirations as either idealistic or realistic. His findings in reference to idealistic educational aspirations indicated that a high proportion (77 percent) of his sample aspired to having a college education. When asked if they planned to continue their education beyond high school, about half of these same youth responded in the affirmative. The students were asked to report their parents' wishes or desires concerning their educational aspirations. One-third of the sample responded that their parents wished that they would finish high school, while over half indicated that they should continue their education beyond high school (De Hoyos, 1961).

Research conducted by Juárez in 1968 found that in comparison with the aspirations and expectations of Anglo youth, those of Mexican Americans differed very little. In 1967, a south Texas study of Mexican Americans, male and female high school sophomores, indicated that even when the adolescent's father's occupation was related to the student's level of occupational aspiration, (1) large proportions of Mexican American youth desired high-level occupations, (2) little differences existed between the level of occupational aspirations and expectations of males and females, (3) occupation expectations of Mexican American youth were high, although lower than their aspirations, and (4) the majority were not very certain of their expectations (Kuvlesky & Monk, 1976).

Another study on Mexican Americans pointed out that ethnic differences vanished when the variable of class was taken into account (Heller, 1969). Miller and Kuvlesky (1976) investigated the status aspirations of migrant and nonmigrant Mexican Americans; their findings suggested that there were no significant differences in terms of their levels of aspirations toward occupation and education. However, it can be speculated that the differences would have been of greater magnitude given a stronger and more extensive indicator for migrant status. The distinctions provided by closed-ended questions which evoke a simple yes or no answer are very gross. A more valuable indicator would include questions that are more descriptive of the migrant experience.

Horacio Ulibarri (1971) conducted a study from a sample of sixty-five migrants and ex-migrants dispersed in Arizona, Colorado, New Mexico, and Texas. His findings indicated that the workers possessed present-time orientations, felt apathy toward the government, and were resigned to poverty. However, Ulibarri did not speculate as to why these attitudes were so pronounced, much less address the frequently debated question as to such orientations being due to environment, class, or culture (Ulibarri, 1971).

In 1973, Venegas conducted a study of El Paso High School students and analyzed his data in terms of ethnicity, sex, grade level, and type of school program in which they were enrolled. The findings indicated (p. 4) that:

> students in all groups regardless of ethnicity, sex, grade, or school program had high aspirations and expectations for education and occupation. Males generally had higher aspiration and expectation levels in comparison to females. Anglo Americans had higher expectation levels than Mexican Americans. The academic group was generally higher than the general and vocational samples.

The rural south Texas border historical study of 1967 was compared (Kuvlesky & Monk, 1976) with Venegas's metropolitan study, and in general it found that rural and metropolitan Mexican Americans are more alike than different. Furthermore, the majority of the Mexican Americans indicated a high level of aspirations and expectations (Kuvlesky & Venegas, 1974). In a similar comparative study that was conducted by Kuvlesky and Edington (1976), the status projections for four ethnic groups (Mexican American, black, Navajo, and Anglo youth) found that regardless of ethnicity, most youth aspire strongly to be upwardly mobile; however, many perceive their aspirations to be blocked. These youth do not suffer from a lack of motivation, but lack the resources to realistically accomplish their goals (Kuvlesky & Edington, 1976).

A comparative study of Mexican American migrant and nonmigrant students at Eagle Pass High School was conducted by Chahín in 1977. The data were analyzed in terms of migrant status, sex, instructional program, and family procreation values. The findings clearly supported Robert Merton's (1957) proposition that all kinds of youth in the United States have high success and achievement goals regardless of ethnicity or migrant status. Furthermore, the study substantiated that parents and teachers are the most influential role models for this youth. The study also indicated that regardless of whether they enrolled in an academic preparatory curriculum or a vocational technical curriculum, Mexican American youth showed high aspirations. But it did not answer the question as to how these students would achieve their high aspirations.

The holistic model of intervention discussed by Hayes Bautista and Harveston in their 1977 medical study placed the pathogenic locus outside as well as inside the individual, and defined the causal elements to be political, economic, social, and psychological. This is perhaps a model that can be used for institutional interventions in the educational system. This model requires individual and institutional interventions with the maintenance and restructuring of systems that take into account the holistic needs of students.

A related study on social class and Chicanos concluded that perhaps cultural and sociolinguistic variables determine forms of consciousness and how Chicanos function within our institutions (García, 1980). Yet, the Santos study of Hispanic youth as emerging workers concluded that if the employment of Hispanics continues to be determined by economic conditions in manufacturing and other related industries, their job prospects are not very favorable unless they receive an education or technical training (Santos, 1985).

In 1987 Moll and Díaz reported on two case studies of elementary and junior high reading and writing classes that demonstrated how instructional conditions constrain what working-class Hispanic students and their teachers are able to accomplish. The study indicated that rearrangements of the instructional procedures that utilize students' skills and that take into account their social, linguistic, and intellectual resources will enhance learning outcomes.

It is quite clear that the divergence in the perspective of recent researchers is reflective of contemporary academicians growing up in minority communities. The research has focused on socioeconomic issues, language, and culture which are critical factors in the development of individuals. This has led to further research that focuses on the needs and strengths of our students. These comprehensive approaches have served to dismantle long held stereotypes that had continued to perpetuate interventions that were ineffective in our communities.

We cannot neglect the accessibility of education and resources. According to a United States youth study on "lost talent," social class and membership in a lower socioeconomic group doubled the risk of youth failing to achieve their aspirations (Hanson, 1994). Matute-Bianchi's (1991) study (as cited in Gibson & Ogbu, 1991) documented the various patterns of achievements among Mexican-descent students in California. Their study pointed to a relationship between academic achievement and students' perceptions of ethnic identity. According to Matute-Bianchi, ethnic identity becomes part of an interactive process which includes the students and the institutions within a social context. The study further pointed out that the intragroup variability that exists among Mexican-descent students needs to be critically examined to ensure we do not continue to use single-cause explanations for the underachievement of Mexican American students. Furthermore, positive self-identity of "Mexicanos" has to be used as an asset in helping students succeed and achieve their aspirations (Gibson & Ogbu, 1991).

Hayes Bautista and Chapa (1988), in their study of young Latinos, argued that demographic facts reflect an emerging Mexican majority that is largely uneducated, unskilled, and politically disenfranchised. Furthermore, resources need to be invested in the development of human capital or else the state of California will experience racial and generational conflict and a lower standard of living. It is quite apparent that as a result of the demographic shift the emerging Mexican American population in the Southwestern states will also require investment and development of human capital.

Stanton-Salazar and Dornbusch (1995) conducted a study to attempt to explain the social attainment of Mexican American youth. They used the concept of social capital rather than classical explanations of social attainments that are based on the process of parental encouragement and assessment of merit by self and others. As used in this study, "social capital" refers to social relationships from which an individual is potentially able to derive institutional support, particularly knowledge-based resources. Even though the findings indicated some evidence for the relation between grades and status expectations and measures of social capital, the strongest relations were among language measures, implying that bilinguals may have special advantages in acquiring the institutional support necessary to succeed and achieve higher or upward social mobility. Even though the research pertinent to the status aspirations and expectations of Mexican Americans is limited, the findings suggest a trend of upward mobility projections. These findings clearly question the cultural deterministic viewpoint which states that Mexican culture produces apathy toward status achievement, and that the values are contrary or antagonistic to achieving upward social mobility. The findings clearly convey that Mexican American youth want the same high levels of achieved status as do other groups of American young people. They are interested in college, technical training, prestige jobs, security, plus all the other opportunities that are available to our middle-class American society. These achievement-oriented projections in essence illustrate that Mexican American youth can delay gratification. Mexican American youth also think of the future and/or not always in the present or in the past. Yet it can also be stated that within the Mexican American population there is considerable heterogeneity with respect to mobility values and orientations. Given the low socioeconomic status of this community, the role of institutional agents in the transmission of knowledge and information is critical to the future educational attainment of Mexican American children.

Quite explicitly, the De Hoyos, Juárez, Miller, Kuvlesky, and Chahin studies provide evidence that Mexican American youth, regardless of migrant background or sex, have high educational and occupational aspirations and expectations. Furthermore, these youth are strongly committed to their goals. The realization of their orientations will require that institutions respond to their needs with intervention strategies that take into account the strengths of the students and the community.

IMPLICATIONS FOR PUBLIC POLICYMAKERS

School districts should design career education programs pertinent to the needs of Mexican American students; even though these programs are recommended for grades K-12, at the secondary level a career education program should be designed so that students can participate on a continuous basis throughout their elementary and secondary education. This will provide the students with a better understanding of what is expected of workers, what occupations exist, and what educational and occupational paths lead to a particular career goal. Career education allows individual students to discover their interests, attitudes, and values toward certain careers.

Counselors should be very careful to ensure that counseling is not solely based on interpretations of standardized tests, since respondents enrolled in the vocational-technical program may have high aspirations, comparable to those respondents in the college preparatory curriculum. Thus, it is conceivable that students who are enrolled in the vocational-technical programs might be playing the system, while at the same time jeopardizing their opportunity to learn the basic cognitive skills which are needed to function in college and which a vocational and technical program might not provide. Therefore, counselors should explore all the possible alternatives before determining the program that most adequately serves the needs of the individual.

Furthermore, the schools need to engage Mexican American parents about the opportunities that their children might have, and engage them in these opportunities so that they in turn may work with their youth on development of career and life plans. Considering the low level of education of parents in the Mexican American community, we must see that a parental involvement program should be designed so that parents themselves can be better informed and empowered to have a greater input into the educational process. The parents should not only be involved in the activities of the program but also in its development, implementation, and evaluation. Such a program should establish the basic framework for planned educational activities which will take into account the holistic needs of families that result in a close rapport between the parents, the community, and the school system. In this manner, parents will have an opportunity to assume a more active role in the education of their children. In undertaking this role, parents will support children and the goals of the school. Thus, parental involvement will not only improve communication between the school and parents, but also enhance the functional well-being of the child at home. This program needs to be continuously evaluated to review the assumptions and ensure maximum participation of parents.

Educational and governmental policymakers concerned with the educational plight of Mexican American children should carefully check their operating assumptions about what youth want or need. A continuous evaluation of present programs and assessment of forthcoming needs should be conducted at the local, state, and federal levels. Surveys can be used to assess the attitudes of parents and students toward school. Accountability and management audits can be used to assess school expenditures, learning, and institutional responses to student needs. This would provide legislators and policymakers with a more realistic appraisal of needs in order to create a more effective procedure for the development of programs and the appropriation of funds. In this manner, existing resources can be used to develop programs that will better equalize the educational opportunities of these isolated communities in the Southwest. Furthermore, we must continue to research and assess the educational needs of Mexican American students and to advocate for their needs.

Mexican American children have the desire, despite the systemic, linguistic, and educational barriers as well as discriminatory barriers and practices which they face. Hence, it is up to educators, community members, and policy innovators, who make up the society and have created these educational institutions, to promote access, opportunities, networks, and learning experiences that will fulfill those desires.

The cooperative efforts of school districts, parents, program planners, culturally competent staff, and legislators will be required to develop institutional policies that reflect the needs of the community and respond with resources and interventions that involve students and their parents as partners in the learning process. In addition to these collaborative efforts, accessibility to policymakers as well as continuous evaluation of institutional programs will determine whether the playing field has been leveled.

REFERENCES

Allport, G. W. (1954). *The nature of prejudice*. Cambridge: Addison Wesley.

Alvarez, R. (1970). The psycho-historical and socioeconomic development of the Chicano community in the U.S. *Social Science Quarterly, 53*, 920–942.

Arciniega, T., & Brishetto, R. (1973). Examining the examiners: A look at educators' perspectives on the Chicano student. In R. O. de la Garza, Z. A. Kruszewski, & T. A. Arciniega (Eds.), *Chicanos and Native Americans: The territorial minorities* (p. 37). Englewood Cliffs, NJ: Prentice Hall.

Blawis, P. B. (1971). *Tijerina and the land grants*. New York: International Publishers.

Cárdenas, B., & Cárdenas, J. A. (1972). The theory of incompatibilities. *Today's Education*, 1–2.

Carter, T. (1970). *Mexican Americans in school: A history of educational neglect*. New York: College Entrance Examination Board.

Chahín, J. (1977). *The educational and occupational aspirations and expectations of Mexican Americans: Are migrants different?* Unpublished doctoral dissertation, University of Michigan, Ann Arbor.

Chapa, J. (1992). *The changing face of America: Future implications of demographic trends* (Monograph No. 2, Underwood Lecture Series). McAllen: University of Texas, Pan American.

Chávez, L. (1991). *Out of the barrio.* New York: HarperCollins.

Darder, A. (1991). *Culture and power in the classroom.* New York: Bergin & Garvey.

De Hoyos, A. (1961). *Occupational and educational levels of aspirations of Mexican American youth.* Unpublished doctoral dissertation, Michigan State University.

De León, A. (1982). *The Tejano community, 1836–1900.* Albuquerque: University of New Mexico Press.

DeVillar, R. A., Faltis, C. J. & Cummins, J. P. (1994). *Cultural diversity in schools: From rhetoric to practice.* Albany: State University of New York Press.

García, H. (1980). *Chicano social class assimilation and nationalism.* Unpublished doctoral dissertation, Yale University.

Gibson, M. A., & Ogbu, J. U. (1991). *Minority status and schooling: A comparative study of immigrant and involuntary minorities.* New York: Garland.

Gordon, C. W. (1970). Educational achievement and aspirations of Mexican American youth in a metropolitan context. In L. Grebler, J. W. Moore, & R. C. Guzman (Eds.), *The Mexican American people* (p. 171). New York: Free Press.

Grebler, L., Moore, J. W., & Guzman, R. C. (1970). *The Mexican American people.* New York: Free Press.

Guerra, I. (1959). *The social aspirations of a selected group of Spanish name people in Laredo, Texas.* Unpublished master's thesis, Texas A&M University.

Hanson, S. I. (1994). Lost talent: Unrealized educational aspirations and expectations among U.S. youths. *Sociology of Education, 67,* 159–183.

Hayes Bautista, D., & Chapa, J. (1988). *The burden of support: Young Latinos in an aging society.* Stanford: Stanford University Press.

Hayes Bautista, D., & Harveston, D. (1977, March-April). Holistic Health Care. *Social Policy,* 7–13.

Heller, C. (1966). *Mexican American youth: Forgotten youth at the crossroads.* New York: Random House.

Heller, C. (1969). *Structured social inequality.* New York: Macmillan.

Heller, C. (1971). *New converts to the American dream.* New Haven, CT: College and University Press.

Horsman, R. (1981). *Race and manifest destiny: The origins of American racial Anglo-Saxonism.* Cambridge: Harvard University Press.

Johnson, K. (1970). Teaching the culturally disadvantaged: A rational approach. *Science Research Associates, 72*, 135.

Johnson, L. (1973). A comparison of the vocabularies of Anglo American and Spanish American high school pupils. *Journal of Educational Psychology, 49*, 135.

Juárez, R. (1968). *Educational status orientations of Mexican American and Anglo American youth in selected low-income counties of Texas.* Unpublished master's thesis, Texas A&M University.

Kahl, J. A. (1957). *The American class structure.* New York: Rinehart.

Kluckhohn, F., & Strodteck, F. (1961). *Variations in value orientations.* Evanston, IL: Row, Peterson.

Knowlton, C. S. (1962, October). Patron-peon patterns among the Spanish Americans of New Mexico. *Social Forces, 40*, 12–17.

Kominski, R., & Adams, A. (1994). *Educational attainment in the United States: March 1993 and 1992* (U.S. Bureau of the Census, Current Population Reports, P20–476). Washington, DC: U.S. Government Printing Office.

Kuvlesky, W. P., & Bealer, R. C. (1966, September). A clarification of the concept occupational choice. *Rural Sociology, 31*, 265–276.

Kuvlesky, W. P., & Edington, E. O. (1976). *Ethnic group identity and occupational status projections of teenage boys and girls: Mexican American, black, Native American, and Anglo youth.* Paper presented at the annual meeting of the Southwestern Sociological Association, Dallas, TX.

Kuvlesky, W. P., & Monk, P. M. (1976). *Historical change in status aspirations and expectations of Mexican American youth from the border area of Texas: 1967–1973.* Paper presented at the annual meeting of the Southwestern Sociological Association, San Antonio, TX.

Kuvlesky, W. P., and Ohlendorf, G. W. (1968, June). A rural-urban comparison of the occupational status of Negro boys. *Rural Sociology, 33*, 274–283.

Kuvlesky, W. P., & Venegas, M. (1974). *Aspirations of Chicano youth from the Texas border region: A metropolitan-nonmetropolitan comparison.* Paper presented at the annual meeting of the Rocky Mountain Social Science Association, El Paso, TX.

Machado, M. A. (1978). *Listen Chicano! An informal history of the Mexican American.* Chicago: Nelson-Hall.

Madsen, W. (1964). *Mexican Americans of South Texas.* San Francisco: Holt Rinehart and Winston.

Martínez, O. J. (1988). *Troublesome border.* Tucson: University of Arizona Press.

Matute-Bianchi, M. E. (1991). Minority status and schooling: A comparative study of immigrant and involuntary minorities. In M. A. Gibson & J. U.

Ogbu (Eds.), *Situational ethnicity and patterns of school performance among immigrant and nonimmigrant Mexican-descent students* (pp. 205–247). New York: Garland.

McWilliams, C. (1948). *North from Mexico: The Spanish-speaking people of the United States*. Philadelphia: Lippincott.

Merton, R. K. (1957). *Social theory and social structure*. New York: Free Press of Glencoe.

Miller, M. V., & Kuvlesky, W. P. (1976). *Status and familial projections of Mexican American migrants and non-migrants: Are migrant youth different?* Paper presented at the annual meeting of the Mexican American Studies Section of the Western Social Science Association, Tempe, AZ.

Moll, L. C., & Diaz, S. (1987). Change as the goal of educational research. *Anthropology and Educational Quarterly, 18*, 300–311.

Montejano, D. (1989). *Anglos and Mexicans in the making of Texas, 1836–1986*. Austin: University of Texas Press.

Nava, J. (1969). *Mexican Americans, past, present, and future*. New York: American Book.

Nava, J. (1973). *Viva la raza*. New York: Van Nostrand.

Parsons, T. (1951). *The social system*. New York: Free Press.

Perloff, H. (1969). *Regions resources and economic growth*. Baltimore: Johns Hopkins University Press.

Sánchez, G. I. (1966). *La raza: Forgotten Americans*. Notre Dame, IN: University of Notre Dame Press.

San Miguel, G. J. (1987). *"Let all of them take heed": Mexican Americans and the campaign for educational equality in Texas, 1910–1981*. Austin: University of Texas Press.

Santos, R. (1985). *Hispanic youth: Emerging workers*. New York: Praeger.

Saunders, L. (1954). *Cultural differences and medical care*. New York: Russell Sage Foundation.

Simmons, O. G. (1969). The mutual images and expectations of Anglo Americans and Mexican Americans. *Daedalus*, 288–299.

Stanton-Salazar, R. D., & Dornbusch, S. M. (1995). Social capital and the reproduction of inequality: Information networks among Mexican-origin high school students. *Sociology of Education, 68*, 116–135.

Stephenson, R. M. (1957). Mobility orientation and stratification of 1,000 ninth graders. *American Sociological Review, 22*, 204–212.

Stoddard, E. R. (1973). *Mexican Americans*. New York: Random House.

Turner, R. H. (1964). *The social context of ambition*. San Francisco: Chandler.

Ulibarri, H. (1971). Social and attitudinal characteristics of Spanish-speaking migrant and ex-migrant workers in the Southwest. In N. N. Wagner & M. J. Haug (Eds.), *Social and psychological perspectives* (p. 165). St. Louis: Mosby.

United States Commission on Civil Rights. (1970). *Ethnic isolation of Mexican Americans in the public schools of the Southwest.* Washington, DC: U.S. Government Printing Office.

United States Commission on Civil Rights. (1971). *The unfinished education.* Washington, DC: U.S. Government Printing Office.

United States Commission on Civil Rights. (1972a). *Mexican American education in Texas: A function of wealth.* Washington, DC: U.S. Government Printing Office.

United States Commission on Civil Rights. (1972b). *The excluded student: Educational practices affecting Mexican Americans in the Southwest.* Washington, DC: U.S. Government Printing Office.

United States Commission on Civil Rights. (1973). *Teachers and students: Classroom interaction in the schools of the Southwest.* Washington, DC: U.S. Government Printing Office.

United States Commission on Civil Rights. (1974). *Toward quality education for Mexican Americans.* Washington, DC: U.S. Government Printing Office.

Vaca, N. C. (1970). The Mexican American in the social sciences. *El Grito, 4,* 46.

Venegas, M. (1973). *Educational and occupational aspirations and expectations of El Paso high school students.* Unpublished doctoral dissertation, New Mexico State University.

Walsh, C. E. (1987). *Pedagogy and the struggle for voice: Issues of language power and schooling for Puerto Ricans.* Westport, CT: Greenwood.

CHAPTER 6

The Multicultural Literacies of Precollege Latino Students

RAIMUNDO MORA

INTRODUCTION

This chapter explores the multicultural literacies of selected Latino adolescents entering college in the United States, and identifies ways in which educators and practitioners might eliminate barriers and create opportunities for these students to succeed. By establishing connections between the language used in the classroom and the lives of students outside school, this chapter seeks to show practitioners ways in which they can promote their students' literacy without alienating them from the educational process. Illustrated are some of the ways in which educational, economic, cultural, and circumstantial factors interact in the development of these students' literacy.

Interpretations of the literacy of precollege non-native English students in the United States abound (Cohen, 1994; Ellis, 1986, 1987; Henning, 1991; Johns, 1991). Yet these studies frequently focus only on the English-speaking competency of students. To seriously understand the development of students' literacy, the factors that shape their learning processes need to be considered (Connor, 1991; Ferdman, Weber, & Ramirez, 1994; Macías, 1994).

The analysis presented herein is based on research that seeks to analyze Latino adolescents' literacy beyond the coding and decoding of words, and which seeks to document the intricate ways in which the factors mentioned above interact. These studies are reported in two sections. The first section, "Language Use in the Context of Three ESL Classes," reports on a research study that combines interviews of students with a pragmatic analysis of the language used in three classes (Mora, 1992). This research documents how first-language literacy, background knowledge, culture, and personal circumstances interact with the language used to develop the academic discourse of the classroom, and it indicates the opportunities and barriers students face in developing the academic discourse of the classroom.

The second section, titled "The Social Contexts of Academic Literacy," is based on two complementary studies to Mora's (1992) research. These case studies show how language attitudes and socioeconomic factors play an important role in the acquisition of academic literacy in a second language in addition to first language literacy, culture, background knowledge, and personal circumstances. The cases present excerpts from interviews with real adolescents, who in the process of bridging their home and academic literacies have to face daily social and economic circumstances which frequently affect their literacy acquisition processes.

BACKGROUND

The students in the research studies from which the excerpts were taken are all limited English-proficiency students who grew up in working-class environments in the New York and New Jersey area.[1] Their experiences are reported through ethnographic studies, because qualitative research, and particularly ethnography, is the appropriate approach for understanding learners and the contexts in which they use literacy.

According to Szwed (1988), ethnography breaks with most past research on literacy because it is the only means available for finding out what literacy really is and what can be validly measured. Likewise, Macedo (1991) argues that traditional approaches to literacy have been ingrained in a positivistic method of inquiry which ignores the interrelationship between the sociopolitical structures of a society and the act of reading.

These ethnographies bring to the foreground perspectives of literacy which are different from those that characterize target culture and language and neglect to prioritize the adolescents' interpretations of their literacy acquisition processes. What it means to become literate in an unfamiliar language and culture is focal. Thus, these case studies are consistent with recent studies of literacy that take into account *the contexts in which people have to use literacy, and the individual traits of the subjects whose literacy is studied* (Solá & Benett, 1991; Ferdman et al., 1994; Macías, 1994; Nespor, 1991).

It should be noted, however, that these studies mainly address first language literacy and not second language literacy. This is in tune with Ferdman's (Ferdman et al., 1994) contention that the complexities of becoming literate in a second language have only recently been considered by scholars. Furthermore, these studies focus only on students from working-class backgrounds and do not purport to represent Latino adolescents' literacy of other socioeconomic and geographical locations. Throughout the chapter, published research which documents the literacy of other groups of Latinos in different contexts is presented.

The intent is to make visible the need to learn about the characteristics of students in order to help them succeed in their academic endeavors and the immediate need for this type of research.

LANGUAGE USE IN THE CONTEXT OF THREE ESL CLASSES

This section covers excerpts from research on language use conducted at a New York community college in three ESL classes (Mora, 1992). Because teachers and students usually rely on oral language to teach and learn literacy in the classroom, the focus is on the classroom discussions. This is much in keeping with Kintgen's (Kingten, Kroll, & Rose, 1988) claim that when studying literacy in a modern setting, we must always be aware that the relations of literacy with orality are likely to be intricate and significant.

The methodology used to gather data consisted of classroom observations, field notes, and videotaping of specific sessions. The videotapes were viewed by the researcher and the participants, and their interpretations of class discussions—in which students explored topics they were going to write about with their teachers—were tape-recorded and analyzed by the researcher. The reason for this focus was that during classroom discussions, participants orally prepared their written compositions, and such discussions shed meaningful light into their different levels of literacy and the differences which existed between their discourse and that of the school.

In keeping with the ethnographic method used by Saville-Troike (1982), when participants commented on aspects of language use, the researcher asked for more specific information and then compared answers to the same questions made by teachers and students. He transcribed class discussions and repeatedly compared different versions of the same discussions: videotapes, transcripts, participant interpretations, and logs. The transcripts were organized into speech acts that were numbered consecutively for each class discussion, with time elapsing between discussions measured. Nonverbal clues as they were interpreted by participants and the researcher were also analyzed. Excerpt 1, which relates to background knowledge as the main finding in this event, follows.

Background Information

Context: ESL class, with Norberto, Marina, Bertha, Juan, and Justine, the teacher, present.

NORBERTO: Norman Bates had a problem of sexual identity, so he developed a double personality. Sometimes he was the son, and sometime he was the mother.

MARINA: The man was under a lot of pressure because he had control on two personalities. It gave him power but also fear. He was scared.

BERTHA: It is a movie about a crazy and his mother.

JUAN: It's boring [in a snapping way].

The teacher, Justine, gave this feedback to the students' comments:

JUSTINE: I studied film at the university, you know, cinema. I teach cinema at my other job, and I find your comments as good as those of my cinema students. You understand the movie much better than me when I watched the movie for the first time. I'm very serious. I'm astonished.

These comments were made during a thirty-minute discussion following the teacher's showing of the film *Psycho*. A few students spoke at length. When Justine tried to end the discussion, Norberto and Marina continued talking to her about the movie. Justine had to make two more attempts to end the discussion and promised to continue it next day.

During Justine's analysis of the videotape containing this discussion, she said that when she stated that she prized the students' comments, she referred to Norberto's and Marina's comments. She had ignored Juan, who had come up with one of his usual negative comments and felt that Bertha had not understood the film yet did not want to embarrass her in front of the class.

In this excerpt, Norberto and Marina were able to impress Justine with their analyses because they had background information about the psychological issues the film addressed. Norberto had taken an introductory psychology course when he attended law school in Argentina, as had Marina when she attended college in Ecuador. This gave them access to vocabulary and psychological concepts which they could use in articulating their analyses. They also had the linguistic competence to integrate this background information into their interpretations.

Both students had high ESL placement scores. In the class discussion, Marina and Norberto asked and answered questions, recounted episodes in the movie, and provided explanations. By contrast, Bertha and Juan confined themselves to one short statement each.

Culture and Appropriateness

In an excerpt from another ESL class, Marvin and Rosa are the students and Janis is the teacher. In a class discussion, Marvin said that in his country it was difficult to get married because of economic problems. Rosa contradicted him, saying that these problems also existed in the United States. This prompted him to shift from the register he was using with the teacher to a more informal, humorous register. Now he said that Rosa just wanted to get married and added that all women like to get married and pointed his finger at his female classmates. The students laughed.

During the analysis of this exchange in the videotape, Marvin said that he wanted to make a joke when he said that all women wanted to get married. On several occasions, Marvin and Rosa contradicted each other and both said it was common "in the way Hispanic men and women talk to each other." However, Janis, the teacher, did not note the humor or the change in register. She expressed distaste during the discussion by making a face and gesturing. During the analysis of the videotape, she said that she could not help but hold Marvin's sexist comments against him. She found his pointing at women "aggravating." Janis considered Marvin "sexist" for saying that all women just wanted to get married. Marvin said he was aware of her dissatisfaction, but not of what had caused it.

This exchange suggests that the student's initial desire to achieve communication goals was not enough, that in fact, his remark made him suspect as being sexist. Given the tenor of sexism in most colleges, making openly racist and sexist remarks is considered inappropriate. Had Marvin known this sociocultural norm, he could have chosen whether to comply with it or disregard it. In essence, his own kidding transgressed the cultural norm that Janis expected. In this sense, Wittgenstein's (1958) notion that when we communicate we play "language games" seems apropos, because to do so we need to know the rules of the games we want to play.

Culture and Personal Circumstances

In this excerpt, Janis interacts with Marvin and Rosa in class:

> Janis read an article about AIDS aloud. She then began a discussion about the AIDS crisis in the United States. At the end of the discussion, she asked students to write an essay about the same subject for the next class. "That's too heavy" was the only comment Marvin made in class. "I don't like to talk about AIDS" was Rosa's explanation of her lack of participation in this class.

Rosa was usually a lively participant in class, but in this class she looked distressed and did not speak. During the analysis of the videotape, she said that she could not speak because she did not have the "right" words. But during this class, the teacher and students focused most of the time on the meaning of words. Rosa could have asked the teacher about unfamiliar vocabulary.

When the researcher spoke about this class to her in Spanish, Rosa said that she did not like to talk about AIDS, and added that "women should not talk about sex." At that point, the researcher could not get her to say anything else about it. Rosa never turned in the composition about AIDS. Her difficulties speaking about the topic may have been personal, but her saying that women should not talk about sex also acknowledged gender differences in her native culture that influenced her class performance.

By refusing to discuss and write a composition on the topic, Rosa showed her disapproval. Janis acknowledged Rosa's silence a few weeks later when she analyzed the videotape. However, she did not seem to have understood the implications of this silence, since she included the topic of AIDS as one of the two topics the students could write about when she prepared the final exam. In none of the classes observed did the students speak directly about the inappropriateness of a topic. It was evident that the teachers decided what was/was not appropriate to say in class.

Marvin explained his saying "That's too heavy" as a comment involving pain about talking about AIDS. During the analysis of the videotape Marvin, who usually participated very actively in class, said that a close friend of his had recently died of AIDS, so it was painful for him to talk about it in class. Initially, the researcher thought that Marvin had used the word *heavy* humorously, to mean "difficult," since he had no-

The Multicultural Literacies of Precollege Latino Students   137

ticed that Marvin constantly used humor when he spoke. The emergence of pain as a theme was totally unexpected. Rosa's and Marvin's interpretations of their participation showed that pain and appropriateness were two reasons for them not to speak in this class.

THE SOCIAL CONTEXTS OF ACADEMIC LITERACY

The case studies reported in this section were conducted in the summer of 1994 and the fall of 1995. They document the literacy acquisition process of Latino adolescents who had just finished high school. They were conducted to complement the findings of the case studies reported in the previous section.

These case studies focused on how the literacy acquisition process of adolescents is influenced by factors external to the classroom. The students in these cases had enrolled in a precollege program at a four-year college in Newark, New Jersey. This program was financed by the Educational Opportunity Fund (EOF). EOF was established by the New Jersey legislature in 1968 to increase access to higher education by providing financial assistance and support services for "needy" New Jersey residents attending the state's colleges and universities. The program is the most comprehensive of state-funded efforts to eradicate inequality in higher education.

The researcher observed one precollege writing class and interviewed students and teachers outside class every week during one semester. The following fall, he observed the same students in a college-level writing class and continued interviewing teachers and students. The class observations were kept in logs that he wrote during and after classes. The interviews were recorded, transcribed, and analyzed.

In this section two students whom the teachers of the precollege program and the researcher considered representative of Latino students registered in ESL classes are presented.

Brenda

By the time this study was conducted, Brenda was the only person in her family and her husband's family who had finished high school. Brenda's writing teacher said that when he first read Brenda's compositions he thought Brenda had committed plagiarism, but later he realized that Brenda was a good writer. He explained that Brenda had been placed in ESL because although she had been born in this country, she had grown up speaking Spanish at home and her community, and sometimes she used Spanish sentence structures when she wrote in English. He added that Brenda nevertheless developed her ideas thoroughly. According to this teacher, this reflected the fact that she was an intelligent and eager reader. In fact, Brenda corroborated the teacher's comment about her reading habits. She said that since she was a child, she had enjoyed reading in both Spanish and English and that her favorite hobby was reading Spanish novels. The teacher in another interview said, "Her appearance was very misleading. She wore so much makeup and dressed so extravagantly that it was hard to believe she could write such thoughtful compositions."

Yet the same teacher commented that Brenda was well informed about current issues, especially women's rights and the political situation in Puerto Rico: "She always had plenty of ideas when she wrote about these issues." The teacher also noticed that at the beginning of the semester Brenda wrote very short compositions, but toward the end of the semester she could write long pieces.

In an interview, Brenda said that when she started the precollege program she did not know how to develop her ideas. She explained that it was not until her teacher told her to find ways to link her compositions to personal experiences and political interests that she could develop her ideas in longer compositions. She said that when she made connections between composition topics and her own experiences she could use what she knew about politics. The teacher, however, focused on the fact that Brenda tended to miss many classes and sometimes she did not do her homework. When asked why she was missing so many classes, Brenda explained that sometimes her in-laws could not baby-sit her son so she had to stay at home and care for him.

Brenda's parents were from San Juan, Puerto Rico, and migrated to Newark, New Jersey, where Brenda was born and attended public school. When she was 15, she got married to her boyfriend, Mario, because she was pregnant. Brenda explained that when they married, Mario and his parents had promised that they would help her finish high school and go to college. Brenda gave birth to a boy. Mario was then a senior, two grades ahead of her, but never finished high school because he had to support Brenda and his son.

After getting married, he dropped out of school and got a job in a garage in Newark, where he has been working as a mechanic ever since. Brenda and Mario lived with Mario's parents. At the time of this program Brenda was 19 and her son was 4.

The Multicultural Literacies of Precollege Latino Students

Brenda's economic limitations and lack of support at home for her academic work seemed to have interfered constantly with the development of her academic literacy. She explained that she and her son had to live on Mario's low salary. It did not allow them to pay for a baby-sitter or a day care center. Mario and his parents took care of the baby when Brenda went to school, so when they could not do it, she had to at stay home and miss school. Brenda said that her husband and his parents had complained that Brenda dedicated too much time to her studies and that she preferred her books to her family and friends. Brenda said that on more than one occasion they had accused her of "putting on airs" because she preferred to read while the rest of the family was watching TV, or she stayed at home on weekends doing her homework rather than go to parties with her husband. "They could not understand that I needed to spend a lot of time reading and writing to do my assignments," Brenda said.

In one of the last interviews Brenda commented that the situation at home was becoming unbearable because the latest complaint from her in-laws was that she did not help her husband economically. According to Brenda, Mario's mother had recently said that she did not understand why she had to go to college—that since she did not contribute to her son's support, she could at least take care of him. Brenda's response was: "I cannot get a job after school because my husband doesn't want me to be alone in the streets at night, especially in our neighborhood which is getting more and more dangerous. Maybe I should quit school." Two months after Brenda made this statement, she dropped out of school, at a time when she was about to finish the writing requirements of the university. Fortunately, in the spring of 1996, one of the administrators of the EOF program, who had taken special interest in Brenda, offered her a scholarship that would supplement her federal assistance and a job that she could do between classes and that allowed her to pay for a baby-sitter. Brenda was then able to go back to school.

Apparently, there were two main factors that helped Brenda develop her academic skills: (1) she was intelligent and was an eager reader in both Spanish and English, and (2) she received appropriate instruction, which used her background knowledge, in her writing class. However, the development of her reading and writing skills was hampered by the lack of family and university support. Her husband and in-laws could not understand that Brenda needed time to achieve the academic standards of the university. The university provided her with adequate academic instruction but did not meet a basic practical need. If the EOF program had not offered Brenda the support it did, she might not have been able to continue with her studies.

Carlos

During the initial interview, Carlos said that he was upset because he had been placed in an ESL class. When asked why he felt so strongly about it, he said that he was a good student and that to be placed in an ESL class was an unfair penalty. By the time this study was conducted, Carlos was enrolled in a precollege program. He was going to start college the following fall and had been placed in ESL classes because of his reading and writing difficulties in English.

Carlos was born in Lima, Perú, where he attended elementary school. When he was 13 years old, he emigrated with his parents to the United States. Upon his arrival in Newark, New Jersey, he started to attend a junior high school in his neighborhood, where he was placed in a bilingual education program. Carlos did not like being placed in this program because the bilingual classes were located in the worst part of the school building and because "regular students" used to call him "spic." "Although I did not understand what these words meant, I knew they meant something bad related to my being Hispanic," he said.

Carlos complained to his parents and they enrolled him in another school where there was no bilingual education program, so he was placed in a regular class. During the following years, he earned good grades but had difficulties with his writing. Carlos explained that some of his classmates used to write his English compositions in exchange for the science and math assignments that Carlos did for them. On some occasions, however, his English teachers noticed his writing difficulties in English and told him to stop using Spanish because it was interfering with his English. Carlos said that he tried to stop "hanging out" with his Latino friends but that at home nobody spoke English. "However," he added, "although my mother did not use English with me, she encouraged me to study it by buying me books in English. She even bought me a television set so that I could watch TV in English in my room."

In a separate interview Carlos said that during the year that he was in the bilingual program he was frequently afraid of being considered learning disabled because all the retarded and leaning disabled students in the school were placed in the bilingual program. He also explained that he had never liked being different, unlike some of his friends who "enjoyed being exotic." Carlos said, for example, that he selected clothes that "all American kids wear." On another occasion he said that in order to blend in with mainstream students he had to get rid of his accent, which apparently was not easy. Carlos described many unsuccessful attempts to sound like a native English speaker. He said that he used to pay close attention to the sounds produced by native speakers and tried to imitate them, but that the responses of native speakers made him realize he was speaking differently from them. This changed one day when he was hanging out with some "American friends" and suddenly he knew that he was speaking like them because they were not "treating him differently."

When Carlos entered college and took placement exams, he scored high in math and science but low in writing. This is why he was placed in ESL. When the researcher analyzed his compositions, he noticed that Carlos had good ideas but did not know how to articulate them according to conventions of standard English. His ESL teacher pointed to occasional literal translations that Carlos had made from Spanish into English in his compositions. "During the conferences that we had to correct his compositions," the teacher said, "he used to despair because he could not focus on grammar and punctuation at the same time that he tried to understand the conventions of English rhetoric. Frequently these sessions took a long time because he wanted to know why he could not express his ideas in writing the way he expressesd them speaking."

When the researcher pointed to literal translations in his compositions from Spanish to English, Carlos looked puzzled and said that this was happening because he was in an ESL class. In the summer of 1996, Carlos satisfied the exit requirements of the ESL program and during the spring semester he started taking English composition courses which are required for all students enrolled at this university.

DISCUSSION

From these case studies, it is clear that these students face several obstacles. Marvin had not been able to figure out some of his teacher's norms for classroom behavior. Bertha's and Juan's limited knowledge of movies and principles of psychology did not allow them to participate fully in the classroom discussions. In another instance, Marvin's emotions did not permit him to articulate his thoughts about AIDS. Rosa could not write about AIDS because of the cultural values she had grown up with.

Brenda and Carlos exemplify how extra-academic factors interact with literacy. Brenda's literacy acquisition process had been periodically interrupted by domestic problems rooted in conflicts between school and family expectations and economic limitations. Carlos's issues were representative of students whose schooling makes them develop negative attitudes toward their native language and who, as a result, tend to develop academic literacy only in a second language. These cases illustrate how linguistic, educational, social, economic, and cultural factors interact in the classroom and at home, creating both opportunities and barriers for students to develop the academic discourse they need to succeed in American universities. To increase retention of Latino students and improve their academic performance, it is imperative that their academic literacies be improved. This requires educators and policymakers to work together to design programs that promote the integration of these students' realities into school curricula and also help them to solve problems rooted in personal circumstances.

According to the General Accounting Office (1994), dropout rates are high among Latino students, particularly among those not born in the United States—43 percent as opposed to 20 percent for U.S.-born Latinos. The higher dropout rate among the former group can be explained in part by the fact that students who are not born in the United States are likely to face a wider cultural and linguistic gap between their primary and secondary discourses. This gap is extreme when the primary discourse is articulated in a language other than the one used in school. To bridge this gap, it is necessary to understand the differences among Latino students and to tap their learning sources, namely their culture, language, and communities. The pedagogical and political implications of the studies reported in the previous two sections follow.

PEDAGOGICAL IMPLICATIONS

In order to use language effectively it is clear that these students need to know what to say, where to say it, how to say it, and to whom. At the university level, they need to know the conventions of English in general and, in particular, of academic discourse. Students involved in the studies reported above, however, were learning these conventions by trial and error because they were not addressed in the curriculum. Frequently students did not know what the academic discourse expected of them. Teachers expected these students to have the same knowledge native English speakers have about cultural conventions underlying the use of English. This happened because teachers did not take into account students' cultural and sociolinguistic backgrounds nor did they explore their backgrounds as a source of information. These teachers' approaches are characteristic of common practices in the teaching of second language literacy.

To exemplify descriptions of literacy that focus only on the target language, the interpretations of Snow (1994), in the field of English as a second language, and Johns (1991), in English composition, are used. Snow (1994) addresses the components of literacy acquisition in a continuum, starting with the coding and decoding of words, and ending with strategic components of academic literacy: (1) letter recognition; (2) word recognition; (3) markers and cohesive relations among sentences (cohesive relations across utterances, anaphora, ellipsis, conjunctions; and complex temporal and conditional relations, past-future, perfect-progressive, subjunctive mood); (4) extraction and evaluation of new information; (5) integration of new information into old information (abstract topics/vocabulary); (6) authorial stance; and (7) development of reaction to material read. These fundamental components of academic literacy have been addressed profusely in linguistics and pedagogy, therefore, they will not be addressed in this chapter. Instead the focus will be on the contextual factors that are ignored.

Johns (1991) documents what some faculty call "ESL students' academic illiteracy" (p. 170) and defines it as (1) a lack of background knowledge; (2) problems with interpreting and producing the macropurposes of texts; (3) lack of planning in approaching reading or writing; (4) a lack of conceptual imagination; (5) a lack of essential vocabulary; and (6) the students' unwillingness to be objective about their value system.

Johns shows us how a group of college professors understand the academic literacy of limited English-speaking proficiency students, which is helpful to determine the skills these students need to succeed in college. However, students' literacy is defined only in terms of students' deficiencies and unwillingness to learn. Having such a conception will hardly allow faculty to use the background knowledge and powers of conceptualization that the students may have in their native language. Such an approach, one that imposes a discourse pattern without bridging the students' discourse, is likely to alienate students away from the curriculum and discourage them from learning.

This understanding of literacy uses a deficiency model that has been consistently used throughout history to discriminate against immigrants and native speakers of non-English languages (Macedo, 1991). What the teachers quoted by Johns (1991) called "lack" can be phrased in terms of "difference" and "ways to access their knowledge and experiences." This deficiency model has been frequently used to address the bilingualism of some linguistic minorities. While mainstream culture students are encouraged to learn other languages, Latino students, for example, have been discouraged from developing their Spanish. Such literacy practices, defined only in terms of English proficiency and ignoring students' skills in their native language, frequently obstruct their literacy development. This results in students' not being able to use their background knowledge to acquire new knowledge and use their communities' sources of knowledge (Moll, 1989).

The more successful approaches to integrating Latino students into the academic curriculum have acknowledged the bases they use to build up their second language literacy. Willinsky (1991) explains that those who recognize that success or failure in school may be related to the distance between the discourse of the learner and the discourse of the school have adopted multicultural approaches to the teaching of literacy, which promote the integration of culturally and linguistically diverse students into the educational process.

Freire (1992) proposes an approach to integrating students into educational processes that has been used successfully worldwide. He claims that the skills of reading and writing are best learned when students are engaged in meaningful interactions with language and when they deal with issues that are significant in their lives. This approach has been variably termed "emancipatory education," "empowering education," or "liberatory education." Elsasser and Irvine (1985) have also shown that when student realities were integrated into a college curriculum, students found effective ways to use their voices in the academic discourse they were learning. The problem, however, is that even in these studies, which attempt to integrate students, specific aspects of language use in the classroom are not addressed. To integrate all students, the teacher must use language in ways that give all students opportunities to articulate their ideas academically. Closer attention must be paid to the role that language plays (1) in teaching and learning, (2) in evaluating students' academic performance, and (3) in the social interactions that take place in school settings.

In college, students are expected to write within a specific genre—a form which serves as a guide to invention, arrangement, and stylistic choices in the act of writing. We acquire genres as we do the vocabulary and grammatical structures of our native language, not through dictionaries and grammars but from receiving and producing discourse (Bartolomae, 1987). Students with low English proficiency who have not been exposed to academic discourses in any language face the difficult task of learning both English and the conventions of language use in academic settings. Even students who have acquired academic literacy in their first language need to learn rhetorical differences between the academic discourses in their primary and secondary languages. Students who have not developed academic skills either in their native language or in English represent the hardest challenge to a teacher. Development of academic skills takes considerably more time than the acquisition of basic interpersonal communication skills. Cummins (1981) explained that while it takes these students an average of two years to learn oral skills, to learn academic skills takes an average of five years. He pointed out that a threshold level of first language structural acquisition must occur before there can be transfer into the second language.

To improve their English and academic literacy, these students need not only to receive appropriate instruction about language use, but also to be afforded plenty of opportunities to use English academically. During the past decade, the importance these opportunities afford has been underscored by research on second language acquisition theories which emphasize the role of speaking in language acquisition (Ellis, 1986, 1987, 1990). Swain's (1985) comprehensible output hypothesis claims learners need to engage in meaningful interactions to test their hypotheses about language. According to Ellis's (1990) topicalization hypothesis, when the learner has some control over the topic there is more classroom acquisition.

These second language acquisition theories indicate that the opportunities to orally articulate academic discourses which teachers give their students, as in the excerpts reported above, have implications for students' second language literacy. According to Zamel (1982), although the literature on a process approach to teaching ESL writing requires revision as the main component of instruction, class discussion needs more emphasis because it generates options for ESL writers and thus gives them more confidence and more to write about. Raimes (1994) claimed that revising is only possible when students have thoroughly explored a topic. She recommended teachers have students compose aloud because it helps them rehearse by bringing a sense of audience. It should be added that to compose aloud in classroom discussions also gives students opportunities to link and organize ideas and acquire new information. The kinds of talk that are more conducive to acquisition can be promoted by teachers. How to do it, however, is not easy because many of the principles underlying language use are subconscious, or are not known. Mora (1995) suggested at least three ways to increase opportunities for students in class discussions: (1) the use of teachers' silence, questions, and interruptions; (2) teachers' awareness of students' background knowledge; and (3) clarifying the cultural relevance of class discussions.

IMPLICATIONS FOR LANGUAGE POLICIES

The above-mentioned approaches to integrating students into educational processes cannot be implemented in a vacuum. To effectively integrate Latino adolescents into institutions of higher education, the teaching methods and principles used in the classroom need to be supported by school and language policies that create an environment conducive to such integration. Both pedagogical approaches and language policies depart from linguistic assumptions that should be carefully examined to avoid cosmetic solutions to the educational problems of Latino students. *Policymakers and educators should make sure that the linguistic and cultural assumptions underlying language policies are in agreement with these approaches. They should also be sure to address economic and social needs of students.*

Many of the current educational practices in the United States that address ESL students' literacy only in terms of their English proficiency do not tap on their other linguistic and cultural resources, nor do they address the social and economic realities that interfere with education. For example, emphasis on monolingualism has led to the creation of language policies that assess literacy only in terms of the individual's ability to use English, thereby ignoring other characteristics of those whose literacy is being assessed and the literacies which they can use in specific contexts.

A literacy survey conducted by the Educational Testing Service (1990, p. 5) for the U.S. Department of Labor states: "Literacy involves using printed and written information to function in society, to achieve one's goals, and to develop one's knowledge and potential." One possible reading of this is that non-native English speakers' literacy in non-English languages should be promoted to develop their knowledge and potential. However, the survey only assessed English proficiency standards. Another reading was provided by Macías (1994), who claimed that because the survey did not assess proficiency in non-English languages, it minimized the existence of these languages and led educators to ignore the learner's non-English resources.

The survey's definition of literacy is also too vague when applied to practical situations. It does not take into consideration two important factors: the characteristics of those whose literacy is being defined and the contexts in which they use literacy. The first factor was not included because the survey was only conducted along three scales: prose, document, and quantitative literacy in English. Not to assess literacy in other languages contradicts the premise that one of literacy's goals is to "develop one's knowledge and potential," especially today when being bilingual (or multilingual) has become an asset in the job market. The second factor was not included in this survey because it did not address differences between literacies used in different situations.

Arguing in the same vein, Farr (1994, p. 92) documented how for some workers to "function in one's society" frequently means filling out forms and answering questionnaires. Students like Brenda, who come to college from settings in which literacy is defined in these terms, are likely not to receive the support at home they need to achieve their academic goals because their families and communities do not understand these needs.

At a macrolevel, it is clear that language policies in the United States reflect two competing ideologies in American society: one which promotes multilingualism, and another which promotes monolingualism. Proponents of multilingualism claim that diversity is what has made the United States strong. They advocate for bilingual education and equal linguistic rights for everybody (Grosjean, 1982; Hakuta, 1986). Proponents of monolingualism claim that many of the United States' problems are caused by the lack of a homogeneous identity which can only be achieved if everyone uses English (Porter, 1990). Extreme factions within this group created the English Only movement, which seeks to eliminate the use of languages other than English. In imposing standard American English, proponents of monolingualism tend to ignore the fact that many groups in the United States communicate in languages other than standard English. When programs designed for students from these groups do not meet the students' linguistic and cultural needs, they alienate students from the curriculum. A logical consequence of such alienation is the high dropout rate among Latino students whose primary language is Spanish.

Brenda's and Carlos's cases serve to illustrate how economic factors and language attitudes can influence literacy. Brenda's case is representative of many students whose literacy acquisition processes are interrupted by domestic problems rooted in conflicts between school, family expectations, and economic limitations. The university met Brenda's needs through a state program for minority students that provided Brenda with a grant, which paid the part of her tuition not covered by federal and state scholarships, and a job that permitted her to continue studying. This program also offered her a network of faculty members, counselors, tutors, and administrators who supported her before she entered college. During the prefreshman summer program, Brenda worked closely with staff to build the basic skills she would need to perform successfully in college-level courses. This academic support continued after she entered college.

Carlos's negative attitudes toward his native language reflect the ideological climate in which he grew up. The negative attitude toward Spanish in his school apparently contributed to his linguistic choices. In this regard, Carlos is representative of many students who arrive in college with a negative image of ESL programs and resent being placed in ESL classes. When asked by the researcher why, Carlos and others refer to the negative stereotypes attached to students enrolled in ESL and bilingual education programs at the elementary and secondary schools they attended in the United States. Students associate these programs with "special education" and low academic achievement. To dissociate themselves from these programs, they tend to avoid using their native language in public or being in situations that bring out their non-native status. As a result, many of them eventually lose their native language. For some, the length of their residency in the United States versus in their native countries is the most important factor—the longer they live in the States, the more they lose their native language. For others, like Brenda, English proficiency is closely related to their proficiency in their native language, and knowing their native language well means they can reach a higher level of English proficiency. They use both languages on an everyday basis in the United States and become fully bilingual and bicultural.

Further compounding the negative stereotypes about bilingual education and ESL is the very location of the programs. In areas where the monolingual ideology prevails, ESL and bilingual education programs are often located in the worst parts of the school buildings and do not receive the same attention or resources as mainstream programs (Rose, 1989). This leads to negative attitudes toward languages as represented in bilingual education and ESL programs. Paradoxically, the same schools that scorn bilingual education and ESL programs frequently emphasize the study of foreign languages. Spener (1994) explained that historically, in the United States, the value of biliteracy has not been denied when the individual possessing it is a native speaker of English.

Such negativism toward language policies and their implementation has led to several consequences. In the United States, it has been traditionally believed that some non-native speakers could only learn English by giving up their native language. Despite strong arguments to the contrary, this view keeps gaining ground in current educational practices. This exclusionary practice has strongly shaped the attitudes of many Latino students toward their native language. It frequently prevents students from capitalizing on what they know because what learners believe about what they are learning and about what they need to learn strongly influences their learning strategies.

Prevailing language attitudes in American society have also discouraged Spanish speakers from developing literacy skills in their first language that might have enhanced their personal and professional growth. Many people grow up speaking English only while other languages are spoken in their homes. According to the Hispanic Policy Development Project (1990, p. 1), seven of ten children whose parents immigrated to the United States from non-English-speaking countries become "English speakers for all purposes," and their children grow up speaking English as their first language. Apparently, Bertha is an exception. Projections of the study show that by the year 2001 there will be 16.6 million Spanish speakers in the United States, both monolingual and bilingual, and that 4.4 million people will have abandoned Spanish and become English monolinguals.

However, there has also been resistance in terms of overcoming the negative portrayal of native language learning. Linguistic minorities have achieved significant rights which are stated in current language policies. In the education of some students involved in the research reported here, there have been support programs for linguistic minorities that have been instrumental in their literacy acquisition. These programs have provided the context for them to learn academic language and content. The need for such support programs and for improving the existing ones is evident if the numbers of students who overcome linguistic and socioeconomic difficulties is to increase. It is also necessary to promote bilingualism among Latino students.

According to Gee (1991), literacy is the control of secondary discourses beyond the primary discourse that we use to communicate with our immediate families. As a result, he claims, there are as many applications of the word *literacy* as there are secondary discourses. Academic literacy refers to the secondary discourses used in academic settings. He explains that when the academic discourse is compatible with the discourse a student uses at home, it becomes a great advantage.

Abundant research shows how mainstream (native English-speaking) middle-class children acquire secondary literacies through experiences at home both before and during school and how in school they practice a discourse they have acquired at home (Wells, 1981, 1985, 1986). In contrast, many school-based secondary discourses conflict with the values and viewpoints contained in some nonmainstream students' primary discourses (Heath, 1983).

If we are to resolve this conflict, students have to deal directly with educational, linguistic, cultural, socioeconomic, and circumstantial factors supported by institutional structures and faculty who create the conditions and contexts for success. This knowledge and understanding is essential to comprehending the processes Latino students go through when acquiring second language academic literacy. Not to consider their daily lives in academic learning is to deny them opportunities for learning and ways in which schools and higher education can meet their needs.

NOTES

The author would like to thank Dr. Martha Montero of the Graduate College of Education at the University Massachusetts in Boston for her encouragement, valuable insights, and editing contributions in the preparation of this chapter.

[1]The teachers and students have been given pseudonyms in order to maintain their confidentiality.

REFERENCES

Bartholomae, D. (1987). Writing on the margins: The concept of literacy in higher education. In D. Bartholomae (Ed.), *A source book for basic writing teachers* (pp. 66–82). New York: McGraw-Hill.

Cohen, A. (1994). *Assessing language ability in the classroom.* Boston: Heinle and Heinle.

Connor, U. (1991). Linguistic/rhetorical measures for evaluating ESL students. In L. Hamp-Lyons (Ed.), *Assessing second language writing in academic contexts* (pp. 215–227). Norwood, NJ: Ablex.

Cummins, J. (1981). The role of primary language in promoting educational success for language minority students. In G. Lopez (Ed.), *Schooling and language minority students: A theoretical framework* (pp. 3–50). Los Angeles: California State University, Evaluation, Dissemination, and Assessment Center.

Educational Testing Service. (1990). *National Adult Literacy Survey* [Brochure]. Princeton, NJ: Author.

Ellis, R. (1986). *Understanding second language acquisition.* Oxford: Oxford University Press.

Ellis, R. (Ed.). (1987). *Second language acquisition in context.* Englewood Cliffs, NJ: Prentice Hall.

Ellis, R. (1990). *Instructed second language acquisition.* Cambridge, MA: Basil Blackwell.

Elsasser, N., & Irvine, P. (1985). English and Creole: The dialectics of choice in a college writing program. *Harvard Educational Review, 45,* 399–415.

Farr, M. (1994). Biliteracy in the home: Practices among Mexicano families in Chicago. In D. Spener (Ed.), *Adult biliteracy in the United States* (pp. 89–110). McHenry, IL: Delta Systems.

Ferdman, B. M., Weber, R., & Ramirez, A. (Eds.). (1994). *Literacy across languages and cultures.* Albany: State University of New York Press.

Freire, P. (1992). *Pedagogy of the oppressed.* New York: Continuum.

Gee, J. P. (1991). What is literacy? In C. Mitchell & K. Weiler (Eds.), *Rewriting literacy* (pp. 3–12). New York: Bergin and Garvey.

General Accounting Office. (1994, July). *Hispanics' schooling: risk factors for dropping out and barriers to resuming education.* Washington, DC: Author.

Grosjean, F. (1982). *Life with two languages.* Cambridge, MA: Harvard University Press.

Hakuta, K. (1986). *Mirror of language: The debate on bilingualism.* New York: Basic Books.

Heath, S. B. (1983). *Ways with words.* Cambridge: Cambridge University Press.

Henning, G. (1991). Issues in evaluating and maintaining an ESL writing program. In L. Hamp-Lyons (Ed.), *Assessing second language writing in academic contexts* (pp. 279–292). Norwood, NJ: Ablex.

Hispanic Policy Development Project. (1990). *The Hispanic almanac III: Handsome dividends.* Washington, DC: Author.

Johns, A. (1991). Faculty assessment of ESL student literacy skills: Implications for writing assessment. In L. Hamp-Lyons (Ed.), *Assessing second language writing in academic contexts* (pp. 167–179). Norwood, NJ: Ablex.

Kingten, E. R., Kroll, B. M., & Rose, M. (1988). Introduction. In E. R. Kingten, B. M. Kroll, & M. Rose (Eds.), *Perspectives on literacy* (pp. xi-xix). Carbondale, IL: Southern Illinois University Press.

Macedo, D. (1991). The politics of an emancipatory literacy in Cape Verde. In C. Mitchell & K. Weiler (Eds.), *Rewriting literacy: Culture and the discourse of the other* (pp. 147–160). New York: Bergin and Garvey.

Macías, R. (1994). Inheriting sins while seeking absolution: Language diversity and national data sets. In D. Spener (Ed.), *Adult biliteracy in the United States* (pp. 15–45). McHenry, IL: Delta Systems.

Moll, L. (1989). *Community knowledge and classroom practice: Combining resources for literacy instruction* (Year One progress report to Development Associates). Washington, DC: U.S. Department of Education.

Mora, R. (1992). *Pragmatic aspects of the language used in three selected ESL classes.* Unpublished dissertation, New York University.

Mora, R. (1995). Silence, interruptions, and discourse domains: The opportunities that ESL teachers give their students to speak. *Applied Language Learning, 6,* 27–40.

Nespor, J. (1991). The construction of school knowledge. In C. Mitchell & K. Weiler (Eds.), *Rewriting literacy: Culture and the discourse of the other* (pp. 169–189). New York: Bergin and Garvey.

Porter, R. P. (1990). *Forked tongue: The politics of bilingual education.* New York: Basic Books.

Raimes, A. (1994). Language proficiency, writing ability, and composing strategies: A study of ESL college student writers. In A. H. Cumming (Ed.), *Bilingual performance in reading and writing* (pp. 139–172). Ann Arbor, MI: Language Learning/Benjamins.

Rose, M. (1989). *Lives on the boundary.* New York: Free Press.

Saville-Troike, M. (1982). *The ethnography of communication: An introduction.* New York: Basil Blackwell.

Snow, C. (1994, April). Plenary speech at the International Conference of Teachers of English as a Second Language, Baltimore.

Solá, M., & Benett, A. (1991). The struggle for voice: Narrative, literacy, and consciousness in an East Harlem school. In C. Mitchell & K. Weiler (Eds.), *Rewriting literacy: Culture and the discourse of the other* (pp. 35–56). New York: Bergin and Garvey.

Spener, D. (1994). Introduction. In D. Spener (Ed.), *Adult biliteracy in the United States* (pp. 1–14). McHenry, IL: Delta Systems.

Swain, M. (1985). Communicative competence: Some roles of comprehensible input and comprehensible output in its development. In M. Gass & C. Madden (Eds.), *Input in second language acquisition* (pp. 76–90). Rowley, MA: Newburry House.

Szwed, J. F. (1988). The ethnography of literacy. In E. R. Kintgen, B. M. Kroll, & M. Rose (Eds.), *Perspectives on literacy* (pp. 303–312). Carbondale: Southern Illinois University Press.

Wells, G. (1981). *Learning through interaction.* Cambridge: Cambridge University Press.

Wells, G. (1985). *Language development in the pre-school years.* Cambridge: Cambridge University Press.

Wells, G. (1986). *The meaning makers: Children learning and using language to learn.* Portsmouth, NH: Heinemann.

Willinsky, J. (1991). Popular literacy and the roots of the new writing. In C. Mitchell & K. Weiler (Eds.), *Rewriting literacy* (pp. 255–270). New York: Bergin and Garvey.

Wittgenstein, L. (1958). *Philosophical investigations* (3rd ed., G. E. M. Anscombe, Trans.). New York: Macmillan.

Zamel, V. (1982). Writing: The process of discovering meaning. *TESOL Quarterly, 16,* 195–210.

CHAPTER 7

Demystifying the Images of Latinos
Boston-Based Case Studies

MARTHA MONTERO-SIEBURTH

INTRODUCTION

Latinos are represented by the media and by educational researchers through overwhelmingly negative images. Clara Rodríguez's (1997) research, reported in *Latin Looks: Images of Latinas and Latinos in the U.S. Media*, captures the degree to which the media and other institutional entities typecast Latinos. Described as illiterate, educationally and culturally disadvantaged, poor, non-English-speaking, welfare burdens, and criminally inclined (Fine, 1990; McDermott, 1989), Latinos are viewed as a "problem" in U.S. society. Research in education represents Latinos as being the most "at-risk" of student populations, with the highest dropout and teen pregnancy rates, the worst HIV-positive health statistics, and one of the highest criminal and delinquency records.

Given such stereotypes, how can Latinos be understood in terms of their actual lives and schooling experiences? What factors influence their educational success or failure, especially within the classroom context? These questions form the basis for the research represented in this chapter. Using case studies of Latino students, their teachers, and their mothers' aspirations, drawn from research conducted in an urban Boston-based high school over a six-year period, the complexities of students' learning experiences and teachers' work lives, and their definitions of success are closely examined.

MODELS FOR THE ACADEMIC ACHIEVEMENT OF LATINOS

Among the explanations which have been proffered in education to identify the ways that Latinos become "failures," or more commonly "at-risk," are models of linguistic match or mismatch between teachers and students, macro- and structural analysis, differential adaptation, cultural compatibility between home and school, the social construction of success and failure, ego rigidification, and affective dissonance. Sociolinguists have identified learning differences based on the linguistic match or mismatch between teachers and students through microethnographic studies of language used in the classroom (Cazden, Hymes, & John, 1972). In addition, there are studies demonstrating the cross-purposes created by communication which also affect learning (Erickson, 1991; Erickson & Mohatt, 1982; Gumperz, 1980). Many of these explanations have been at the microlevel of analysis of speech patterns and classroom interactions. Gibson and Ogbu (1991), on the other hand, have demonstrated the effects of social and economic structures in their research on immigrant and involuntary minorities at a macrolevel of analysis. They argue that immigrant minorities are incorporated into a host society by their own choice, leaving their countries of origin in search of socioeconomic and social betterment where they are more in control of their destinies, and involuntary minorities are incorporated through colonization, exploitation, and slavery. However, Ogbu (1987) points out that involuntary minorities experience historically induced limitations on employment, which often relegate them to a job ceiling that affects their perception of schooling.

De Vos and Suárez-Orozco (1990) take the analysis further, and argue that free from generational depreciation, immigrant minorities adapt readily and develop what Suárez-Orozco (1989) refers to as a dual frame of reference—interpreting their newfound experiences on the basis of their experiences back home. Such experiences give rise to a folk epistemology of "making it" which differs from that of other nonimmigrant working-class Latinos.[1] Within the articulation of both these micro- and macroanalyses for Latinos lies the cultural difference or cultural ecological model of understanding success and failure in schooling, promoted by anthropologists (Spindler & Spindler, 1987; Trueba, 1989). Culturally compatible programs such as the Kamehameha Early Education Program in Hawaii have been examples of specifically engineered matches between the family, the community, and the school. Yet these cultural adaptation matches and explanations tend to be limited.

Research indicates that some immigrants fare much better than U.S.-born Latinos and even Anglos (Matute-Bianchi, 1991; Mehan, Villaneuva, Hubbard, & Lintz, 1996; Ogbu & Matute-Bianchi, 1986; Suárez-Orozco & Suárez-Orozco, 1995). Such research points to underlying motivational factors, such as nationalism, identification with group, and level of education in the country of origin. Yet the understanding that Trueba (1989) makes of academic success and failure as "socially constructed phenomena" adds a dimension which has not been analyzed previously. Failure to learn, he acknowledges, is a "consequence of a given sociocultural system which denies the opportunity for social interaction and for cognitive development" (p. 28). De Vos and Suárez-Orozco's (1990) psychosocial framework for understanding the effects of cumulative depreciation or failure of learning in the classroom complements Trueba's explanation by characterizing the experience of negativism over time as ego rigidification. Nonlearning strategies become a defense mechanism which is set into motion. The continued depreciation of students which occurs in schools leads to defensive nonlearning in which the traditional schooling system is not only irrelevant, but threatens the student's sense of ethnic belonging. The overall result is what De Vos and Suárez-Orozco (1990) call "affective dissonance, whereby students realize that to become engaged in learning as a successful act may be interpreted by peers and others as passing, to act white and leave one's group behind" (p. 42). This sense of alienation from one's own group, according to De Vos and Suárez-Orozco (1990), appears to have different outcomes for immigrants than for involuntary minorities, with the former using the dual frame of reference in making their choices in education and the latter succumbing to limited options. Immigrant students make choices to partake of the educational system, without having reached the "ceiling" of academic and economic opportunities, mostly because of external factors, namely, immigration and academic grounding. For involuntary minorities, the category under which many Puerto Ricans and Mexicans are found, the choices, although available, may also be limited by other internal factors: primary language maintenance, cultural fidelity, and fulfillment of social roles, among others.

Research on Latino adolescents in bilingual and mainstream classes at a Boston high school are summarized as a backdrop to the current discussion of how images of Latinos become contextualized in schools.[2] The degrees of engagement or disengagement of Latino students can best be analyzed in the classroom context, not only because of the types of interactions, roles, and responses which ensue, but more importantly, because it is in this context that the issue of quality of interactions to tasks, and engagement or disengagement of learning, is linked to achievement.

QUALITATIVE ANALYSIS OF A LATINO SOCIOCULTURAL SYSTEM

Following an initial study on overall attendance patterns at Townsend High School,[3] a second study focusing on potentially at risk Latinos was conducted from 1989 to 1992. Eight Latino students, four in bilingual math and four in civics mainstream classes, were followed, interviewed, and observed at different intervals during two years to uncover the conditions under which they could become at risk. In addition, 32 administrators, teachers, and staff were interviewed about their perspectives on potential at-risk students. Of the eight students, two were promoted in bilingual education, and only one in the mainstream program. The remaining five students (two in bilingual and three in mainstream classes) repeated classes due to cumulative absences, lack of makeup work, and marginal grades.

These findings were reported in two publications, one identifying schooling practices and processes, and the other identifying implicit thinking of administrators, teachers, and staff about at-risk Latino students (Montero-Sieburth, 1993, 1996). Predictably, Latino students who were absent a good part of the year and lacked basic knowledge in math failed. But it could not be explained why Latino students who had been in the system since the early grades had been mainstreamed, spoke English well, and knew what to expect also failed. This required a more in-depth analysis of the contexts and experiences of the students' classrooms and teachers. Data from the previous research were analyzed with a focus on the classroom contexts of the bilingual and mainstream civics classes, as well as students' and teachers' definitions of success.[4] Interviews with the students' mothers were included to gain a clearer understanding of the educational experiences and expectations students had at home. From such analyses, case studies of two Puerto Rican students, one island-born and the other U.S.-born, their mothers, and their respective teachers were developed. These cases were informed by the notion of dual reference and affective dissonance, from De Vos and Suárez Orozco's research and Trueba's notion of social construction of success and failure.

CASE STUDIES OF STUDENTS, PARENTS, AND TEACHERS

Irene

Irene is an attractive 16-year-old Puerto Rican female who arrived in the United States in January 1990 to join her mother and two siblings, a sister in the sixth grade and a brother in the eighth grade. Upon her arrival, she was placed at level 2 of the Lau categories[5] and in the lower group (group B) in Ms. López's bilingual math class. While Irene felt confident with the math she had in Puerto Rico, she expected to be in group C, the more advanced math group, by the end of the year.

When she first arrived, Irene spoke only about her Puerto Rican roots, the beaches, the countryside, the rivers, and local beauty. She showed up several times in fancy dresses, dangling earrings, and colorful makeup without a coat or a sweater in the middle of January, believing that if the sun was out, it would be warm as it was in Puerto Rico. Irene made constant comparisons between life in the U.S. and Puerto Rico:

> In Puerto Rico, we [referring to friends] understood each other because friends spend so many years together in elementary and high school. Here people don't know you. I said good-bye to one of my friends who has gone back to Puerto Rico and she said she won't forget me because we are comfortable together. I am *chévere* (great) and we cried.

She felt uncomfortable not speaking Spanish. She commented:

> I don't like Puerto Ricans in the U.S. Here they change, they learn English and when you arrive, they know that you do not know English, and yet they speak to you in English anyway, just to bother you. There are a few Puerto Ricans who treat you well.

She also noted:

> Here we are all Puerto Rican, and we are more problematic because we look for trouble and we are envious [of others]. I always had a problem with other girls in school, because if you are pretty or have a boyfriend, you pay a price. However, I make friends here. There are some Puerto Ricans, Salvadorans, and Mexicans.

She still missed the grandmother, family, friends, and boyfriend she had left behind in Puerto Rico, even though she was glad to be with her mother.

Nevertheless, Irene settled into her new life. She felt accepted and was able to gain the confidence of her friends, with whom she developed close friendships, knowing she could ask for their help when needed. Irene became known for her well-groomed fingernails and her primping, which she would do each day in Ms. López's class. She earned the respect of the girls from Colombia, Nicaragua, El Salvador, and Puerto Rico, who set the dress code and behavioral norms as well as the gossip network. On one occasion, when Irene read a letter from a friend, her female peers responded cattily: "Mira cómo hablan de tí" (Look how others are talking about you). Irene disregarded their comments and diverted their attention by talking about a drawing she was making: "Qué lindo está esto . . ." (How lovely this is).

She began to distinguish between good and bad teachers. When asked what made Ms. López different from her other teachers, Irene responded:

> She talks to you and explains things, and she is understanding. The good teachers are the ones who give *easy* classes [meaning accessible to students, with teachers willing to explain], not strict (like in English class) and when one needs their help they are available.[6]

Irene grew to dislike one of the teachers at the school who had been her mother's teacher in Puerto Rico, because he often made comparisons between her and her mother, asking Irene if she was going to study like her mother, who had been a terrible student in high school.

Irene helped with the family chores after school, and after completing her homework, watched television. She did not often go out since she did not know how to get around the city and her mother did not allow her to participate in any activities after school, since she needed to be home by a certain time. When Irene left in the morning, her mother made sure she got on the first bus and her aunt met her before taking the second bus home. On weekends, Irene accompanied her mother to the church, a ritual to which she grew quite accustomed.

By the third term Irene's grades, which had been A's, B's and C's in Puerto Rico, began to slide. She received B's and C's with an F in English, which was her worst subject. Irene attributed her poorer grades to testing, which she felt was harder in the States. She recognized she needed additional help even though she completed all of the assignments. But not having anyone to turn to with her homework, she asked her neighbor who spoke English to help her. Her mother, who had not finished high school, studied English in the morning but did not speak it well enough to help her. By the end of the year, Irene received A's in computer literacy, speech, and U.S. history; a B in mathematics; C's in ESL 2, earth science, and physical education, which she disliked because she had to change in front of other girls; and a D in health education, her lowest grade.

Despite the initial culture shock and adjustments, Irene took things in stride. She developed goals of her own during the first year. She met a boyfriend she was serious about:

> My goals are to get married. After high school I don't want to go to school any longer, I want to have two kids and raise them here. But the most important thing is my studies now.

Notwithstanding, the following year, Irene became pregnant, but continued to come to school until she graduated. This was perhaps an outcome which may have represented her own coming to terms with balancing school and home demands, and best represented her own sense of success.

Irene's Mother

After divorcing Irene's father, who remarried and had two other children in New York City, Irene's mother moved to Puerto Rico, where she lived rent-free, used food stamps, and did not work. When her brother, who was a minister of a church in Boston, insisted she move, she decided to come to Boston, because at least she could count on her brother, her sister-in-law, and a religious network which she contacted every Tuesday, Thursday, and Sunday. She left Puerto Rico with her youngest siblings, leaving Irene behind in the care of her mother. She found housing soon after her arrival, but could not find work. After several months, Irene's mother became a welfare recipient. Although she expected her children to help her out by learning English in school, she nevertheless took English during the time they were in school.

The move helped Irene and her mother become closer, but at the same time the mother became more protective of Irene. Her relationship with Irene was described as being trustful:

> Irene tells me everything about her life, and I have given her my trust. She tells me the good and bad things.

Irene's mother recognized that some of Irene's friends considered her *antipática* (not sympathetic), but she felt Irene stood up for herself. She said: "Porqué ella no le ríe las gracias a todos, sabe a quién se las ríe" (Because she does not simply please everyone, she knows to whom she has to respond). About her aspirations for Irene, she was quite clear:

> I want her to learn in school, to learn English. Her mind is more awakened than my mind. I respond to crisis by crying and I fix everything crying. I don't want my children to lose their language. I expect the best from Irene. If she wants to continue studying, I will support her. I ask God that she don't give me much trouble because I don't have anyone to help me, just my brother and he is with the things of the Lord, not with things of the world. I want God to take care of her.

Irene's mother was also concerned about sex in the United States:

> I told her the U.S. is a very advanced country, and the boys at twelve have sex. I hope you can take care of yourself. If you have a boyfriend, and you have self-respect, you don't allow them to touch you and they won't. You are 16 and nobody has to talk about you. If you have a friend, I hope you will introduce him to me.

Under Irene's mother's protective guidance, Irene completed the school year, but when her mother considered changing schools as an option for her, Irene refused, because she had grown to love the school.

Ms. López

Ms. López, a native of Costa Rica, was a newcomer to Townsend High School, where she was a bilingual teacher for four years. Ms. López went to elementary school in Costa Rica, where she lived with her mother and five sisters and brother. Her father had passed away when she was 4. At the age of 10 she asked her mother to allow her to teach religion, a feat which she accomplished quite well. Thus, when she arrived in the United States at age 15, Ms. López had already developed a strong sense of *mística* (commitment to teaching) in Costa Rica. Her brother, who was the first to emigrate to the States, was able to bring each member of the family to Boston, so Ms. López was able to complete her high school in Boston after being in a bilingual program for two years.

Within a short time after her arrival, an American teacher who grew fond of Ms. López paid for her English classes, and with English under her belt she enrolled in a preadmission program which led her to the completion of a bachelor's degree. She worked in a shelter using her sociology and psychology background, and became involved in an adult education training program, doing student intake. This led her to a middle school, where upon the advice of teachers who watched her cover classes she decided to teach in the Boston public schools as a noncertified teacher. Townsend High School was her first assignment. During the years she taught at Townsend, she continued to study, completing first a master's degree in education and then a second master's in administration.

Unlike other teachers, Ms. López had five preparations a day. Yet in addition to this, she prepared work for her more advanced students and for those needing extra help. She taught the Spanish bilingual basic math class, biology, and literature classes for all ninth and tenth graders and she also attended classes at night in order to complete her bilingual teacher certificate. Her previous teaching in elementary, secondary, and adult education, as well as her previous training in social work and with battered children, proved to be useful at Townsend.[7]

Luke

As the oldest of three children, Luke lived with his mother, father, sister, and brother in a heavily concentrated Latino community from which he was bused to Townsend. A U.S.-born Puerto Rican, Luke attended kindergarten, was placed into a regular program, and continued into high school, where he was placed in level 4 of the Lau categories although he spoke Spanish and English at home.[8] Luke transferred from another high school into Mr. Laferty's mainstream civics class as a sophomore at age 16. He also used the free lunch program at school at the request of his parents, and worked eighteen hours a week after school in order to help the family with finances. Luke preferred work and television to constantly having to complete his homework when he got home. He was usually tired, unable to study or make up tests, which became reflected in his grades.

While in ninth grade, Luke's overall grades fluctuated from F to B-plus, but over the four terms they were consistently C's or D's. His reading scores were at least one to two years behind in grade equivalency for grades 6 and 7 and at least three to four years behind by grades 8 and 9. His math scores were more closely aligned to grade level except for a three-year grade equivalency difference in ninth grade. Luke enjoyed science, math and Chapter I reading, where he not only received B-pluses, but was also with his friends. Civics and English were boring because the teachers either talked only about laws or English, or were classes he "hated." For Luke, classes had to be first and foremost fun. He often said of civics, "I don't get that class." His teacher's message, however, was: "It may be great to do what is of interest to you, but to get an education, you have to take the boring with the interesting." Getting ahead in English was epitomized by Luke with the following:

> To pass you really did not need to work. All you gotta do in English to pass that class is be quiet. The teacher never teaches. He just gives you a page a day. "Here, do that page, when you're finished, be quiet." You could be doing your work and get straight A's on your test or book report and just get an F 'cause you're talkin' and that's what happened to me. He failed me first term 'cause I was talkin'. That's how it is.

Clearly Luke understood what was required of him from the school and teachers. He planned to finish high school, and to "have something good in the future." Yet how he was to accomplish such goals eluded him. Luke expected to get at least C's in his major subjects:

> It's important to get good grades sometimes. When I'm in a failing position—that is, when I work hardest and especially in the last term—I pay attention, and listen to the teacher, and I never cut when I wanna get good grades.

He also recognized that beyond having good grades and attendance, the ways that he and his friends were perceived by the school made a difference:

> The school, they treat us bad 'cause every time there's a problem, they always looking for us. They started looking for me 'cause they said they had some kinda list, and they started looking for me and my other friends, like we're always involved in things. They got us like gang members in that school. They looked for me and my other friends. So when one of my friends went to the bathroom, then a teacher said, "Watch out for these guys," and another said, "Oh we also gotta watch out for . . ." and you know, 'cause he went to the bathroom then they thought he went to get a weapon, so they kicked him out of school. It's

like if there's a fight, [the disciplinarian] is always looking for me, I don't know why, and it's all of us.

Although Luke's disciplinary record from his previous high school was solid, the transition to Townsend was difficult. Within the first few months at Townsend, he was involved in several fights. Luke attributed the fights to the fact that while at the other high school, "There was school spirit and teachers seemed interested and willing to help," allowing him to speak Spanish, but at Townsend, "It's like the white people, they wanna take over the school." Among the many gripes Luke expressed about homework, teachers, and classes, the major frustration was the fact that he couldn't speak Spanish in Mr. Laferty's class. He expressed his frustration by exploding after being silent: "I don't like that, that's my language."

Clearly Luke understood what was expected of him, what the rules were, and what he needed to do, yet sustaining the requirements for passing "all of the time" was something he did not want to do. By the end of the third marking period, Luke's academic fate was clearly at risk. While Luke passed every test, did most of his homework, and was absent only three days, his behavior placed him "on thin ice for the semester." To overcome the odds, Luke needed higher grades and better behavior for the fourth marking period.[9] While he was able to maintain average grades (except for two tests), and was absent only three days, his cumulative scores and poor behavior contributed to his failing civics.

Luke's Mother

Luke's mother eloped with his father when she came to the States at a young age. She completed ninth grade in Puerto Rico but continued her education by attending college for two years. His father completed seventh grade, and later completed a GED in the States. Luke's mother was a family service worker and his father drove two trucks in a maintenance company. During the nineteen years the family had lived in the States, they visited relatives in Puerto Rico each summer, sending the children to visit their grandmother. The next summer was Luke's turn.

At the time of the study, Luke's mother complained that things had changed in Boston over the years; there were too many problems and it was time to go back to Puerto Rico. Drugs, shootings, and gangs made her feel uneasy about Luke's safety at school and in the streets. She feared for his life and felt distressed about the violence in the school.

Whenever fights broke out between students at school, she kept him at home:

> I don't wanna send my Luke to Townsend where they are having problems with white and Hispanic or black against white, you know? It's a chance that he's taking, and I told them, until you get rid of the problem, Luke will not go to school. He's supposed to go 'cause he's gonna get a good education and he's gonna be coming home maybe shooting or wounded. No, come on, gimme a break.

She felt so strongly about the school, although she had visited Luke's previous high school, that she stated:

> I will never go. Maybe it's fear, but when Luke has a problem, I usually call, I leave messages, they call me back, but like, to visit and stuff like that, never.

She also complained about the education Townsend offered, which she compared with the education she herself had in Puerto Rico. She felt Luke was being cheated out of a good education:

> Teachers in Puerto Rico really teach and they often have large groups of forty to sixty students. Teachers here complain when they have nineteen or twenty students. In Puerto Rico, students have their own notebooks and you have to keep them in order and clean because they grade you for that, too. And you take notes. I remember I used to go home and study and everything was right there. In here, it's not like that, just papers, papers, papers.

The choice plan, she felt, simply did not work. Although she selected other high schools, with Townsend being her last choice, when Luke got in she pushed him since she felt that if he didn't want to go to Townsend, he was not going to do a good job in learning. "Schools don't give you what you choose," she commented. "They think they own the children and that they can do whatever they want. It's not like that, c'mon."

Mr. Laferty

Mr. Laferty, a twenty-four-year veteran of the Boston public schools, of Irish-American descent, began teaching late in November of 1990 at

Townsend. He had been shuffled from one school to another since school started, but by using his seniority and filing a grievance to maintain his teaching position at the school, he was back at his school. However, he now had to teach ninth- and tenth-grade civics instead of the juniors and seniors which he had taught during his eight years at Townsend. This was, in his words, "A different ball of wax," and "I'm finding that I'm in a learning process again and I have to make some changes."

Mr. Laferty had also been a coach for basketball and baseball, had run a store for the senior class, had advised seniors, had been a counselor coordinator, and was currently involved in the teachers' union. One of his major concerns was that even though he enjoyed teaching, out of the 180 students only 38 had passed his classes; in this particular class, 18 students flunked and 8 failed because they did not complete homework. He did not really understand what was happening and he tried to figure out how to best help his students by (1) digging up information on students who were not doing well academically, (2) approaching them personally, and if that didn't help, (3) talking to their peers or other staff members who had these students in their class as a way to reach them. Mr. Laferty rarely looked at his students' discipline records in order not to prejudice himself until he had direct problems with a student. Teaching Latino students was a new experience for Mr. Laferty. He admitted he had a lot to learn about Latinos, and underscored that he appreciated having his class studied. He noted:

> I may definitely be doing something that I shouldn't be doing. I treat Latinos the way I treat others. I treat them the way I hope teachers treat my three children.

His view was:

> My problem is, I don't compartmentalize my students. I don't care if their name is Hermione Gingold, Twan Too, Joel Hernández, or James Patrick O'Grady. They're just five kids in my class and I have the same rules for all five kids. I don't have a special rule for people because of their ethnic background. Why should I give special treatment to a specific group of kids?

Notably, Mr. Laferty's background was quite different from that of his students. His father was a physician and his mother an elocution teacher who checked the homework of his nine brothers and sisters every night until they graduated from high school. All his siblings were successful, in that they all completed college and several had advanced degrees. Thus, for Mr. Laferty, his expectations of close parenting and checking of students' homework represented an education of value. His own parents read to him "since he was old enough to sit down and pay attention." Yet he realized parental involvement today was not the same as when he grew up. His own ethics were that parents would help their children. He expected his students to do what he did, and his students' parents to do what his own parents had done with him. He modeled this in his class, by transcending the role of being a teacher and by being a guide, reinforcing some of the things his own parents taught him: courteousness, not swearing, dressing appropriately, expressing standards of behavior. By the time students left his classes, he expected them to share standards of behavior which he hoped they learned at home and he simply reinforced in school. Thus, for him, his role was to teach what parents weren't doing.

While he "enjoyed opening students' minds," Mr. Laferty also wanted to point them "in a God-fearing, correct direction in life." Part of his mission was to teach his students how to appreciate life in America and to understand what it meant to be an American. He insisted:

> This is an English-speaking country. Customs, however, are a blend of many different and diverse groups . . . And I don't have a problem with someone trying to preserve their culture . . . I have a real problem when I am told I have to teach Latin American history or Vietnamese geography. I'm in the United States of America, and I want to try and make these new immigrants understand the country they're coming to and be able to work and be accepted by it.

He felt schools could do a better job in helping parents become aware of educators and the problems they faced, and educators could become aware of the problems parents faced. Yet the current state of education demoralized him. His philosophy of education was that schools were for the betterment of kids, but in his opinion:

> There are very poor facilities to deal with the real recalcitrant youth of society. That spills over into the schools and hurts us, and society itself is partly to blame, as are the students, and the parents who do not come to PTA meetings. Even when report cards get home and the kid has an F in conduct and effort, we don't even get a phone call.

CLASSROOM CONTEXTS OF THE CASE STUDIES

Bilingual Math Context

Ms. López's bilingual classroom was located in a well-lit bright and cheery room decorated with Chinese posters, since the classroom was shared between the Chinese and Latino bilingual teachers. On any given day, close to 21 students were present, 8 girls and 13 boys, most of whom were from El Salvador, Nicaragua, Honduras, Guatemala, and Puerto Rico. Ms. López always arrived at 6:30 A.M., often staying after school to tutor students or run the Spanish Club, and she often left the school after 10:00 P.M.

Her corner desk was flanked by sets of desks clustered into several rows. Each set of rows represented a designated group of math abilities. Rows A and B, the lower achievement group, worked on basic multiplication tables, fractions, addition and subtraction, while group C worked on long division as the more advanced group. Each group faced a different side of the classroom, thereby allowing students to write math examples on the blackboard.

Ms. López rotated from class to class each day. On her way to each classroom, she was usually trailed by students who greeted, kissed, or hugged her and hovered around till she reached her door. Irene would pick up the scent of her perfume and tell Ms. López what the brand was. Once in class, Ms. López immediately took roll call at her desk in the corner of the room—a cue which students regarded as a signal for the class to begin. After a twenty-minute whole-class presentation on a specific topic, students were expected to work on their own in each of the groups. Ms. López first checked in with group A, and then attended to groups B and C, who faced the back blackboard. She allowed students to seek help from their peers. Irene, like the rest of the students, gravitated freely from desk to desk and paired up with Luis or Teresa, with whom she would work on multiplication tables. Other students in Ms. López's class worked silently and diligently, and even when they did not all complete their schoolwork or homework they paid attention and worked collaboratively.

During class, Ms. López invited students to show the results of their math problems on the board. Those who did not want to come to the blackboard she coerced through personal or verbal requests. For students who had difficulty with the placement of the decimals, she would create stories such as the following:

El señor decimal no va a estar contento si no lo ponen en su lugar. Hay que asegurarnos que está directamente sobre el otro señor decimal puesto que tiene que unirse a él. (Mr. decimal won't be happy if he isn't placed where he belongs. We need to make sure he is on top of the other Mr. decimal in order to be properly added):

35.5
15.5

Once students showed how they solved problems and checked for errors, they were openly praised, and at times applauded as a group, a ritual which Irene enjoyed since it built group coherence. During the period, Ms. López gave out assignments to each group. The first group would work on completing the ditto sheet exercises before she rotated to the next group. Once Ms. López completed her drill with the last group, she asked them to share with the class how they solved the math problems. Five minutes before the bell rang, she gave out the homework assignments, handed out extra ditto sheets for students to practice, and shouted notices to students as they left from the front of the room. Such consistency in routines from day to day made it possible for students to anticipate Ms. López's next move. When she forgot what came next, they often reminded her.

Ms. López used multiple instructional approaches to accommodate each student's math level, although they were grouped. She used a basic textbook as a resource book, to aid the more advanced students; but she also used xeroxed worksheets and dittos taken from English language resource books, and imported sixth and seventh grade Spanish textbooks from Costa Rica, to help the students who knew less. Directions were always given in Spanish, while students used the written English materials during seatwork. She even translated the English written exercises in the Metropolitan Math Test to Spanish, since it was the only version available at the school, although Ms. López had asked for a translated version early during the school year. She admitted that her students were being tested more on their English-speaking and -writing abilities than their knowledge of mathematics, hence she used a series of tests such as homework and quizzes to make sure they knew. When homework was handed in on time, she gave extra points after checking in with each student.

To control classroom behavior, Ms. López used verbal cues. Students who put their feet on a chair were reminded by Ms. López: "Está cogiendo muchas alas, y se las voy a cortar, baje los pies de la silla" (I see you've sprouted wings and want to fly; however, I'm going to clip your wings. Take your feet off the chair). When students chewed gum, which was not allowed except for "downtime," she used metaphors to anthropomorphize objects in order to get her point across. She referred to the wastepaper basket as a person in need of being fed. Rather than directly reprimand and demand students throw their gum out, she would simply say: "Caballero, entiendo que el basurero como que le está diciendo algo" (Sir, I believe the wastepaper basket is telling you something). Other times she would say, "Hay que darle de comer al basurero" (We need to feed the wastepaper basket). When she overheard students swear, she simply admonished them by saying: "Who said that word?" and then she would gently say, "Cuidado, mi amor" (Be careful, my love).[10] No doubt, Ms. López was *polifacética*, capable of doing two or three tasks at the same time. She talked to one student while she scanned the room to check on other students' behaviors. She often remarked she had eyes in the back of her head.

Beyond schooltime, Ms. López spent an inordinate amount of time talking about students' academic progress, events and happenings at the school, and providing feedback to students and parents by telephone. This served to keep her in touch with what was going on at home. She also relied heavily on the student social networks, as *comadres* and *compadres* (godparents), to inform her about individual students and their whereabouts. When students did not come to school, she called them at home, even showing up at their doorstep. She was like a mother, sewing, washing the clothes for those who had no means, cooking when they had no food, or visiting them in the hospital when they were ill. Yet throughout such interactions, she also shared personal information about herself with the students so as to gain their trust. Students commented on her weight loss, her clothes, and her perfumes.

During lunch, which took place in her classroom, one student would normally bring lunch paid for by Ms. López from the nearby deli to be shared with all students. While eating, Ms. López heard many of the personal issues students shared. Irene knew that Ms. López checked on her much like her mother and aunt did, but by openly and safely talking to Ms. López about her concern for dress, makeup, and the new boys she met in school, issues she reluctantly shared with her mother, she could test out her ideas before confiding in her mother. In this manner, Ms. López became well informed about each of her students; she could keep abreast of their needs and know how to mediate between their concerns and those of their parents and administrators.

The class rituals, while consistent, also changed even though she checked in with the three groups every day. On the days students had a birthday, or there was a holiday or simply the need for students to have a break from their routines, Ms. López would bring food she had cooked for the class, would allow students to chew gum and talk while completing tasks, and would have them listen to music. Such rewards were taken as special, and students came to expect a card from Ms. López or some type of special activity in class. There were also special celebrations such as Mother's Day, which were planned jointly by Ms. López and the students and included all of the students' parents. In anticipation of an evening event Ms. López would call all the parents to make sure they would attend, and if they did not have transportation she had taxis bring them to school, paid for by the administration. Ms. López organized the after-school rehearsals for the dance presentations and poetry readings, and on those occasions many students gave up their jobs to perform. To make sure female students could stay after school for the rehearsals, Ms. López interceded by calling the parents when their daughters would take the second bus home. Such vigilance and communication with parents served to prevent several pregnancies from occurring. Ms. López earned the prestigious title of "Ms. Contraception."[11] The night of the event, students performed, and prizes were awarded to the youngest and oldest mother, and to the mother with the most children. Ms. López even asked students who did not have their mother with them to select a person from the audience to be their mother for the evening, an activity which brought many tears, especially for those students whose mothers were not present. Students also celebrated the non-Latino holidays, such as Thanksgiving, St. Patrick's Day, and Valentine's Day, with Ms. López, who would remind students of the meaning of Thanksgiving: "Today is a day which allows all peoples to be thankful, not only for this day, but every day," to which students responded: "We should be thankful to be here in America, and for the teacher we have." Such celebrations served to refuel students, but more importantly, to keep the culture of the students alive, or as Ms. López would say, "to make them aware and proud of who they were." However, as significant as these celebrations were, there were also other issues which arose at the school that were not as controllable.

The fact that different types of Latinos all converged in the school was a new experience for many Latinos accustomed to seeing their own counterparts in their home countries or communities. Intragroup differences between Latinos appeared to become accentuated in school. Physical appearances, language differences, dress, and the like, as well as expressions of closeness or distance, were used to label each other. Irene, for example, remarked:

> The Colombians are *muy orgullosas* (proud); they believe they are the best. There are also some Puerto Ricans who are like that. Some of the girls I can't stand, but not the boys. They are *enamorados* (fall in love easily, lovers) and they are nice and develop friendships easily.

Idiomatic expressions served to create value clashes and conflicts. While on the surface some terms served to bond Latino male students, such as *cabrón* (literally referring to a goat, but also used to refer to a man who is being cuckolded by his wife), *pendejo* (literally meaning "pubic hair," but used to mean "dumb"), or *fregar/joder* (to bother someone, to hassle), they could also be used to jest, be cool, or insult someone. For Puerto Ricans these words were offensive and disrespectful, while for Mexicans and other Central Americans they were acceptable. On the other hand, words such as *contra* (darn it) or *coger* (to take something) used by Puerto Ricans could elicit strong reactions from Mexicans and Central Americans, for whom such words refer to fornication. At other times, language differences resulted in students distancing themselves, being disruptive, confronting, making fun of each other, harassing each other, or saving face.

Irene witnessed a fight between a Puerto Rican student who insulted a Colombian female student on the bus. Colombian students ganged up on the student the moment he got off the bus. She also saw fights erupt between white and black students, where the Latino students were more likely to bond with blacks over whites as a show of solidarity. In the fights between Latinos, Ms. López could arbitrate. For example, when she asked students to do something, some of the Puerto Rican students grumbled under their breath: "¿Porqué carajos tengo que hacer esto?" (Why in the hell do I have to do this?), to which Central Americans would shout across the room: "¿Ya ve, missy, lo que piensan los puertorriqueños?" (Do you see, missy, how Puerto Ricans think?). Ms. López ignored the comment and restated her request.

Even more pernicious was the perceived racism to which Latino students were exposed for the first time when they encountered intragroup differences in the school and the community. On her first day at school, Irene heard, "There was racism from the whites. The projects belong to the whites and the fights are with the blacks." Not surprisingly, her mother would not come to school to meet with teachers and administrators.

Differences between ethnic groups were rarely confronted in the school. It was evident that Latinos knew little or nothing about Chinese people or their culture, and yet were comforted by their presence without having any orientation or explanation about who they were. For many Latinos, Chinese people represented all Asians, so that distinctions between Vietnamese or Cambodians were unknown. Many simply did not know how to relate to Chinese students, since they had become more accustomed to black and white students. Irene remarked:

> You can understand a *moreno* (African American) or *americano* (Anglo), but the Chinese are *frescos, se le pegan a uno* (They are fresh, they come close to you). The Latinos do, too, but when they are of your same country, you understand them.

Mainstream Civics Class

Mr. Laferty's mainstream civics class consisted of 28 students. Of these, 23 were freshmen, 4 were sophomores, and 1 was a junior. Five students were 14-year-olds, eleven were 15-year-olds, eight were 16-year-olds, two were 17-year-olds, and two were 18-year-olds. On any given day, you could expect anywhere from five to seven students to be absent.

Mr. Laferty's class was organized with eight long desk tables, seating four students each, angled at a slant facing the front. A large world map hung on the wall next to the hallway. In one corner of the room, a large golf club (driving wood) stood, and Mr. Laferty used it as a pointer or as an object he could fidget with as he paced around the room, lectured, or conducted question-and-answer periods. On the other wall, notes of the lecture of the day were usually written and these were referred to during class lectures. On the desks of students, one 1983 civics textbook could usually be seen. This textbook presented synoptic factual information on the U.S. form of government. Some of the information was biased and inaccurate. For example, the presentation on the immigration laws of 1880–1924 did not have any explanations of their being directly aimed at the exclusion of Asians. Furthermore, the illustrations represented mostly middle-class whites.[12] One of the illustrations on who is called an American asks: "Aren't the people of Canada, or Mexico or Brazil called Americans too?" This is answered by: "The United States was the first independent nation in the hemisphere. By the time Mexico and other nations won their independence in the 1800s, the 'American' label already had a specific meaning. It means a citizen of the

United States" (*American Civics* [Boston: Harcourt Brace Jovanovich, 1987]). Some historians would argue that citizens of Mexico and Central America also are considered American, as opposed to North American. Class topics focused on issues of government (either local, state, or federal) through whole-group instruction combined with individual seatwork directed to quizzes, exams, and homework. Students learned about court cases, the establishment and function of various forms of government (democracy, dictatorship, etc.) as well as specifics on voting, lobbying, public interest groups, and so on. However, for the Latino students the topics under discussion seemed alien not only in their lives, but because they did not know how to connect with the topics. They answered with single words when drilled. The few occasions in which they seemed engaged were when the content of the lesson dealt specifically with personal issues. Mr. Laferty would comment on an issue: "I'm not going to fight you, but what if . . ." or "The Congress could decide to vote against the President; is there anything that he can do?" or he might say, "Let's assume that you can pass this bill, what would your opposition show?" Using these hypothetical situations, and playing devil's advocate, Mr. Laferty engaged students. On these occasions, Latino students came alive, adding their own ideas to the content and asking questions. However, there was rarely any discussion pertaining to the students' own backgrounds. Issues of what it means to be a citizen of the United States while still being considered a Latino, or the pros and cons of Puerto Rican statehood, were never addressed.

Mr. Laferty met students at the door as they streamed in from the hallway. He waited until they were seated before taking roll call, and after roll call he read the school's announcements. He then lectured from either the front of the class or from his desk in the middle of the room. The lecture was already synthesized into notes written on the blackboard, which were copied by students as Mr. Laferty spoke. As Mr. Laferty moved about the room, he picked up trash from the floor, moved to the back corners of the room, and directed questions from there for homework reviews. Some of the questions were: "Luke here thinks I believe that the government should . . ." and then he would turn to the inattentive student and ask: "What do you think, or say?"

While this strategy was used to elicit students' attention, those used to his style might respond, but those who were not aware of how this strategy functioned, mostly Latinos, simply remained quiet. Another frequently used strategy was reminiscent of a quiz show. Mr. Laferty asked questions such as: "Who were the stars of the movie *Patton*?" "What was the name of John Wayne's last movie?" Although these strategies worked for Mr. Laferty, they were often out of the students' realm, particularly if they were not familiar with quiz show approaches or had not seen *Patton* or the last John Wayne movie.

When students did not respond, Mr. Laferty taunted them. During a class review in which students were silent, he remarked: "You know, it's going to give me great pleasure to put some of you into your third failure this marking period, and you're going to sit there like jerks and let me." While these remarks may have been used to elicit their response, the bolder students spoke while others seemed to be discouraged. Students not paying attention would frequently be ignored by Mr. Laferty, who allowed them to place their heads on the table until the class came to an end. For those who had fallen asleep, he alerted students with comments such as "Luke, the period's over, wake up." Students could also study on their own, but when they were noisy, they could expect to be kicked out of class. When a student did not know a specific word, Mr. Laferty had the student look up the word in the dictionary, a process which took up precious class time. Sometimes the whole period went by before the student explained the definition to the whole class. Other times sarcasm was used to provoke inquiry, as in the following example:

MR. LAFERTY: I apologize to those of you who are trying to learn today for the buffoonery of people like Jerry.
STUDENT: I ain't no buffoon. What's a buffoon?
MR. LAFERTY: There are two dictionaries . . . Look it up.

After one student found the word in the dictionary, it was handed to Jerry, who read it silently as being "idiotic." On another occasion, Mr. Laferty wrote *verbatim* on the board and asked students what they thought it meant. When no one answered, he responded: "For you Latinos, that's Latin, it's a dead language, like some of the minds and bodies in here." While his statement targeted Latinos, others were obviously included. One white student, whose face turned red, was asked by Mr. Laferty: "Are you blushing, or are you part Indian?"

The routines in class were essentially the same each day. Homework was orally reviewed, with students calling out answers for about fifteen to twenty minutes, and then the lecture would commence. If students had not completed their homework assignments Mr. Laferty would forgo this routine. The last ten to fifteen minutes of the class were spent writing down the homework assignment. This was also a cue for "free time," in which Mr. Laferty and the class talked openly about the subject or anything else, and students conversed freely or completed homework to be handed in for other classes. On occasion, when the review of a quiz, test, or homework went poorly, either because students were talking or had not participated, Mr. Laferty would announce that the class was over—students were to "study." Mr. Laferty would open the door, leave the room, go into the hallway, and wait till the bell rang, at which time he would return. During those periods, Latino students maintained a running commentary in Spanish, and although the content of what they said was about their school lives, they sometimes talked about things they didn't want Mr. Laferty to know—having a copy of a test they needed to make up, or girl and boy issues.

Since handraising was rare, students learned to take turns in speaking up. On those occasions, Mr. Laferty conceded the floor and students would be acknowledged with comments such as "OK, you're on, Mr. Martinez," or for the question-and-answer periods he would say, "Let's pick on a Spanish student for this one." When students did not answer questions after ten seconds, Mr. Laferty answered himself. While Mr. Laferty prided himself on being clear, at times he gave mixed messages to his students. On the one hand, he would say, "I don't care if you copy what's on the board. If you don't, I don't care." On the other hand, he would deride students for not doing their homework or studying hard enough for quizzes. Setting low expectations and creating an "us and them" situation within the classroom made it difficult for students to know exactly what to expect. There was a carryover of the "I don't care attitude" message by students who didn't see the point of studying civics:

JOSÉ: I don't care about elected officials . . .
MR. LAFERTY: In response to your not caring, José . . . Why elected officials are important because they affect lives indirectly.

Or:

The fact remains that many citizens are complainers, and when I hear kids like you complain it bothers me because ninety-nine and four one-hundredths don't understand what's going on . . . There are more complainers than doers.

The use of negative reinforcement to elicit responses from students at times resulted in silence, sometimes in partial answers, or at times open contestation manifested through verbal dueling, which would start with retorts, become a heated discussion, and escalate into some type of explosive reaction. The Latino students' use of Spanish, which students knew upset Mr. Laferty, created the most inflammatory situations. Mr. Laferty remarked:

> I resent the fact that you guys who are much smarter than I am and can speak two languages speak Spanish in here. It makes me feel like you're talking behind my back. Look, I'm stupid. I understand English and only English. As a result, I always want to know what's going on in my classroom. So I don't wanna hear a foreign language—foreign to me—spoken in this classroom. And if that upsets you, fine. Go downstairs and complain.

On one occasion when Mr. Laferty overheard Latino students using Spanish, he said: "If you wish to talk in here, you will talk in English . . . if you don't you will go out. That's an ultimatum." Luke snapped back: "He's just saying that 'cause it's his stupid language—go to hell." After calming down, Mr. Laferty responded: "I am sorry, and I am ignorant, plus I am not stupid. There is no need to use swear words in Spanish or English, nor for you to talk behind my back." To which another Latino student responded: "I was born that way . . . I want to talk that way." Mr. Laferty responded in exasperation: "English is the language of this country. You picked the wrong day, you're outta here." As Luke was sent to the dean of discipline, the other students quietly resumed class. On another occasion, Mr. Laferty remarked to one student: "When have you heard me ask you to speak Spanish?" A Latino male student replied: "Never, and I still speak it." Mr. Laferty threw his hands in the air, walked out into the hallway, and said, "I'm going out for peace and quiet. I've had it."

Despite such differences, Mr. Laferty communicated with his students, most often bantering with the Latino males more than with other students, including whites, African Americans, and females. At times, the interchange was amicable, and at other times, it became a heated debate escalating into immediate standoffs. Mr. Laferty joked around with students; however, his attempt at using snide remarks to draw their attention often put students off. Some of the Latino students responded by verbally teasing Mr. Laferty—using only Spanish or acting out. On one occasion, Luke stabbed Mr. Laferty's lunch banana with a pencil while Mr. Laferty was out of the room. Mr. Laferty returned and inquired who the perpetrator was; when no response came he angrily said: "What you don't realize is that you're a disgrace to your families." Luke finally came forth, only to be sent immediately to the office.

On another occasion Mr. Laferty used a Gaelic word, *pugumaho* (which he did not translate), to show that he, too, knew another language as a means to connect up with the Latino students. As he did this, he jestingly made an aside to the researcher: "They're so cocky with their Spanish, let's give them some Gaelic." When Luke first heard the word, he responded, "*Pugumaho* to you, too." Mr. Laferty playfully swatted him on the shoulder, saying, "Hey, I know what you said to me."[13]

Underlying such bantering and retortful exchanges was an expressed sense of mission, values, and morality which Mr. Laferty upheld. From his role as an adult and his authority as a teacher, he thought that what had worked for him would be emulated by his students. For him, students who could not keep the "common rules of decency in a classroom, who did not routinely perform the tasks and assignments given to them, and who used foul language in class" shouldn't be in his class. Thus, when students did not make up their exams on time, Mr. Laferty automatically gave zeros, without realizing that on the days he set up the makeup exams based on his schedule, students could not attend, either because they worked or because they could not take the 6:00 A.M. bus to arrive at school by 7:00 A.M. for the exam.

Mr. Laferty also felt frustrated by his students' general lack of knowledge, especially about Andrew Young or Thurgood Marshall. He was discouraged that even the African American students in his class didn't know who they were. His outrage was evident when he said: "Not only was Thurgood Marshall a justice of the Supreme Court, but he was the first black [to hold that office]." The fact was that unless students had opportunities to learn about such cultural figures directly from their parents or teachers, their only exposures were the schoolwide celebrations held by each cultural club. Each club was responsible for performing, making bulletin displays, or serving special food to celebrate different ethnic groups. Such celebrations took place during Black History Month, Mother's Day, Chinese New Year, and St. Patrick's Day. On St. Patrick's Day, Mr. Laferty wore a green tie and joked about the Irish with students and teachers. His students joined in these celebrations and participated in the clubs or after-school functions, but Luke could not even participate in the Spanish Club since he went to work and then home after school.

Thus, for Mr. Laferty, being present in class, complying with homework assignments, conforming to his standards of behavior, passing quizzes and tests, being compliant and nondisruptive, being good Americans, and having the right disposition and attitude toward learning and home-school values were all criteria he expected students to have in order to pass. Students not adhering to these expectations would not likely experience success. For students who were borderline but showed improvement, particularly during the fourth term, even with accumulated zeros, Mr. Laferty gave the benefit of the doubt and a slight edge. As Mr. Laferty pointed out, he was quite confident that his students were capable of doing the work, and especially the Latino students: "None of these [Latino] kids have an ability problem. They all can do the work, every single one of them. It's a question of will."

ANALYSIS OF BOTH CLASSES, TEACHER AND STUDENT INTERACTIONS, AND TEACHER EXPECTATIONS

To understand the types of situational and contextual issues which might explain the meaning of success and failure for these students, it is necessary to analyze their experiences and interactions embedded within the contexts of their classrooms. "Situating" the students also helps us to understand the role their teachers played as they responded to the structural pressures and bureaucratic culture of the school, which influenced their teaching. Thus, both classrooms are first analyzed for their contributions to opportunities for success, and then the two students' meaning of success are presented. Taken together, Ms. López and Mr. Laferty's classes were distinctively different even though they served Latino students at the same grade levels. Such differences were noted in the types of students, languages used, teacher-student interactions, gender differences, and social and cultural rules that each class maintained.

Ms. López's students came from varied backgrounds and with different skills and knowledge, ranging from no schooling or limited third and fourth grade experiences to basic mathematics exposure. Many of the Latino students from Latin America, particularly war-torn countries such as El Salvador or Guatemala, had either been out of school or attended only from first to third grade. Many of these students had not been exposed to textbooks, workbooks, or instructional materials except those provided by teachers. Thus, their experiences of schooling were basically formed in the United States. Other Latino students, mainly those with families in Puerto Rico, often experienced circular migration, going back and forth as many as four times a year. Thus, their education was in constant adaptation. In contrast, Mr. Laferty's civics class was composed of African American, white, and Latino students, most of whom had been in the system for several years. Even the U.S.-born Latinos in class knew what to expect since they had already been socialized into mainstream classes.

In terms of teaching styles, Ms. López tended to be directive in carefully preparing for her students in each group. She expected students to work independently once she reviewed the concepts in class. Mr. Laferty tended to lecture and then raise questions much as in a college format, giving students tests as a means to assess how much they had learned. Thus, from the perspective of students, Ms. López's style of moving around, working directly with students, and constantly asking questions was viewed as the appropriate form to teach. Mr. Laferty's teaching, on the other hand, was viewed as talking to students since he rarely asked for their opinions but instead voiced his own. This sense of information sharing, whether directive or through talk, became a means by which students categorized their teachers, either as *those who taught* or as *those who only talked*, reviewing information for tests.

Ms. López's social interactions with students on a day-to-day basis could best be described as firm but supportive. Her gregarious, joking demeanor gave way to calm and firm disciplinary action. Students involved in arguments were sent to the office. When the students' lack of discipline and other behavior upset her, she responded by giving them the "cold silent treatment," a practice known to most Latinos from their interactions with their families. Once apologies and recognition of responsibilities were made by the students, Ms. López renewed her interactions with them.

Mr. Laferty's social interactions with his students depended on how he felt that day. On the days Mr. Laferty felt positive or euphoric about something, interactions went smoothly; but on the days he was upset by pressures from the school office, hearing about layoff notices, or by having difficulty with students from the previous class, Mr. Laferty was tense and disinterested. On those days he dismissed class early, walked out into the hallway, or simply sat while students doodled, put their heads down, or dozed off.

At the same time, friction was also evident, with some students more than others, in Mr. Laferty's class. While Luke was quiet most of the time, he erupted whenever speaking Spanish was disregarded or belittled. Students also had a hard time making it to Mr. Laferty's 7:00 A.M. detentions, given the bus schedules, and became upset when Mr. Laferty added other penalties for not being present. In his attempt to make students aware of their own folly, Mr. Laferty's style was often based on negative reinforcement and use of condescension. Remarks such as "When the Spanish connection shuts up down here" or "Why are there so many of you people [referring to Latinos] with a gold tooth?" left students silent.[14] Other remarks, such as "I figure I'm going to get less from you in the future anyway—from all of you. I can see the writing on the wall," portended just such reactions from the students.

Spanish was used extensively in Ms. López's class. Not only were students taught in Spanish with worksheets in Spanish from Latin American textbooks personally procured and paid for by Ms. López, but Spanish was used as the medium of instruction and social life. Students who did not know Spanish well were given basal readers in Spanish; those who used Spanish and English interchangeably were presented with an array of instructional materials at different levels in both languages, and those who had English language skills but needed the security provided by the bilingual class had the option of mastering mathematics using English and Spanish through a variety of tests, including multiple choice. This obviously meant more work in preparation for Ms. López, but it also meant she had more than one way to find out what students knew, how to best align tests for them, and how to pace their learning. Compared to regular basic mathematics classes, where students tend to be more homogeneous and use the same textbook and the same types of drills for whole-group instruction, this class presented multiple challenges.[15]

Mr. Laferty's class, in contrast, was conducted entirely in English, expressive of the modalities of behaviors and values maintained by the teacher, even though the U.S.-born Latinos reverted to speaking Spanish as the norm. Here the issue of language did seem to be related not only to class differences, in that Mr. Laferty came from a white, middle-class background and his Latino students came mostly from working-class backgrounds, but also to the status differences of English and Spanish, where English is a high-status language and Spanish is viewed as low-status. When asked directly about why they used Spanish knowingly if it irritated and upset Mr. Laferty, Latino students including Luke responded by saying: "It's because it's our language."

Clearly Latino students in his class perceived the use of Spanish as a right and privilege which they could use in the hallways and in class. The comments and side remarks they made in Spanish seemed appropriate to them, yet for Mr. Laferty the use of Spanish was perceived as a direct affront, as a denial of his power, as backstabbing, and most importantly, as loss of control. For Luke, using Spanish was a way he expressed his identity, but for Mr. Laferty the use of Spanish instead of English was perceived as rude, exclusive, and an infringement of his authority, especially because he did not speak Spanish nor did he have a clue as to what was being said.

While both teachers acknowledged the need to incorporate culture into the lives of their students, Ms. López generally understood the Latino cultures her students came with, whereas Mr. Laferty hardly knew anything about his students' backgrounds. Ms. López demonstrated a great deal of cultural sensitivity in that she taught students to be proud of their cultures and themselves and to honor their own culture and that of the United States. At the same time, Ms. López was conscious of the common traditional values that many of the students brought with them from their home countries and the value conflicts some were experiencing in their newfound culture. Values regarding sexual behaviors and courtship patterns were differentiated along immigrant, rural, and urban lines by males and females.[16] Thus, Ms. López was constantly helping students to negotiate between their own cultures from their home countries or homes and those they were learning in school.

In contrast, Mr. Laferty's role as a cultural broker was to emphasize culture to his students through his own assimilationist lens and his value experiences, mostly developed from a middle-class Irish American perspective. Mr. Laferty did not really share much in common with his students and, given his own upbringing, had set ideas of how they should succeed in the United States, and in particular in his class.

His views on bilingual education shed light about his own understanding of bilingual students. Mr. Laferty believed that bilingual classes did not allow students to become absorbed into "the national picture of the U.S. as a melting pot." He understood people wanting to preserve their ethnic backgrounds, but he was opposed to the idea that it should be through bilingual education at the taxpayers' expense. Moreover, he felt that such classes lowered expectations and academic standards, which only placed Latino students at a disadvantage compared to other students. Moreover, he felt bilingual education gave special rules for people based on their ethnic background. In his classroom, "All students have to adhere to the standards I set in this room; and they all have to pass under the same rules and regulations."

Such differences in incorporating language and culture raised questions about how students situated themselves in each class. Irene, on the one hand, received a great deal of reinforcement of Latino basic values and cultural norms through her peers and Ms. López's efforts; she also was learning how to adapt both value systems, as a sense of her future survival and success. Luke, on the other hand, was constantly reminded by Mr. Laferty that in order to "fit" into the mainstream culture, he could not use his native language or rely on his culture if he expected to succeed.

Gender issues regarding males were curiously treated the same by Ms. López and Mr. Laferty, who recognized male students more often and paid greater attention to their demands. In Ms. López's class, male students received the lion's share of her attention through their boisterous and demanding behaviors, shouting across the room, screaming out of turn, talking while Ms. López taught, or simply misbehaving and upsetting the tenor of the class. Girls, by contrast, were compliant, tended to be quiet, stuck more to themselves, and were absorbed with primping behaviors—putting on makeup, straightening their clothes, cleaning their desks, and so on. The few occasions on which girls openly sought Ms. López were for help about specific "female issues," boy problems, or issues with their parents.

Because Mr. Laferty's class had one of the highest concentrations of Latinos in a mainstream class, Latinos were proportionately called upon more frequently than other students. His class reflected a more prevalent male culture, partly because his class was composed mostly of more males than females and because males engaged in outspoken, heavy verbal jest and ribbing to gain Mr. Laferty's attention. Female students, while treated respectfully by Mr. Laferty—who insisted males treat girls fairly—were placed at a social distance.

Ms. López maintained a personal role outside of the school and a professional role within the school. She became one of the few anchors for her students and their demands. At any given moment, she might take a student who thought he might have a sexually transmitted disease to a clinic, or she might intervene in an argument between mother and daughter, or defend students in court, or simply feed students and their families when they had no food. She responded immediately and directed her attention to those most in need. But within the school, Ms. López's role was precarious. As part of the bilingual staff of the school, Ms. López interacted with the mainstream teachers, helping them to pace students with language and behavioral issues, but she was also quite protective of her students. Although highly esteemed within the bilingual program, she was considered "too caring" of her students by many of the mainstream teachers—an issue which set her apart from them. Her nurturing was often seen as "solicitous" and she was shunned by some teachers for teaching after school, seeking parents, and defending her students. Within the bilingual program, Ms. López stood out as a leader by running the Spanish Club, counseling students, teaching after school, and creating new projects with the students and teachers. The fact that the principal relied heavily on her advice, translation with parents, and views on bilingual students had garnered her a place within the school as an irreplaceable member whose position was secure, yet she was perceived as a threat by her own peers who saw her as having too much power and influence.

Mr. Laferty also had a significant role within the school. However, tensions for Mr. Laferty were derived from the changing tides in administration. From day to day he did not know how long he would be at the school, making his situation tenuous, even though Mr. Laferty was part of the network of senior teachers, had earned a special place within the teachers' union, and had contributed widely to teacher stability and union rules at the school. Despite such successes, Mr. Laferty's situation was vulnerable since he had been moved around, displaced, and could expect to receive a "pink slip" (notification of loss of job) or be bumped into another school. He felt the administration devalued teachers' work. This lack of stability made his classroom a site where many of these pressures became evident. Latino students' refusing to use English made the antagonism even more apparent, since Mr. Laferty had little control over his life outside of the classroom.

Attempting to maintain such control, Mr. Laferty insisted on Latino students' speaking English, learning civics, and becoming Americanized as the major modalities of success. These were all controllable concerns. Lacking was understanding the role that status of the students' language and their culture had within the school's dominant and subordinate relationships. More important is the degree to which Spanish tends to be devalued within such school settings. This was certainly the case with Irish Gaelic speakers at the turn of the century, who left their brogue behind in order to adopt the English of the Anglos. The Latinos in Mr. Laferty's class, as the nondominant students, also suffered the experience of language denial and rejection much as Mr. Laferty's ancestors did. But unlike the African American students in the class who were racially visible and used English, these U.S.-born Latinos were racially invisible but became visible through their use of Spanish, despite the expectation that they use only English as the medium of communication. When they resisted, they became scapegoats.

Such scapegoating can be explained as the deflection of stresses and the teachers' inabilities to deal with the inordinate demands they had on a daily basis, yet a deeper explanation may be found in the analysis of the multiple pressures which the institution exerted on Mr. Laferty and his teaching. Mr. Laferty's remarks can be construed as being snide, sarcastic, and even discriminatory, bordering on racist.[17] Yet such a denouncement would be one-sided and would not explain why Mr. Laferty demonstrated any caring for his students, willingness to be flexible, or meeting their needs. Through our research we witnessed such concern and care on several occasions.[18] Mr. Laferty felt he treated students equally. He let students know he was available to talk with them after school when they needed help, and was quite baffled when they did not show up or take advantage of his offers for help. He was aware that his responses might misinterpret some cultural nuances for Latinos, which he admitted might be out of ignorance, but he was open to learning about Hispanic cultures and becoming a more effective teacher.[19]

Observations of Mr. Laferty's demeanor beyond his class, within the school, are indicative of a teacher highly regarded by his peers. Mr. Laferty was not an ill-intentioned or negative person, but he did share the same color-blind perspective of many of his white peers who believed they were doing the best for their students by treating them "all the same." Such assumptions belied the fact that Mr. Laferty and his mainstream peers embodied the very power structure of the school, seasoned with over twenty years of teaching experience at the same school, coming from European ethnic groups, and enjoying white privilege. Until 1991, the top administration of the school had always been white, and the student body, while diverse, was bused into a community which was not their own due to desegregation plans which had been in force since 1974. Students at Townsend conformed to the policies and cultural traditions which had been developed at the school since that era, and teachers like Mr. Laferty were encapsulated in a cultural milieu which had not changed with the shifting demographics, despite the introduction of bilingual and special needs students and teachers to the school. Mr. Laferty's responses, based on his teaching and example, were to assimilate and educate students through Americanization. Yet he was unaware of who his students were and what they needed. His concern for students was colored by his own interpretations of success and his family's ideology of hard work. He did not understand that students in his class were totally different from those he taught during the 1970s, and that the demands of schooling, knowledge, and basic skills for academic achievement for his current students were greater. Furthermore, it is my contention that Mr. Laferty's issues about Spanish and maintaining control in his class had less to do with discrimination and racism and more to do with a white teacher's lack of recognition of the shifts in cultural paradigms for himself and his students. In some respects, Mr. Laferty could be professionally trained to understand how his students were different, that the groupings he had been accustomed to had now shifted from being homogeneous to heterogeneous, that in addition to the language he was responsible for using in the past he now needed to consider the multiple languages his students brought to class, that the power differences created by competing within a job ladder now meant competing with bilingual teachers, and that the security and seniority of his job now was being shared with new teachers of different types of learners. Yet such training was not available even though Townsend was undergoing school-based management.

In essence, Mr. Laferty's sense of success was based on his specific vision about becoming American and using English. His rejection of Spanish in an all-English-speaking environment and culture was symptomatic of the fear that students might use Spanish to swear and say things behind his back that he would not be able to control. Thus, in Mr. Laferty's class Latino students were required to shed their language and culture and adapt to his defined norms of success as the only available route.

Success for Ms. López, however, was based less on being recognized by the school and more on how she succeeded and advanced her professional career through credentials in a system which viewed bilingual teachers as interlopers and minorities which were not fully integrated. "To advance despite adversity" was the message she transmitted to her students. Their success, she believed, began with their own self-respect and engagement in learning, and with the support of teachers who were willing to understand their culture, and model that commitment through honest teaching and care. As she often said, "Their [Latino students'] success is my success, and their fate is my fate." Thus, Ms. López's role in the success of her students was both as a mediator of culture and language and as an advocate within the school. In Ms. López's class the teacher was the negotiator of the Anglo culture and their own, whereas in Mr. Laferty's there was no negotiation, simply accommodation and adaptation to a monocultural and monolingual norm. Such dualities along language lines represent the very dualities that existed between the bilingual and mainstream programs.

THE STUDENTS' DEFINITIONS OF SUCCESS

In the analysis of both students' meaning of success, it is clear that Irene adapted readily to meeting Ms. López's academic requirements since the first days in class. She attended class every day, completed her homework, and submitted her written work. She also dutifully followed what she was told, although she sometimes read letters in class from her friends and spent at least five minutes each day applying makeup. She used her primping, chatting, and emulating of Ms. López's own femininity as a ready means to step into the social culture of the classroom, where she was accepted and liked. She also used her time carefully, leaving her homework until the evening when she could get help from her neighbor, and using the time in school to socialize with her peers. In essence, Irene learned to balance the academic and social dimensions of her school life quite well in comparison to the more sedate and confined existence she had at home. On the one hand, Townsend provided Irene with greater freedom than she had at home, and on the other hand, Irene complied with her mother's religious and social demands at home. In this respect, Irene had no reason to rebel. She was able to conform at home, since she had established a social and cultural network which sustained her at school. In the final analysis she was able to fit the expected behavior of completing high school while at the same time becoming a mother.

Luke, on the other hand, struggled to maintain any such balance. Although clearly aware that he needed to attend school, get good grades, and be attentive in class in order to "succeed," he responded with sporadic attendance, did not keep up with the assignments, did not take tests, showed disrespect, and had poor grades. Luke complied by attending and being physically present at school, but he hooked[20] (cut classes) every opportunity he had, to relieve some of the pressures at school, even though he was aware of the consequences. His own belief was "People who hook are people who don't do good, don't care about the school." His grades were also totally inconsistent, with F's in general social science classes and English, and B-pluses in math, communication, and personal growth. In one term his test grades varied from 60 to 87 points, making his academic attempts look feeble.

Unmotivated after working eighteen hours a week after school, Luke came home tired and watched television instead of completing assignments. Yet just as the marking periods were ending, Luke would apply himself and study. One of the researchers in our team helped Luke with his academic work, which he appreciated, especially after receiving advance warnings that he might fail during the third marking period. Such support was not evident at home. Luke attempted to please his family by "being a good student" and "complying—studying for tests, and getting good grades," but his mother's constant complaints made him feel unsuccessful as well. She complained about his education at Townsend and made comparisons with her own education in Puerto Rico; she also complained about the violence in the community and the lack of safety in the school, and kept Luke home every time there was a ruckus at school. Such complaints and actions gave Luke reason to doubt the advantages that the school offered him. Thus, it appears that the meaning of success for Luke was more likely determined by his prowess to "outwit the system" than by complying with the demands placed upon him. Luke could study under pressure, but he did so as a last ditch effort. Luke also knowingly challenged Mr. Laferty, by using Spanish in civics class, despite Mr. Laferty's continuous threats and belittling remarks. While he was aware that using Spanish placed him at a disadvantage, such opposition seemed to reflect his resistance to the imposed culture of the classroom; it was one of the few arenas which Luke controlled. How far such resistance served Luke's personal and future interests, especially when he failed civics, does raise several questions: Did Luke intentionally set himself up? Were his skills so limited that his outward behavior was to cloak his own fears, and in turn, immobilize his learning? Or were the messages of his mother and Mr. Laferty self-fulfilling prophecies? While Luke was determined on all counts to complete the school year and go on to the next grade, it is not likely that most students would succeed against the odds which Luke faced.

THE SPIRAL EFFECTS OF AFFECTIVE DISSONANCE AND SOCIAL CONSTRUCTION OF SUCCESS

In retrospect, both Irene's and Luke's outcomes raise several obvious questions: What are the intrinsic meanings of success for students like Irene and Luke? Under what conditions are their own meanings of success accepted? How might Irene and Luke have balanced the academic demands of their classes and the demands of their families given the situational context and interactional dynamics of each class and of home? How does the legitimacy and identity of language and culture affect Latino students' opportunities to succeed? Using De Vos and Suárez-Orozco's (1990) notions of ego rigidification and affective dissonance as well as the dual frames of reference which Suárez-Orozco characterizes for immigrants, and Trueba's concept of social construction of success, the situations of both of these students were analyzed.

Irene's success was more closely aligned with that of an immigrant, in that her adaptation was helped in many ways by the fact that she grew up in Puerto Rico with the social and cultural capital of her Latino culture and family. Her social construction of success was based on what had been traditionally accepted in her family—the role of feminine women, beauty, and motherhood. Such exposure gave her the confidence to make her transition into the mainstream culture a smooth one. Luke, by contrast, had been exposed to the erosion of his own culture and language in U. S. schools over the years. His social construction of success was based on how he constructed his own identity which was closely linked to the use of Spanish. Yet it was this very identity which was silenced in his school, especially during his adolescent years. Thus, the growing and spiraling sense of failure he experienced is much like that which befalls involuntary minorities, in that the social, economic, and academic ceiling of opportunity is viewed as not being readily accessible or sustainable. His major basis of control and power, despite his academic standing, was his use of Spanish, but even that became contested terrain in Mr. Laferty's class. One needs to question, What is being lost by having students use Spanish as a social means of communication in English-based classrooms? While the answer may be nothing but control, the issue points to how Townsend, as an institution, responded to students like Luke and Irene through policies and practices. If students were to experience success at Townsend, they needed to have the opportunities to construct that identity of success.

First, like most high schools, Townsend used the label *Hispanic* as a monolithic term generically applied to all Spanish-speaking and monolingual students with Hispanic backgrounds. Yet this was confusing, in that even though Townsend provided the context in which diverse Latinos converged for the first time, in ways that might not have occurred in their countries of origin or even in their communities, it did so disregarding the variability that existed within each Latino group, and the identities which many Latino students might have chosen for themselves. For immigrants, being "Hispanic" became a newfound experience in school, since many preferred to use their nationality as their identity. But to apply the same rubric to cases like Irene's and Luke's, who as Puerto Rican migrants were categorized in ways which did not aptly represent their situations, created an identity quagmire. Mainstream teachers at

Townsend tended to identify Puerto Ricans as Hispanics because of their use of Spanish, and the administration included them in their Hispanic quotas, but as nonimmigrants Puerto Ricans share a distinct status with Anglos by virtue of being U.S. citizens. These subtle distinctions were undetected by the teachers, who relegated Puerto Rican students to being like other Latinos. Only those teachers, some of whom were in the bilingual program, and administrators who were willing to explore and learn about their students' backgrounds and languages could become privy to such experiences. Even more significant was how Puerto Ricans, whether island- or U.S.-born, were perceived by their Latino counterparts. For many Central and South Americans, encountering Puerto Ricans in the school as an extension of Latino cultures was a new experience.

Second, the school did not include time for personal interactions in its academic agenda. Personal interactions occurred either early in the morning as buses arrived, or after school, and only in those cases where teachers decided to break union rules by staying after school to meet with students. The lack of built-in social time beyond celebrations did not allow teachers to know their students. Furthermore, such divisions between what constituted academic and social time paralleled the same divisions that students experienced between their own communities and the school and similarly what their own parents felt. The values, language, and cultural learning that the students should have brought to school remained at home, except for the occasional school celebration or festivity in which the students' ethnicity was displayed in front hall exhibits, or through dance performances or food presentations. Rarely were the cultural values of students included as part of the curriculum or the instructional program.

Third, the realities of Latino students' lives were rarely known. Since teachers had few facts on hand, limited access to undocumented student records, limited contact with parents, and few references to other successful cases which would help them respond more appropriately to these students, they relied on hearsay. The opinions of teachers were used in the assessment of Latino students, rather than facts from complete student profiles. Latino students became characterized by test scores for reading, math, and English-speaking proficiency—achievement scores and grades—instead of focused knowledge to explain whether those students could read and write, had been in schools, had come from urban environments or rural areas, knew their way around, and were in extended or single-headed households.

Fourth, the perceptions which teachers, administrators, and staff held about Latinos were often misfounded. Such perceptions shaped the environment in which the Latino high school students succeeded or failed. Even though over 50 percent of the administrators, teachers, and staff interviewed in Townsend reported Latino students were perceived as being positive, using adjectives such as "friendly, outgoing, courteous, and respectful," several others mentioned Latinos were also perceived as being "lazy, cliquish, and potential dropouts." In the absence of factual and complete student profiles and informed awareness of cultural differences, negative images of Latinos weighed heavily in their assessment and created color blindness. Such images set up rank orders and hierarchies in which Puerto Ricans were identified by some of the school personnel as being below other Latinos in academic performance and social adaptation. Indeed, a comment from Mr. Laferty represented the common and widespread generalization of other teachers in the school:

> Hispanic students from other environments and other countries—these seem to be more of a mix, where you have strong familial ties and strong familial influences. And they just seem to be more into the work ethic . . . It's my experience in the system, not just here at this high school. I've dealt with Colombians, Ecuadoreans, Venezuelans, Costa Ricans, Hondurans, and probably kids from other countries that I'm not aware of, and had far more success in at least getting them to do what you would expect an average high school kid to do. I find the biggest line of resistance coming, in my personal experience, from the Puerto Rican community . . . I find a much higher failure rate among the Hispanics from the island of Puerto Rico than I do from any other part of North America.

Fifth, this self-fulfilling prophecy of failure engendered negativism which contributed to lack of support for Latino students on the part of teachers and administrators. Townsend teachers and administrators believed that assimilation into the dominant culture for Latinos was dependent on their adaptive behaviors. For some of the teachers, the longer Latino students were in the States, the quicker they adopted certain negative attitudes. In fact, the shared belief was students were fine until they became Americanized. Such a process of "Americanization," they believed, could occur within a matter of months, and definitely within a school year, and it occurred for immigrants as well as for second-generation Puerto Ricans. Thus, becoming "Americanized" in this case embodied displaying lazy behavior, disrespect for adults and peers, and not taking school seriously, the very antithesis of its democratic meaning.

A CALL TO ACTION

All of this requires a call to action about the very democratic principles and values which teachers believe are being embodied in becoming American. Not understanding the complexities of acculturation and assimilation, a cycle of negativism is contextually kept alive by unfounded and biased perceptions of single individual situations applied to Latino groups. Trapped in this pattern of negativism, Latino students respond through silent, passive responses; to active rebellion in the form of cutting classes, leaving school, hookin', engaging in verbal dueling and escalating retorts with teachers; to the final statement of resistance—dropping out. Such expressions are about contestation, identity, and power, and in these situations, it may well be that the students who speak Spanish view themselves as having power over their limited monocultural/monolingual teachers. With such limited choices, students fall into the very self-fulfilling pattern which they openly protest. Instead of being proactive, acting with reasoned thinking, being compliant with the teachers' rules, or colluding by simply being quiet, some Latino students resist by acting out of default. In so doing, some "shoot themselves in the foot." Students in these situations lack the awareness and knowledge of how they contribute to setting up no-win situations, and the results come as a surprise. If there are teachers like Ms. López around, students receive some advice and support; otherwise, they are on their own. Thus, dropping out and failing become a form of liberation, rather than annihilation, after experiencing several frustrated attempts at "succeeding."

The effects of this downward spiral have implications which extend far beyond single student situations of resistance, reaction, and control. A school's mission is to keep the school safe, and to do this, policies are created to keep out-of-control situations in check. A reactionary cycle for control on the part of the administration and teachers sets in at the same time that students clamor for recognition and legitimacy. Teachers not knowing what to do revert to controlling their students, through lock-step policies and decisions from the administration which students, parents, and other teachers cannot override. They clamor for behavior codes and conformity to rules. Such a cycle does not reinforce respect for what the students bring nor does it help students understand what is clearly expected of them. Instead, the need to *control* rather than to *educate* such students prevails over the best intentions of teachers and administrators, and it intensifies and sets into motion a cycle of repression, reaction, and failure. The consequences of maintaining this kind of cycle intact left Irene and Luke not knowing what they could truly call their own in Townsend.

CONCLUSION

Being successful in American high schools requires more than academic know-how: it also requires specific dominant mainstream knowledge, skills, and attitudes regarding how institutional structures explicitly and implicitly operate. Being Latino in such a system requires that one learn not only the explicit rules of the mainstream dominant culture, but more importantly, the implicit know-how that allows one to navigate the school system. Success in this sense has more to with the attitudes and perceptions which teachers and administrators have of Latinos—how they are perceived, how they are acculturated, how Spanish is accepted and given status, how students conform to school, how well they behave in the classroom, deal with teacher interactions, and engage in the curriculum—than what they bring from home. How well Latinos "fit" the current system becomes the overriding measure of their success from the perspective of mainstream educators. Yet for Latinos, how well they balance the social and academic demands of their own native culture and language with the demands of the dominant culture, how well they develop personal relationships of meaning with their teachers and administrators, how well they use the power of their own language in social ways, how well they learn to cope with the cumulative sense of failure they experience versus opportunities for success, and how well they are supported to seek those opportunities become the internalized meanings of their success.

This study's analysis suggests that while teachers like Ms. López may enhance the learning of Latino students because of the cultural and linguistic matches and the positive climate which has evolved in and out of her classroom, the situation in which students find themselves when they come to school, or are mainstreamed into a class like Mr. Laferty's, requires they be able to negotiate through the rules and regulations and demands of the school using their own and limited resources for "making it." What this requires for some students is being able to first and foremost speak their mother tongue in social ways, and in other cases, finding advocates and supportive teachers who will enhance their chances and teach them about the implicit culture of schooling. Identifying the perceptions and attitudes of high school educators who—even though they may be well intentioned and caring yet are fearful of losing control and their jobs—denigrate, scapegoat, and isolate Latinos is another way that the negativism which these students experience can be reduced. Inservice training of the realities of such students' lives and the composite re-creation of social identities that they go through in American schooling is yet another way to reach their teachers.

Schooling as presently formulated by its "deep structure" consisting of "the physical uniformity of classrooms, overall control orientation of policy, program, and pedagogy; the general similarity of curriculum and of schedule; the reliance on test scores as measure of 'success;' and the practice of tracking . . ." (Benham Tye, 1987, p. 281) tends to be not only tedious, boring, and unexciting, but pedagogically irrelevant for these students. It is not surprising that the concrete experiences rendered by work after school may be a greater enticement than schooling.

Required of schools like Townsend to become attractive for students like Irene and Luke are the following: (1) Deconstructing the ways in which schools erode Latino students' identity, language and culture and historical situatedness may result in engagement in learning. Thus, identifying the ways Latino students currently cope well within the institution is a beginning. Also required are (2) acknowledging the use of native language so that students like Luke, who continue to struggle despite mounting odds, can be validated even through their use of Spanish, which is one of the few arenas they can fully control; (3) supporting and maintaining core values from the home, where such values can be openly discussed and acknowledged, as the new values come into play in their lives; (4) finding advocates who will support student endeavors and will speak for them; and (5) developing a professional workforce that is more sensitive, sensible, and responsive to their issues.

Townsend's school philosophy emphasized "opportunities [which were] . . . flexible, continuous, and meaningful" and a curriculum which strove "to accentuate free thinking and creativity on the part of the student in order to assist in the development of the powers of observation, imagination, and reasoning." Where in this philosophy were the needs of Latino students represented? Instead, a spiral of embedded negativism prevailed, where Latino students faced the bureaucratic maze of a school burdened with stressed, fearful, and burned-out teachers, except for those who "lived the lives of their students." In this spiral, students readily became scapegoats, particularly for teachers who had difficulty in accepting the changes brought on by shifting demographics, and facing their own situations within the institutional changes. Through this traditional philosophy, Latino students were viewed as raw inputs into an impersonal system in which they were expected to academically achieve through completion of grades K-12. To that end, administrators, faculty, and staff were concerned about making sure Latino students "fit and fulfill" the criteria laid out for them to constitute appropriate outputs of the system and success. This is an outdated and ineffective image. Latinos do not wish to continue to support such outcomes, but rather foster an image of success gained from negotiating different cultural and linguistic needs, building personal relationships with teachers, curricular structures which include their experiences, a sense of obligation, responsibilities and respect to self, the group, and others, and the advocacy of teachers to ensure their well-being. This is the socially constructed image of success that is needed.

NOTES

The research for this study was made possible through a grant from the Inter-University program for Latino Research and the Social Research Council during 1989–1990. Subsequent research was conducted on a volunteer basis during 1990–1994.

I would also like to acknowledge the participation of Dr. David Whitenack of Stanford University and Dr. Ada Gonzalez, a practicing psychotherapist in Boston, who at the time of this study were my research assistants. Their ideas and contributions are recognized for their significance.

I also want to thank Ms. López and Mr. Laferty, as well as Irene and Luke and their mothers, whose names appear as pseudonyms for reasons of confidentiality. Without your sharing of knowledge, your struggles and wisdom, none of this research would be possible. *Mil gracias.*

[1] See Carola Suárez-Orozco and Marcelo Suárez-Orozco's *Transformations: Migration, Family Life, and Achievement Motivation among Latino Adolescents* (Stanford, CA: Stanford University Press, 1995), and Maria Eugenia Matute-Bianchi's article "Situational Ethnicity and Patterns of School Performance among Immigrant and Nonimmigrant Mexican-Descent Students," in Margaret Gibson and John Ogbu (Eds.), *Minority Status and Schooling: A Comparative Study of Immigrant and Involuntary Minorities* (New York: Garland, 1991), for an extensive in-depth review comparing immigrant and U.S.-born Latinos.

[2] The Latino population at this school numbered close to 250 and of these about 135 were in bilingual classes while the rest were in mainstream or regular classes.

Demystifying the Images of Latinos 197

³Beginning in 1988–1989, a six-year qualitative research study in different states took place at a Boston-based high school. The quantitative and qualitative collaborative study with Townsend teachers arose from their concerns about student absenteeism at their school. Over 150 students from all ethnic backgrounds and over 45 teachers were interviewed. The findings from this initial study indicated that Asian students had the highest attendance, followed by Latinos and blacks, and whites had the lowest attendance even though many came from the neighboring community. Attendance overall was higher for students in the bilingual program than for students in regular mainstream classes, and Latino students reported feeling safer, more cared for, and understood in bilingual than mainstream classes (Collaborative Inquiry of Townsend High School and Harvard Graduate School of Education School Experienced Teachers' Program, unpublished report, 1989).

⁴Data from the potentially at-risk Latino students had been extensively collected to include the school policies and practices, the classroom contexts, student and teacher backgrounds, and parent aspirations. Thus, the raw data were analyzed for the purpose of this chapter.

⁵The Lau categories grew out of the Lau vs. Nichols ruling in California, which guarantees the right to be educated in a language that allows you to compete in school. The categories refer to levels of English exposure from I to IV before being entirely mainstreamed.

⁶The English class Irene referred to had a teacher who did not allow students to use Spanish or other native languages. If students were caught they had to write 150 times on the board that they would not use their native languages. Two years after Irene completed high school, this teacher's contract was not renewed.

⁷In 1993, Ms. López left Townsend for Snedden High School, leaving the low morale of the school behind. Conflicts with one of the bilingual teachers became overbearing, and she felt unappreciated by the new principal, who leaned on her heavily with bilingual students and families but did not promote her during her last two years at Townsend. Yet in the years Ms. López was at Townsend High, she was highly regarded especially by her peers, her students, and their parents. Today, Ms. López is a lead teacher and an assistant headmaster at Snedden, where she has found a niche.

⁸The Lau categories range from 1 to 5, with the lowest level of English proficiency being at level 1 and the highest at level 5, at which point students could simply be totally mainstreamed (have all of their classes in English). In Luke's case, at level 4, he needed reinforcement in English skills.

⁹Luke was absent 28 times during the four terms, along with the other three Latino students of this study who averaged 28.5 absences. During the last quarter, Luke was absent 3 times.

[10]Recognizing that teachers tend to use the repertoires by which they were socialized, it may be that Ms. López was using repertoires which are common in Costa Rican schools. The "indirect" form of making requests, or admonishing behavior using metaphors and terms of endearment when being firm, are commonly used in Costa Rican schools.

[11]The faculty complained that Ms. López was breaking union rules and she was therefore not allowed to keep many of the after-school activities the following year. A graduate student replaced her and tutored students after school; however, without the same degree of vigilance two of the female students became pregnant.

[12]Tallies on the civics textbook in terms of its illustrations indicated that the total number of illustrations (40) in three different units of the book per category were as follows: men of color in leadership roles (2); women of color in leadership roles (1); white men in leadership roles (7); white women in leadership roles (7); whites and people of color (35); whites only (37); people of color only (13).

[13]In fact, it became clear after checking with Mr. Laferty that he did not know the meaning of *pugumaho* which he used so gingerly. In checking its meaning with Gaelic speakers, *pugumaho* is used to mean "kiss my behind."

[14]This reference to a Latino student's use of a gold tooth prompted other students to say it was fashionable, but one student made the comment that it was to identify you as a gang member. At that point, the jesting proved to be too much for the student with the gold tooth; one week later, he had pulled it out.

[15]The one arena where Ms. López was not in agreement with her students was when she insisted on using Costa Rican terms over Puerto Rican terms for objects, such as *bus* for *la guagua* (the bus), and colors such as *purpura* for violet (purple). She corrected Puerto Rican Spanish speakers by insisting they use the final *d* and *r* at the ends of words, which Puerto Rican speakers tend to drop, and also to substitute *r* with *l* when they speak. Ms. López also insisted that students use the mathematical notation she had learned in Costa Rica which is extensively used throughout Central America and Mexico (e.g., $8 \times 24 =$ for multiplication or $824 \div 7$ for division, rather than the methods which had been taught to Puerto Ricans which are displayed as follows:

$$24 \times 8 = \text{(multiplication)}$$

$$7 \overline{)824} \text{ (division)}$$

While these demands appeared to be lingusitic in nature, they had more to do with class differences than language per se, and with Ms. López's maintaining her middle-class status among her students and other Spanish-speaking teachers.

[16]For some of the immigrant male students, expressing *piropos* (flattering verbal remarks) to girls in the hallways, while commonplace in their countries of origin, created difficulties among their U.S.-born Latino friends and Anglos who

did not accept such expressions. Similarly, distinguishing between virgins and marriageable girls from *libertinas*, loose or promiscuous girls who wore tight-fitting clothes and heavy makeup in school, were criteria which the immigrant male students upheld but which the more urban and U.S.-born Latinos were not as concerned with. For most of the Latinas there was a newfound freedom from their traditional values which they experienced in school, and welcomed. For some, this gave them permission to experiment, but for others, like some of the immigrant Latinas, the degree of push and pull of familial bonds and obligations, the hold their parents had on them, and their degree of religiosity, determined their conformity, adaptation, or resistance.

[17]The notion of unintended racism may be pertinent here because it seems to be a common phenomenon among white educators who, in the best interest of students, attempt to teach using the practice from which they themselves learned. However, much of that practice is embedded within dominant mainstream cultural values derived from a Eurocentric perspective and class paradigm.

[18]Mr. Laferty often conveyed how touched he was by students' comments when they felt helped by him. On several occasions, we saw him shed tears.

[19]As a researcher one wonders why a teacher would even agree to have people in his classroom for a whole year, if not to uncover ways in which to better his own teaching and schoolwork.

[20]The notion of *hookin'* was identified by David Whitenack while he was a research assistant collecting data for this study. Hookin' refers to actually cutting class, missing a specific class, and cutting all day, but it does not refer to dropping out of school or being off the premises of the school. From the students' comments, they were concerned about the degree of hookin' which might cause them to fail, and readily understood that attendance equaled passing all classes and hookin' equaled failure.

REFERENCES

Benham Tye, B. (1987, December). The deep structure of schooling. *Phi Delta Kappan,* pp. 218–283.

Cazden, C., Hymes, D., & John, V. (1972). *Functions of language in the classroom.* New York: Teachers' College.

Coleman, J. (1987). Families and schools. *Educational Researcher, 16*(6), 32–38.

Cummins, J. (1986). Empowering minority students: A framework for intervention. *Harvard Educational Review, 56,* 18–36.

Darder, A., & Upshur, C. C. (1993). What do Latino children need to succeed in school? A study of four Boston public schools. In R. Rivera & S. Nieto

(Eds.), *The education of Latino students in Massachusetts: Issues, research, and policy implications* (pp. 127–146). Boston: University of Massachusetts, Mauricio Gastón Institute for Latino Community Development and Public Policy.

De Vos, G., & Suárez-Orozco, M. (1990). *Status inequality: The self in culture.* Newbury Park, CA: Sage.

Erickson, F. (1991). Conceptions of school culture: An overview. In N. Wyner (Ed.), *Current perspectives on the culture of schools* (pp. 1–12). Brookline, MA: Brookline Books.

Erickson, F., & Mohatt, G. (1982). Cultural organization of participation structures in two classrooms of Indian students. In G. Spindler (Ed.), *Doing the ethnography of schooling* (pp. 133–174). New York: Holt, Rinehart, and Winston.

Fine, M. (1990). Making controversy: Who's at risk? *Journal of Urban and Cultural Studies, 1*(1), 55–68.

Gibson, M., & Ogbu, J. (1991). *Minority status and schooling: A comparative study of immigrant and involuntary minorities.* New York: Garland.

Gumperz, J. (1980). Conversational inference and classroom learning. In J. L. Green & C. Wallat (Eds.), *Ethnography approaches to face to face interaction in educational settings* (pp. 3–43). Norwood, NJ: Ablex.

Matute-Bianchi, M. E. (1991). Situational ethnicity and patterns of school performance among immigrant and nonimmigrant Mexican-descent students. In M. A. Gibson & J. U. Ogbu (Eds.), *Minority status and schooling: A comparative study of immigrant and involuntrary minorities* (pp. 205–248). New York: Garland.

McDermott, R. (1989). Making dropouts. In H. Trueba, G. Spindler, & L. Spindler (Eds.), *What do anthropologists have to say about dropouts?* (pp. 16–26). New York: Falmer Press.

Mehan, H., Villanueva, I., Hubbard, L., & Lintz, A. (1996). *Constructing school success.* New York: Cambridge University Press.

Montero-Sieburth, M. (1993). The effects of schooling processes and practices on potential "at risk" Latino high school students. In R. Rivera & S. Nieto (Eds.), *The education of Latino students in Massachusetts: Issues, research, and policy implications* (pp. 217–239). Boston: University of Massachusetts, Mauricio Gastón Institute for Latino Community Development and Public Policy.

Montero-Sieburth, M. (1996). Teachers, administrators, and staff's implicit thinking about "at risk" urban high school Latino students. In F. Rios (Ed.), *Teacher thinking in cultural contexts* (pp. 55–84). Albany: State University of New York Press.

Ogbu, J. (1987). Variability in minority performance: A problem in search of an explanation. *Anthropology and Education Quarterly, 18,* 312–334.

Ogbu, J., & Matute-Bianchi, M. E. (1986). Understanding sociocultural factors: Knowledge, identity, and school adjustment. In California State Department of Education, Bilingual Education Office, *Beyond language: Social and cultural factors in schooling language minority students* (pp. 73–142). Sacramento: Author.

Rivera, R., & Nieto, S. (Eds.). (1993). *The education of Latino students in Massachusetts: Issues, research, and policy implications.* Boston: University of Massachusetts, Mauricio Gastón Institute.

Rodríguez, C. (1997). *Latin looks: Images of Latinas and Latinos in the U.S. media.* Boulder, CO: Westview Press.

Spindler, G., & Spindler, L. (Eds.). (1987). *Interpretive ethnography of education at home and abroad.* Hillsdale, NJ: Erlbaum.

Suárez-Orozco, M. (1989). *Central American refugees and U.S. high schools: A psychosocial study of motivation and achievement.* Stanford, CA: Stanford University Press.

Suárez-Orozco, C., & Suárez-Orozco, M. (1995). *Transformations: Migration, family life, and achievement motivation among Latino adolescents.* Stanford, CA: Stanford University Press.

Trueba, H. (1989). Rethinking dropouts: Culture and literacy for minority student empowerment. In H. Trueba, G. Spindler, & L. Spindler (Eds.), *What do anthropologists have to say about dropouts?* (pp. 27–42). New York: Falmer Press.

CHAPTER 8

The Development of Coping Strategies among Urban Latino Youth
A Focus on Help-Seeking Orientation and Network-Related Behavior

RICARDO D. STANTON-SALAZAR

INTRODUCTION

Interest in research on urban Latino youth in the United States is closely associated with a growing national concern with what Dryfoos (1990) describes as a new class of "untouchables" emerging in our inner cities, on the social fringes of suburbia, and in some rural areas. Dryfoos describes them as "young people who are functionally illiterate, disconnected from school, depressed, prone to drug abuse and early criminal activity, and eventually, parents of unplanned and unwanted babies. These are the children who are at high risk of never becoming responsible adults" (p. 3). Recent reports indicate that of the 28 million 10- to 17-year-olds in the United States, 1 in 4, or 7 million, are prone to multiple high-risk behaviors and experiences, such as school failure, substances abuse, delinquency, and unprotected intercourse (Dryfoos, 1990). Yet these key and well-cited risk behaviors do not adequately articulate the harm done to developmental processes. Perkins and Villaruel (this volume) provide us with a more precise and expanded definition of *risk* behavior—that is, as behaviors/actions that can compromise or impede six basic areas of human development.[1]

Although Latino youth represent about 10 percent of the entire national adolescent population (1986 figures), along with African American youth, they may be disproportionately represented in that subgroup engaging in multiple high-risk behaviors. In fact, current social trends foretell that the vulnerability of minority youth is increasing dramatically. From 1984 to 2020, the number of children (under 18) living in poverty will increase from 14.7 to 20.1 million, an increase of 37 percent. As of 1990, 37.1 percent of Mexican-origin children (under 18), 48.4 percent of Puerto Rican children, and 44.8 percent of African American children were living below the official poverty line. Gottlieb (1975) states that the number one source of turbulence in the social world inhabited by today's youth is divorce, and reports that 60 percent of children will, at some point in their childhood, experience living in a single-parent household. Chapa and Valencia (1993) report that 27 percent of Mexican-origin children and 43 percent of Puerto Rican children currently do not live with both parents; and 51 percent of African American children will never live with their two parents.

These statistics correspond to current research on urban minority communities and their increasing marginalization from mainstream society (Wilson, 1987). Large urbanized environments have become the domain not only of prosperous, well-educated, liberal-minded Americans, but also of the dispossessed (Fischer, 1982; Brookins, 1991). Black and Latino youth growing up in our central cities are expected to make the transition into productive adulthood in communities increasingly fraught with urban decay, unemployment, violence, and hopelessness. One indicator of our changing urban character is the increasing violence witnessed by children in urban neighborhoods. A survey of Chicago's Community Mental Health Council found that nearly 40 percent of Chicago's high school and elementary children had witnessed a shooting, 33 percent had seen a stabbing, and 25 percent had seen a murder. In Los Angeles, as many as 20 percent of the county's annual homicides may be witnessed by children (Garbarino, Dubrow, Kostelny, & Pardo, 1992). The risk is certainly real; embeddedness in family, school, and community environments plagued by deteriorating economic and social conditions not only increases the lure and perceived inevitability of high-risk behaviors and events, but also increases the chances of personal catastrophe associated with these behaviors: suicide, chronic drug addiction, homicide, unplanned pregnancy, AIDS, incarceration, chronic unemployment, and poverty.[2]

Research conducted by a number of educational anthropologists (e.g., Gibson & Ogbu, 1991; Trueba & Delgado-Gaitán, 1988) has greatly contributed to our understanding of how cultural forces within an ethnic community play their role in differentiating those youth who are at risk and often resistant to educational and social interventions, and those who appear to be highly resilient and who successfully steer away from high-risk experiences. Especially significant is the research on

The Development of Coping Strategies among Urban Latino Youth 205

Latino youth and on ethnic communities in the United States which are stratified generationally (i.e., immigrant, second generation, etc.) (e.g., Buriel, 1984; Matute-Bianchi, 1989).

The adaptive responses of many inner-city Latino youth are varied, influenced by the multiple and often competing ideologies and "social characters" around them. While many adaptive responses among youth have their rational basis, and all are certainly meaningful, adaptive responses are seldom neutral in their consequences. What often distinguishes research on Latino youth is the significant proportion of youth who become heavily invested in school and who steer away from illegal activity; such youth manage to achieve literacy as well as proficiency in two languages and are able to maintain high educational expectations and optimism throughout the high school years—all this, in spite of their enrollment in poorly funded schools and their residence in segregated, economically depressed, and violence-prone communities. When such adaptive responses take on a political dimension, they often promote social integration for other community members, usually through political mobilization and social change in the larger society (see Gurin & Epps, 1975; Sánchez-Jankowski, 1991; Willie, 1985). Most "positive" adaptive responses or coping strategies though, particularly among immigrants, are apolitical; and yet, they do often serve to promote individual success in the educational system and some successful measure of individual social integration within the mainstream (Buriel, 1984; Ogbu, 1991).

Other adaptive responses are anomic in character, often harmful to self and others, and over the long haul serve to exacerbate the individual's already marginal position in society.[3] These adaptive responses, particularly among poor African American, Chicano, and Puerto Rican youth, are often oppositional and defiant in character; yet, while such responses are geared toward warding off the psychologically painful aspects of anomie, they often embody the most alienating aspects of the dominant culture, leading to hard-boiled and highly individualistic forms of resiliency.

In light of these differences in the Latino youth community, this chapter addresses the following questions: (1) Do such differences in risk status point to differences in coping strategies and ideology? (2) Is the development of positive coping strategies and high motivation associated with particular cultural traits found among certain sectors of the Latino population? (3) If so, what are these traits, and how are they understood by group members? (4) What sociocultural forces are responsible for the development of coping strategies which are antisocial and entail high-risk behaviors? In the following pages, I discuss how variations in coping strategies can be understood in terms of young people's help-seeking orientation, that is, perceptions, attitudes, beliefs, and correspondent behaviors that either motivate or inhibit youth from actively seeking help and support from available and resourceful adults in the community, the school, and other mainstream institutions. I trace the developmental origins of these orientations to various cultural and societal forces, including historically rooted cultural patterns and ideologies, the corrosive conditions of poverty, and social relations between Latinos and dominant group members. I conclude by addressing the implications of research in this area to the success of current and future educational and social welfare interventions.

CURRENT ATTEMPTS TO UNDERSTAND RESILIENCY IN CHILD AND YOUTH DEVELOPMENT: RESEARCH ON THE MOBILIZATION OF SOCIAL SUPPORT

Research on the role of cultural and structural forces in influencing coping strategies or vulnerability to risk factors in minority or low-income communities is sorely lacking in the psychological and social welfare literature. A number of researchers, however, are now investigating the possible negative effects of rapid acculturation on educational achievement, social mobility, and mental health.[4] An increasing number of studies have suggested that integration within traditionalist ethnic networks may provide the necessary support and stability to cope effectively with detrimental societal forces affecting minority communities (see Buriel, 1984, for review; see also Portes & Bach, 1985, p. 299).[5]

The work necessary to further our understanding of those protective factors operating within different low-status and subordinated communities is evident in a number of disciplinary and scholarly circles. One especially promising line of research focuses on the developmental experiences of "resilient" children, that is, children who develop high levels of competency and sociability, and who demonstrate positive coping patterns, in spite of growing up in stressful and problem-plagued environments. A number of researchers have documented the positive coping styles of resilient children (Werner & Smith, 1982; see also Garbarino et al., 1992, for a review). Among the many descriptions of these children, Garbarino et al. (1992) stress:

> Resilient children are able to manipulate and shape their environment, to deal with its pressures successfully, and to comply with its demands.

They are able to adapt quickly to new situations, perceive clearly what is occurring, communicate freely, act flexibly, and view themselves in a positive way. Compared to vulnerable children, they are able to tolerate frustration, handle anxiety, and ask for help when they need it. (Anthony & Cohler, 1987, in Garbarino et al., 1992, cited p. 103)

Investigations into the developmental experiences of these children have revealed the critical role of early attachment experiences, specifically, "a stable emotional relationship with at least one parent or other reference person" (Garbarino et al., 1992, p. 103). Garbarino et al.'s (1992) review of cross-cultural studies also emphasizes three other important factors: consistent access to an open, supportive educational environment; the presence of a parental model of behavior which encourages constructive problem-solving; and social support from persons outside the family.

Communities also are capable of fostering conditions leading to resiliency, most obviously through the provision of material resources and supportive services. Yet, access to such resources and services is normally difficult in economically depressed communities (Williams & Kornblum, 1985). In such environments, community influences are usually much more subtle, having their effect through social networks, where affiliates exchange resources and support and promulgate certain cultural ideologies. Garbarino et al. (1992) state that ideology can potentially contribute to resilience by giving substance and meaning to adverse or dangerous circumstances and events. Ideology is, therefore, a psychological resource, even when it may not lead to final societal solutions. The important role of ideology is more fully addressed further along in this chapter.

The findings derived from the research on resilient children underscores the importance of social support in child and adolescent development. The questions posed by researchers in this area are markedly similar to those posed by researchers within the area of adult social support. In this latter area, we find a considerable and growing body of research which underscores the potential of social support networks in mediating the impact of stress-related events on physical and mental health (see d'Abbs, 1982; Hirsch, 1981; and Vaux, 1988, for reviews).

Two major areas of interest dominate the research on social support: the first addresses how people's routine interactions with those in their personal network affect their vulnerability to stress-related events and illness; the second, how and under what conditions people mobilize their social ties as a coping strategy. In the first area, among the most noteworthy findings are that supportive relationships can, under the appropriate conditions, reduce the risk of suicide (Kaplan, Cassel, & Gore, 1977), prevent clinical depression (Lin, Dean, & Ensel, 1986), and relieve both the psychological and the physiological stress symptoms associated with work-related pressures (Gore, 1978), immigration and resettlement (Kim, 1986; Portes & Bach, 1985), and bereavement (Walker, MacBride, & Vachon, 1977).

Underlying the proposed role of social support in "buffering" the individual from the symptomatic consequences of stressful events is the notion that effective coping strategies entail the successful acquisition of information from significant others. Albrecht and Adelman (1987) state that effective support provides information which enables the individual to better evaluate the current situation, to become aware of alternative and potentially effective solutions, and to instill a heightened sense of personal adequacy and progressive optimism. The process by which this information is delivered is also considered crucial. Albrecht and Adelman stress that supportive actions, to be effective, must validate the emotions of the individual as well as provide the opportunity for emotional ventilation; this not only serves to relieve internalized pressures, but also communicates genuine empathy.

In the second area, researchers have mainly looked at the conditions which deter people from mobilizing their network and from seeking help. This research may be key to our understanding those factors which, under one set of conditions, promote resilience among minority children and adolescents, while under different conditions, lead them to engage in high-risk coping responses (Stanton-Salazar, 1997; Valenzuela, 1997). Nelson-Le Gall (1985) emphasizes a view of help-seeking as an effective alternative for coping with difficult and stressful life events. She states that eliciting assistance from a specific person is really a matter of social problem solving, and requires a set of social skills that are best learned during childhood.[6]

In their review of the literature on adult help-seeking, Gross and McMullen (1983) identified three major thresholds individuals must cross in seeking and obtaining support: (1) the perception and assessment of the problem and their need for outside aid; (2) the decision to seek or not seek help, particularly the assessment of the costs and benefits associated with seeking help; and (3) the exercise of interpersonal skills necessary to engage in potentially supportive others. Much of the research on help-seeking has been fixed on the second threshold, that is, on the problem of ambivalence—that people in need of help often do not ask for it. Many individuals are willing to forgo help when they perceive that the act of seeking or obtaining assistance may be too psychologically costly. Gross and McMullen (1983) have classified these potential costs or risks into two general categories: (1) perceived threats to self-esteem and self-concept, and (2) social costs associated with perceived effects on interpersonal relationships. In recent years, specific theories have emerged for addressing each of these two types of risks. A great deal of attention has been paid to what is perhaps the most significant personal risk, that of injury to self-esteem. This threat arises when individuals interpret their request for help as an admission of incompetence or inadequacy, which in turn would serve to damage their sense of competency and self-esteem. Following this logic, two opposing predictions have been made (Nadler, 1983). The first involves individuals with low self-esteem, while the second involves those with high self-regard. Low self-esteem individuals are geared toward defense against any further injury to their psychological self; thus, low-self-esteem individuals would be expected to avoid the situation of seeking help more than those with high self-esteem. The second scenario provides a quite different view. High-self-esteem individuals have many positive self-cognitions regarding their ability to accomplish difficult tasks. When their self-evaluations of ability become closely associated with their concept of self, the act of seeking help appears inconsistent or threatening to both. Thus, high-self-esteem individuals would be less expected to seek assistance in times of need. Nelson-LeGall (1985) reports that the research literature tends to support the second scenario more than it does the first (see Fischer, Nadler, & Whitcher-Alagna, 1982, for a comprehensive review).[7]

The threat of embarrassment may be another major factor in explaining young people's ambivalence toward seeking help. Goffman (1955, 1956) stressed that people are greatly concerned about being seen and evaluated favorably by others, and that people will often go to great lengths to avoid being seen in a negative light. Thus, to a large degree, daily social interaction may be governed by the desire to avoid embarrassing moments. Goffman (1956) went to great lengths to describe all the internal and external physical symptoms which accompany embarrassment. Building on the work of Goffman and also of Modigliani (1968, 1971), Shapiro (1983) describes embarrassment as "an acute, uncomfortable emotional state" (p. 145), and defines it as a noxious psychological state that arises from the belief that others, who know of one's behavior, evaluate one unfavorably because one's behavior violated situational expectations. Modigliani states that this violation results in the loss of "situational subjective public esteem" (1968, pp. 315–316). This definition raises the issue regarding the contrasting bases of self-esteem, one general and the other situational.

Shapiro (1983) distinguishes between loss of self-esteem due to behavior which fails to meet the individual's internal standards (as discussed earlier) and the loss of self-esteem due to behavior which the individual perceives will cause public others to render negative evaluations. Thus, the conditions for embarrassment to occur are situational; a referent audience or public is necessary. The conditions for general loss of self-esteem, in contrast, are internal—here, the audience is oneself. Asking for help may raise the threat of embarrassment when it provides public information about unsatisfactory performance, particularly under conditions in which poor performances are normatively attributed to the lack of intelligence and ability, to faulty character (e.g., laziness), or to defective mental health (Ames, 1983; Philips, 1963).

Although virtually all of the research on embarrassment and help-seeking has focused on adults, the threat of embarrassment may be expected to be intensified among adolescents, who are known for their often acutely painful self-consciousness, and their paramount need to appear normal—particularly when "the public" is composed of their peers. Gottlieb (1975) believes that due to their greater self-consciousness and their lower threshold for defining stigma, attempts to seek assistance may be disguised or indirect, and therefore, adolescents are more likely to experience difficulty in obtaining the necessary support early in the coping process. Ambivalent feelings regarding seeking help due to threats to self-esteem may be a problem specific to cultural sites where individualism rather than communalism is stressed. We return to this issue later in the chapter.

Apart from the burden of personal costs on help-seeking, researchers have also sought to understand how perceived social costs underlie the ambivalence toward seeking support. Most formulations have drawn from both equity theory (Adams, 1965; Wallston, Walster, & Bercheid, 1978, cited in Gross & McMullen, 1983) and indebtedness theory (Greenberg & Westcott, 1983, cited in Gross & McMullen, 1983). Simply stated, the prospect of indebtedness, combined with anxieties that one may not be able to reciprocate within a reasonable period of time, raises the possibility of long-term indebtedness, attendant guilt, and/or embarrassment over not being self-sufficient. At least for middle-class North Americans, the excessive adherence to norms for maintaining equity in social relationships often undercuts the possibility of forming and participating in resource-flowing exchange networks.

THE IMPORTANT ROLE OF HELP-SEEKING ORIENTATION IN COPING BEHAVIOR

The proclivity among some individuals to focus on the potential risks of help-seeking, while others tend to focus on benefits, may in fact be rooted in the individual's developmental history and personality structure. People's psychological orientation to problem-solving through the mobilization of ties and networks, or help-seeking orientation, has begun to receive some attention in community psychology (Wallace & Vaux, 1993). This concept, originally coined as "network orientation," was formally defined by Tolsdorf as "a set of beliefs, attitudes, and expectations concerning the potential usefulness of [an individual's] network in helping him cope with a life problem" (Tolsdorf, 1976, p. 413). A number of recent works draw attention to a more expanded conception of network orientation (Phelan, Davidson, & Yu, 1998; Stanton-Salazar, 1997), yet most explicit treatments of this phenomenon in the literature have focused on help-seeking beliefs and practices. In order to provide some conceptual clarity to this and related phenomena, we use the term *help-seeking orientation* here to specifically address issues of help-seeking and social support, and treat it as one key dimension of a more complex constellation of network-relevant dispositions and skills related to adaptation to environmental demands, stressors, and opportunity structures.

Empirical studies on the subject, although sparse, have shown that help-seeking beliefs appear to be quite consequential. Eckenrode (1983) found that, independent of the number of potential sources of support, those with positive orientations toward help-seeking received relatively more assistance. Vaux, Burda, and Stewart (1986) found that persons with negative help-seeking orientations reported significantly smaller networks, meaning less people (ties) they could potentially call on for support. There was some evidence that a negative help-seeking orientation was associated with receiving less advice and guidance, and less material, financial, and emotional support, suggesting that available others were reluctant to be supportive to those with negative orientations. Substantial evidence emerged to show that those with negative orientations did perceive themselves as having less support from significant and available others.

Vaux and associates (1986) also found help-seeking orientation associated with a number of separately measured personality traits, specifically, low affiliation, low trust in institutions, and low nurturance. Those who scored high on femininity tended to have a positive orientation toward help-seeking, although the separate masculinity measure showed no significant relationship with help-seeking orientation. Similar evidence surfaced in a subsequent study by Vaux and Wood (1987). Persons with a negative help-seeking orientation were less likely to develop, maintain, and utilize supportive relationships, and tended to feel less cared for and involved. In line with predictions, such persons were more likely to experience symptoms associated with psychological distress.

Regrettably, only a few studies to date have been conducted specifically on the network and help-seeking orientations of adolescents.[8] In a study of middle-class whites, East (1989) investigated how early adolescents' help-seeking orientation related to their psychological functioning and perceptions of social support. Measures of perceived risk and perceived social benefits were derived. The results showed that those adolescents who believed that social benefits accrue from the seeking of support tended to perceive more support from nonfamily members; the association between perceived benefits and family support was only evident for boys. Perceptions of interpersonal risk, however, did not appear to be consequential in regard to support from family or nonfamily members, with one exception. Boys sensitive to risk reported less support from their fathers, suggesting that a negative orientation among sons may deter fathers from offering support.

East (1989) did not address the possibility that adolescent perceptions of interpersonal risk may have different effects depending on social class and parental resources. Middle-class family members and associates may provide nurturance and other forms of support regardless of the adolescent's hesitancy to elicit support. In contrast, lower-income families, particularly those experiencing high degrees of stress, may reserve their supportive responses for those who actively and persistently seek attention and support, regardless of risk.

On par with research on adults, East (1989) also found that early adolescents who evaluated interpersonal situations as involving more risks did report lower self-worth. However, evaluations of high risk may have different bases across income levels and ethnic groups. Adolescents who perceive family and community members as limited in emotional and material resources may interpret risk in terms of strains on providers (DePaulo, Leiphart, & Dull, 1984) rather than in terms of risk to their psychological selves. Research that examines social class and ethnic group differences in help-seeking and help-giving is needed to bear this out.

The influence of social class and subculture on helping-seeking behavior among adolescents is well illustrated in Gottlieb's (1975) study of high school senior boys. Gottlieb identified central members of four different social cliques in the senior class, and conducted intensive interviews focusing on the students' preferences for informal sources of help and on the nature of the support they actually received from these sources. One group called the Elites was composed of boys regarded by their peers as highly competitive and successful in the academic realm and in athletics. These youth actively sought the support of school personnel, who in turn acted in ways that recognized and reinforced the boys' prestige within the school. The help-seeking orientation of another group, called the Outsiders, provided a remarkable contrast. These boys came from working-class families, were not well known by their classmates, and did not participate in school and community activities; many had already left home and were working full-time jobs. Rather than seek the support of school personnel, these youths preferred the support of peers who shared similar backgrounds and life experiences. Gottlieb's (1975) study strongly suggests that supportive contact with mainstream institutional agents is significantly related to the degree of overlap in subcultural values and norms. Gottlieb further shows that teachers, coaches, guidance staff, and secretaries were clearly less responsive to marginal students and often acted in ways that discouraged them from seeking their support. Thus, access to institutional resources and support is reserved for those who conform to and embrace the cultural logic of the status quo.

THE SOCIAL AND CULTURAL ORIGINS OF HELP-SEEKING ORIENTATION

The above research strongly suggests that individual differences in help-seeking orientation do influence access to potential sources of support. A deeper inquiry into this issue leads to other important questions which also await further research—perhaps most importantly, the sociocultural origins of help-seeking orientation. Researchers have begun to suggest that an individual's propensity to seek support in times of need may be contingent upon both early and cumulative experiences with network exchanges.

Looking to Bowlby's (1969) attachment theory, Wallace and Vaux (1993) hypothesize that help-seeking orientation among adults originates in early attachment experiences with caregivers. According to Bowlby (1969), the development of normal resiliency among children is dependent upon a caregiver's emotional availability and responsiveness to the child's emerging and changing needs. Different experiences among children in the quality of caregiving experiences lead to different attachment styles, which researchers have now identified as *secure, avoidant,* and *anxious/ambivalent* (Ainsworth, Blehar, & Wall, 1978, cited in Wallace & Vaux, 1993). A number of studies have demonstrated stability into middle childhood (Main & Cassidy, 1988; Waters, 1978; both cited in Wallace & Vaux, 1993). Studies have also shown that children classified as securely attached—relative to their counterparts classified as insecurely attached—exhibited more empathy, more sociability, and less shyness; they also were better adjusted, exhibiting greater resiliency, higher self-respect, and less hostility (Arend, Gove, & Sroufe, 1979; Main & Weston, 1981; Pastor, 1981; Waters, Wittman, & Sroufe, 1979; all cited in Wallace & Vaux, 1993). As might be inferred, securely attached children were also more likely to seek assistance when confronted with difficult tasks and to heed the directives provided by helpers (Matas, Arend, & Sroufe, 1978, cited in Wallace & Vaux, 1993). Other studies on adults have demonstrated that those classified as having secure attachment styles—relative to those classified as having avoidant or anxious/ambivalent styles—reported more trusting and satisfying romantic relationships, displayed more prosocial conflict resolution strategies, and overall tended to rate higher on self-esteem and altruism (Hazan & Shaver, 1990; Pistole, 1981; Collins & Read, 1990; all cited in Wallace & Vaux, 1993).[9]

This leads us to the important question of whether help-seeking orientation should be viewed along a singular and generalizable dimension, or whether avoidant or anxious/ambivalent styles become activated situationally, for example, in instances where people must interact with gatekeepers and institutional agents, and where such interactions have been historically marred by cultural conflict or class-based antagonisms and social distance. It may very well be that avoidant or anxious/ambivalent styles do reflect the general orientation of some individuals, but that certain social domains serve to aggravate or intensify such styles.

Questions regarding whether particular attachment styles endure from infancy to childhood to adulthood, and whether such styles are normally generalizable across social domains, have yet to be resolved through empirical research. Yet, Wallace and Vaux (1993) argue that adult attachment styles, regardless of whether they are traceable to early childhood, do affect the nature and quality of close relationships. They report empirical findings which provide qualified support for the notion that adults with insecure attachment styles "are more likely to endorse beliefs and expectations reflecting the risks, costs, and futility of seeking help from network members" (p. 362). Wallace and Vaux (1993) focus on two subscales of their help-seeking orientation scale (again, the term "network orientation" is used [Vaux, 1988]), "independence" and "mistrust," and their respective relation to attachment style. Those individuals classified as having an avoidant attachment style—relative to those classified as secure—scored significantly higher on both independence and mistrust. Those classified as anxious/ambivalent scored significantly higher on mistrust, but not on independence. Wallace and Vaux (1993) state that the combination of independence and mistrust among avoidant respondents points to the development of an unhealthy and excessive self-reliance. In contrast, ambivalent respondents tend to shy away from utilizing their network resources not so much due to their commitment to self-reliance, but rather to their feelings that available sources of support cannot be trusted—in other words, a sense of distrust and feelings of vulnerability prevent them from seeking help.

INSTITUTIONAL AND SUBCULTURAL INFLUENCES ON HELP-SEEKING ORIENTATION

Casting help-seeking orientation as a personality trait rooted in the person's early developmental history does not preclude the possibility of cultural and institutional influences on help-seeking behavior, although research which addresses these influences is quite limited. The lack of attention to social context and cultural processes, and the overall "psychologizing" of the social support literature, is quite consonant with the field of social psychology (within the discipline of psychology), where social cognition has traditionally taken precedence over the study of social transactions embedded in institutional and cultural contexts (Eckenrode & Wethington, 1990; Wellman, 1983).

What attention has been paid to the sociocultural and contextual influences on social networks and help-seeking falls into one of three distinctive research areas. The first directs our view to institutional and organizational arrangements—the nature and organization of tasks, including rules, procedures, and norms for carrying out these tasks; the allocation of roles; opportunities for publicly demonstrating diverse competencies; and finally, evaluation procedures. These structures, whether within the workplace or the school site, not only dictate the conditions and norms under which resources are shared and how the transfer of support is interpreted (Ames, 1983; Nelson Le-Gall, 1985), but also how individual performance and competency is socially interpreted (Simpson & Rosenholtz, 1986). When institutional arrangements and norms lead to a stress on competition and individual merit, and when ability is seen along a singular and generalizable dimension, the risk of seeming less than competent is high, and the impulse to seek help is weakened.

A second area of research directs our attention to social forces that determine the material conditions to which people must adapt, including restrictions on the composition and structure of their social networks. This second area of research takes as its starting point what Wellman (1983) refers to as the social distribution of possibilities, a term referring to the unequal distribution of opportunities for entering different social and institutional contexts and for forming relationships with people who hold valued institutional resources, such as career-related information, vital social services, and bureaucratic influence (De Sola Pool & Kochen, 1978; Fischer, 1982; Lin et al., 1986; Stanton-Salazar, 1997; Stanton-Salazar & Dornbusch, 1995).

At the intersection of these social forces, we also find distinctive belief systems and sets of norms—often set within a subcultural milieu—which govern supportive interactions (Vélez-Ibáñez, 1980, 1983). Communal subcultures, for example, whether they encapsulate kinship networks or urban community life, contribute to shaping people's help-seeking orientation and behavior—in other words, how people orient themselves to the needs of others and to their own needs for support (Eckenrode & Wethington, 1990). With this in mind, the two constructs discussed above, "independence" and "mistrust"—together with their logical counterparts—can be understood not merely as attributes of individual psychology, but as constructs learned within a social collective sharing a common position within the larger social structure and a distinctive cultural history and character.

INDIVIDUALISM AS THE FOUNDATION FOR THE GENERAL HELP-SEEKING ORIENTATION OF ANGLO-AMERICANS

In any one metropolitan area, we find multiple communities, each with its own subculture and networks (Fischer, 1982). Such plurality is also found within a particular ethnic group which shares a geographic space. Using terminology proposed by Erich Fromm, we can say that a key aspect of the subculture within any one group is the "social character" shared by members. "The concept of social character," Fromm observes, "does not refer to the complete or highly individualized, in fact, unique character structure as it exists in an individual, but to the 'character matrix,' a syndrome of character traits which has developed as an adaptation to the economic, social, and cultural conditions common to that group" (Fromm & Maccoby, 1970, cited in Sánchez-Jankowski, 1991, p. 23).[10]

We can say, then, that a group's distinctive "social character" reflects—at a deeper level—a framework which members depend upon for interpreting events, situations, and experiences revolving around the interactions with mainstream institutions (e.g., the school), and for guiding their behavior within these interactions (Ogbu, 1991). Urban social scientists have stressed that social characters—and the ideologies they embody—are never right or wrong (e.g., Fischer, 1982; Ogbu, 1991): "Their purpose is to guide behaviors and interpretations" (Ogbu, 1991, p. 7). They are neither totally rational nor totally emotional, but they are always meaningful; that is, they "make sense" to group members. They are a social construction based on a history of intra- and intergroup relations and meaning-making.

While the social character of any particular social group corresponds to its position in the intersection of social statuses, it is also shaped and textured by ideologies historically rooted in a group's traditional ethos. The prevailing social character of middle-class Anglo-America has been profoundly shaped by the ideology of individualism, which can be understood as a psychodynamic worldview that interprets people's social status, life condition, and material wealth as consequences of individual natural talents, choices, and actions. The rise of this ideology appears to be historically rooted across different societies in their respective economic development and modernization, leading, in turn, to mass literacy, the decline of traditional authority, and the rise of new forms of social organization (Eames & Goode, 1973).

Across the globe, the rise of individualism has accompanied the transition from a closed stratification system to a relatively open one. An individual's social station, potential for productivity, and overall life condition are no longer perceived to be ascribed or divinely ordained by a transcendent God. Accordingly, the individual is perceived as exercising control over his or her life chances, in part through the letting go of traditional mores and the adoption of new and nontraditional practices. This process usually entails the weakening of the bonds which tie the individual to the corporate group. Familial ties are often reassessed as liabilities rather than assets. Social attachments and relations tend to become more calculated, sustained mainly by common personal interests and goals, and ultimately expendable and substitutable (Fischer, 1982; Tonnies, 1887/1963). The individual is expected to chart his or her own path, to take risks, to be geographically mobile, to be motivated by self-interest and the potential for individual gain; principal responsibility for both achievements and failures is attributed to the individual, not to society (Turner, 1960).

Social morality in society now rests in people's individual character rather than in the character or moral legitimacy of institutions and collective social arrangements. Under the ideological cloak of individualism, the lack of social mobility and long-term poverty are cast as deficits in individual motivation, virtue, or innate ability (Davis & Moore, 1945; Turner, 1960). In societies where individualism is strong, "self-trust and self-reliance are institutionally articulated as values of esteem and self-reference" (Vélez-Ibáñez, 1980). To replace natural or communalistic support systems, formal institutional mechanisms are established to met people's personal and social needs and to provide a safety net for those whose unmet expectations under individualism lead to various pathologies (i.e., anomie).

Socialization to principles of individualism has never occurred to the same degree among those living within the boundaries of Westernized societies. The adoption of these principles has, in fact, been particularly weak among non-Western (nonwhite) people and the economically disenfranchised, in spite of formal institutional attempts to reinforce and legitimate these principles (Boykin, 1986; Willie, 1985). For these groups, the promises of individualism are overshadowed by the risk of alienation and social death. The assumptions which underlie the ideology of individualism may also be questioned, particularly whether social mobility and prosperity rest in individual effort and talent. Rather than sustain a belief in divinely ordained causation or individual talent, people on the fringes of mainstream society often see causation in terms of man-made power structures rooted in a corporate capitalist economic system (Eames & Goode, 1973). Quite often, communal and familial social arrangements are sustained as safeguards against economic woes and the threat of anomie, which is perceived as lurking within the shadow of excessive individualism. Many non-Western ethnic groups in Western societies continue to engage in communalistic social relations and to maintain natural support systems.

COMMUNALISM, RECIPROCAL NETWORKS, AND *CONFIANZA EN CONFIANZA* AS AN ALTERNATIVE HELP-SEEKING ORIENTATION

In contrast to the strong psychodynamic valuation given to individualism (and in its extreme, to narcissistic self-trust and self-reliance), non-Western groups continue to adhere, in varying degrees, to communalism. Boykin (1986) defines *communalism* as "a commitment to social connectedness which includes an awareness that social bonds and responsibilities transcend individual privileges" (p. 61). This cultural feature may be sustained due, in part, to its defensive and practical functions in contemporary Western societies, but it must also be seen as an enduring feature of any particular ethnic group's traditional and indigenously rooted ethos (Boykin, 1986; Boykin & Toms, 1985). Over the past fifteen years, researchers has provided sizable evidence that communalism continues as an enduring cultural feature of many Mexicano and other Latino communities in the United States (Gilbert, 1978; Keefe, 1979; Keefe & Padilla, 1987; Keefe, Padilla, & Carlos, 1979; Sena-Rivera, 1979; Vélez-Ibáñez, 1983; Williams, 1990).

The organizing principle underlying the formation of Mexican/Latino interpersonal networks and the continuance of social relationships can be understood by the term *confianza en confianza,* translated by Vélez-Ibáñez (1980, 1983) to mean "trusting mutual trust." *Confianza en confianza* is a construct learned through socialization in family and community, and serves as a predominant mode of survival as much as it serves as a vehicle of self-reference, social esteem, and cultural meaning-making.[11] While individualism emerges within the context of calculated exchange relations with formal institutions, *confianza en confianza* emerges within natural support systems of family and community. It denotes a psychocultural expectation for ongoing exchange, mutual generosity, and reciprocity in the context of trusting and intimate relations. It reflects the view that life is sustained, and well-being ensured, only through embeddedness and participation in multiple networks where trusting relations are fostered and where intimacies, goods, services, and access to organizational privileges and resources are regularly exchanged. In sum, *confianza en confianza* reflects the propensity of many Mexicanos/Latinos to construct and sustain social structures which interweave people in a system of mutual obligations—a trust that engagement in such social structure will provide more effective returns than individual efforts (Coleman, 1988).

In reality, social groups within complex urban systems are neither absolute individualists nor communalists. Rather, groups display tendencies which indicate their position along a cultural continuum between two ideal-typical points; furthermore, it is certainly feasible that a group's position on this continuum may change across social domains—in other words, it may be situational and domain-driven. Nonetheless, the general salience of one or the other construct is dependent upon the intersection of experiences rooted in multiple social statuses, principally, ethnic origin, generational status, social class, gender, and region.

This view complements the framework proposed by Wallace and Vaux (1993) and other social psychologists who see affiliation, attachment, and trust as rooted in early developmental experiences during childhood. What I add to their framework is the notion that developmental experiences occur within a cultural and historical context, positioned at the intersection of statuses, and within a complex and socially divided society. The case made here is that for a large segment of the Mexicano/Latino population in the United States, the intersection of their multiple statuses fosters a help-seeking orientation which continues to place a social value on affiliation, attachment, and trust, at least at the level of family and community. Such an orientation among adults, along with the exchange behaviors which stem from it, may have a lot of do with buffering children from excessive environmental stress and with fostering in them a high degree of resilience. And yet, for a growing segment of urban minority poor in our inner cities, particularly among marginalized youth, the intersection of statuses produces a help-seeking orientation which reflects neither the individualism embodied in Anglo mainstream institutional life, nor the communalism reflected in immigrant or more traditionalist ethnic enclaves.

VARIATIONS IN THE ADAPTIVE RESPONSES OF LATINO YOUTH

The mode of adaptation among nonimmigrant minority youth in low-income urban communities is usually the most visible, audible, and distressing. Yet, the current attention paid to these youth is due not merely to their oppositional character and apparent rejection of mainstream standards of morality, features which have been historically present, but to the sights and sounds of violence and increasing destructiveness. Even within community boundaries, the oppositional and sometimes violent character of youth behavior is often perceived as disruptive to those community members pursuing more conventional or traditional means of survival.[12] With the increase of violence and gang involvement in inner-city communities has come a refocus of attention on how low-income, disenfranchised minority communities embody alternative, often competing, subcultures, each reflecting distinctive modes of adaptation to social oppression and marginalization (e.g., Gibson & Ogbu, 1991; McLaughlin & Heath, 1993).

The adaptive responses and defiant behavior of a growing segment of inner-city Latino youth and young adults appear to stem from a social character which rejects the accommodation and conformity of immigrants, while adopting the most excessive aspects of individualism, sustained only by a highly adapted, defensive, and acutely concentrated peer-focused communalism (Vigil, 1988). The causes and meaning of their defiant behavior are typically portrayed by the mainstream using the logic of deviance, individual pathology, and learned helplessness, thus ignoring the marginalization of many minority youth rooted in the class and racial inequalities and antagonisms which characterize our society (Giroux, 1983, p. 107). In reality, what we find is a continuum whereby youth can be distinguished by the degree to which they embody what Sánchez-Jankowski (1991, p. 23) terms a "defiant individualist" character. The greater the experience of marginality among youth, and the more it is shared by similar and significant others who likewise lack institutional supports, the greater the probability that youth will assume and express such a character.

CHARACTERISTICS OF DEFIANT INDIVIDUALISM

Sánchez-Jankowski (1991, p. 24) outlines the principal attributes and developmental trajectory of the defiant individualist character. The first attribute is an intense sense of competitiveness, which he argues emerges from the scarcity of resources in low-income communities. The choice between competition or communalism begins in the family domain where material resources are insufficient to provide for the needs of all children. This scarcity may extend to affective or emotional resources, particularly when parents or adult caretakers exhaust themselves trying to shelter their children from often horrific environmental conditions including violence and drugs (Garbarino et al., 1992). Under such conditions of scarcity, the ground becomes fertile for either the seeds of intensive communalism (Eames & Goode, 1973; Lomnitz, 1977; Stack, 1974) or of competition.

Due to the segregation and concentration of poor families in low-income neighborhoods and housing projects, the prospect of obtaining support and assistance is often restricted to others coping with the same resource-poor conditions. Although reciprocal and communalistic relations are clearly visible in these communities, such relations or networks are organized around survival rather than optimal well-being. These networks take many forms, from kinship networks to adult female-centered neighborhood networks (Lomnitz, 1977; Eames & Goode, 1973). Along with the humaneness and mercy that is generated within many of these networks, participation often requires many psychic and material costs (e.g., privacy, dependence, inability to accumulate resources (Stack, 1974). For many youth, a competitive and individualistic help-seeking orientation appears to be a more rational and potentially profitable type of coping behavior.

Yet, competition within family and community domains serves to implant the seeds of mistrust or wariness, another core trait of defiant individualism (Sánchez-Jankowski, 1991, p. 24). Under conditions of scarcity and competition, and outside the realm of *confianza en confianza*, "trust is not simply a given, but something to be calculated" (p. 24). Persistent calculations and wariness, in turn, lead to self-reliance, a trait regularly romanticized within the mainstream media, which depict self-reliance and rugged individualism as core American values. Yet, self-reliance among resource-rich middle-class Americans is categorically and qualitatively different from the same trait under conditions of scarcity and poverty, particularly in the case when entire urban communities become isolated from members of the mainstream, including members of the stable labor force (Wilson, 1987). Under these adverse conditions, self-reliance leads to individual social isolation, an emotional detachment from others that only further minimizes the possibility of association with networks and institutions (both indigenous and mainstream) that may attempt the infusion or sharing of resources and assistance.

Mistrust of others, self-reliance, and social isolation do not leave open many possibilities for prosocial coping strategies. While young people observe many adults struggling to survive through participation in reciprocal networks, they also "observe, confront, and negotiate with people" whose mode of survival, although predatory, often reaps greater material benefits (Sánchez-Jankowski, 1991, p. 24). We must remind ourselves here of how the media and commercial industry promulgate the view that the acquisition of commercial goods is a viable route to higher social status and individual happiness.

It is also important to point out that predatory modes of survival usually require continued identification and integration in the community. Drug addicts, pimps, gang members, those engaged in armed robberies, and those working within the underground street economy usually depend on vulnerable members of their respective communities to make their own mode of survival successful (Sánchez-Jankowski, 1991; Sullivan, 1989). Under conditions of scarcity, marginalization from the mainstream, and predatory-type danger, coping and the management of stress becomes a principal life activity: "the goal is to fight, to survive, to overcome" (Sánchez-Jankowski, 1991, p. 25). The adoption of this means of survival, however, is not so much a "cost-benefit decision" or "choice," but rather an adaptational strategy adopted from the social character of others who share similar social biographies. One rides the bus one is already in. Full-blown defiant individualism is one such bus. Leaving it to board another, more socially acceptable one requires a radical and transformational experience—clearly possible, but usually highly improbable without major outside social intervention.

Sánchez-Jankowski's (1991) description of the developmental progression of defiant individualism overlaps considerably with Wallace and Vaux's (1993) discussion of the developmental origins of avoidant and anxious/ambivalent attachment styles. Both suggest a coping strategy not geared toward the mobilization of available social supports within community or mainstream networks or institutions. While Sánchez-Jankowski (1991) alerts us to how "distrust" and "excessive independence," as coping mechanisms, are often rooted in early familial experiences with poverty, other researchers have documented the existence of more communalistic coping mechanisms which stress mutual trust and interdependence in the face of similar material conditions (e.g., Gibson & Ogbu, 1991; McLaughlin, Irby, & Langman, 1994; Williams & Kornblum, 1985). The work of Vigil (1988), on Latino gangs in southern California, points outs that barrio gangs continue to stress communalism and interpersonal supportive exchanges as an individual coping strategy, but only among themselves. The barrio gang may, in fact, serve to keep defiant individualistic tendencies in check, becoming a substitute for family and community, and providing norms and mechanisms for personal security, social support, and attachment needs.

Within Latino communities in the United States, the path taken by individual youth may depend much upon the "social character" of their own extended family and community networks. The existence of alternative help-seeking orientations within Latino communities can perhaps be best understood in terms of how different generational groups exhibit distinctive social characters and social orders. By this I refer to differences between immigrants and second-generation Latinos, and those whose families have resided in the United States for many generations. Within each subgroup, distinctive social characters and social orders emerge as organizational responses, not only to the immediate exigencies collectively experienced (e.g., poverty, segregation) within family and neighborhood domains, but also to the historical intergroup relations with the dominant society. Two separate forces may, therefore, be operating to distinguish the social character of lower-income, generationally established Latino communities from that of immigrants. The first is their degree of coerced acculturation, particularly the loss of both familistic and communalistic patterns of behavior; and the second, the meanings attached to their lack of social integration within the mainstream. I address the second of such forces below.

A FRAMEWORK FOR UNDERSTANDING INTERGENERATIONAL DIFFERENCES IN ADAPTATION

John Ogbu (1978, 1991) suggests that explaining key differences in minorities' coping styles requires an understanding of their cultural models, employed to make sense of their experiences. Ogbu's definition of "cultural model" overlaps considerably with Fromm and Maccoby's (1970) "social character." A crucial dimension of this cultural model entails how a group perceives its relationship with (and often exclusion from) public institutions and with the people who control them, for example, the school system and its gatekeepers. While one group reveals its basic trust in, or even acquiescence to, such institutions, another group may reveal a deep-seated distrust and resentment, developed over a significant historical period.

Ogbu has argued that adaptations to discrimination, poverty, and low social status among minority groups have always been a function of the type of minority community in question. According to Ogbu, differences in national origin and nativity (i.e., whether members of a community were born in the United States or elsewhere), and most importantly, the historical and political circumstances surrounding initial intergroup contact, go a long way in explaining how different groups adapt to their situation as minorities in the States. Group responses to discrimination and stigmatization have their correlates within the youth population, and have been linked to divergent behaviors and attitudes observable to those who work within our public schools and urban communities.

Particularly revealing are a group's strategies for dealing with discriminatory treatment and with institutional obstacles which inhibit their upward mobility in society. These strategies include the group's educational strategies, which Ogbu defines in terms of attitudes, plans, and actions that deal with employing the school system to satisfy the desire for economic stability, upward mobility, and general well-being. The case of Chicanos and Mexicanos is illustrative (Matute-Bianchi, 1989). In contrast to native-born Chicanos, Ogbu argues that Mexican immigrants—as with other immigrant groups—tend to exhibit a "trusting or acquiescing relationship with schools and members of the dominant group" (Ogbu, 1991, p. 21). Immigrants possess a cultural model which promotes a perception of the educational system as a viable route around discriminatory structures, and one which will ultimately lead to economic security and upward mobility. Discriminatory treatment is seen as temporary rather than permanent. In contrast to low-income, U.S.-born minority members, immigrants believe that the burden is on them to prove their worthiness and entitlement to institutional privileges and resources. Unlike immigrants, involuntary minorities, particularly African Americans, native-born Chicanos, Puerto Ricans, and Native Americans, are more likely to develop a distrust of those who are perceived as representing the dominant group's interests, and often question whether strict conformity to mainstream norms defining good citizenship and hard work will lead to equal treatment and social advancement within society's major institutions—principally, the educational system and the labor market.

Native-born Latino children and youth growing up in economically distressed families and communities are far more vulnerable to the lure of either defiant individualism or peer-focused communalism (i.e., gangs). Rapid acculturation and social distance from immigrant-based networks may diminish the chances of becoming socialized within a larger, adult-based communalistic environment governed by the principal of *confianza en confianza* (Buriel, 1984; Vélez-Ibáñez, 1980, 1983). Reared within families outside the realm of immigrant influences, and lacking the economic resources to properly sustain middle-class individualism, the development of avoidant and anxious/ambivalent attachment styles becomes highly likely.

For native-born Latino youth, the development of a negative help-seeking orientation in later years continues to be fostered when they learn of the nature of intergroup relations with dominant group members and institutional gatekeepers—teachers, school officials, welfare agents and social workers, police, landlords, and city officials. The culture of distrust, and the existence of class-based and racial antagonisms which pervade relations between native-born, low-income Latinos and dominant group members, serves to justify and reinforce a help-seeking orientation which emphasizes self-reliance and distrust, and possibly, alliance with other marginal youth (Stanton-Salazar, 1997). The effects of rapid acculturation or deculturation (Berry, 1980), combined with initiation into interclass and interracial group antagonisms, however latent, serves to marginalize youth from the only two viable adult sources of social support.

For many youth, the reciprocal exchanges and communalistic networks visible among immigrants and more conservative members of Latino communities remain survivalist in appearance, and unrealistically optimistic; because there is often no clear political dimension, communalism rarely appears to alter the material conditions of community members or the economic and political status of the community. Neither does it serve to validate their sense of defiance, nor their own "penetrations" into the oppressive character of the societal opportunity structure (Willis, 1977).[13]

IMPLICATIONS FOR SOCIAL WELFARE AND EDUCATIONAL POLICY AND INTERVENTION

Institutional programs and interventions designed to promote the school success and overall well-being of Latino and other minority youth are taking on a greater burden in light of rapidly changing social conditions within our urban centers, conditions which are plainly deleterious to healthy social development (Dryfoos, 1990; Garbarino et al., 1992). The future success of these interventions may depend on a thorough and theoretically grounded understanding of how minority children and youth, across geographic and national contexts, develop different coping styles.

Defiant individualism, and restricted or expanded forms of communalism, as distinctive help-seeking orientations, regularly play a decisive role in determining young people's life chances, particularly by shaping their receptivity to sound institutional interventions, especially within the context of school. Latino children from low-income families, but reared within more adult-oriented communalistic networks, are much more likely to develop the classic characteristics of resilience. They learn the verses of *confianza en confianza,* the value and necessity of trust, caring, and reciprocity. They develop the requisite skills of sharing, cooperation, and exchange as well as associated strategies for managing relations with different caregivers and personalities. They learn that the steady flow of support from significant others entails reciprocal obligations and the occasional (prosocial and tactful) resolution of conflict. Such children tend to fare well when fortunate enough to find themselves within a competently staffed and resource-rich classroom, school, or educational or social program. Social attachments to school and program personnel readily follow and become the conduits for the flow of institutional resources and emotional support.[14] Children with secure attachment styles, and alert to the social benefits which accrue from help-seeking, are open to the potential benefits of social support; they become better able to evaluate stressful situations and possible threats, and are more aware of alternative and potentially effective solutions to stress-producing situations and problems; they also become aware of their own developing mastery and sense of personal adequacy.

However, these are not the children who most challenge us as a society. Educational and community-based interventions serving predominantly Latino immigrant groups do need to provide sound institutional resources in a way that is sensitive to their language and cultural background; and they do need to tailor services in ways that meet the special needs of people new to the host society (Portes & Rumbaut, 1990; Vásquez, Pease-Alvarez, & Shannon, 1994). Although many have argued that this necessitates a considerable change in how schools and other institutions provide services to immigrant communities, I would argue that what is needed is no less than the transformation of the institutional culture of school, that is, a radical change in the very nature of intergroup relations between institutional agents and community members, from that of hierarchy and exclusion to that of trust and reciprocity. Such a transformation may not necessarily come from the top, but may require political organization and mobilization from below; in any case, the two surely must occur before it can really happen.

Such a transformation is all the more necessary when we address the needs of those Latino youth who exhibit the type of social character associated with nonimmigrant and marginalized communities in the United States. Unlike Latino immigrants, these youth often behave in ways which undermine well-intentioned intervention efforts. Attempts to provide support to such youth may appear futile, and under present circumstances, this may well be the case. However, this is only so because the transmission of support and resources, in order to be effective, must occur in the context of trusting and genuinely supportive relations (see Stanton-Salazar, Vásquez, & Mehan, 1996).

The task appears prodigious, considering that what is necessary is essentially the reversal of many young people's help-seeking orientation; in effect, it requires establishing the groundwork so that young individuals with attachment styles that are avoidant and/or ambivalent become secure and prosocial, reflecting interdependency and reciprocity—in other words, the internalization of *confianza en confianza*. One can easily become pessimistic, given the traditional emphasis on discipline and punishment in our society, and given program models which insist on locating "the problem" in minority group members rather than in oppressive social structures. The cultural/class differences between minority youth and many institutional agents represent an additional factor, although such differences do not necessarily preclude the development of trusting and nurturing relations; they often translate into undue burdens placed on children, making supportive relations contingent on their rapid acculturation and prerequisite conformity to mainstream cultural standards. More problematic is that which is rarely discussed in educational and social welfare circles: that social distance, distrust, and latent antagonisms rooted in our stratified society often manifest themselves in subtle ways in interpersonal relations between people who occupy dominant and subordinate positions in the social system. It is, therefore, quite reasonable to expect that these tensions often interfere with the development of trust and rapport between institutional agents and older minority youth (Stanton-Salazar, 1997; Valenzuela, 1997).

Relationships of genuine trust will be difficult if not impossible to establish until two things occur (Stanton-Salazar & Dornbusch, 1995): (1) Children and youth must feel assured that close and open interactions with institutional agents are securely grounded in the agent's genuine commitment to their welfare, and that such a commitment will not be easily fractured. In other words, the risks of vulnerability must be powerfully overshadowed by a sense of security that social support, resources, and enriching experiences are to be had through social attachments to institutional agents. (2) Feelings of marginalization in society, and in the school system, must be validated, publicly recognized, and discussed.[15]

Again, this may seem a tall order; and yet, the gravity of the problem found in poor urban schools and communities across the country require us to concede that conventional reforms, programs, and policies have not worked. We often hear that the vast amounts of money channeled to minority-populated schools and community programs have not produced dividends, and thus, have been wasted. First of all, such funds, relatively speaking, have not been vast, particularly when compared to other national priorities and investments (e.g., military), and secondly—and most importantly—such funds have not always been utilized for the purpose of building long-lasting supportive networks around children and youth.[16] Network-analytic theories and theories of social support currently found in sociology and social psychology have not been the essential building blocks of school interventions and youth programs—with a number of notable exceptions.[17] A new computer lab may be a great resource for any school, but a computer is not a relationship; alone, it cannot affect consciousness and help-seeking orientations as genuinely supportive relationships can. As long as reforms and youth-directed policies fail to focus on the building of personal communities of support around minority children and youth, and as long as they negate the importance of minority consciousness in the developmental process, they are doomed to failure. And with this failure comes a great and terrible tragedy, a whole new generation deprived of hope.

NOTES

[1]These areas are (1) physical health, physical growth; (2) the accomplishment of normal developmental tasks; (3) the fulfillment of expected social roles; (4) the acquisition of essential skills; (5) the achievement of a sense of adequacy and competence; and (6) the appropriate preparation for the next developmental period of the life span (i.e., young adulthood for adolescents).

[2]See Dryfoos (1990) for studies on each of these problem areas.

[3]Anomie is a social condition both of a population and of individuals, and is often characterized by a sense of failure, futility, and loss of control over one's life. Building on Durkheim, Merton (1949) argued that deviant or aberrant behavior is, in many cases, the consequence of social pressures to achieve certain culturally prescribed goals without the provision of adequate resources or means to achieve them.

[4]See Amado Padilla (1980) for examples are early research on acculturation stress.

[5]One notable example is a study by Buriel, Calzada, and Vásquez (1982), who investigated the cultural and social antecedent factors which led to deviant behavior among a trigenerational sample of Mexican-origin adolescents.

[6]Nelson-Le Gall (1985), in fact, has argued for a reconceptualization of help-seeking that shifts the focus away from a view of help-seeking as stigmatizing, self-threatening behavior to a view of help-seeking as an effective alternative for coping with current difficulties (p. 65).

[7]See Nelson Le-Gall (1985) for limitations of the research using the self-esteem approach.

[8]See Belle, Dill, & Burr (1991) and Gottlieb (1975).

[9]A number of scholars have found Bowlby's theory on attachment style seriously problematic (Burman, 1994; Clarke-Stewart, 1988; White & Woollett, 1992), essentially arguing that it contributes to and reflects dominant ideologies and myths about contemporary families and that these biases render the methodology used in typical attachment studies highly questionable. One serious problem is that the theory does not take into consideration extended family forms, and implies that other caretaking arrangements, apparent across different cultural and economic groups, are detrimental to the healthy development of the child. Citing criticisms made by Burman (1994), Spina (1998, personal conversation) points out that attachment theory gained popularity after World War II, when motherhood began to be glorified just as women were being asked to leave behind their war-industry jobs and to return to men the task of financially supporting the family. In the mid-1980s, when asked to address the various challenges to his work, Bowlby "strongly maintained that motherhood and career were irreconcilable and that child care by anyone other than the mother was a terrible and dangerous thing" (Spina, 1998). With the majority of mothers now working, and with women a dominant part of the workforce (Baca Zinn & Eitzen, 1996), the raising of children today entails various strategies where children are cared for by multiple caretakers, across different contexts, without any deleterious effects on attachment or development.

[10]The concept of "social character," of course, overlaps considerably with Pierre Bourdieu's notion of "habitus," which he uses to refer to "a system of internalized structures, schemes of perception, conception, and action common to all members of the same group or class" (Bourdieu & Passeron, 1977). These two concepts also overlap with the concept of "cultural model" employed by Ogbu (1991, p. 7) to explain why different minority groups who share similar social conditions adapt in very different ways, and how these distinctive adaptations ultimately affect the group's experience within the school system, the labor market, and other mainstream institutions.

[11]There are, of course, other related dimensions of Latino families that have their roots in premodern society, and which contribute to the persistence of natural support systems (*personalismo, compadrazgo* are but two) (see Keefe & Padilla, 1987; Williams, 1990).

[12]This has emerged in my current ethnographic research in several Latino communities in San Diego, California.

[13]My colleague Angela Valenzuela adds that disaffected youth judge the communalistic tendencies of the adult community in a negative light because

they see this cultural behavior as a sign of weakness. She states that this may very well be an outcome of media and school influences which socialize Latino youth to look down upon what is traditionally and characteristically Latino (see Valenzuela, 1997).

[14]See Garbarino et al. (1992, chapter 6, "School as a Refuge," and chapter 8, "Developing Supportive Settings for Children").

[15]Fine (1991) discusses instances within an urban school where students' efforts to discuss their own marginality in society are thwarted by the teacher.

[16]See Jonathan Kozol's (1991) *Savage Inequalities: Children in America's Schools* (New York: Crown).

[17]See Comer (1980); Ansen, Cook, Habib, Grady, Hayes, & Comer (1991); McLaughlin et al. (1994).

REFERENCES

Adams, J. S. (1965). Injustice in social exchange. In L. Berkowitz (Ed.), *Advances in experimental social psychology* (Vol. 2). New York: Academic Press.

Ainsworth, M. D., Blehar, S. M., & Wall, S. (1978). *Patterns of attachment.* Hillsdale, NJ: Erlbaum.

Albrecht, T. L., & Adelman, M. B. (Eds.). (1987). *Communicating social support.* London: Sage.

Ames, R. (1983). Help-seeking and achievement orientation: Perspectives from attribution theory. In B. M. DePaulo, A. Nadler, & J. Fisher (Eds.), *New directions in helping: Vol. 2. Help-seeking* (pp. 165–186). New York: Academic Press.

Ansen, A. R., Cook, T. D., Habib, F., Grady, M. K., Hayes, N., & Comer, J. P. (1991). The Comer School Development Program: A theoretical analysis. *Urban Education, 26,* 56–82.

Anthony, E., & Cohler, B. (1987). *The invulnerable child.* New York: Guilford Press.

Arend, R., Gove, F., & Sroufe, L. A. (1979). Continuity of individual adaptation from infancy to kindergarten: A predictive study of ego-resiliency and curiosity in pre-schoolers. *Child Development, 50,* 950–959.

Baca Zinn, M., & Eitzen, D. S. (1996). *Diversity in families* (4th ed.). New York: HarperCollins.

Belle, D., Dill, D., & Burr, R. (1991). Children's network orientations. *Journal of Community Psychology, 19,* 362–372.

Berry, J. W. (1980). Acculturation as varieties of adaptation. In A. Padilla (Ed.), *Acculturation: Theory, models, and some new findings* (pp. 9–25). Boulder, CO: Westview Press.

Bourdieu, P., & Passerson, J.-C. (1977). *Reproduction in education, society, and culture*. London: Sage.
Bowlby, L. (1969). *Attachment and loss*. New York: Basic Books.
Boykin, A. W. (1986). The triple quandary and the schooling of Afro-American children. In U. Neisser (Ed.), *School achievement of minority children: New perspectives* (pp. 57–92). London: Erlbaum.
Boykin, A. W., & Toms, F. (1985). Black child socialization: A conceptual framework. In J. McAdoo & H. McAdoo (Eds.), *Black children* (pp. 33–51). Beverly Hills, CA: Sage.
Brookins, G. K. (1991). Families in urban environments: Psychosocial, structural, and policy implications. In M. Lang (Ed.), *Contemporary urban America: Problems, issues, and alternatives* (pp. 153–172). New York: University Press of America.
Buriel, R. (1984). Integration within traditional Mexican American culture and sociocultural adjustment. In J. L. Martinez & R. Mendoza (Eds.), *Chicano psychology* (pp. 95–130). New York: Academic Press.
Buriel, R., Calzada, S., & Vásquez, R. (1982). The relationship of traditional Mexican American culture to adjustment and delinquency among three generations of Mexican American male adolescents. In J. L. Martinez & R. Mendoza (Eds.), *Chicano psychology*. New York: Academic Press.
Burman, E. (1994). *Deconstructing developmental psychology*. London and New York: Routledge.
Chapa, J., & Valencia, R. (1993). Latino population growth and demographic trends: Implications for education. *Hispanic Journal of Behavioral Science, 15*(2), 163–164.
Clarke-Stewart, K. A. (1988). The "effects" of infant day care reconsidered. *Early Childhood Research Quarterly, 3*, 293–318.
Coleman, J. S. (1988). Social capital in the creation of human capital. *American Journal of Sociology, 94*, S95-S120.
Collins, N., & Read, S. J. (1990). Adult attachment, working models, and relationship quality in dating couples. *Journal of Personality and Social Psychology, 58*, 644–663.
Comer, J. P. (1980). *School power: Implications of an intervention project*. New York: Free Press.
d'Abbs, P. (1982). *Social support networks: A critical review of models and findings* (Monograph No. 1). Melbourne: Institute of Family Studies.
Davis, K., & Moore, W. (1945). Some principles of stratification. *American Sociological Review, 10*, 242–249.
DePaulo, B. M., Leiphart, V., & Dull, W. R. (1984). Help-seeking and social interaction: Person, situation, and process considerations. In E. Staub, D. Bar-

Tal, J. Reykowski, & J. Karylowski (Eds.), *The development and maintenance of pro-social behavior* (pp. 337–357). New York: Plenum.

De Sola Pool, I., & Kochen, M. (1978). Contacts and influence. *Social Networks, 1,* 5–51.

Dryfoos, J. (1990). *Adolescents at risk: Prevalence and prevention.* New York: Oxford University Press.

Eames, E., & Goode, J. G. (1973). *Urban poverty in a cross-cultural context.* New York: Free Press.

East, P. (1989). Social risks in adolescent help-seeking. *Journal of Early Adolescence, 9,* 376–395.

Eckenrode, J. (1983). The mobilization of social supports: Some individual constraints. *American Journal of Community Psychology, 11,* 509–528.

Eckenrode, J., & Wethington, E. (1990). The process and outcome of mobilizing social support. In S. Duck (Ed.), *Personal relationships and social support* (pp. 83–103). London: Sage.

Fine, M. (1991). *Framing drop-outs: Notes on the politics of an urban public high school.* Albany: State University of New York.

Fischer, C. S. (1982). *To dwell among friends.* Chicago: University of Chicago Press.

Fischer, J. D., Nadler, A., & Whitcher-Alagna, S. J. (1982). Recipient reactions to aid. *Psychological Bulletin, 91,* 27–54.

Fromm, E., & Maccoby, M. (1970). *Social character in a Mexican village.* Englewood Cliffs, NJ: Prentice Hall.

Garbarino, J., Dubrow, N., Kostelny, K., & Pardo, C. (1992). *Children in danger: Coping with the consequences of community violence.* San Francisco: Jossey-Bass.

Gibson, M. A., & Ogbu, J. U. (1991). *Minority status and schooling: A comparative study of immigrant and involuntary minorities.* New York: Garland.

Gilbert, J. (1978). Extended family integration among second generation Mexican Americans. In J. M. Casas & S. E. Keefe (Eds.), *Family and mental health in the Mexican American community* (Monograph No. 7). Los Angeles: University of California at Los Angeles, Spanish Speaking Mental Health Research Center.

Giroux, H. (1983). *Theory and resistance in education.* London: Heinemann Educational Books.

Goffman, E. (1955). On face work. *Psychiatry, 18,* 213–231.

Goffman, E. (1956). Embarrassment and social organization. *American Journal of Sociology, 62,* 264–271.

Gore, S. (1978). The effect of social support in moderating the health consequences of unemployment. *Journal of Health and Social Behavior, 19,* 157–165.

Gottlieb, B. H. (1975). The contribution of natural support systems to primary prevention among four subgroups of adolescent males. *Adolescence, 10,* 207–220.

Greenberg, M. S., & Westcott, D. R. (1983). Indebtedness as a mediator of reactions to aid. In J. D. Fisher, A. Nadler, & B. M. DePaulo (Eds.), *New directions in helping: Vol. 1. Recipient reactions to aid* (pp. 86–112). New York: Academic Press.

Gross, A. E., & McMullen, P. A. (1983). Models of the help-seeking process. In B. M. Depaulo, A. Nadler, & J. D. Fisher (Eds.), *New directions in helping: Vol. 2. Helpseeking* (pp. 47–70). New York: Academic Press.

Gurin, P., & Epps, E. (1975). *Black consciousness, identity, and achievement.* New York: Wiley.

Hazan, C., & Shaver, P. (1990). Love and work: An attachment-theoretical perspective. *Journal of Personality and Social Psychology, 59,* 270–280.

Hirsch, B. J. (1981). Social networks and the coping process: Creating personal communities. In B. Gottlieb (Ed.), *Social networks and social support* (pp. 149–170). London: Sage.

Kaplan, B. H., Cassel, J. C., & Gore, S. (1977). Social support and health. *Medical Care, 15*(5, Supplement), 47–58.

Keefe, S. E. (1979). Urbanization, acculturation, and extended family ties: Mexican Americans in cities. *American Ethnologist, 6,* 349–365.

Keefe, S. E., & Padilla, A. M. (1987). *Chicano ethnicity.* Albuquerque: University of New Mexico Press.

Keefe, S. E., Padilla, A. M., & Carlos, M. L. (1979). The Mexican American extended family as an emotional support system. *Human Organization, 38,* 144–152.

Kim, J. (1986). *The strength of weak ties: A conceptual elaboration at the dyad level.* Unpublished doctoral dissertation, Stanford University, Stanford, CA.

Kim, Y. Y. (1987). Facilitating immigrant adaptation: The role of communication. In T. L. Albrecht & M. B. Adelman (Eds.), *Communicating social support* (pp. 192–211). London: Sage.

Kozol, J. (1991). *Savage inequalitites: Children in America's schools.* New York: Crown.

Lin, N., Dean, A., & Ensel, W. (Eds.). (1986). *Social support, life events, and depression.* Orlando, FL: Academic Press.

Lomnitz, L. A. (1977). *Networks and marginality: Life in a Mexican shantytown.* New York: Academic Press.

Main, M., & Cassidy, J. (1988). Categories of response to reunion with the parent at age six: Predictable from infant attachment classifications and stable over a one-month period. *Developmental Psychology, 24,* 415–426.

Main, M., & Weston, D. R. (1981). The quality of the toddler's relationship to mother and to father: Related to conflict behavior and the readiness to establish new relationships. *Child Development, 52,* 932–940.

Matas, L., Arend, R. A., & Sroufe, A. (1978). Continuity of adaptation in the second year: The relationship between quality of attachment and later competence. *Child Development, 49,* 547–556.

Matute-Bianchi, E. (1989). Ethnic identities and patterns of school success and failure among Mexican-descent and Japanese-American students in a California school. *American Journal of Education, 95,* 233–255.

McLaughlin, M. W., & Heath, S. B. (Eds.). (1993). *Identity and inner-city youth: Beyond ethnicity and gender.* New York: Columbia University, Teachers' College.

McLaughlin, M. W., Irby, M. A., & Langman, J. (1994). *Urban sanctuaries: Neighborhood organizations in the lives and futures of inner-city youth.* San Francisco: Jossey-Bass.

Merton, R. K. (1949). *Social structure and anomie.* New York: Free Press.

Modigliani, A. (1968). Embarrassment and embarrassability. *Sociometry, 17,* 313–326.

Modigliani, A. (1971). Embarrassment, facework, and eye contact: Testing a theory of embarrassment. *Journal of Personality and Social Psychology, 17,* 15–24.

Nadler, A. (1983). Personal characteristics and help-seeking. In B. M. DePaulo, A. Nadler, & J. D. Fisher (Eds.), *New directions in helping: Vol. 2. Help seeking* (pp. 303–340). New York: Academic Press.

Nelson-LeGall, S. (1985). Help-seeking behavior in learning. In E. W. Gordon (Ed.), *Review of research in education* (Vol. 12, pp. 55–90). Washington, DC: American Educational Research Association.

Ogbu, J. (1978). *Minority education and caste: The American system in cross-cultural perspective.* New York: Academic Press.

Ogbu, J. U. (1991). Immigrant and involuntary minorities in comparative perspective. In M. A. Gibson & J. U. Ogbu (Eds.), *Minority status and schooling: A comparative study of immigrant and involuntary minorities* (pp. 3–33). New York: Garland.

Padilla, A. M. (Ed.). (1980). *Acculturation: Theory, models and some new findings.* Boulder, CO: Westview Press.

Pastor, D. L. (1981). The quality of mother-infant attachment and its relationship to toddlers' initial sociability with peers. *Child Development, 52,* 932–940.

Phelan, P., Davidson, A. L., & Yu, H. C. (1998). *Adolescents' worlds: Negotiating family, peers, and school.* New York: Teachers' College Press.

Philips, D. (1963). Rejection: A possible consequence of seeking help for mental disorders. *American Sociological Review, 20,* 963–972.

Pistole, M. C. (1981). Attachment and adult romantic relationships: Style of conflict resolution and relationship satisfaction. *Journal of Social and Personal Relationships, 6,* 505–512.

Portes, A., & Bach, R. L. (1985). *Latin journey: Cuban and Mexican immigrants in the United States.* Los Angeles: University of California Press.

Portes, A., & Rumbaut, R. G. (1990). *Immigrant America: A portrait.* Berkeley: University of California Press.

Sánchez-Jankowski, M. (1991). *Islands in the street: Gangs and American urban society.* Berkeley: University of California.

Sena-Rivera, J. (1979). Extended kinship in the United States: Competing models and the case of *la familia Chicana. Journal of Marriage and the Family, 41,* 121–129.

Shapiro, E. G. (1983). Embarrassment and help-seeking. In B. M. DePaulo, A. Nadler, & J. Fisher (Eds.), *New directions in helping: Vol. 2. Help-seeking* (pp. 143–163). New York: Academic Press.

Simpson, C. H., & Rosenholtz, S. J. (1986). Classroom structure and the social construction of ability. In J. G. Richardson (Ed.), *Handbook of theory and research for the sociology of education* (pp. 113–138). New York: Greenwork Press.

Spina, S. U. (1998). A review of R. J. Haggerty, L. R. Sherrod, N. Garmezy, & M. Rutter (Eds.), "Stress, risk, and resilience in children and adolescents: Processes, mechanisms, and interventions." *Mind, Culture, and Activity, 5,* 235–239.

Stack, C. B. (1974). *All our kin: Struggles for survival in a black community.* New York: Harper and Row.

Stanton-Salazar, R. D. (1997). A social capital framework for understanding the socialization of racial minority children and youth. *Harvard Educational Review, 67,* 1–40.

Stanton-Salazar, R. D., & Dornbusch, S. M. (1995). Social capital and the social reproduction of inequality: The formation of informational networks among Mexican-origin high school students. *Sociology of Education Journal, 68,* 116–135.

Stanton-Salazar, R. D., Vasquez, O. A., & Mehan, H. (1996). Engineering success through institutional support. In A. Hurtado, R. Figueroa, & E. E. García (Eds.), *Strategic interventions in education: Expanding the Latina/Latino pipeline* (pp. 100–136). Santa Cruz: Regents of the University of California.

Sullivan, M. (1989). *Getting paid: Youth, crime, and work in the inner city.* London: Cornell University Press.

Tolsdorf, C. (1976). Social networks, support, and coping: An exploratory analysis. *Family Process, 15,* 407–417.

Tonnies, F. (1963). *Community and society.* New York: Harper and Row. (Original work published 1887).
Trueba, H., & Delgado-Gaitan, C. (1988). *School and society: Learning content through culture.* New York: Praeger.
Turner, R. H. (1960). Sponsored and contest mobility and the school system. *American Sociological Review, 25,* 855–867.
Valenzuela, A. (1997). Mexican American youth and the politics of caring. In E. Long (Ed.), *From sociology to cultural studies: Vol. 2. Sociology of Culture Annual Series* (pp. 322–350). London: Basil Blackwell.
Vásquez, O. A., Pease-Alvarez, L., & Shannon, S. (1994). *Pushing boundaries: Language and culture in a Mexicano community.* New York: Cambridge University Press.
Vaux, A. (1988). *Social support: Theory, research, and intervention.* New York: Praeger.
Vaux, A., Burda, P., & Stewart, D. (1986). Orientation toward utilization of support resources. *Journal of Community Psychology, 14,* 159–170.
Vaux, A., & Wood, J. (1987). Social support resources, behavior, and appraisals: A path analysis. *Social Behavior and Personality: An International Journal, 15,* 107–111.
Vélez-Ibáñez, C. G. (1980). Mexican/Hispano support systems and *confianza*: Theoretical issues of cultural adaptation. In R. Valle & W. Vega (Eds.), *A natural resource system for health: Mental health promotion to Latino/Hispano populations* (pp. 45–54). Sacramento, CA: Department of Mental Health.
Vélez-Ibáñez, C. G. (1983). *Bonds of mutual trust: The cultural systems of rotating credit associations among urban Mexicans and Chicanos.* New Brunswick, NJ: Rutgers University Press.
Vigil, J. D. (1988). *Barrio gangs: Street life and identity in southern California.* Austin: University of Texas.
Walker, K. N., MacBride, A., & Vachon, M.L.S. (1977). Social support networks and the crisis of bereavement. *Social Science and Medicine, 11,* 35–41.
Wallace, J. L., & Vaux, A. (1993). Social support network orientation: The role of adult attachment style. *Journal of Social and Clinical Psychology, 12,* 354–365.
Wallston, B. S., Walster, G. W., & Bercheid, E. (1978). *Equity: Theory and research.* Boston: Allyn and Bacon.
Waters, E. (1978). The reliability and stability of individual differences in infant-mother attachment. *Child Development, 49,* 483–494.
Waters, E., Wittman, J., & Sroufe, L. A. (1979). Attachment, positive affect, and competence in the peer group: Two studies of construct validation. *Child Development, 50,* 821–889.

Wellman, B. (1983). Network analysis: Some basic principles. *Sociological Theory,* 155–200.

Werner, E. E., & Smith, R. S. (1982). *Vulnerable but invincible: A longitudinal study of resilient children and youth.* New York: McGraw-Hill.

White, D., & Woollett, A. (1992). *Families: A context for development.* New York: Falmer Press.

Williams, N. (1990). *The Mexican American family: Tradition and change.* Dix Hills, NY: General Hall.

Williams, T., & Kornblum, W. (1985). *Growing up poor.* Lexington: Lexington Books.

Willie, C. V. (1985). *Black and white families: A study in complementarity.* Bayside, NY: General Hall.

Willis, P. (1977). *Learning to labor: How working class kids get working class jobs.* New York: Columbia University Press.

Willis, P. (1981). *Learning to labor: How working class kids get working class jobs.* New York: Columbia University Press.

Wilson, W. J. (1987). *The truly disadvantaged: The inner city, the underclass, and public policy.* Chicago: University of Chicago Press.

CHAPTER 9
Family Values of Latino Adolescents

HEIDIE A. VÁZQUEZ GARCÍA, CYNTHIA GARCÍA COLL, SUMRU ERKUT, ODETTE ALARCÓN, AND LINDA R. TROPP

Latino families have been described in the literature as adhering to family values and styles of interactions that are different from those of other ethnic groups and the dominant middle-class, Anglo, North American culture. Familism, or the strong identification, loyalty, attachment, and solidarity of individuals with their families, is considered one of the most important culture-specific values of Latino families (Andrade, 1980; Garrison & Weiss, 1979; Gurak, 1981; Moore, 1970; Sabogal, Marín, Otero-Sabogal, VanOss-Marín, & Pérez-Stable, 1987; Triandis, Marín, Betancourt, Lisansky, & Chang, 1982). Similarly, the phrase "normal enmeshment" has been coined to describe the pattern observed within Latino families of overinvolvement, dependence, and discouragement of self-differentiation among family members (Canino & Canino, 1980; Badillo Ghali, 1982). *Respeto*, as a value and as a behavior, also serves in the preservation of generational and gender role boundaries in families, moderating how individual family members interact based on age and sex (García-Preto, 1982). Accordingly, child-rearing values also emphasize strict sex roles, respect for elderly and other authority figures, discouragement of independence, and avoidance of conflict with significant others (Borrás, 1989; García-Preto, 1982).

However, recent research has started to document the variability and diversity observed among Latino families living in the mainland United States. For example, Zayas and Palleja (1988) describe how different levels of acculturation and upheavals in employment and relocation affect the cultural values and functioning of families. Generation, language preference, level of acculturation, and ethnic identity have also been found to be related to individual differences among Latinos in terms of adherence to these traditional family values (Garza & Gallegos, 1985; Szapocznik, Kurtines, & Fernandez, 1980). Therefore, there seems to be a wide range of normative values among Latino families as a result of migration, socioeconomic changes, and contact with other views and ways of functioning.

While these studies do document variability and diversity among Latino families, most of the research to date has concentrated on adult populations (with the notable exception of Szapocznik and his colleagues' work, 1980). Thus, very little information is available on the Latino adolescent population living in the United States. Adolescents are an important and yet generally neglected group of the Latino population. While population reports indicate that by the next millennium the adolescent population in the United States as a whole will decline, it is projected that by the year 2030 Latino youth will number 9.6 million, more than double the number in 1980. In other words, one in every five youths in the United States will be Latino (Children's Defense Fund, 1990). In addition, Latinos tend to be younger than the population at large. Latino adolescents are twice as likely to have a parent who is younger than 30 and there is a higher percentage of Latino teenagers who are parents themselves (Children's Defense Fund, 1990; Ventura, 1982).

Not only are adolescents an understudied and marginalized group, but, more often than not, research tends to focus on the negative outcomes of this population and the pathology that results from said outcomes. This is due in part to the fact that Latino youths are overrepresented in high-risk groups. For example, Latinos are two and a half times more likely than whites to be two or more grades behind in school (Children's Defense Fund, 1990). In addition, they have the highest rate of school dropouts: 35.3 percent, compared to 13.6 percent for black non-Latinos and 8.9 percent for white non-Latinos (National Center for Education Statistics, 1993). Unemployment rates are also higher for Latino males: 28 percent and 14 percent for 16- to 19-year-olds and 20- to 24-year-olds, respectively (National Center for Education Statistics, 1993). Similarly, the teenage pregnancy rate for all Latinos (17 percent) is almost double what it is for white non-Latino teenagers (10 percent) (Ventura, 1994).

Although it is true that Latino youths are overrepresented in these at-risk groups, the majority of Latino adolescents do not exhibit high-risk behaviors. However, the literature does not address the developmental pathways of the groups that are not exhibiting behavioral and developmental problems. This lacuna suggests the critical need for normative studies. We need research that examines how the family values of Latino adolescents are influenced by their daily realities on the U.S. mainland, and how factors such as acculturation, migration, education, and socioeconomic status affect the outcome of Latino adolescents in relation to their individual as well as family development.

We also need to take into account the notion of Latino adolescents being caught in multiple worlds. While adolescence itself is a period of change, adjustment, growth, and discovery for human beings (for both the adolescent and his or her family), Latino adolescents in the United States are also confronted with the potential for additional conflicts with their family due to differences in migration, acculturation, and discrimination. A useful framework to understand the experience of Latino adolescents and their families is that of Boykin and Toms (1985). In their framework, African American child socialization has to prepare children to cope with the experiences of (1) mainstream America, (2) African Americans, and (3) minorities. Similarly, Latino adolescents often function within and between two or more value systems and frames of reference. Zavala Martínez (1994) coins the term *entremundos* as the experience of being caught between two worlds, forced to "forge multiple identities within these contexts . . . while simultaneously adapting to the taxing demands of a constantly changing, highly urbanized technological society" (p. 30). By examining the variables that impact the lives of Latino adolescents we can explore how these factors influence the family values and views of Latino adolescents. These variables in turn affect adolescents' outcomes, namely, their own mental health, academic achievement, employment opportunities, and interaction with their parents as well as their own functioning as young parents.

In this chapter, we address the current conceptualization and measurement of family values and functioning within minority groups in the United States and within Latino families in particular. Subsequently, we describe the process of developing a scale for measuring family values and functioning among Latino adolescents. Finally, we present data on an exploratory study of eighty Latino adolescents and discuss the implications of such data on understanding the family functioning and values of Latino families.

CONCEPTUALIZATION OF FAMILY VALUES AND FUNCTIONING

Most aspects of a given society or culture are based on its worldview; some examples include work style, mode and style of communication and interaction, and dynamics of human relationships, to name a few. Similarly, a society's worldview which is historically, culturally, and socially defined is at the root of family organization, family values, and family functioning. For the most part, this worldview as defined by the cultural context is not only upheld by the family itself, but is also reinforced by the immediate community in which a family lives as well as by the greater population of that culture (Brislin, 1993). Stability within the family depends on (1) its adherence to the same worldviews through patterns of interactions with one another as well as others (Reiss, 1981), and (2) the transmission of family values and functioning from one generation to the next. Furthermore, the ways in which these values are to be transmitted to future generations are considered sacrosanct. Thus, as a culture perfects the child-rearing and socialization techniques and attitudes that will be most beneficial to the next generation, those practices are preserved at all costs (LeVine, 1977; Triandis, Bontempo, Villareal, Asai, & Lucca, 1988).

One basic dimension of worldviews and a primary difference between Latino and Anglo culture is the notion of collectivism versus individualism. Collectivist cultures view self-definition as a group process, subordinate personal goals to in-group goals, show concern for the integrity of the in-group, and form intense emotional attachments to the in-group (Triandis et al., 1988). Individualist cultures emphasize self-definition as an entity that is distinct and separate from group(s), maintain personal goals even if pursuit of such goals inconveniences the in-group, and show less concern and emotional attachment to the in-group (Triandis et al., 1988, p. 335). With regard to family relationships and systems, Triandis and colleagues (1988, p. 325) state that:

> . . . in collectivist cultures the most important relationships are vertical (e.g., parent-child), whereas in individualist cultures the most important relationships are horizontal (e.g., husband-wife, friend-friend) . . . interdependence is maximized between parent and child by frequent guidance, consultation, socializing in which the children are included, and penetration into the child's private life. In individualist cultures, there is emotional detachment, independence, and privacy for the child.

Psychological and emotional distance characterize the relationships between family members in individualist cultures, whereas the familial relationships and values of persons in collectivist cultures are characterized by a close-knit relationship between the individual and the extended family (Brislin, 1993). Integrally related to this unique conceptualization of relationships and to their maintenance in family structures is the communication and the expression of emotions. According to Gudykunst and Nishida (1989), people in collectivist cultures are more aware of, and pay more attention to, context when communicating than people in individualist cultures. Touching, emotional expression, physical distance between people, and eye contact are essential in interactions but differ as a function of context. Unlike individualists, directness and clarity is not a particular goal of collectivists when communicating. Rather, the ability to maintain harmony by avoiding contradiction (i.e., saying what the other wants to hear) is highly valued (Triandis, 1994).

Therefore, given certain cultural ideals, values, and worldviews, societies will emphasize the provision of certain childhood experiences that will lead to the internalization of these values. Brislin (1993) states that children are able to behave in many different ways and to engage in many types of experiences. Yet it is the guidance away from a *total* set of possible behaviors and an encouragement of a particular, more limited set of behaviors that are "considered acceptable and important within any one culture" that is an important part of socialization (Brislin, 1993, p. 95). Similarly, Serpell (1994, p. 163) states that:

> ... culture structures the effective opportunities for intellectual developments, defines the goals of socialization, and constitutes the context within which the definition of goals and opportunities for attaining them is debated among the people who collectively own, belong to, and construct that culture.

In other words, as the norms, boundaries, and construction of cultures vary, so will the acceptable, meaningful behavior of people in that culture with regard to communication, social behavior, child rearing and socialization, and family values and functioning.

Mainstream child development researchers, on the other hand, have only recently realized that family values and functioning are influenced and shaped by cultural values, competencies, and defined tasks. Moreover, the lack of understanding of cultural differences as differences and *not* as deficits has hampered the theories and research with non-Anglo populations. For example, Kluckhohn and Strodtbeck (1961), Mead (1953), and Saunders (1954), to name a few, suggested that Mexican

American families were dysfunctional because their cultural values and orientations (1) were incompatible with Anglo-American values, (2) contributed to their low socioeconomic status, and (3) ultimately, impeded their own success and the successful socialization of their children. Similarly, Lewis (1965) and Thomas (1967) depicted the Puerto Rican family as an inferior, "high-risk," dysfunctional institution, pointing to inherent flaws in the structure of the Puerto Rican family as the primary reason for poor socialization patterns as well as poor developmental outcomes of Puerto Rican children. Early studies with Latinos also argued that they lacked self-direction, had low self-esteem, had cognitive and linguistic deficits, and a low need for achievement. Carter (1979), Jensen (1962), and Reisman (1962) theorized that Latino youths' school performance was related not only to the students' deficits but to the inferiority of their families. These deficiencies, in turn, were often attributed to presumed problems in the children's family lives and to the flawed family functioning and value system which has often been portrayed not only as "bleak, disrupted, and impoverished" (Stevenson, Chen, & Uttal, 1990), but as a process which is inherently flawed. Thus, rather than focus on explaining the variability between cultures and the relativity of values outlining the strengths of a particular family or of the structure of families within a particular culture, most of the extant research has used a comparative model to focus on the weaknesses of non-majority culture families.

However, while deficit-oriented models and comparative studies have predominated the research and continue to be used (see Harrison, Serafica, & McAdoo, 1984; McLoyd & Randolph, 1985), there is a paradigmatic shift with regard to the family values and functioning of ethnic minority families and their children. This new wave of research moves away from deficit-oriented models and comparative studies and focuses on cross-cultural elements. Frameworks such as the socioculturally relativistic paradigm (Laosa, 1989), the cultural-ecological model (Ogbu, 1981), and the developmental-contextual model (Lerner, 1989) are being used to study minority children and families in their own right. These frameworks suggest that different cultures with different child-rearing practices promote competencies which, while different from those of middle-class Anglos (Ogbu, 1981), are valued and adaptive given their past and present contextual demands. In this work, competence is culturally defined, and these culturally defined competencies (e.g., gender, social, and familial roles) are transmitted to new generations through child-rearing practices and techniques (LeVine, 1977; Berry, 1980; Ogbu, 1981).

Similarly, from an organizational perspective (see Cicchetti & Schneider-Rosen, 1986; Sroufe, 1979; Werner, 1948) as well as other frameworks that study human development and family processes within context (LeVine, 1977; Super, 1981; Whiting, 1977), competence is described as a series of interlocking social, emotional, and cognitive competencies that facilitate an individual's broad adaptation to his or her environment. In other words, competence is not defined in relation to the "average" prototype, which in the case of the United States is considered the white middle class. Rather, competence is defined as the ability to perform age-appropriate and culturally defined tasks under specific environmental circumstances. Therefore, cultural differences in parenting and teaching behavior which are consistent with cultural values form part of adaptive strategies within the family context.

ADAPTATION AND DIVERSITY IN LATINO FAMILY VALUES

As stated previously, broad generalizations can be made about Latino families in terms of family values, behaviors, and familial roles. Yet several factors can be identified as introducing and influencing variability within this population. Documenting some of the differences within subgroups of Latinos is important in understanding how certain variables have a greater or lesser impact on the development and outcome of Latino adolescents in the United States. This section specifies a number of forces which we believe modify the traditional Latino family values and functioning. Some of these factors include migration, acculturation, and gender.

Migration

Even though two-thirds of the Latino population in the United States was born here, with Mexican Americans being the largest subgroup, amounting to 75 percent of the Latino population living in the States (Children's Defense Fund, 1990), migration of Latinos to and from the U.S. mainland continues to shape the family values of those who migrate as well as those who do not. Various patterns of migration for Latino groups in the United States have been documented. According to Aponte (1993), rapid migration by Puerto Ricans has long ceased, whereas Mexican immigration continues at a fairly rapid pace. These patterns are influenced by differences in opportunity, sociodemographics, and accessibility to country of origin.

Puerto Rican families, for example, with their ability to come and go from the U.S. mainland because of its colonial status with the United States, are constantly dealing with the issue of migration and the changes that result from "circular migration" or the "revolving door" phenomenon (Bonilla & Campos, 1981; Bonilla, 1985). In the early nineteenth century most of the Puerto Rican migration was due to political factors. After 1917, Puerto Ricans received U.S. citizenship and for the most part the migration to the States was motivated by economic reasons (Comas Díaz, 1989). Originally developed to refer to the need of surplus labor to go back and forth from Puerto Rico to the United States, the term *circular migration* has now been used to describe the lack of progress resulting from the constant migrating to and from Puerto Rico and the United States (Rodriguez, 1989). Researchers such as Rogler, Cooney, and Ortiz (1980) have documented how circular migration has affected not only the family values of Puerto Ricans (from traditional island to contemporary mainstream U.S.), but how changes in ethnic identity (parents feeling stronger than their children about traditional Puerto Rican values and culture) have also resulted.

Similarly, Cuban migration to the United States has and continues to be motivated by political factors. While there are differences in terms of the fluidity of return migration to the country of origin (i.e., the ability of Puerto Ricans to return to Puerto Rico and the inability of Cubans to return to Cuba), studies have shown some similarities between the two groups in the cultural adaptation process of adolescents and their families. Research with Cuban American adolescents and their families has documented that adolescents, more so than their parents, tend to overacculturate to the host culture. In thus rejecting the values and customs of the culture of origin they bring about major changes and potential conflicts in family as well as intrapersonal identity (Szapocznik et al., 1980; Szapocznik, Scopetta, Kurtines, & Arnalde, 1978).

In addition, immigrant families and children are also faced with further challenges due to generational boundaries between family members (Cornille & Brotherton, 1993). Immigrant families, and especially second-generation families, feel that in order to succeed in the new (host) culture they must give up their own coping mechanisms and adopt new problem-solving strategies offered by the host culture. Baptiste (1993) states that adolescent immigrants tend to be more malleable and impressionable than their parents, and quickly acculturate and assume "American" behaviors, attitudes, values, and habits which are different from the usual ones expected for adults and children in the family's native country.

Consequently, conflicts with adolescents (especially with Puerto Ricans because of citizenship status and the ease of movement to and from the island to the U.S.) are sometimes managed with a quasi return migration to their country of origin (e.g., Puerto Rico), if only for a short time, in an attempt to instill the traditional values that are being lost as a result of acculturation. According to Badillo Ghali (1982), adolescents in particular, because they are caught between conflicting parental and societal values, may rebel and become defensive about who they are, possibly resenting and rejecting the characteristics and the values of their own group and family which they interpret as being the culprit for having caused the rejection from the host culture. Because of the strong ties to extended family members, and possibly many still living on the country of origin, this process is considered quite common and whenever possible is practiced in the hopes of diminishing the "Americanization" of their children. Martinez (1981) states that this process is practiced by parents who believe that cultural sanctions will have a stronger impact in the country of origin.

Research suggests that conflict ensues when collectivist families, where interdependence, obligation, consultation, and guidance are valued, such as in Latino cultures, encounter individualistic cultural values which foster independence, emotional detachment, and privacy for and between family members (Triandis et al., 1988). For Latino adolescents and their families, such conflicts can manifest themselves in adolescents' modification of ties to parents (Inclán & Herron, 1990), adolescents' autonomy (see Szapocznik, Santisteban, Río, Pérez-Vidal, Kurtines, & Hervis, 1986) and self-differentiation. According to Baptiste (1993) the following are some issues that affect Latino parent-adolescent relations: (1) changes in familial and generational boundaries; (2) lessening of parental authority because of changing roles; (3) fear of losing children to the new culture; (4) unpreparedness for change and conflict; and (5) extended family engagement-disengagement problems.

In other words, it is not only the *contact* with a different culture or values per se that affect parent-adolescent relations in Latino families, but also the fear that the interaction and the exchange between cultures might produce conflict within the adolescent as well as in the family.

Acculturation

Acculturation is another factor in addition to migration that influences family values of Latino adolescents. Acculturation is defined as the process by which a particular set of attitudes, behaviors, and values changes or is modified as it comes into contact with another different set of values and behaviors (Lin, Masuda, & Tazuma, 1982). While many equate acculturation with migration, the process of acculturation may actually result from exposure to a set of norms different from one's own culture. For example, a Latino child might go through a process of acculturation as he or she moves from a predominately Latino neighborhood to a predominately Anglo neighborhood. Or a child who has been in a bilingual class might go through the process of acculturation when entering a monolingual mainstream class. Therefore, acculturation can be conceptualized as a psychosocial adaptation to any particular, previously unfamiliar, cultural environment.

Reuschenberg and Buriel (1988) found that people acculturate in a variety of ways to different settings. They suggest that the acculturation of some individuals only affects their outside social interactions, while their internal family interactions remain intact. Similarly, Laosa (1977) has stated that a person who learns to function in more than one cultural context will do so and behave accordingly as called for by the situation and the cultural standards. In clinical practice, Inclán (1985) has reported differences in value orientations for Latino clients who express interest in more egalitarian sex roles in family relationships while maintaining traditional affective values.

Yet while the melting pot theory of minority assimilation to white mainstream U.S. values and culture is being challenged by the "salad bowl" theory, whereby acceptance and maintenance of cultural, religious, racial, or ethnic diversity is slowly becoming a societal norm, the process of acculturation is not without obstacles. As stated by Tropp and colleagues (Tropp, Erkut, Alarcón, García Coll, & Vázquez, 1994, p. 1), "cultural change does not necessarily intimate a smooth transition." Whether voluntary or forced, aspects of the process of acculturation (or lack of acculturation) can affect the adaptation of the individual to the host culture, resulting in a number of changes in areas such as language use, cognitive style, personality, identity, attitudes, and stress (Berry, 1980). Fitzpatrick (1988) points to three patterns that may result from the acculturative process. He suggests that an individual may attempt to become more like the people in the host culture as quickly as possible, may resist the host culture's values and behaviors, and withdraw to his or her own culture, or may find a middle point between his or her own culture and the host culture, negotiating between his or her own traditional cultural values and the host culture's values and customs. Koteskey, Walker, and Johnson (1990) state that the ability to negotiate between two cultural value systems and to retain customs and traditions that are labeled or considered obsolete within the traditional culture may help achieve a cultural and personal identity.

Furthermore, the acculturation process affects groups of people and systems as well as individuals. For example, research suggests that to a large extent parents and other family members mediate children's ability to acculturate to various situations and environments (Caudill, 1973; García Coll & Meyer, 1993; García Coll, Meyer, & Brillon, 1995). Rueschenberg and Buriel (1988) found that the more acculturated Mexican-descent families became to U.S. culture, the more they used formal social support services (i.e., outside the family system). Similarly, Sabogal and colleagues (1987) found that as the level of acculturation increased in Mexican American families, the perception of the family as referents decreased. Interestingly, while certain behaviors and values were reported as changing with increasing acculturation, other cultural values and practices such as the maintenance of the internal family system and the maintenance of the perception of family support remained constant. In other words, individuals as well as families may learn to acculturate in certain spheres of life without necessarily relinquishing the cultural values of their original culture.

Theorists suggest that acculturation permeates physical, psychological, linguistic, emotional, and cultural areas of development. Ogbu (1987), on the one hand, suggests that school performance, academic achievement, language proficiency, and social development such as peer and familial relationships for children and adolescents are all affected by acculturation. Moreover, how parents themselves adapt to differing cultural values, practices, and attitudes, as well as how they negotiate conflicts resulting from contrasting traditional and host culture values, will affect their children's academic achievement, psychological adjustment, and social competence. On the other hand, Szapocznik et al. (1980) suggest that as children prepare to go into adolescence, they become more active in their own acculturation—a process that continues throughout the adolescent period. As the adolescent becomes more dynamic in his or her own acculturation, parental opinion and power to control the level of acculturation in certain situations may be overshadowed and ignored by the adolescent. An intergenerational gap in acculturation can produce conflict in the form of feelings of guilt, loss, rejection, and alienation for both the parent and the adolescent.

While it is very important to note the potential conflicts, maladaptation, and even pyschopathology that can result from overacculturation to mainstream values and behaviors relative to their parents, it is also critical to consider how these factors may result from underacculturation. Szapocznik and colleagues (1978, 1980) suggest that adolescents who are underacculturated tend to become withdrawn, isolated, and at times depressed due to the internalization of the trauma of adapting to the host culture. Similarly, Rogler and colleagues (1991) suggest that low acculturated individuals experience pervasive isolation from the host culture because they feel they cannot reconstruct the social networks that they had established in their country of origin, which in turn produces higher levels of stress, acculturative strain, and low self-esteem. Acculturation, as Gil, Vega, and Dimas (1994) and others suggest, is not a bipolar mechanism. Rather, it is a continuum that serves to mediate the effects of adaptation (whether positive or negative) to a host culture.

Gender

Along with migration and acculturation, gender affects how and to what degree Latino adolescents will adhere to traditional family values and functioning. As has been documented in the literature, in traditional Latino culture strict gender roles dictate appropriate behaviors and values within the structure of the nuclear as well as the extended family. Díaz Guerrero (1955) states that two of the central themes upon which the Mexican family value system is based are "the unquestioned and absolute supremacy of the father and the necessary and absolute self-sacrifice of the mother" (p. 411). Similarly, Badillo Ghali (1982) states that martyrdom and self-sacrifice are the characteristics that are expected of a good Puerto Rican woman and wife while men have unquestioned supremacy and freedom. While the male's role is to discipline the children as well as to provide for and protect the family, it is the woman's sacrifice and selflessness that sustains the reciprocity of family obligations, relationships, and ties throughout generations (Nieves Falcón, 1972; Bernal & Alvarez, 1983).

These gender roles, however, are not only ascribed to women and men solely within the context of the family, but rather they become cultural categories which are socially prescribed and upheld through social institutions such as school, church, and other organizations. There is very little empirical and theoretical work that examines the relationship between familism and women's role in Latino societies, or how these familial relationships reinforce women's dependency and subordination to the patriarchal family system. However, there are some studies which explore how sociocultural context influences women's roles. For example, in a study conducted with middle-class Puerto Rican women, Margarida Juliá (1989) found that 75 percent of the women felt that there was an implicit social assumption that self-fulfillment and self-actualization for women only came in their role as caretakers. Academic achievement, professional development, and economic independence were not seen as accomplishments for women by society. In other words, the sexually based dichotomous expectations that shape the traditional family value system of Latinos were found to also dictate appropriate gender role behavior in society.

On the other hand, Latinos are confronted with factors such as migration and acculturation, gender role expectations, and behavioral change. In fact, Ginorio (1979) suggests that Latino women acculturate faster to the host culture's gender roles than they do to anything else. For example, the submissiveness and loyalty that is expected to be exhibited by Puerto Rican women (Minuchin, Montalvo, & Guerny, 1967) begins to erode as opportunities for increased autonomy and assertiveness increase. O'Reilly (1985) states that while Puerto Rican men in the United States return to Puerto Rico to regain their social status, which is for the most part gender-based, most women choose to stay in the States, regardless of economic and social hardships, in order to achieve and retain the autonomy which is not culturally or economically available to them on the island.

Another factor that has an impact on gender roles is employment. It has been documented that immigrant Latino females find employment faster than males (Borrás, 1989), thereby changing the traditional women's role of solely providing for the family in an emotional capacity to the role of breadwinner. As this reversal occurs, it challenges the male's role of providing for the family and the male's authority over economic and monetary matters. This shift subsequently causes low self-esteem in men and increases tensions within the relationship which can lead to separation and possibly divorce (Borrás, 1989).

As gender roles shift, the patriarchal structure of the Latino family is challenged. Mendoza and colleagues (1994) state that Latino families are more likely than non-Latino Caucasian families to be headed by a single parent, which more often than not is female. Several researchers have postulated that the single Latina mother has to assume the complex dual role of mother and father, which changes the conditions for dealing with single parenthood in the original cultural context (Borrás, 1989).

The difficulty in assuming this role does not come from the inability of the women to fulfill its responsibilities, but rather from the socialization process in the culture of origin which clearly defined gender roles within the family and society. Children and adolescents face similar transitions and cultural transformations as a result of migration and acculturation. Several empirical studies have shed light on how migration affects Latino adolescent males and females differently. For example, Hardy-Fanta and Montana (1982) found that Puerto Rican female adolescents who migrated to the United States had increased parent-adolescent conflicts due to differing levels of adherence to cultural values. Some of the ways in which the adolescents manifested their ambivalence toward their traditional values included sexual or aggressive acting out behavior, depression, withdrawal, poor school functioning, and male-female relationships that were "impulsively established" (p. 352). Similarly, in a study examining gender differences in stress among Mexican immigrant adolescents in California, Zambrana and Silva-Palacios (1989) found that while all adolescents experienced stress related to social change (e.g., language, immigration status, social expectations), females experienced higher levels of stress compared to males. These responses on the part of the adolescent female may have resulted from role conflict between appropriate gender role behavior in the host culture versus allegiance to their own traditional cultural values.

Dissonance between home and school values (as a function of acculturation) also challenges traditional Latino family values and traditional gender roles for children and adolescents. Some of these home/school cultural, familial, and gender value conflicts include (1) girls do not need to be as educated as boys/both sexes should be educated equally; (2) admonishment of immodesty in girls/physical education requires changing in front of others; (3) promotion of ignorance of sexual matters/advocates sex education; (4) segregation of sex groups/nonsegregated sex groups; (5) nurturance of dependency/values independence; (6) nurturance cooperation/values competition (Vázquez Nuttall & Romero-García, 1989).

While it seems that gender socialization and role expectations may be altered by factors such as migration and acculturation, the opposite might also be true. Espin (1987) suggests that instead of adopting the host culture's gender roles, immigrant families might "become entrenched in traditional social and sex-role norms as a defense against the strong pressures to acculturate" (p. 493). However, for adolescents, this adherence to "old," traditional ways and views of gender roles might be problematic. In some cases, adolescents may become isolated and withdrawn, develop low self-esteem, and become marginalized as they cannot negotiate between their traditional gender roles and the gender roles of the host society (Zavala Martínez, 1994).

Thus, traditional gender socialization, gender role expectations, and behaviors of Latino families are challenged as dominant mainstream gender socialization patterns fostering egalitarian sex roles are espoused by the host culture. Goldscheider (1993) states that as gender roles change for family members, the interpretation and the adherence to traditional familism values also changes. However, while some would argue that these changes are contributing to the decline of the family and to family values, others suggest that reinterpretations or reconfigurations in gender roles in Latino families may be an adaptive strategy in the preservation of some sense of familism for Latino families (Zavala Martínez, 1994).

MEASUREMENT OF FAMILY FUNCTIONING AND VALUES IN LATINO ADOLESCENTS: AN EXPLORATORY STUDY

Unfortunately, culturally appropriate research as well as measures in this area are limited. A thorough examination of the available instruments revealed that traditional family values and functioning of Latino families and adolescents as measured by standard instruments may be seen as "pathological" or "deviant." Consequently, we generated our own items as well as adapted items from the McMaster Family Assessment Device (FAD) (Epstein, Baldwin, & Bishop, 1983) and the Familism Scale (Sabogal et al., 1987). The final scale consists of 51 items, whose responses are on a 7-point Likert scale (1 = strongly agree to 7 = strongly disagree), measuring prescriptive family values, family roles and relationships, degree of enmeshment and communication, and affective expression in Latino families. The higher the number chosen on the response scale, and the higher the total scores, the less adherence to traditional Latino family values.[1]

An Exploratory Study

An exploratory study was conducted in the Boston metropolitan area, and included a sample of eighty adolescents (mean age = 15.4 ± 1.97 years, ranging from 11 to 19 years of age). Forty-seven subjects (59 percent of sample) were females. Ninety-six percent of the sample reported that they were currently in school (mean grade level = 10.05 ± 2.05). Thirty-five percent self-identified as Puerto Rican and the other 64.3 percent self-identified as Mexican, Salvadoran, Guatemalan, Nicaraguan, Dominican, Latino/Latina, Other (Latino), or Other. Regarding migration histories, 18.8 percent of the sample migrated to the United States when they were younger than 5 years old, 26.2 percent migrated when they were between the ages of 5 and 12, 22.5 percent came to the States between the ages of 13 and 17, and 32.5 percent of the sample were U.S.-born.

The subjects were recruited primarily through various community organizations and schools in the greater metropolitan area of this large Northeastern city. Informed consent from the parents of the adolescents as well as from the adolescents themselves was obtained prior to administration. The questionnaires were administered individually as well as in groups, although subjects worked independently, reading and answering the questions on their own. Two language versions of the questionnaire were available and subjects were able to complete the questionnaire in the language of choice. Forty-four percent of the adolescent respondents chose to fill out the questionnaire in Spanish.

A principal component analysis with a varimax rotation was conducted on the data yielded by the eighty respondents. This yielded two main factors which accounted for 31 percent of the variance. Twenty items loaded in the first factor, which resembles the familism construct so frequently identified in the literature (Cobb, 1976; Keefe, Padilla, & Carlos, 1979; Moore, 1970; Sabogal et al., 1987; Triandis et al., 1982). Examples of the items which loaded in this factor are (1) "The family should consult with close relatives, uncles, aunts, grandparents, concerning its important decisions"; (2) "I don't bring up things I know my parents don't want to talk about"; (3) "The most important role for parents is to discipline their children well"; and (4) "It is important to me to protect my family's reputation." This factor has an Eigenvalue of 8.72, accounts for 19.8 percent of the variance, and has good internal reliability (alpha = .88).

The second factor also reflects a previously identified dimension of Latino family values, that of *respeto* (Inclán & Hernández, 1992). Nine items loaded in this factor. Examples of the items that loaded in this factor are (1) "People in my family are not comfortable hugging and kissing each other to show that they care"; (2) "Kids should not question adults"; (3) "Much of what a son or daughter does should be done to please their parents"; and (4) "People in my family don't say what they feel but they make it known." This factor accounts for 10.8 percent of the variance, has an Eigenvalue of 4.77, and also has good internal consistency (alpha = .83).

Factor scores were generated for each respondent and used for subsequent analyses. The sample's mean and standard deviation for the familism factor (1) was 2.69 ± .86, while for the *respeto* factor (2) it was 4.28 ± 1.22, suggesting a higher adherence to familism than to *respeto* ($t = -12.11$, $p < .0001$) in this sample of Latino adolescents.

Several analyses were conducted to assess the impact of migration on the respondent's scores on familism and *respeto*. Adolescents who had lived in the U.S. mainland for a longer period of time scored higher on the familism factor ($r = .34$, $p < .01$) and on the *respeto* factor ($r = .34$, $p < .01$), indicating less adherence to familism and *respeto* values with longer residence in the United States. Familism and *respeto* scores did not differ by age at which subjects first moved to the U.S. mainland, nor did they differ by whether subjects were U.S.-born.

We then broke down the length of time living on the U.S. mainland variable into two groups: 8 years or less versus 10–19 years. The two groups differ on the *respeto* factor ($F(1,73) = 8.14$, $p < .01$) but not on the familism factor. The group that had been in the U.S. mainland for 8 years or less had a mean of 3.87; the group that had been in the U.S. mainland for 10–19 years had a mean of 4.68. These findings suggest that the group that had been in the U.S. mainland longer endorsed *respeto* less than the other group. Thus, it seems that while adherence to *respeto* decreases as the length of time in the U.S. mainland increases, adherence to familism does not. This finding, which is similar to the findings of Sabogal and colleagues (1987), suggests that while adolescents support familism values (e.g., enmeshment, family support), they do not endorse the more patriarchal system of the Latino family which maintains strict gender roles, and age and authority boundaries.

Acculturation and Family Values

Finally, adolescence is a time when gender effects are pronounced given differences in physical growth, social expectations, sexual and emotional development, and identity formation. Gender differences among adolescents have also been observed in the area of behavioral acculturation (Szapocznik et al., 1978). In a one-way analysis of variance, we found that girls were lower on the *respeto* factor than boys ($F(1,78) = 7.37$, p <

.01). There was no gender effect on the familism factor. This finding supports the previous findings as a function of migration, of a decrease in adherence to *respeto* values due to the desire to break away from the patriarchal structure of family functioning while maintaining the familism values component.

IMPLICATIONS FOR LATINO ADOLESCENTS AND THEIR FAMILIES

This chapter examines family values of Latino adolescents and explores how tradional Latino family values may be changing as a result of intrinsic as well as extrinsic forces. The findings from the exploratory study presented in this paper suggest that Latino adolescents' adherence to family values changes as a result of contextual and developmental demands including migration, acculturation, and gender role expectations and behaviors. They also suggest that the influence of these factors on adolescents' view of family values may be related to the exposure to the host culture, migratory experiences, and level of acculturation. In addition, the findings suggest that there are some dimensions of traditional Latino family values and functioning (i.e., familism) that adolescents adhere more to regardless of the impact of other influences.

While these findings do suggest changes in how Latino adolescents in the United States are viewing traditional family values, they do not intimate a breakdown in the traditional Latino family system. In fact, research suggests that a variety of buffers come into play when families are faced with conflicting economic, social, and cultural circumstances, and that constructive developmental pathways can be followed for adolescents as well as their families so as to facilitate cultural transitions. For example, Szapocnik and colleagues (1980) examined how bicultural involvement through the learning of communication and negotiation skills can increase and enhance Latino adolescents' "bicultural survival skills." In short, the adaptive strategies such as biculturalism that Latino families utilize (1) to combat the stressful aspects of prejudice, discrimination, and segregation, and (2) to gain access to Anglo-American resources, result from cultural patterns that encourage the well-being and the survival not only of the individual but of the family and community as well (Harrison, Wilson, Pine, Chan, & Buriel, 1990).

In addition, Latino adolescents, faced with multiple and often conflicting environments and values (e.g., school values, family values, cultural norms, etc.), must negotiate various contextual and cultural demands to successfully complete developmental and culturally defined tasks. Laosa (1989) states that understanding the child environment organization of the family is crucial in making children's extrafamilial environments developmentally compatible with the home environment. On the one hand, rigidity, defined as the "impermeability in the boundaries of one or more system's components" (Laosa, 1989), on the part of Latino adolescents and/or their families may result in lack of functional modification to certain social, cultural, and familial demands. On the other hand, individuals might adopt and adapt to several cultural orientations and situations simultaneously, minimizing the detrimental effects of under- or overacculturation which can manifest themselves in the form of psychosocial, emotional, or behavioral disorders (Szapocznik et al., 1980). Recent work has elaborated on the benefits of biculturalism, suggesting flexibility in roles, cognitive style, adaptability, and creativity (Ramírez & Castañeda, 1974).

While various factors were presented in this chapter as forces that affect the family values and functioning of Latino adolescents, future research must explore how other factors such as socioeconomic status affect Latino adolescents' family values. According to the U.S. Bureau of the Census (1990), 40 percent of Latino children grow up in poverty as compared to 17 percent for white non-Latino children. In addition, other statistics indicate that Latino children experience more extreme poverty and for longer periods of time when compared to other white non-Latinos (U.S. Bureau of the Census, 1990). Various researchers and theorists have pointed to poverty as a source of risk that exacerbates physical, mental, and social problems in children (see Sameroff, Seifer, Barocas, Zax, & Greenspan, 1987). Furthermore, in addition to environmental factors that may affect children's outcome, such as the lack of adequate nutrition, housing, health care, and education, research points to poverty as a mechanism which inhibits parenting ability by decreasing the capacity for supportive parenting in a consistent fashion (McAdoo & McAdoo, 1990). McLoyd (1990) suggests that the limited number or complete lack of material resources indirectly affects children's psychological distress through parental behavior. In other words, it is important to examine how contextual factors not only affect behavioral and emotional outcomes in children but also how they affect family functioning.

In conclusion, it is suggested that while Latino adolescents in the United States may be exposed to a variety of influences which may change their perspective of traditional family values, for the most part Latino adolescents are maintaining to some degree the basic dimensions that are characteristic of Latino family values and functioning. This maintenance of some traditional family values may be an indication that there is something within the family value system of Latinos which aids transition and adjustment to new surroundings. It may also be an indication of a fusion of traditional and modern family values within a different cultural context as a means of facilitating psychosocial and bicultural adaptation.

NOTE

[1] See Alarcón, Erkut, García Coll, & Vázquez García (1995) for a detailed description of the development of the family values and functioning scale.

REFERENCES

Alarcón, O., Erkut, S., García Coll, C. T., & Vázquez García, H. A. (1995). *Engaging in culturally-sensitive research on Puerto Rican youth* (Working Papers Series No. 275). Wellesley, MA: Center for Research on Women.

Andrade, S. (1980). Family planning of Mexican Americans. In M. Melville (Ed.), *Twice a minority: Mexican American women* (pp. 17–32). St. Louis: Mosby.

Aponte, R. (1993). Latino families in poverty: Diversity, context, and interpretation. *Journal of Contemporary Human Services, 74,* 527–537.

Badillo Ghali, S. (1982). Understanding Puerto Rican traditions. *Social Work, 27,* 98–102.

Baptiste, D. A. (1993). Immigrant families, adolescents, and acculturation: Insights for therapists. *Marriage and Family Review, 19,* 341–363.

Bernal, G., & Alvarez, A. (1983). Culture and class in the study of families. In J. Hansen (Ed.), *Cultural perspective in family therapy* (pp. 33–50). London: Aspen.

Berry, J. W. (1980). Acculturative stress: The role of ecology, culture, and differentiation. *Journal of Cross Cultural Psychology, 5,* 382–406.

Bonilla, F. (1985). Ethnic orbits: The circulation of people and capital. *Contemporary Marxism, 10,* 148–167.

Bonilla, F., & Campos, R. (1981, Spring). A wealth of poor: Puerto Ricans in the new economic order. *Daedalus, 110,* pp. 133–176.

Borrás, V. A. (1989). Dual discipline role of the single Puerto Rican head of household. In C. T. García Coll & M. De Lourdes Mattei (Eds.), *The psychosocial development of Puerto Rican women* (pp. 200–213). New York: Praeger.

Boykin, A. W., & Toms, F. P. (1985). Black child socialization: A conceptual framework. In H. P. McAdoo & J. L. McAdoo (Eds.), *Black children: Social, educational, and parental environments* (pp. 33–51). Newbury Park, CA: Sage.

Brislin, R. (1993). *Understanding culture's influence on behavior.* New York: Harcourt Brace College.

Canino, I. A., & Canino, G. (1980). Impact of stress on the Puerto Rican family: Treatment considerations. *American Journal of Orthopsychiatry, 50,* 535–541.

Carter, T. P. (1979). *Mexican Americans in school: A history of educational neglect.* New York: College Entrace Examination Board.

Caudill, W. A. (1973). The influence of social structure and culture on human behavior in modern Japan. *Journal of Nervous and Mental Disease, 157,* 240–257.

Children's Defense Fund. (1990). *Latino youths at a crossroads.* Washington, DC: Adolescent Pregnancy Prevention Clearinghouse.

Cicchetti, D., & Schneider-Rosen, K. (1986). An organizational approach to childhood depression. In M. Rutter, C. E. Izard, & P. B. Read (Eds.), *Depression in young people: Developmental and clinical perspectives* (pp. 71–134). New York: Guilford.

Cobb, S. (1976). Social support as a moderator of life stress. *Psychosomatic Medicine, 38,* 300–314.

Comas-Díaz, L. (1989). Puerto Rican women's cultural transitions: Developmental and clinical implications. In C. T. García Coll & M. de Lourdes Mattei (Eds.), *The psychosocial development of Puerto Rican women* (pp. 166–199). New York: Praeger.

Cornille, T. A., & Brotherton, W. D. (1993). Applying the developmental family therapy model to issues of migrating families. *Marriage and Family Review, 19,* 325–240.

Díaz Guerrero, R. (1955). Neurosis and the Mexican family structure. *American Journal of Psychiatry, 112,* 411–417.

Epstein, N., Baldwin, L. M., & Bishop, D. S. (1983). The McMaster Family Assessment Device. *Journal of Marital and Family Therapy, 9,* 171–180.

Espín, O. M. (1987). Psychological impact of migration on Latinas. *Psychology of Women Quarterly, 11,* 489–503.

Fitzpatrick, J. P. (1988). The Puerto Rican family. In C. H. Mindel & R. W. Habenstein (Eds.), *Ethnic families in America: Patterns and variations* (pp. 192–217). New York: Elsevier.

García Coll, C. T., & Meyer, E. C. (1993). The sociocultural context of infant development. In C. H. Zeanah (Ed.), *Handbook of infant mental health* (pp. 56–59). New York: Guilford.

García Coll, C. T., Meyer, E. C., & Brillon, L. (1995). Ethnic and minority parenting. In M. H. Bornstein (Ed.), *Handbook of parenting* (Vol. 2, pp. 189–209). Hillsdale, NJ: Erlbaum.

García Preto, N. (1982). Puerto Rican families. In M. McGoldrick, J. K. Pearce, & J. Giordano (Eds.), *Ethnicity and family therapy* (pp. 164–186). New York: Guilford.

Garrison, V., & Weiss, C. I. (1979). Domincan family networks and United States immigration policy: A case study. *International Migration Review, 13,* 264–282.

Garza, R. T., & Gallegos, P. I. (1985). Environmental influences and personal choice: A humanistic perspective on acculturation. *Hispanic Journal of Behavioral Sciences, 7,* 365–379.

Gil, A. G., Vega, W. A., & Dimas, J. M. (1994). Acculturative stress and personal adjustment among Latino adolescent boys. *Journal of Community Psychology, 22,* 43–54.

Ginorio, A. (1979). *A comparison of Puerto Ricans in New York with native Puerto Ricans and Caucasian- and Black-Americans on two measures of acculturation: Gender role and racial identification* (Doctoral dissertation, Fordham University). *Dissertation Abstracts International, 40,* 983B-984B.

Goldscheider, F. K. (1993). Familism: Parental and gender relationships. In F. K. Goldscheider & C. Goldsheider (Eds.), *Leaving home before marriage: Ethnicity, familism, and generational relationships* (pp. 80–95). Madison, WI: University of Wisconsin Press.

Gudykunst, W., & Nishida, T. (1989). Theoretical perspectives for studying intercultural communication. In M. Asante & W. Gudykunst (Eds.), *Handbook of international and intercultural communication* (pp. 17–46). Newbury Park, CA: Sage.

Gurak, D. T. (1981). Family structural diversity of Latino ethnic groups. *Research Bulletin of the Latino Research Center, 4*(2–3), 6–10.

Hardy-Fanta, C., & Montana, P. (1982). The Latino female adolescent: A group therapy model. *International Journal of Group Psychotherapy, 32,* 351–366.

Harrison, A. O, Serafica, F., & McAdoo, H. (1984). Ethnic families of color. In R. D. Parke (Ed.), *The family: Review of child development research* (Vol. 7, pp. 329–371). Chicago: University of Chicago Press.

Harrison, A. O., Wilson, M. N., Pine, C. J., Chan, S. Q., & Buriel, R. (1990). Family ecologies of ethnic minority children. *Child Development, 61,* 347–362.

Inclán, J. (1985). Variations in value-orientation in mental health work with Puerto Ricans. *Psychotherapy, 22,* 324–334.

Inclán, J., & Hernandez, M. (1992). Cross-cultural perspectives and codependence: The case of poor Latinos. *American Journal of Orthopsychiatry, 62,* 245–255.

Inclán, J. E., & Herron, D. G. (1990). Puerto Rican adolescents. In J. T. Gibbs & L. N. Huang (Eds.), *Children of color* (pp. 251–277). San Francisco: Jossey-Bass.

Jensen, J. V. (1962). Effects of childhood bilingualism, I. *Elementary English, 39,* 132–143.

Keefe, S. E., Padilla, A. M., & Carlos, M. L. (1979). The Mexican American extended family as an emotional support system. *Human Organization, 38,* 144–152.

Kluckhohn, F., & Strodbeck, F. (1961). *Variation in value orientations.* Evanston, IL: Row and Peterson.

Koteskey, R. L., Walker, J. S., & Johnson, A. W. (1990). Measurement of identity from adolescence to adulthood: Cultural, community, religious, and family factors. *Journal of Psychology and Theology, 18,* 54–65.

Laosa, L. M. (1977). Cognitive styles and learning strategies research. *Journal of Teacher Education, 28,* 26–30.

Laosa, L. M. (1989). Social competence in childhood: Toward a developmental, socioculturally relativistic paradigm. *Journal of Applied Developmental Psychology, 10,* 447–468.

Lerner, R. M. (1989). Individual development and the family system: A life-span perspective. In K. Kreppner & R. M. Lerner (Eds.), *Family systems and life-span development* (pp. 15–31). Hillsdale, NJ: Erlbaum.

LeVine, R. A. (1977). Childrearing as cultural adaptation. In P. H. Leiderman, S. R. Tulkin, & A. Rosenfeld (Eds.), *Culture and infancy: Variations in the human experience* (pp. 15–28). New York: Academic Press.

Lewis, O. (1965). *La vida.* New York: Vintage.

Lin, K. M., Masuda, M., & Tazuman, L. (1982). Adaptational problems of Vietnamese refugees: III. Case studies in clinic and field: Adaptive and maladaptive. *Psychiatry Journal of the University of Ottawa, 7,* 173–183.

Margarida Julía, M. T. (1989). Developmental issues during adulthood: Redefining notions of self, care, and responsibility among a group of professional Puerto Rican women. In C. T. García Coll & M. L. Mattei (Eds.), *The psychosocial development of Puerto Rican women* (pp. 115- 140). New York: Praeger.

Martínez, A. L. (1981). The impact of adolescent pregnancy on Latino adolescents and their families. In T. Ooms (Ed.), *Teenage pregnancy in a family context: Implications for policy* (pp. 326–344). Philadephia: Temple University Press.

McAdoo, H. P., & McAdoo, J. L. (Eds.). (1990). *New directions for child development: Vol. 46. Economic stress: Effects on family life and child development.* San Francisco: Jossey-Bass.

McLoyd, V. (1990). The impact of economic hardship on black families and children: Psychological distress, parenting, and socioemotional development. *Child Development, 61,* 311- 346.

McLoyd, V., & Randolph, S. (1985). Secular trends in the study of Afro-American children: A review of child development, 1936–1980. *Monographs of the Society for Research in Child Development, 50* (4–5, Serial No. 211).

Mead, M. (1953). *Cultural patterns and technical change.* Paris: UNESCO.

Mendoza, F. S., Takata, G. S., & Martorell, R. (1994). Health status and health care access for mainland Puerto Rican children: Results from the Latino Health and Nutrition Examination Survey. In G. Lamberty & C. T. García Coll (Eds.), *Puerto Rican women and children: Issues in health, growth, and development* (pp. 119–136). New York: Plenum.

Minuchin, S., Montalvo, B., & Guerny, B. R. (1967). *Families of the slums: An exploration of their treatment.* New York: Basic Books.

Moore, J. W. (1970). *Mexican American.* Englewood Cliffs, NJ: Prentice Hall.

National Center for Education Statistics. (1993). *Youth Indicators, 1993.* Washington, DC: U.S. Government Printing Office.

Nieves Falcón, L. (1972). *Diagnóstico de Puerto Rico.* Río Piedras: Editorial Edil.

Ogbu, J. U. (1981). Origins of human competence: A cultural-ecological perspective. *Child Development, 52,* 413–429.

Ogbu, J. U. (1987). Variability in minority school performance: A problem in search of an explanation. *Anthropology and Education Quarterly, 18,* 312–334.

O'Reilly, J. (1985). Adapting to a different role. *Time, 126*(1), 82–83.

Ramírez, M., & Castañeda, A. (1974). *Cultural democracy, bicognitive development, and education.* San Diego, CA: Academic Press.

Reiss, D. (1981). *The family's construction of reality.* Cambridge: Harvard University Press.

Reissman, F. (1962). *The culturally deprived child.* New York: Harper and Row.

Reuschenberg, E. J., & Buriel, R. (1988). *The effects of acculturation on relationship patterns and system variables within families of Mexican descent.* Unpublished manuscript, Claremont Graduate School, Claremont, CA.

Rodríguez, C. E. (1989). *Puerto Ricans born in the U.S.A.* Boston: Unwin Hyman.

Rogler, L. H., Cooney, R. S., & Ortiz, V. (1980). Intergenerational changes in ethnic identity in the Puerto Rican family. *Intergenerational Migration Review, 14,* 193–214.

Rogler, L. H., Cortes, D. E., & Malgady, R. G. (1991). Acculturation and mental health status among Latinos. *American Psychologist, 46,* 585–597.

Sabogal, F., Marín, G., Otero-Sabogal, R., VanOss Marín, B., & Perez-Stable, E. (1987). Latino familism and acculturation: What changes and what doesn't? *Latino Journal of Behavioral Sciences, 9,* 397–412.

Sameroff, A. J., Seifer, R., Barocas, B., Zax, M., & Greenspan, S. (1987). IQ scores of 4-year-old children: Social-environmental risk factors. *Pediatrics, 79,* 343-350.

Saunders, L. (1954). *Cultural differences and medical care: The case of the Spanish-speaking people of the Southwest.* New York: Russell Sage.

Serpell, R. (1994). The cultural instruction of intelligence. In W. J. Lonner & R. Malpass (Eds.), *Psychology and culture* (pp. 157–163). Boston: Allyn and Bacon.

Sroufe, L. (1979). The coherence of individual development: Early care, attachment, and subsequent developmental issues. *American Psychologist, 34,* 834–841.

Stevenson, H. W., Chen, C., & Uttal, D. H. (1990). Beliefs and achievement: A study of black, white, and Latino children. *Child Development, 61,* 508–523.

Super, C. M. (1981). Cross-cultural research on infancy. In H. C. Triandis & A. Heron (Eds.), *Handbook on cross-cultural psychology: Vol. 4. Developmental psychology* (pp. 17–53). Boston: Allyn and Bacon.

Szapocznik, J., Kurtines, W. M., & Fernandez, T. (1980). Bicultural involvement and adjustment in Latino American youths. *International Journal of Intercultural Relations, 4,* 353–365.

Szapocznik, J., Santisteban, D., Rio, A., Perez-Vidal, A., Kurtines, W. M., & Hervis, O. (1986). Bicultural effectiveness training (BET): An intervention modality for families experiencing intergenerational/intercultural conflict. *Hispanic Journal of Behavioral Sciences, 8,* 303–330.

Szapocznik, J., Scopetta, M. A., Kurtines, W., & Aranalde, M. (1978). Theory and measurement of acculturation. *International Journal of Psychology, 12,* 113–130.

Thomas, P. (1967). *Down these mean streets.* New York: Knopf.

Triandis, H. C. (1994). Culture and communication. In H. C. Triandis (Ed.), *Culture and communication* (pp. 181–206). New York: McGraw-Hill.

Triandis, H. C., Bontempo, R., Villareal, M. J., Asai, M., & Lucca, N. (1988). Individualism and collectivism: Cross-cultural perpectives on self-ingroup relationships. *Journal of Personality and Social Psychology, 54,* 323-338.

Triandis, H. C., Marín, G., Betancourt, H., Lisansky, J., & Chang, B. (1982). Dimensions of familism among Latino and mainstream Navy recruits (Technical Report No. 14). Champaign: University of Illinois, Department of Psychology.

Tropp, L. R., Erkut, S., Alarcón, O., García Coll, C. T., & Vázquez, H. A. (In press). Psychological acculturation: Development of a new measure for Puerto Ricans on the U.S. mainland. *Educational and Psychological Meaasurement.*

Tropp, L. R., Erkut, S., Alarcón, O., García Coll, C. T., & Vázquez, H. (1994). *Toward a theoretical model of psychological acculturation* (Working Papers Series No. 268). Wellesley, MA: Center for Research on Women.

U.S. Bureau of the Census. (1990). *Census of population and housing. Massachusetts.* Massachusetts Summary Tape File 1A. Washington, DC: Author.

Vázquez-Nuttall, E., & Romero-García, I. (1989). From home to school: Puerto Rican girls learn to be students in the United States. In C. T. García Coll & M. L. Mattei (Eds.), *The psychosocial development of Puerto Rican women* (pp. 60–83). New York: Praeger.

Ventura, S. J. (1982). Births of Latino Parentage, 1979. *Monthly Vital Statistics Report* (National Center for Health Statistics, Public Health Service, Hyattsville, MD), *32*(2), Supplement.

Ventura, S. J. (1994). Demographic and health characteristics of Puerto Rican mothers and their babies, 1990. In G. Lamberty & C. García Coll (Eds.), *Puerto Rican women and children: Issues in health, growth, and development* (pp. 71–84). New York: Plenum.

Werner, H. (1948). *The comparative psychology of mental development.* New York: Harper and Row.

Whiting, J. W. M. (1977). A model for psychocultural research. In P. H. Leiderman, S. R. Tulkin, & A. Rosenfeld (Eds.), *Culture and infancy: Variations in the human experience* (pp. 29- 48). New York: Academic Press.

Zambrana, R. E, & Silva-Palacios, V. (1989). Gender differences in stress among Mexican immigrant adolescents in Los Angeles, California. *Journal of Adolescent Research, 4,* 426–442.

Zavala Martínez, I. (1994). Entremundos: The psychological dialectics of Puerto Rican migration and its implications for health. In G. Lamberty & C. T. García Coll (Eds.), *Puerto Rican women and children: Issues in health, growth, and development* (pp. 29–38). New York: Plenum.

Zayas, L. H., & Palleja, J. (1988). Puerto Rican families: Considerations for family therapy. *Family Relations, 37,* 260–264.

CHAPTER 10

Authority Plus Affection
Latino Parenting during Adolescence

MARIBEL VARGAS AND
NANCY A. BUSCH-ROSSNAGEL

The search for an identity and the accompanying questions that arise about one's own group, behaviors, values, and traditions are an important undertaking for all adolescents. A sense of ego identity provides a feeling of being one and the same to oneself and to continue being the same in other people's views (Erikson, 1963). As Archer and Waterman (1994) point out, "the multiple components of the individual's identity need to become integrated or synthesized for there to be a sense of continuity, stability, and effectiveness within one's social environmental context" (p. 78). The primary social context for this synthesis is that of the family, with parents playing a key role. Erikson (1968) suggests that the process of identity development involves questioning of authority figures, especially parents. Indeed, Marcia's (1966) conceptualization of identity achievement requires an exploration of the impact of parents on the self, and research shows that parents' behavior has a tremendous influence on identity development (Marcia, Waterman, Matteson, Archer, & Orlofsky, 1993).

Parents and the family environment may be especially important for minority youth, who balance the demands of two divergent cultural systems while trying to resolve the identity crisis. As Spencer, Dornbusch, and Mont-Reynaud (1990) have indicated, minority youth often have to tackle additional issues, not faced by majority youth, in the process of identity development. Comparisons between one's group and the majority culture may represent a painful undertaking for the minority adolescent. Spencer et al. (1990) state that one's "family environment is a mediating factor that strongly shapes the development of minority youth" (p. 135), but the nature of this influence has not been widely explored in Latino families.

The Latino population is diverse in place of origin, racial characteristics, length of residence in the United States, and political and migratory background; thus, distinct attributes may be found within the different groups which fall under the term *Latino*. However, Latinos also share various characteristics, namely language, religious beliefs, and values (Marín & VanOss-Marín, 1991), which differentiate them from other major ethnic groups. In this chapter we will address some of the qualities that a number of Latino subgroups have in common as these relate to the family, parenting practices, and parent-child relations during adolescence. The sparse literature that exists on Latinos mainly includes Mexican and Puerto Rican samples; thus, these two groups will be the primary focus of this chapter. Although various other Central American, South American, and Caribbean people have established themselves in the United States and are considered to be part of the panethnic label "Latino," research efforts have not kept abreast of this migratory trend. It should be noted that efforts are being made to change this scenario (i.e., Shelley-Sireci's work, 1995, on Central American infant-mother attachment; Duany's work, 1994, on the transnational identity of Dominicans; and Fracasso's work [Fracasso, Busch-Rossnagel, & Fisher, 1994] on Dominican infant-mother attachment, to name a few). In our discussion of research findings, subgroups will be identified when the information is available. However, we will also be making some generalizations in this chapter as these relate to the experience of the Latino youth within the family system based on cultural commonalities that have endured through the years and are related to the historical experience of these people. It is important to note that as a result of the limited amount of empirical developmental research which includes other Latino subgroups, these cultural patterns are the only cross-group evidence for such generalizations.

This chapter focuses on the reality of Latino youth and their families who experience the demands of two cultural systems frequently at odds with each other. In the first section we will present some of the most salient attributes of the Latino culture found in the literature. The next section will relate a set of specific attributes to the process of socialization in Latino families. Next, we will compare these processes to Euro-American parenting models appearing in the scientific literature. In particular we will examine Baumrind's initial parenting prototypes and research, which has assessed family processes in Latino families. Studies discussing the relationship of parenting behavior to adolescent outcomes, particularly school performance, will also be presented. We will conclude by identifying a set of issues which should be addressed in future research on parent-adolescent relationships in Latino families.

IDENTIFICATION OF LATINO CULTURAL BELIEFS

When delving into the roots of behavioral patterns of ethnic groups it is common to go back and examine cultural beliefs and cultural scripts, even though research seems to indicate that the relationship between beliefs, values, and behaviors is not as strong as we would expect or want it to be (Sigel, 1992). Various Latino cultural beliefs have been identified in the scientific literature. Allocentrism, for instance, refers to the "cultural trait associated with the preference for interpersonal relationships in ingroups that are nurturing, empathetic, loving, intimate, respectful and willing to sacrifice for the welfare of the group" (Yep, 1995). *Simpatía*, another important value, deals with the emphasis in "needing to promote and maintain harmonious and pleasant interpersonal relationships" (Triandis, Marín, Lisansky, & Betancourt, 1984). *Marianismo*, referred to by some as the virginity cult, has been labeled as the cultural counterbase of machismo; it stipulates that the woman should be chaste before marriage and when married conform to the husband's macho behavior. In addition to, and consistent with, *marianismo* is viewing the role of the mother as self-sacrificing in favor of her family and children (Comas-Díaz, 1982). In this chapter we will focus on three cultural values identified in the literature as a significant influence in the lives of Latino youth and styles of interaction within the family system. These values are familism, *respeto*, and machismo. Our focus on these values does not negate the relevance of other beliefs as representative of Latino culture, but our interest is in exploring how these three appear to define roles and styles of interaction within the family unit.

The significant role that the family plays in the lives of Latinos has been often examined and discussed in the scientific literature (e.g., Fitzpatrick, 1987; Fracasso & Busch-Rossnagel, 1992; Ramos-McKay, Comas-Díaz, & Rivera, 1988; Sabogal, Marín, Otero-Sabogal, Marín, & Pérez-Stable, 1987). *Familism*, the term commonly used to refer to this cultural value, is described as representing the strong identification and attachment that exists among family members and the strong feelings of loyalty, reciprocity, and solidarity shared with each other (Canino, Earley, & Rogler, 1988). Among Puerto Ricans, the family has traditionally occupied a central place in the organizational structure of society (Rogler & Santana-Cooney, 1984). Again referring to Puerto Ricans, the needs of the individual are described as being subordinate to those of the family, with many family functions being shared by extended family members (Ramos-McKay et al., 1988). Sandoval and De La Roza (1986) point out that regardless of national or social background, Latinos share a very strong family orientation, and they add: " The important place that the family plays in the lives of Hispanics clearly overrides the importance of, loyalty to, and participation in other institutions most cherished by white Americans, such as the community, school, churches, and clubs" (p. 154). Even among individuals who have high levels of acculturation, familism seems to be an important characteristic as indexed by perceived high levels of family support (Sabogal et al., 1987). Díaz-Guerrero and Szalay (1991) also talk about the significance attributed to the family by both Mexicans and Colombians, as evidenced from their data with undergraduate students in Mexico, Colombia, and the United States. Their findings indicate that Mexicans, Colombians, and Americans emphasize the cohesive nature of the family, with the Latino groups placing a greater emphasis on the establishment of close bonds and the subordination of individual interests to those of the group. Thus, although the family also constitutes an important element in the lives of Americans, it is expressed in a different way (Díaz-Guerrero & Slazay, 1991, p. 2):

> To Americans family relations are particularly important as a major source of emotional satisfaction: joy, happiness, good times. To Mexicans family relations are exceptionally affect laden, with a great emphasis on love, reflecting a strong emotional interdependence. While love is important in the American family as well it has a lower salience, and there is little indication of its use as an instrument of influence.

Respeto, or respect for one's parents and other authority figures, is yet another important cultural value which we can relate to the development and upbringing of Latino youth. Lauria (1964) has described *respeto* as that quality of the self which must be presented in all social encounters. It pertains to the recognition that there are certain norms of behavior in the interactions characteristic of human activity. In the case of *respeto*, it specifically refers to the proper demeanor demonstrated in social encounters. From a broad perspective, it establishes that every individual must be treated with respect, regardless of whether the individuals are social equals, superiors, or subordinates. *Respeto* gives honor and dignity to all no matter what their social rank. In a more restrictive usage or within the context of child rearing, *respeto* essentially refers to the expectation that children will obey and show deference to their parents and other adult authority figures within and outside the confines of the family system. As Fracasso and Busch-Rossnagel (1992) indicate, "*[R]espeto* accentuates the unique dignity each person possesses" (p. 87), and violations of this value by children may lead to scoldings and punishment which could even be carried out by other relatives besides the parents (Ramos-McKay et al., 1988). In Latino cultures, the emphasis on respect to elders in the child-rearing process may be related to their collectivistic nature, where it is usually the elders of the group who are viewed as authority figures and thus knowledgeable and worthy of respect.

The third cultural value, known as *machismo*, refers to a set of attributes, beliefs, and behaviors traditionally ascribed to men in Latino cultures. Included here are beliefs concerning the male's higher social status, as well as cultural expectations of strength and the ability to fulfill the provider role and take care of the family. Madsen (1964) indicates that there is a cultural expectation for men to be dominant in social relations. Furthermore, machismo is believed to play a major role in the rearing of male and female children, both of whom are socialized to carry on traditional roles, with females as homemakers and mothers while males are encouraged to seek greater independence, display physical courage, and protect the family (Fracasso & Busch-Rossnagel, 1992; Marín & VanOss-Marín, 1991; Millan & Chan, 1991). In rejecting the notion of macho dominance in decision making, Cromwell and Ruiz (1979) argue that joint decision making is common in Mexican and Chicano families. In further examining this issue, it would be interesting to investigate whose position or point of view prevails when decisions are made jointly. Anyhow, although there are those who argue that the female has a significant amount of power within the family system, it seems that this power is subordinate to that of the male and not openly acknowledged in or outside of the household. Thus, the female's power may be manifested in more subtle ways. Additionally, within the family system, Mexicans tend to identify the female more with the role of mother than that of wife, as do Americans; thus, within the hierarchy of the home she commands greater authority and respect than other family members aside from the husband/father (Díaz-Guerrero & Szalay, 1991). Other research also appears to indicate that Mexican American women are redefining their roles and relationships, with working-class females trying to attain separate identities from those of their husbands (Williams, 1988). Research on Dominican migrating females also appears to show changes as a result of the greater financial independence they attain when they become the main economic providers in their families as a result of the greater job opportunities for women immigrants (Duany, 1994). Taking into account the differences across Latino subgroups and that contact with the host culture has eroded the strength of these values, research continues to suggest that they are still a part of the upbringing of Latino adolescents. For example, DesRosiers, Zayas, and Busch-Rossnagel (1995) conducted a study with college students to assess ethnic differences in their beliefs about familism and reciprocity. Eighty-five Euro-American and Latino students completed various scales on these issues. Communal reciprocity was defined as concern for the welfare of the other in a relationship that is cooperative with mutual goals and where gains by either person are experienced as a benefit to both. Communal reciprocity can be contrasted with exchange reciprocity in which each individual maintains a mental balance sheet of support given versus support received. Results showed that communal reciprocity was correlated with familism. Main effects for ethnic group membership on familism and communal reciprocity were also found, with Latino students scoring significantly higher than Euro-American students on both familism and reciprocity.

Likewise, the work of Vázquez-Garcia, García Coll, Erkut, Alarcón, and Tropp (this volume) suggests that adolescents continue to adhere to cultural values such as familism and *respeto,* although their expression may be modified by contextual and developmental demands, particularly during the process of acculturation. In addition, the traditional values themselves may be in conflict because of the contact with the new culture during this process. For instance, some demands that family ties place on Latino youth, such as a child serving as an interpreter for parents who do not speak English, may be in conflict with *respeto* and machismo, the expectation of children showing deference to the parent, particularly the father. Such a situation may give the child more power in the relationship than is comfortable for the father. Casas, Wagenhaim, Banchero, and Mendoza-Romero (1994) point out, "[H]aving the children assume such a role is humiliating because he [the father] is accustomed to a position of authority, power and respect" (p. 324).

The effect of the conflict among cultural values and the demands of the larger society on the identity development of Latino youth is particularly intriguing. How do Latino males reconcile parental and societal encouragement to be independent and assertive outside the confines of the family setting with the dependent and subservient role they may be expected to play within the confines of the family? A similar issue arises with the female child. What is the real message being conveyed to the Latino girl socialized to be submissive and traditional in her beliefs and her interactions with others while being raised in a female-headed household with her mother as the sole provider? This issue may be even more complicated in migrant families when often "to be male is to be 'the authority' with no power or economic potential and to be female is to be 'submissive' but autonomous financially and overwhelmed by responsibilities. Thus a cultural pattern once adaptive and socially syntonic has become a myth which no longer has a base in reality and may create, at times, an area of stress to family members who enter into conflict over their sexually defined roles" (Canino et al., 1988, p. 28).

We expect that these examples illustrate how traditional Latino values are challenged by the values and behavioral demands of the host society and impact the interactions of Latino youth and their parents. As Szapocznik and Kurtines (1993) propose, adolescent development must be placed in the context of the family, and that family must be understood in the context of the culture, and to complicate matters further, that culture itself is embedded in a culturally diverse context. Thus, any conclusions that are drawn when relating cultural values to family processes must recognize the complexity of the different systems at play and the demands which these systems place on the family and the individual by altering traditional roles and styles of interaction.

SOCIALIZATION IN LATINO FAMILIES

This set of traditional beliefs (familism, *respeto*, and machismo) has long been identified as and continues to remain a unique part of Latino cultures in spite of interaction with non-Latino communities. Furthermore, we presume that these beliefs considerably influence the child-rearing patterns in Latino families, thus having a significant impact on family processes and the home experience of Latino adolescents. These values appear to lead to the use of rearing techniques consistent with the socialization goals of maintaining cohesion and interdependence among family members found in the group of origin.

For instance, interdependence may be evidenced in the expectation of having older children assume certain household duties, such as taking care of younger siblings. Although the youth may take the initiative to engage in such activities that benefit the family, thus showing independent behavior, the act itself will work toward maintaining kinship ties and ensuring the well-being of the family. In a study with Anglo, Chicano, and black parents, Chicano parents were more likely than Anglos to press for early assumption of responsibilities in their children while at the same time creating more permissive home environments (LeVine & Bartz, 1979). Hence, early assumption of family responsibilities, as shown by a person's role as an active, sharing family member, reflects the interdependence valued by Latino families (Delgado-Gaitán, 1994).

Displays of affection among family members, particularly toward young children, are also commonplace in Latino families. For instance, Quirk et al. (1986) found that Puerto Rican mothers ascribed great importance to affection in contrast to creativity or productivity. Furthermore, secure attachment, particularly emphasizing relatedness, is encouraged among Puerto Rican children (Harwood, 1992), and children are rewarded for being close to their parents and other adults (Vázquez-Nuttal & Romero-García, 1989). Minturn and Lambert (1964) also rated Mexican American mothers among the highest when it came to the manifestation of affection toward their children in comparison to mothers from other cultures.

Thus, also intimately tied in with this seemingly austere parenting emphasizing parental power, respect, and male dominance, we find a patterning of behavior indicative of the high regard in which children are held in Latino cultures. That is, the strict parenting commonly associated with the values we have highlighted are tempered by an overriding concern for the well-being of children, often bordering on overprotectiveness. For instance, Ramos-McKay et al. (1988) and Ortiz-Archilla (1992) discuss how in Puerto Rican families child rearing is shared among members of the extended family and the well-being of young ones is a very important concern shared by all. On yet another level, work conducted with Mexican populations indicates that parents have the strong desire for their children to be successful in school, but also to be kind and considerate of others, to have respect for elders and authority, to be cooperative, and thus, to master the values of the group (Delgado-Gaitán, 1992). Hence, there is an expressed desire for the child to be well educated, not only as this pertains to formal education but in the ways of the traditional culture as well.

In contrast, we also find parents in Latino subgroups who in some situations express no qualms about responding to transgressions with the use of corporal punishment. In this context we would define corporal punishment as acts by parents or caregivers which carry the intent to cause the child pain or discomfort, but not injury, to correct or control the child's behavior. For instance, in a study conducted during the 1970s with Puerto Rican families residing on the island, almost all of the mothers indicated that they used physical punishment with their children and more than three-fourths indicated that they did so once a week or more (Rodríguez, González, & Muñoz, as cited in Bird & Canino, 1982). Similar findings were reported for Mexican American mothers, who, compared to mothers from other cultures, were rated highest in the use of physical punishment (Minturn & Lambert, 1964). What appears to be most striking about this action from observing or talking to parents is their sense of ownership and absolute right in reprimanding their child in this manner without much questioning or concern for the child's feelings as a separate individual. Given the loving nature of the parent-child relationship it seems hard to understand that corporal punishment is viewed as a sensible parenting behavior. In pondering the issue this may reflect the parent's concern for the well-being of the child and particularly for the manner in which the child will be perceived by others. A child who is respectful and *simpático* is likelier to be perceived well by others. That is, a well-behaved child will be held in high esteem and make the family proud. The child who does not adhere to the values of the culture will bring shame upon himself or herself and the family as well.

Another interpretation may lie in the urban environments in which many Latinos live. Fracasso et al. (1994) found physical interventions to be related to secure attachment in Puerto Rican and Dominican American families, while Ainsworth, Blehar, Waters, and Wall (1978) found them to be related to insecure attachment in Euro-American infants. The dense housing of the Latinos may have necessitated physical interventions to ensure the safety of children, and the physical interventions were often used as an opportunity for affection. This relationship may hold for adolescents as well: the urban environment contains threats to the safety of adolescents, so parents may respond by curtailing activities outside the family home.

A MODEL OF PARENTING

In her early work on child development and family interaction patterns, Baumrind (1967) delineated three styles of parenting behavior: authoritative, authoritarian, and permissive. Authoritative parents are both demanding and responsive, balancing nurturant behavior with high control. Parental demands are usually accompanied with clear statements about what is expected from the child and a directive is usually accompanied with a rationale or explanation. Furthermore, authoritative parents were described as affective, conscientious, and secure in their interactions with their children. Independence and individuality are encouraged in children and there is open communication and a recognition of the rights of both parents and children. The authoritarian parent is described as being less nurturant and having lower levels of involvement with his or her children than the authoritative parent. In the authoritarian family, the parent is the one with the superior power in the relationship. There is an emphasis on obedience and respect for authority, along with the expectation that orders are to be followed without question and without the child receiving any form of explanation. The permissive style is characterized by being nondirective, less controlling, allowing greater self-regulation on behalf of the child, and placing few demands on the child for mature behavior (Dornbusch, Ritter, Leiderman, Roberts, & Fraleigh, 1987; Baumrind, 1967, 1991a).

In her work with children prior to adolescence, Baumrind (1967, 1991b) concluded that these styles of parenting were related to particular child behaviors and characteristics. Children of authoritative parents were described as being socialized and independent. Authoritarian parents had children that were described as being significantly less content, more insecure, and less affiliative toward their peers. In addition, children of authoritarian parents were described as having low levels of independence and social responsibility. The children of permissive parents were said to be immature and low in self-control and self-reliance. The implication of these studies is that the authoritative parenting style was "better" than the authoritarian or permissive styles for child outcomes. This evaluation must be interpreted in light of the value placed on independence in North American society. Baumrind (1978) has noted that this definition of competence as independence was restricted to the qualities that facilitate successful adaptation by middle-class white Americans to industrial society. While these qualities may be associated with success for Anglos, their importance for other groups is not clear. For instance, in examining her data on African American girls, Baumrind (1978) found that "where high control is normative, as it is in the black community, nondemocratic control can be associated with independence in girls" (p. 265). Thus, different styles of parenting may have different meanings and child outcomes when the context in which development is taking place is taken into account.

At the risk of oversimplification, Vargas (1992) and DesRosiers et

Table 10.1 Comparison among Baumrind's Parenting Styles and Latino Parenting

Parenting Quality	Baumrind's Styles			Latino
	Authoritative	Authoritarian	Permissive	
Nurturance	High[a]	Low	?	High
Control	Parental[a]	Parental[a]	Child	Parental
Type of parental power	Reasoning	Obedience[a]/ no reasons	Limited	Obedience
Demands on child	Independence/ individuality	Many, especially for conformity[a]	Few[a]	Few, but expect conformity

[a]Indicates correspondence between Baumrind's style and Latino parenting.

al. (1995) suggest that Baumrind's model can be understood as four clusters of parenting qualities: nurturance, control, type of parental power, and demands on the child. *Nurturance* refers to the amount of warmth and affection that are present in the parent-child relationship and is evaluated along a continuum from high to low nurturance. *Control* reflects the center of power or the source of decision making in the relationship and has a continuum that ranges from parental to child control. *Type of parental power* indicates the methods parents use to exert their influence on the child; type is usually evaluated by the category of methods used, although there is also variety in the amount of parental power across the parenting styles. Finally, *demands on the child* is a cluster that indicates what expectations for the child are held by the parent; the demands may vary both in amount and categories of behaviors expected. The characterization of each style using these qualities is presented in Table 10.1.

Application of Baumrind's Model to Latino Families

Again, recognizing the possibility of oversimplification, we state that these qualities can be used to compare Baumrind's styles to traditional Latino parenting (see Table 10–1). As noted above, researchers have remarked on the high level of affection and attachment in Puerto Rican and Mexican American families (Minturn & Lambert, 1964; Quirk et al., 1986; Vázquez-Nuttal & Romero-García, 1989). Therefore, we have characterized traditional Latino parenting as being high in nurturance. Although children are cherished in Latino families, there is no question that the decisions are made by the parent, who expects obedience from the child and may use physical punishment to exert control (Minturn & Lambert, 1964; Rodriguez et al., cited in Bird & Canino, 1982). Latino parenting thus places control in the parents, whose power is related to obedience and corporal punishment. The overprotectiveness and permissiveness which is characteristic of Puerto Rican and Chicano families (Canino et al., 1988; LeVine & Bartz, 1979) suggests that few demands are placed on the children; existing demands are usually related to family responsibility and conformity to keep from bringing shame to the family (LeVine & Bartz, 1979).

The comparison with Baumrind's styles seems to indicate that traditional Latino parenting exhibits qualities of all three styles. Latino parenting has the high nurturing of authoritative parenting, the parental control of authoritative and authoritarian parenting, few demands on the child, like permissive parenting, and couples an expectation of obedience with physical punishment like authoritarian parenting.

This combination of parenting styles in Latino parenting suggests two nonexclusive possibilities when attempting to apply Baumrind's styles to Latino families. One possibility is that Baumrind's patterns are not valid for Latinos because parenting qualities do not cluster the same as with Euro-American samples. The second possibility is that an attempt to identify a *normative* Latino parenting pattern (i.e., the pattern used by Latino parents, such as characterizing Latino parenting as authoritarian) is inconsistent with the differential approach of Baumrind, who found three patterns (not one) in her Euro-American sample.

Linking Parenting Behaviors to Child and Adolescent Outcomes

In one of the few empirical studies to use Baumrind's typology with adolescents, Dornbusch et al. (1987) provide a description of the parenting styles and an examination of ethnic differences. Parenting style was assessed by means of a questionnaire administered to a sample of close to 8,000 students enrolled at six different high schools in California. Families were classified as having a "pure parenting style" when they scored high on any one of the three parenting styles (authoritarian, authoritative, permissive) and not so on either of the remaining two. Only half of the families in the sample met this criteria for pure parenting style, with 18 percent classified as permissive, 17 percent as authoritative, and 15 percent as authoritarian. (No breakdown by ethnicity was given for the pure styles.)

The findings indicated that Latino youth had families with higher authoritarian and permissive indices and a lower authoritative index than white families. However, these ethnic differences might be explained by demographic differences because high levels of education in parents were related to a more authoritative style of parenting and a lower score on the remaining two styles. Single parents (both mothers and fathers) were found to be more permissive than families where the two natural parents were present. Dornbusch et al. (1987) did not explore whether controlling for differences in these sociobiographic characteristics would eliminate the ethnic differences in parenting style (as was true in Laosa's 1980 comparison of Chicano and Anglo maternal teaching behaviors).

Dornbusch et al. (1987) also attempted to establish links between Baumrind's parenting styles and adolescent outcome variables, specifically school performance with high school grades as the operational definition. They did find that parental education was a strong predictor of grades, but that the significant relationships found between parenting style and high school grades held across all levels of parental education. For the total sample, the highest mean grade point average was found in the group experiencing the pure authoritative style, closely followed by the no high index style. Higher levels of an authoritarian parenting style were significantly related to lower grades; findings for a permissive parenting style were similar although less strong.

The results also showed that there were ethnic differences in the strength of the relationship between parenting styles and grades, with sex differences emerging in the Latino sample. The best predictors of grades in the Latino sample were being female (positive relationship) and the interaction of the authoritarian index and female (negative relationship). This interaction reverses the effect of authoritarian parenting from negative in the total sample to insignificantly positive within the Latino sample. The authors suggested that the cause of these sex differences lies in cultural orientations with specific reference to the disobedience from adolescent males that is allowed in the Latino family. They also note that the findings are also evidence of the "difficulty in applying the parenting typology across diverse cultures" (Dornbusch et al., 1987, p. 1254).

Because the results of the Dornbusch et al. analyses seemed to indicate positive effects of authoritative parenting, Steinberg, Mounts, Lamborn, and Dornbusch (1991) used a slightly larger, overlapping data set to assess the authoritative style of parenting, taking into consideration various ecological variables. They were interested in learning whether the ecological context of the youth (assessed by ethnicity, socioeconomic status, and family structure) moderated the relation between an authoritative style of parenting and adolescent outcome variables, operationalized by GPA, self-reliance, psychological distress, and delinquency. For the total sample, those adolescents reared in authoritative homes earned higher grades, were found to be more self-reliant, to report less psychological distress and to be less involved in delinquent acts. These findings were most consistent among white middle-class adolescents who came from intact families, but the findings held for most of the Latino analyses as well. For the Latino subsample, all of the sixteen planned comparisons between the authoritative and nonauthoritative families (broken down by SES, and intact versus nonintact) were in the expected direction, and ten showed significant differences in the adolescent psychological outcomes that favored the authoritative families. The lack of other effects mirroring the white comparisons may be the result of small but consistent effect sizes.

Steinberg, Lamborn, Dornbusch, and Darling (1992) obtained a longitudinal follow-up on this sample to examine the mediating effects of parental involvement and encouragement on the relationship between parental authoritativeness and adolescent school performance and school engagement. Approximately 15 percent of the follow-up sample was Latino, but the published results did not include analyses for the separate ethnicities. The authors noted that the results for the Latino samples were different from the overall results in that parental encouragement and authoritativeness enhanced school engagement, which was not well predicted by parental behaviors in the entire sample. Overall the results of the studies of Dornbusch and his colleagues show that the relationship between adolescent outcomes and parenting is most consistent among the Euro-American middle-class adolescents who are overrepresented in the research literature. Research with other cultural and ethnic groups is sorely needed.

A Look at Two Cultures

Many of the questions left unanswered by the series of studies by Dornbusch and his colleagues are illuminated by a study conducted by Holtzman and his colleagues (1964). The purpose of the study was to compare the personality development of American and Mexican children with families from Austin, Texas, and Mexico City, Mexico. Because of the problems inherent in cross-cultural comparisons, especially the possible influence of multiple variables besides culture, the researchers used subcultural variation in SES and individual development (chronological age) to highlight cultural effects. The longitudinal study followed three groups of children and their families for a period of six years, thus employing what is today known as a sequential design. Children ranged in age from 6.7 to 12.7 years at the start of the study and were from both lower- and upper-class families. Approximately 450 families and their children were tested and followed in each country. Children from private schools in Mexico were oversampled to have a group believed to be more comparable to the sample from the United States. Various aspects of child development were assessed; here, we will only discuss significant parent and home variables that differed across groups and were related to parent-child interaction and child development. Mothers were interviewed about three years into the study to obtain information on various topics, including household composition, parent's occupation and educational level, religion, recreational and leisure-time activities, and parental involvement with their children.

There were numerous significant differences between the Mexican and American families in the study. Comparisons indicated that the level of intellectual stimuli provided to children in the home was lower for Mexican families than for American families. For instance, Mexican mothers reportedly read less to their children prior to school entry, and for the most part their children had not acquired any reading, writing, or counting skills prior to school entry. However, Mexican parents did encourage their children to read once they had entered school. One may interpret this finding as indicating that these parents did not place any major demands on their children during the preschool years and simply allowed them to be children without placing any significant restrictions or responsibilities on them at this developmental stage. The fact that once the children entered school parents did encourage their children to read may be the result of the parents seeing school entry as representative of a major transition in the child's life toward greater responsibility which resulted in greater concern for their academic future.

In the case of Mexican fathers, fewer of them and particularly fewer from lower classes shared activities with their sons, evidence that the division of labor by sex associated with machismo influenced family socialization practices. Mexican children were given fewer responsibilities in the home than their American counterparts. They were also more likely to experience parental involvement in their selection of friends. Mexican mothers were described as being less accepting and more controlling of their children, with children having less freedom to express their views or to participate in adult conversations. Mexican mothers described discipline practices that were more authoritarian and they placed a higher value on strict obedience than did American mothers. Mexican mothers also placed more value on the personal characteristic of "desiring to make a name in the world," a value that can be seen as making the family proud (familism) and as being worthy of respect (*respeto*). There was also a greater value placed on the development of independence and a higher degree of intellectual curiosity in the American mothers than was typical of the Mexican mothers.

Other significant cultural differences which had an impact on parenting were a lower educational level among mothers and a larger nuclear family size with the inherent competition for attention among siblings in the Mexican families. Extended family members residing in the household were also a common occurrence in the Mexican sample, leading to an increase in "affiliative activities while de-emphasizing solitary intellectual pursuits" (Holtzman et al., 1964, p. 315), a behavioral manifestation of familism. The investigators commented on how the findings indicated that American children regardless of social class were encouraged toward independent thinking and intellectual activities in which individual achievement is stressed rather than interpersonal fulfillment, a situation in contrast with the Mexican emphasis on familism.

The private school population in Mexico City was most complementary to the Austin population, so this population was oversampled to provide initial control of SES. When comparing the samples, Holtzman et al. dropped the third of the Mexican sample lowest on SES and the highest third of the Austin sample. With this control for SES, many of the variables that showed cultural differences also showed social class differences as well. Lower-class individuals were found to be the most traditional and the ones who showed a tendency to hold on to the traditional sociocultural premises inherited from the past. However, there were few culture by social class interactions. In particular the lower- and higher-SES families in Mexico could be distinguished, with the former expressing more traditional views and the latter considered to look like the middle-class Anglo families with their high, independent achievement values. One exception to this was the finding that the value "getting good grades in school" was ranked most important by lower-class Mexican mothers in contrast to the upper-class American mothers who discounted its importance.

The results of this study suggest that there were differences between Mexican and American parenting beyond what might be explained by social class. More recent work by LeVine, LeVine, Richman, Tapia Uribe, Correa, & Miller (1991) suggests that maternal education has an effect on maternal caregiving and child outcomes, beyond the influence of other SES factors. Husband's school attainment was a predictor of fertility, but not child outcomes, indicating the continuation of machismo in reproductive issues. Their findings of smaller families, with greater investment in each child, may be seen as a modern expression of familism. The findings of Holtzman et al. support the position that the values of familism, *respeto*, and machismo made a significant contribution to the way in which Mexican parents were bringing up their children, while the findings of LeVine et al. (1991) suggest that these values continue to have a significant impact on parenting behavior in Mexican families.

IMPLICATIONS FOR ADOLESCENTS' VALUES

More current work suggests that the cultural differences continue to exist and affect not only school outcomes (as indicated by Dornbusch et al., 1987) but also the acquisition of cultural values themselves. Adolescence is a critical time for the examination and integration of significant individual values. As the work of Vázquez-García et al. (this volume) demonstrates, some basic dimensions of core Latino values are maintained by adolescents which may facilitate their adjustment to the demands of balancing two distinct sets of cultural values.

In a study of Mexican and Mexican American mothers, adolescents, and preadolescents, Díaz-Guerrero (1987) found that mothers endorsed machismo more for their preadolescents than for their adolescents. Interestingly, he did not find a difference between the Mexican and Mexican American adolescents, suggesting the strong pressures of gender-appropriate behavior during this period. He also found age differences in endorsement of cultural rigidity regarding the role of parents and women and beliefs in abnegation (women suffer more). Preadolescents were found to have greater commonality with their mother in their beliefs, while older youth were more self-assertive and less strict in endorsing the traditional cultural values. Díaz-Guerrero interpreted his results as confirming the importance of the mother in the transmission of cultural values.

The findings of DesRosiers et al. (1995) suggest, additionally, that the parenting style may influence the effectiveness of this socialization. They found that the parenting styles perceived by adolescents affect their endorsement of cultural values. Specifically, adolescents who were more acculturated and perceived their parents as being higher in the use of an authoritative parenting style showed lower levels of familism and communal reciprocity. Interestingly, the adolescents who perceived their parents as being higher in the use of an authoritarian parenting style showed a contrast (discrepancy) between the levels of familism and communal reciprocity.

CONCLUSION

The most often used description of parenting, namely, the typologies associated with Baumrind's model, does not fit observations of Latino parenting, so a new model should be developed to guide work in this area. This reflection is consistent with the ongoing work of Baumrind, Dornbusch, and others which shows that the original parenting styles identified continue to need revision to account for the variations seen in parenting styles. However, the paucity in research with diverse samples in this area makes it difficult to construct a new model of parenting which will do justice to the ethnic diversity characteristic of society today.

Such research with diverse samples should not be primarily comparative in nature. Studies which are comparative will be hampered by small sample sizes (as was the case with the studies of Dornbusch and colleagues) and by the likely confounds between the variable of ethnicity and the variables of social class, parental education, and so on (Busch-Rossnagel, 1992). Most importantly, in using ethnicity as an independent variable, comparative studies give inadequate consideration to the psychological processes of the probably unique underlying dynamics of the interactions between minority youth and their parents. Discussing the study of minority child development, Ogbu (1981) suggested that we study minority child development as minority child development, not in comparison to majority child development. That is, the experiences of minority and majority youth are not truly comparable. Although adolescence is a normative process in Western societies, the life experiences and interactions of minority youth within society differ from those of majority youth. Likewise, there are likely to be differences among minority groups (e.g., African American versus Latino) as well, so each group must be studied in its own right.

Several implications about Latino parenting may be derived when we take this position. Comparative studies often result in the identification of a modal behavior—in this case, one parenting style—for each ethnic group. However, this is probably not the appropriate approach since each of the various parenting styles most likely can be identified in different cultures. The identification of a modal behavior neglects within-group variation, both across Latino subgroups and across the developmental processes of adolescence. Instead, the differential approach may be most appropriate in addressing a series of questions. In examining the precursors of individual differences, the differential approach is consistent with the developmental contextual approach emerging as the dominant model in developmental psychology. For instance, it is possible from this stance to assess what parenting qualities appear to cluster in Latino parents and what behaviors express these qualities. We can then explore what adolescent outcomes are associated with the parenting clusters identified. Further, we can determine the antecedent characteristics which lead to the Latino parenting clusters identified. The answers to these questions may be most effectively sought by looking at within-group differences in parenting in the Latino population. Such an endeavor should help in the formulation of a comprehensive parenting styles model and in the assessment of child and adolescent outcomes related to parenting. Similar to the work that is still needed with Euro-American parents and adolescents, there is still the need to explore which characteristics or circumstances, such as level of education, national background, and/or acculturation, lead to these parenting clusters. The result should be nothing less than a model addressing both the developmental nature of adolescence and the understanding of contextual influences on behavior.

REFERENCES

Ainsworth, M. D. S., Blehar, M. C., Waters, E., & Wall, S. (1978). *Patterns of attachment.* Hillsdale, NJ: Lawrence Erlbaum.

Archer, S. L., & Waterman, A. S. (1994). Development and validation of ego-identity status. *Journal of Personality and Social Psychology, 3,* 551–558.

Baumrind, D. (1967). Child care practices anteceding three patterns of preschool behavior. *Genetic Psychology Monographs, 75,* 43–88.

Baumrind, D. (1978). Parental disciplinary patterns and social competence in children. *Youth and Society, 9,* 239–276.

Baumrind, D. (1991a). The influence of parenting style on adolescent competence and substance use. *Journal of Early Adolescence, 11,* 56–95.

Baumrind, D. (1991b). Effective parenting during the early adolescent transition. In P. A. Cowan & M. Hetherington (Eds.), *Family transitions* (pp. 111–163). Hillsdale, NJ: Erlbaum.

Bird, H. R., & Canino, G. (1982). The Puerto Rican family: Cultural factors and family intervention strategies. *Journal of the American Academy of Psychoanalysis, 10,* 257–268.

Busch-Rossnagel, N. A. (1992). Commonalities between test validity and external validity in basic research on Hispanics. In K. F. Geisinger (Ed.), *Psychological testing of Hispanics* (pp. 195–214). Washington, DC: American Psychological Association.

Canino, I. A., Earley, B. F., & Rogler, L. H. (1988). *The Puerto Rican child in New York City: Stress and mental health* (2nd ed.). Bronx, NY: Hispanic Research Center.

Casas, J. M., Wagenheim, B. R., Banchero, R., & Mendoza-Romero, J. (1994). Hispanic masculinity: Myth or psychological schema meriting clinical consideration. *Hispanic Journal of Behavioral Sciences, 16,* 315–331.

Comas-Díaz, L. (1982). Mental health needs of Puerto Rican women in the United States. In R. E. Zambrana (Ed.), *Work, family, and health: Latina women in transition* (pp. 1–10). Bronx, NY: Hispanic Research Center.

Cromwell, R. E., & Ruiz, R. A. (1979). The myth of macho dominance in decision making within Mexican and Chicano families. *Hispanic Journal of Behavioral Sciences, 1,* 355–373.

Delgado-Gaitán, C. (1992). School matters in the Mexican American home: Socializing children to education. *American Educational Research Journal, 29,* 495–513.

Delgado-Gaitán, C. (1994). Socializing young children in Mexican American families: An intergenerational perspective. In P. M. Greenfield & R. R. Cocking (Eds.), *Cross-cultural roots of minority child development* (pp. 55–86). Hillsdale, NJ: Erlbaum.

DesRosiers, F. S., Zayas, L. H., & Busch-Rossnagel, N. A. (1995). *Familism and communal reciprocity in Hispanic and Anglo undergraduates.* Manuscript submitted for publication.

Díaz-Guerrero, R. (1987). Historical sociocultural premises and ethnic socialization. In J. S. Phinney & M. J. Rotheram (Eds.), *Children's ethnic socialization: Pluralism and development* (pp. 239–250). Newbury Park, CA: Sage.

Díaz-Guerrero, R., & Szalay, L. B. (1991). *Understanding Mexicans and Americans: Cultural perspectives in conflict.* New York: Plenum.

Dornbusch, S. M., Ritter, P. L., Leiderman, P. H., Roberts, D. F., & Fraleigh, M. J. (1987). The relation of parenting style to adolescent school performance. *Child Development, 58,* 1244–1257.

Duany, J. (1994). Quisqueya on the Hudson: The transnational identity of Dominicans in Washington Heights. *Dominican Research Monographs.* New York: CUNY Dominican Studies Institute.

Erikson, E. H. (1963). *Childhood and society.* New York: Norton.
Erikson, E. H. (1968). *Identity: Youth and crisis.* New York: Norton.
Fitzpatrick, J. P. (1987). *Puerto Rican Americans: The meaning of migration to the mainland* (2nd ed.). Englewood Cliffs, NJ: Prentice Hall.
Fracasso, M. P., & Busch-Rossnagel, N. A. (1992). Parents and children of Hispanic origin. In M. P. Procidano & C. B. Fisher (Eds.), *Contemporary families: A handbook for school professionals* (pp. 83–98). New York: Teachers College Press.
Fracasso, M. P., Busch-Rossnagel, N. A., & Fisher, C. B. (1994). The relationship of maternal behavior and acculturation to the quality of attachment in Hispanic infants living in New York City. *Hispanic Journal of Behavioral Sciences, 16,* 143–154.
Harwood, R. L. (1992). The influence of culturally derived values on Anglo and Puerto Rican mothers' perceptions of attachment. *Child Development, 63,* 822–839.
Holtzman, W. H., Díaz-Guerrero, R., Swartz, J. D. (1964). *Personality development in two cultures.* Texas: University of Texas.
Laosa, L. M. (1980). Maternal teaching strategies in Chicano and Anglo-American families: The influence of culture and education on maternal teaching behavior. *Child Development, 51,* 759–765.
Lauria, A. (1964). "Respeto," "Relajo," and inter-personal relations in Puerto Rico. *Anthropological Quarterly,* 53–67.
LeVine, E. S., & Bartz, K. W. (1979). Comparative child-rearing attitudes among Chicano, Anglo, and black parents. *Hispanic Journal of Behavioral Sciences, 1,* 165–178.
LeVine, R. A., LeVine, S. E., Richman, A., Tapia Uribe, F. M, Correa, C. S., & Miller, P. M. (1991). Women's schooling and child care in demographic transition: A Mexican case study. *Population and Development Review, 17,* 459–496.
Madsen, W. (1964). The agrinado. *American Anthropologist, 66,* 355–361.
Marcia, J. E. (1966). Development and validation of ego-identity status. *Journal of Personality and Social Psychology, 3,* 551–558.
Marcia, J. E., Waterman, A. S., Matteson, D. R., Archer, S. L., & Orlofsky, J. L. (1993). *Ego identity: A handbook for psychosocial research.* New York: Springer-Verlag.
Marín, G., & VanOss Marín, B. (1991). *Research with Hispanic populations.* Newbury Park, CA: Sage.
Millán, F., & Chan, J. (1991). Group therapy with inner city Hispanic acting-out adolescent males: Some theoretical observations. *Group, 15,* 109–115.
Minturn, L., & Lambert, W. (1964). *Mothers of six cultures: Antecedents of child rearing.* New York: Wiley.

Ogbu, J. U. (1981). Origins of human competence: A cultural-ecological perspective. *Child Development, 52,* 413–429.
Ortiz-Archilla, S. (1992). Families in Puerto Rico: An analysis of the socialization process from a macrostructural perspective. In J. L. Roopharine & D. B. Carter (Eds.), *Annual Advances in Applied Developmental Psychology, 5* (pp. 159–171). Norwood, NJ: Ablex.
Quirk, M., Ciottone, R., Minami, H., Wapner, S., Yamamoto, T., Ishii, S., Lucca-Irizarry, N., & Pacheco, A. (1986). Values mothers hold for handicapped and non-handicapped preschool children in Japan, Puerto Rico, and the United States mainland. *International Journal of Psychology, 21,* 463–485.
Ramos-McKay, J. M., Comas-Díaz, L., & Rivera, L. A. (1988). Puerto Ricans. In L. Comas-Díaz & E. E. H. Griffith (Eds.), *Clinical guidelines in cross-cultural mental health* (pp. 204–232). New York: Wiley.
Rodríguez, L. V., González, J. L., & Muñoz, R. A. (1978). *Study of child rearing practices, parents' information and child development outcomes in Puerto Rico.* Hato Rey, PR: Health and Social Studies, Inc.
Rogler, L. H., & Santana-Cooney, R. S. (1984). *Puerto Rican families in New York City: Intergenerational processes.* Maplewood, NJ: Waterfront.
Sabogal, F., Marín, G., Otero-Sabogal, R., Marín, B. V., & Perez-Stable, E. J. (1987). Hispanic familism and acculturation: What changes and what doesn't? *Hispanic Journal of Behavioral Sciences, 9,* 397–412.
Sandoval, M. C., & De La Roza, M. C. (1986). A cultural perspective for serving the Hispanic client. In H. P. Lefley & P. B. Pendersen (Eds.), *Cross-cultural training for mental health professionals* (pp. 151–181). Springfield, IL: Thomas.
Shelley-Sireci, L. M. (1995). *Social and instrumental interaction styles across age and context: A longitudinal study of Central American and Euro-American mother-infant dyads.* Unpublished dissertation, Fordham University, Bronx, NY.
Sigel, I. E. (1992). The belief-behavior connection: A resolvable dilemma? In E. Sigel, A. V. McGillicuddy-DeLisi, & J. J. Goodnow (Eds.), *Parental belief systems: The psychological consequences for children* (2nd ed., pp. 433–456). Hillsdale, NJ: Erlbaum.
Spencer, M., Dornbusch S. M., & Mont-Reynaud, R. (1990). Challenges in studying minority youth. In S. S. Feldman & G. R. Elliot (Eds.), *At the threshold: The developing adolescent* (pp. 123–146). Cambridge, MA: Harvard University.
Steinberg, L., Lamborn, S. D., Dornbusch, S. M., & Darling, N. (1992). Impact of parenting practices on adolescent achievement: Authoritative parenting,

school involvement, and encouragement to succeed. *Child Development, 63,* 1266–1281.

Steinberg, L., Mounts, N. S., Lamborn, S. D., & Dornbusch, S. M. (1991). Authoritative parenting an adolescent adjustment across varied ecological niches. *Journal of Research on Adolescence, 1,* 19–36.

Szapocznik, J., & Kurtines, W. M. (1993). Family psychology and cultural diversity: Opportunities for theory, research, and application. *American Psychologist, 48,* 400–407.

Triandis, H. C., Marín, G., Lisansky, J., & Betancourt, H. (1984). *Simpatia* as a cultural script for Hispanics. *Journal of Personality and Social Psychology, 47,* 1363–1375.

Vargas, M. (1992). *Predictors of maternal teaching strategies in Puerto Rican mothers.* Unpublished dissertation, Fordham University, Bronx, NY.

Vázquez-Nutall, E., & Romero-García, I. (1989). From home to school: Puerto Rican girls learn to be students in the United States. In C. T. García Coll & M. L. Mattei (Eds.), *The psychosocial development of Puerto Rican women* (pp. 60–83). New York: Praeger.

Williams, N. (1988). Role making among Mexican American women: Issues of class and ethnicity. *Journal of Applied Behavioral Sciences, 24,* 203–217.

Yep, G. A. (1995). Communicating the HIV/AIDS risk to Hispanic populations. In A. M. Padilla (Ed.), *Hispanic psychology: Critical issues in theory and research* (pp. 196–212). Beverly Hills, CA: Sage.

CHAPTER 11
Migrant Adolescents
Barriers and Opportunities for
Creating a Promising Future

BERTHA LÓPEZ, LUCILA NERENBERG,
AND MARINA VALDEZ

The information presented in this chapter focuses on the issues pertinent to migrant adolescents. It has been gleaned from ten years of clinical experience as well as a comprehensive review of the literature that has focused on migrant life in the United States, specifically in Michigan. The objective of this chapter is to examine the assets of migrant life for Latino adolescents, and as well, to introduce dimensions that contribute to less than healthy development.

In this chapter we will therefore present issues that impact the development of migrant adolescents with respect to what is known of their conditions and what is necessary to achieve "positive and healthy outcomes" in their intrapersonal development. We will specifically look at health and education as two of the most important factors that affect opportunities for promising futures.

The information presented within this chapter is derived from three primary sources. First, a comprehensive review was undertaken to summarize the literature that exists on Latino migrant families and adolescents. Second, information was obtained from migrant families living and working in southeast Michigan. Finally, the information is also based upon the combined experiences of the authors who have worked with migrant families and youth over the last decade. The final section of this chapter highlights several dimensions of programs that have created healthy environments for migrant adolescents and their families. Various recommendations that practitioners, researchers, and policymakers should keep in mind if the well-being of migrant adolescents is to be further enhanced are also presented.

DEMOGRAPHICS

The origins of migrant labor can be traced to the bracero programs, an agreement between the United States and Mexican governments which brought thousands of Mexicans to the fields to fill the labor shortage caused by World War II (Rochin, Santiago, & Dickey, 1991). The few documented studies available show that little has been done since that time to change the circumstances of Mexican American migrant workers. Griffith and Kissam (1995) report that almost all Mexican American migrant families live in poverty, earning approximately half the poverty-level income. They also noted that most migrants live in substandard housing and have inadequate access to medical care. The average life expectancy of a migrant worker is estimated at under 50 years (Rochin et al., 1991).

The majority of migrant families in the United States, and specifically in Michigan, are of Hispanic origin (Rochin et al., 1991). Typically, these migrant families bring with them unique cultural traditions, beliefs, and biases which serve as the foundation of their individual and familial development.

With respect to immigration status, the erroneous perception of the general population is that most of the migrants are foreigners. Yet statistics indicate that 54 percent are citizens of the United States, 30 percent are documented immigrants, and only 16 percent are undocumented (Michigan Department of Agriculture, 1996). It is estimated that there are approximately 1.7 million migrant farmworkers in the United States, with approximately 409,000 being children and adolescents who must travel with their families (Morrissey, 1996). Most of the migrant teens in southeastern Michigan today were born in the United States and are of Mexican descent.

Within the state of Michigan, similar trends can be noted. From the 1940s through the mid-1960s, the majority of migrant laborers participated in the bracero program and generally increased the labor force in Michigan during the 1960s, and subsequently in the 1970s. The 1980s, however, were found to be unstable and marked with declines in the migrant workforce (Rochin et al., 1991). Michigan's migrant population has decreased; as of this writing, the reported numbers are down from 45,000 to 43,000 (Michigan Department of Agriculture, 1996).

Migrant teens come to Michigan with their families or by themselves from Texas, Florida, and most recently in increasing numbers from Georgia, Alabama, Arkansas, and the Carolinas. There are also a number of migrants from the countries of El Salvador, Guatemala, and Honduras (Rochin et al., 1991).

EDUCATION

A frequently cited myth related to the educational aspirations of migrant families and adolescents holds that neither parents nor children value education. School personnel and community leaders often contend that Mexican Americans prefer to work in the fields and lack motivation to achieve an education. Yet, the reality of life in the migrant stream presents a set of life-issues that can be frequently misinterpreted. Because of the various growing seasons, for example, migrant adolescents and their families must frequently move across and between counties, states, and regions of the country for economic survival (U.S. Department of Education, 1995; National Commission on Migrant Education, 1992). In some instances, climatic changes that affect growing seasons (e.g., excessive rain or unusually long and hot periods) result in crop damages, thus impacting employment. As a consequence, families must move to areas where less damage has occurred in order to maintain a level of income. In these situations, adolescents and children are unable to complete an entire school year within one school district (Morrissey, 1996), or for that matter, cannot predict how long they will be within a particular school district.

When not confronted with seasonal changes that negatively impact growing seasons, many adolescents must work in addition to attending school. Because of the physical nature of this work, which demands long hours, students are unable to devote much time to studying, are frequently tired, and even when able to attend class are inattentive, or worse yet may fall asleep. This is interpreted as a lack of motivation and/or interest in education.

Further difficulties are confronted by children and adolescents who must attend schools, albeit for a short period of time, where they have few if any peers. In addition, language may be an issue. In other cases, being pulled out of school results in having to leave friends behind. As a consequence, migrant adolescents who are in school tend to isolate themselves. This isolation can be seen either as a weakness or as a strength. As a consequence, they tend to stick together for safety. For example:

> For Ana school may be the only place for her to socialize because of her isolation as the only adolescent in her camp. When she is at school she does not seek out friendships from other peers with the exception

of other migrant adolescents who attend the same school. She prefers to be with others who are like her and understand what she may be experiencing as a migrant adolescent.

Another challenge confronting migrant adolescents is the issue of acceptance by their peers in a school setting:

> Eight high school migrant adolescents were nervous about the first day of school. They were feeling ambivalent by their own report. They were excited, but also feeling anxious. Steve was worried about what he wore to school that day. His family had not received their pay that week so he was unable to shop for school clothes. He wore an old T-shirt and an old pair of shorts. He hoped that his peers would not notice and ridicule him. All through the school day, he imagined that all his peers were making fun of the way he was dressed and he was looking forward to the end of the school day.

A third issue that frequently confronts the educational performance and motivation of migrant adolescents has to do with repetitive assessment and entry procedures (Morrissey, 1996). Because school records do not always follow an individual in a timely manner, students must undergo a series of assessments in order to correctly place them. All too often, these assessments lead to recommendations for adolescents to be placed in remedial or special education classes, and in other cases, in classes which they may have already had in another school district. In other circumstances, students may be placed in classes that are below their ability until they undergo assessments or records are transferred—which may take several weeks.

A typical conversation between two migrant high school students illustrates the above point.

> Carlos asks his friend Sandy if she is taking health class again. He is angry because he has already taken health twice and he does not understand why he has to take it again. He is interested in taking psychology, but his counselor is worried that he may not be able to do the work and assigns him to another health class. Sandy understands his frustration and supports his interest in psychology, but does not know how to help him.

In addition to the aforementioned issues which impact the educational success of migrant youth, other aspects of their lifestyle also minimize their chances of school success. Poverty, for example, is a risk factor that many migrant adolescents and their families confront (Edelman & Solow, 1994). In addition to the dehumanizing aspect of poverty, the effects of a life of constant migration negatively impacts the health status of youth and their families, contributes to poor health care, and creates tenuous ties with schools (Allen-Meares, Washington, & Welse, 1996).

A frequently misunderstood "barrier" is the family. Specifically, migrant families, like other Latino families, tend to have strong family ties, a good work ethic, rich cultural traditions, and respect for authority (Morrissey, 1996). The impact of these strong ties is illustrated in the following scenario:

> Norma, a 16-year-old migrant adolescent, was viewed by her teachers as a fairly good student. She always appeared to enjoy school, worked hard, and got along well with her peers. This year, however, her attendance and participation at school were sporadic, and considered to be unlike her. A number of concerns had come up, including her inattentiveness during various classes (especially those in the earlier parts of the day), failure to submit homework, and sporadic attendance. Upon discussing this with Norma, the school social worker uncovered the difficult dilemma that was confronting her. While she wanted to be in school, her parents needed her to work with them in the fields. The crops were not as plentiful as they had been in years past, and as a consequence, more assistance was needed to maintain the family income. Norma did not protest her parents' decision, as she understood her obligation to financially contribute to and assist her family.

As in this situation, when parents are struggling to maintain a basic living, they must frequently turn to, and depend on, their children for additional help. Thus, participation in school may be a familial hardship (Leon, 1996). The dependence of the parents on the adolescent to increase family income is seen as a collective way to improve the family's living condition.

MIGRANT HEALTH ISSUES

Data related to the health status, needs, and access for migrant populations have several shortcomings. Most data sets, for example, have a "missing denominator" factor (Rust, 1990). In other words, because no real population estimate exists, it is difficult to determine an accurate prevalence rate of injury, illness, or health status.

Health Barriers

Barriers to health prevention include economic, political, legislative, and social factors (Friedman-Jiménez & Ortiz, 1994). Due to the lack of research on barriers related specifically to migrants in the adolescent age group, data on migrant farmworkers of all ages will be presented.

Contrary to popular belief and similarly to the general Latino population, most migrants seen in southeast Michigan underutilize services. Estimates show that less than 20 percent of farmworkers are served by clinics nationwide (Sakala, 1998). Economic factors include the adolescent migrants' pressing need to help support themselves and their families. Living in poverty also affects families' ability to afford health insurance or pay for out-of-pocket medical expenses. As a consequence, migrants tend to try to postpone or cancel medical appointments rather than miss a day of work (Friedman-Jiménez & Ortiz, 1994). Rochin et al. (1991) note that additional barriers include geographic inaccessibility of clinics, hours that do not coincide with fieldwork, and staff who may not be bilingual or bicultural. Sakala (1988) adds that underutilization of services can also be due to underservice in rural areas, migrants' not being aware of services, and the reluctance of many providers to serve this population.

> In one such case, an adolescent did not even mention his major medical concerns during an on-site visit, until his friends approached the treatment team. They stated that he had recent difficulty sustaining the demanding pace that they all needed in the fields, as well as poor appetite and significant weight loss. Part of their rationale in initiating the consultation was that their friend was "shy and would probably not dare to ask about this." Despite his having an on-site evaluation and receiving a strong recommendation to have further testing done, he was ambivalent about coming to a clinic. He was reluctant to miss further work hours and worried about when and how he could go to the nearest clinic, as well as how he would pay for services.

This case also illustrates other health care barriers for adolescents, such as legislative issues. For example, if this young man was "undocumented," he may have forfeited care due to fear of deportation. Political barriers to health care have included migrant teens being an "invisible population," even less studied than the migrants in general. Therefore, there are few if any health programs that target migrant teens. They also have virtually no advocates or lobbyists to improve their chances of obtaining care.

Health Advantages

Ruducha (1994) wrote that migrant child health is confronted with overwhelming challenges. Yet, she adds, the effects are mediated by cultural strengths and adaptations of migrant families. This includes more frequent two-parent families and larger households than nonmigrant children of the same ethnic origin, leading to more social support in both material and emotional matters. Ruducha examines a possible positive role of work-related isolation, leading to decreased acculturation. Decreased acculturation is thought to protect cultural norms, including health behaviors (Vega & Amaro, 1994).

Vega and Amaro (1994) also note that a number of health indicators improve with decreased acculturation of Hispanics, including infant mortality, low birth weight, adolescent pregnancy, high blood pressure, and overall cancer rates. Negative health behaviors also increase with acculturation, including low fiber consumption, decreased breast-feeding, and increased use of cigarettes, alcohol, and illicit drugs.

Vega and Amaro (1994) suggest that the stress of acculturation is due to the disruption of social support systems, difficulties adapting to the host culture, and likely discrimination. One subtype of acculturation is by assimilation, by which a person rejects his or her own identity and cultural values. This route may leave the individual without protective resources and place him or her at greater risk.

Occupational Diseases

Agriculture is frequently cited among the nation's most dangerous occupations (Friedman-Jimenez & Ortiz, 1994; Wilk, 1986). Farm-related deaths are usually due to machine-related accidents and appear to be related to age as well as occupation (Friedman-Jiménez & Ortiz, 1994; Heyer, Franklin, Rivara, Parker, & Haug, 1992). Youth working in agriculture can legally perform hazardous jobs at a younger age than in any other industry. Unfortunately, even the insufficient legal protection is frequently violated due to little existing or enforced legislation and a critical need for more income (Occupational Health Subcommittee, 1990; Wilk, 1986).

Other hazards include pesticide exposure resulting in acute poisoning or chronic sequelae such as dermatitis, increased risk of cancer, or birth defects (Friedman-Jiménez & Ortiz, 1994). Although data on adolescents are lacking, Gold, Gordis, Tonascia, and Szklo (1979) found an excess risk of both brain cancer and leukemia in children of migrants, which was also associated with pesticide exposure.

An increasing number of studies link pesticide exposure to cancer in nonfarmworker children, adolescents, and adults (Davis, Brownson, García, Bentz, & Turner, 1993; Leiss & Saritz, 1995; Mulder, Drijver, & Kreis, 1994).

Substance Abuse

The National Migrant Resource Network Program (1991) noted the lack of formal research on substance abuse among migrant teens and discussed anecdotal information gathered from the National Coalition of Advocates for Students, spanning fifteen states. During a number of regional and national meetings, migrant youth and adult service providers identified substance abuse as a priority issue.

Lovato, Litrownik, Elder, Núñez-Liriano, Suárez, and Talavera (1994) did one of the few studies on migrant adolescents, on 214 high school students in San Diego County, California. They surveyed the use of alcohol and cigarettes, correlating these with acculturation. The results showed that overall smoking and binge drinking rates were less than the national norms for their age group.

Significant correlations were also found between alcohol use and acculturation in migrant youth. Male and female binge drinkers tended to be more acculturated, coinciding with findings in the general Hispanic population (Marks, Garcia, & Solis, 1990).

Mental Health

The National Advisory Council on Migrant Health (1995) notes that the need for mental health services in the farmworker population is usually overlooked. They point out that this is despite the increased incidence of mental health problems associated with brutal living conditions. As with other health problems, access is a major issue, exacerbated by a critical lack of funds for treatment of mental illness.

Problems encountered by migrants seeking health care include communication difficulties, the present structure of service delivery and billing in traditional mental health agencies, a lack of networking with other multiservice types of agencies by the mental health agencies, relatively little preparation in effective cross-cultural medical practice, and the lack of integrated psychiatry and general medical care. This has been observed for many years by frontline staff and confirmed to be true by studies that were conducted in California while studying Mexican American agricultural workers (Vega, Scutchfield, Karno, & Meinhardt, 1989). These studies were undertaken to better understand the underutilization of established mental health services by this population.

A decade of working and trying different treatment modalities has shown that the most effective method of diagnosis and treatment with this population is that which can be done in an outreach format (Torres, 1994). Other factors found to be effective arise when those doing the diagnosis are culturally competent, bilingual, and bicultural. Not as much information was found regarding migrant teens; however, clinical observation for this same decade has shown that migrant teens very seldom present themselves for services. When they do seek services, it is frequently related to referrals from other health or social professionals.

Atzlan: The Dreams and Bridges of Migrant Adolescents

Like other adolescents, migrant youth have dreams and aspirations that frequently are not captured. In 1991, the National Coalition of Advocates for Students invited providers and adolescent farmworkers to participate in a youth forum in Florida. By the end of the conference, the youth participants had generated the following joint statement (Camacho de Schmidt, 1994, p. 1):

> We, the youth, imagine a healthy future. We imagine a health clinic that we helped build and is responsive to the needs of adolescents. We imagine a health center that is still open after school and after work, where our language is spoken, where we are not strangers or foreigners seen with condescension. We would like to see doctors, nurses, secretaries, and administrators who have done farm labor in the past and who know what our life is like from the inside . . .
>
> For those of us who live and work in labor camps, we imagine outreach programs that come without intimidation and with staffers speaking like we do, to tell us about the dangers that we are up against.
>
> We imagine materials that we like to pick up and read, or cassettes and videos that we can check out and enjoy watching, but from which we may learn good things about health and life.

The difficulties they confronted were attributed to their experiences with peer pressure, culture shock, low self-esteem, and living in isolated rural communities. To combat these issues, they proposed peer support groups with professional support for substance abuse, obesity, family alcoholism, adolescent parenthood, child abuse, and sexuality.

> In a local peer support group in southeast Michigan, a group of teenage girls were discussing what they felt could be better in their camp, school, and community. One of the girls reported that she would like to see people not be so surprised that she was interested in going to college. "It must be the first time they heard that a migrant actually wanted to be more; even the teacher seemed surprised."

Based on the aforementioned model, a migrant community in southeast Michigan attempted to capture the voice of youth through a survey. The results indicated that like the Florida youth, those working in the migrant communities of Michigan had high aspirations for themselves; teens reported that they wanted to be doctors, nurses, teachers, and police officers. They reported that the things that most helped them to achieve their goals were support from their families and education.

These same teens, interviewed later specifically for this chapter, pointed out that their parents were their partners "in wanting better for us." Seemingly in contradiction to this the parents and teens were having a major struggle. Parents wanted them to go to school either after work and/or when there was no work, but not during the high-intensity harvest time. This was despite the teens' report that their parents wanted them to learn and prosper. Lack of teen labor during the high-intensity harvest time can create a great deal of financial stress for the family. One father's genuine concern was recently voiced regarding his children's desire to stay behind and find a job in the family's home base as evident in the following scenario.

> If all my children follow the first one's footsteps, I won't be able to make enough to keep up with the cost of living, even in the South where it is definitely cheaper to live. Years ago when I came with my parents, it was very profitable. There were five of us working with my father. We gave all our money to our parents, and they gave us what we needed as our needs came along. You had no choice; this was just how it was. Nowadays, my children do not agree with this. They talk to me about their needs and whether or not it is fair of me to keep all the money. I want them to be happy and healthy, but I worry about what will this mean to the family and how will we survive? I want to do what is best for us all.

CULTURAL STRENGTHS

A number of authors have noted a tendency for service providers and researchers to focus on needs and problems, rather than assets of target populations (Delgado, 1996; Freire, 1983). Regarding Latino populations in particular, Ramírez (1983) points out that European paradigms have tended to devalue and overlook unique assets of the mestizo worldview. He defines the latter as a way of seeing the world that developed as a result of combinations of indigenous and immigrant cultures in the Americas. In keeping with the above author's observations, almost no literature on assets of Latino youth was found and even less concerning migrant youth. Yet the few studies published, accompanied by anecdotal reports, point to a number of little-recognized assets.

Resourcefulness

Youth in migrant families bring with them extraordinary resilience and strength in that they tend to be more resourceful and responsible than their nonmigrant peers (U.S. Department of Education, 1989). An example of culturally determined resourcefulness, as described by Ramírez (1983), is survival in new environments while searching for new beginnings and surmounting obstacles. He notes this as a theme for both the Aztecs and the European settlers. In the case of a migrant youth seen in Michigan, an obstacle requiring resourcefulness was attending school in different states. At times, states refuse to accept reciprocity for courses previously agreed upon. This can be very problematic, and a reason for some migrant teens to feel that summer school is not worth the effort. Without summer school, however, they are at a disadvantage upon returning to their home state well after school begins. The following case covers a number of strengths in dealing with these challenges.

> Daniel was 18 years old and had been struggling with school, due to feeling rejected by his non-Latino classmates in the small, rural town. The double load of working and not knowing if another move would be necessary also interfered with his schoolwork. Nevertheless, he persisted with his goal of graduation. His father had finished high school and his mother was working on completing her own high school degree. She was actively supportive of his efforts and had stood up for his Michigan school credits being validated in Texas, despite resistance by the school system. He was further encouraged by a peer at school. He decided that in order to finish his senior year, he needed to find a way to return to Texas in time for the beginning of class, instead

of returning with his family, when the crops were finished. He worked extra hours and his family also contributed toward an airplane ticket. He was able to finish high school successfully.

This case illustrates both individual resourcefulness and the value of support systems. For instance, Daniel was individually responsible for finding a highly unusual path to graduation. Few if any of his family had ever flown back to Texas or had family members return on their own. The price of the ticket was another challenge for a family living below poverty-level income. Daniel was resourceful in finding and following through with his choice. His support system was also critical in wanting him to graduate and contributing their scarce funds toward this. A social worker's offer of support and transportation to the airport was also considered and accepted, showing a willingness to find bridges in less traditional support systems also.

Support Systems

Migrant teens, along with their families, frequently return to the same areas on a seasonal basis. As a consequence, relationships are frequently established with farm owners, community residents, and former migrant laborers and relatives who have "settled out" (meaning they are now part of the permanent neighborhoods of the host communities). When not in close proximity, peer relationships are maintained through letters, word of mouth, telephone calls, and most recently, through computer networking. These relationships have been seen as fundamental to the sense of self and well-being for these teens. Many times the relationships made at migrant camps have led to either formal or common-law marriages.

Migrant community relationships have also led to other forms of support, such as two families becoming strongly meshed together by becoming *padrinos* (i.e., godparents) of each other's offspring. As *padrinos*, connections between families are not only formalized, but also strengthened and enlarged. According to Griswold del Castillo (1984), *padrinos* also serve a formal role as *compadres* (co-parents), providing discipline and emotional and financial support when needed (Ramírez & Arce, 1981). And as *compadres*, they are expected to become the closest of friends with parents and members of the extended family (Griswold del Castillo, 1984). These extended social networks can prove critical in migrant teens' development, as in the following example:

Juan is a 17-year-old Mexican youth who came to the United States to work in the fields a year ago. He sends his earnings home to his parents and younger siblings. He is well known in the camp for being one of the best and hardest workers. The only other person who matches his reputation for productivity at work is his "cousin," Pablo. Pablo is not a blood relative, but his family has "taken Juan in" for the past year, working and traveling together. But the relationship goes farther than cohabitation; Pablo's parents have been encouraging Juan to attend school. In September, both boys would head off to the classroom and obtain good grades on exams, but the teacher was concerned about poor follow-through with homework. After school, they would both head home, eat, get changed, and go straight to work. Juan would not spend time socializing or doing any activities other than those that took him toward his goals. In Florida, Pablo and Juan had attended a high school program oriented toward becoming Marines, which was currently a shared dream.

Self Discipline

Adolescents who work in the migrant stream contribute to their families in multiple ways, most notably economic. Thus, participation in the labor force is not a rite of passage, but rather, an issue of familial and economic necessity and survival (Buirski, 1994).

Ramírez (1983) discusses the attributes of self-control and firmness of purpose in traditional Mexican American values. Valle (1994) also refers to the strong sense of responsibility in migrant teens. One adolescent summed up the assets of work and self-discipline as follows:

Manuel is an 18-year-old who lives with his family, who have traveled between Michigan and Florida for many years. He stated that he does not feel pressured to work by his parents:
I've learned from my parents, by working in the fields. They are helping me learn to be responsible. I earn what I spend, even on clothes for school. Being a hard worker will help me during all my life, even though I had to miss school at times. Many kids my age are lazy; they have a bad attitude; they don't want to work and are not respectful to their parents. My parents have taught me to be respectful, to work, to take care of myself. When I see kids whose parents give them lots of things, I don't understand why they do that. They are not helping them with all those gifts that they didn't work for.

OVERCOMING THE ODDS: DIMENSIONS OF EFFECTIVE PROGRAMS FOR MIGRANT YOUTH

Most programs for migrants usually emphasize improving access to health care, education, housing, a safe workplace, and furthering community involvement. Only a few refer to adolescents specifically. The Student with Action Farmworkers (SAF) is one such program that attempts to meet the needs of migrant adolescents by including them in multiple dimensions of their outreach and programmatic efforts. The SAF has been specifically designed to work with migrant adolescents and their families in North Carolina, recruiting host communities, migrant teens, and young adults enrolled in local universities to participate in a unique summer internship program. Projects have included interns working with rural health clinics, migrant summer schools, legal service agencies, county health departments, and community-based organizing projects. Students also taught driver's education classes in Spanish for farmworker women, translated for migrants in courtrooms, and organized a health fair. A new program for teens is Project Levante, an SAF project working on school retention for farmworker youth. The project had interns from farmworker families present a play about challenges that farmworker teens face when planning to pursue college studies. The play was presented bilingually to over 250 farmworker students and their families (Wiggins, 1996).

Viviremos/Se Pou Nou Viv/Learn to Live (1988) is a project targeted toward prevention of AIDS in migrant, immigrant, and rural teens. Their outreach is made through clinics, schools, and community organizations. A critical part of their philosophy is to see themselves as providing guidance but not direction to the community and teens, who must now decide how best to respond to the AIDS crisis.

The Cornell Migrant Program in New York State also involved migrant teens, and used their creative abilities in community art projects (Henderson, 1992). In an oral history project, teenage children of migrant farmworkers were recruited to gather histories of their families and those of other farmworkers in the community. With general community participation, the document developed from a slide show into a book over the course of six years. The book publication was thought to increase a feeling of pride and local inclusion from the teens and the families interviewed, as well as lending a more cooperative atmosphere in the community.

A local program also explored oral histories. The project had teens and others share their life histories and was subsequently aired on local television. The interviews included why they continue to live the life of migrants despite the hardships. It brought forth a great deal of discussion by migrants and community residents as well. More goodwill and pride was generated by that one project than was ever expected. Teens in school listened, perhaps for the first time in some cases, to their parents or a friend's grandparent tell about why they work in the fields. Increased acceptance and communication were developed, not only within families but within whole communities as well.

A key factor of the above programs is migrant teen involvement and outreach. Outreach programs are internationally recognized as an effective strategy for improving health access for hard-to-reach populations (U.S. Department of Health and Human Services, 1994).

Locally, a psychoeducational program run by the Midwest Migrant Health Information Office worked with teens, using theater to address drug abuse and AIDS. This was reported by the teens that participated to be a most enlightening program. The teens spoke of the project as being the reason that they were thinking of careers in teaching, law enforcement, and medicine.

For the past several years Lenawee County Community Mental Health in Adrian, Michigan, has provided an outreach team that is bicultural as well as bilingual. The team spends all its time out in the migrant camps, working on providing education and need/resource matching. Treatment is also provided to migrant teens in their homes and schools as well as medical clinics. The noted outcomes have been fewer medical emergencies, quicker resolutions to camp interrelational difficulties, and decreased need for formal mental health services. Migrants and farmers (by self-report) have found the program useful in being able to access help information readily as an answer to their daily concerns. Having the team do simple medical triaging with the nurse practitioner and the physician cuts down on the need for appointments in medical and mental health clinics. This in turn cuts down on time migrants spent away from their work and school. Therefore, the migrant teens, their families, and the farmers can see the concrete benefits of the program immediately.

Other programs in education and health that have been reported by the migrant teens to be the most helpful are the English as a second language project, which allowed teens to receive school credits. This enabled the teens to receive their diplomas once back in their home base, a dream come true for many teens.

Another program run by Siena Heights College and Community Mental Health had college students and migrant teens "Walking in Each Other's Shoes." This program was noted by both the college students and the migrant teens as being a "horizon-broadening experience," one that increased the insight of both groups regarding the lifestyles and the different struggles each group goes through to realize their goals. Both groups wanted to make sure the program would continue.

RECOMMENDATIONS

The purpose of this chapter is to enhance awareness of issues confronting migrant teens and their many strengths, and to present approaches that have been found to complement their assets. Beyond that it is written as a challenge to those who are doing work in the important field of migrant health and education. As seen throughout this chapter, there are little or no data found in the literature. Therefore, it is vital to the future of this work that service providers make a greater commitment to identify needs and strengths. This should help in making the food harvesters of the world become more visible as well as to be offered a louder voice in the market place that will always need food and people to tend to it.

An important recommendation to be of help to migrant teens' developing brighter futures is that programs be designed with as much input by the teens as possible. Such programs must be culturally competent and staffed by bicultural, bilingual workers. They must be collaborative and integrative with community multiservice groups, and they must be rooted in outreach in their format and implementation. Not many people know better what it takes to enhance the world of migrant teens more effectively than the teens themselves.

It is hoped that our effort to present the realities and aspirations of migrant youth and communities that we have worked with will result in other communities developing effective, innovative programs for migrant youth and their families. Much has been accomplished, but there is much more to do.

REFERENCES

Allen-Meares, P., Washington, R. O., & Welse, B. L. (1996). *Social work services in schools.* Boston: Allyn and Bacon.

Buirski, N. (1994). *Earth angels: Migrant children in America.* Rohnert Park, CA: Pomegranate Artbooks.

Camacho de Schmidt, A. (1994). *Cultivating health: An agenda for adolescent farmworkers.* (Available from the National Coalition of Advocates for Students, 100 Boylston Street, Suite 737, Boston, MA 02116)

Davis, J. R., Brownson, R. C., Garcia, R., Bentz, B. J., & Turner, A. (1993). Family pesticide use and childhood brain cancer. *Archives of Environmental Contamination and Toxicology, 24,* 87–92.

Delgado, M. (1996). Community asset assessments by Latino youths. *Social Work in Education, 18,* 169–178.

Edelman, M. W., & Solow, R. M. (1994). *Wasting America's future.* Boston: Beacon Press (Children's Defense Fund).

Freire, P. (1983). *Pedagogy of the oppressed* (rev. ed.). New York: Continuum.

Friedman-Jiménez, G., & Ortiz, J. S. (1994). Occupational health. In C. W. Molina & M. Aguirre-Molina (Eds.), *Latino health in the US: A growing challenge* (pp. 341–389). Washington, DC: American Public Health Association.

Gold, E., Gordis, L., Tonascia, J., & Szklo, M. (1979). Risk factors for brain tumors in children. *American Journal of Epidemiology, 109,* 309–319.

Griffith, D., & Kissam, E. D. (1995). *Working poor.* Philadelphia: Temple University Press.

Griswold del Castillo, R. (1984). *La Familia.* Notre Dame, IN: University of Notre Dame Press.

Henderson, Z. P. (1992). Migrant program breaks down social barriers. *Human Ecology Forum, 20,* 28–31.

Heyer, N. J., Franklin, G., Rivara, F. P., Parker, P., & Haug, J. A. (1992). Occupational injuries among minors doing farm work in Washington State: 1986–1989. *American Journal of Public Health, 82,* 557–560.

Leiss, J. K., & Saritz, D. R. (1995). Home pesticide use and childhood cancer: A case-control study. *American Journal of Public Health, 85,* 249–252.

León, E. (1996). *Challenges and solutions for educating migrant students.* East Lansing: Michigan State University, Julian Samora Research Institute.

Lovato, C. Y., Litrownik, A. J., Elder, J., Nuñez-Liriano, A., Suarez, D., & Talavera, G. A. (1994). Cigarette and alcohol use among migrant Hispanic adolescents. *Family and Community Health, 16,* 18–31.

Marks, G., Garcia, M., & Solis, J. M. (1990). Health risk behaviors of Hispanics in the United States: Findings from HHANES, 1982–84. *American Journal of Public Health, 80,* (Suppl.), 20–26.

Michigan Department of Agriculture, Agricultural Statistics. (1996). *Michigan crops on which migrants work (1995).* Lansing, MI: Michigan Family Independence Agency, Migrant Services Department.

Morrissey, M. (1996). Migrants struggle to overcome barriers to educational achievement. *Counseling Today, 38,* 8–10.

Mulder, Y. M., Drijver, M., & Kreis, I. A. (1994). Case-control study on the association between a cluster of childhood haematopoietic malignancies and local environmental factors in Aalsmeer, the Netherlands. *Journal of Epidemiology and Community Health, 48,* 161–165.

National Advisory Council on Migrant Health. (1995). *Losing ground: The condition of farmworkers in America.* Austin, TX: National Migrant Resource Program.

National Commission on Migrant Education. (1992). *Invisible children: A portrait of migrant education in the United States.* (Available from the U.S. Department of Education, Office of Migrant Education, Washington, DC)

National Migrant Resource Program. (1991). *Farmworker substance abuse: An action plan for the year 2000.* Austin, TX: Author.

Occupational Health Subcommittee, Migrant Clinicians Network. (1990, May/June). Issues paper on child labor in agriculture. *Migrant Health Newsline,* clinical supplements, 1988–1990, p. 81.

Ramírez, M., III. (1983). *Psychology of the Americas: Mestizo perspectives on personality and mental health.* Elmsford, NY: Pergamon.

Ramírez, O., & Arce, C. H. (1981). The contemporary Chicano family: An empirically based review. In A. Baron, Jr. (Ed.), *Explorations in Chicano psychology* (pp. 3–28). New York: Praeger.

Rochin, R. I., Santiago, A. M., & Dickey, K. S. (1991). *Migrant and seasonal workers in Michigan's agriculture: A study of their contributions, characteristics, needs, and services.* East Lansing: Michigan State University, Julian Samora Research Institute.

Ruducha, J. (1994). *Migrant child health: The role of social, cultural, and economic factors.* Austin, TX: National Migrant Resource Program.

Rust, G. S. (1990). Health status of migrant farmworkers: A literature review and commentary. *American Journal of Public Health, 80,* 1213–1217.

Sakala, C. (1998, February/March). Migrant and seasonal farmworkers in the United States: A review of health hazards, status, and policy. *Migrant Health Newsline,* clinical supplements, 1988–1990, pp. 3–5. Austin, TX: National Migrant Resource Program.

Torres, C. C. (1994, Spring). What works: Increasing the delivery of primary health care to low income rural residents. *Western Wire,* pp. 19–22.

U.S. Department of Education. (1989). *Characteristics of secondary migrant youth: The Migrant Education Secondary Assistance Project.* (Available from the Board of Cooperative Education Service, Geneseo Migrant Center, Geneseo, NY 14454.)

U.S. Department of Education, Bureau of Migrant Services. (1995). *Giving migrant students an opportunity to learn.* (A National Association of State Directors of Migrant Services publication, Baton Rouge, LA. Available from Department of Education, Bureau of Migrant Services, Baton Rouge, LA)

U.S. Department of Health and Human Services, Health Resources and Services Administration, Bureau of Primary Health Care, Office of Migrant Health, Division of Community and Migrant Health. (1994). *Community outreach guidance: A strategy for reaching migrant and seasonal farmworkers.* Rockville, MD: Author.

Valle, I. (1994). *Fields of toil: A migrant family's journey.* Pullman, WA: Washington State University Press.

Vega, W. A., & Amaro, H. (1994). Latino outlook: Good health, uncertain prognosis. *Annual Review of Public Health, 15,* 39–67.

Vega, W. A., Scutchfield, F. D., Karno, M., & Meinhardt, K. (1989, May/June). The mental health needs of Mexican American agricultural workers. *Migrant Health Newsline,* clinical supplements, 1988–1990, pp. 44–46. Austin, TX: National Migrant Resource Program.

Viviremos/Se Pou Nou Viv/Learn to Live. (1988, November/December). Teenagers and AIDS. *Migrant Health Newsline,* clinical supplements, 1988–1990, p. 28.

Wiggins, M. (1996, July/August). Internship program places students into farmworker service roles. *Migrant Health Newsline, 13,* p. 3.

Wilk, V. A. (1986). *Occupational health and safety of migrant and seasonal farmworkers in the United States* (2nd ed.). Washington, DC: Farmworker Justice Fund.

CHAPTER 12
Child Welfare and Latino Adolescents
ROBERT M. ORTEGA

Child welfare services have endured as the cornerstone of the nation's social service system with the primary goal of providing a permanent, safe, and stable living environment for every child (Pecora, Whittaker, Maluccio, Barth, & Plotnick, 1994). Since the enactment of the Adoption Assistance and Child Welfare Act of 1980 (PL96–272), child welfare services have enlarged considerably to include family preservation, kinship and nonkin foster care, family foster care, reunification, adoption and other permanent living arrangements, child care and school care programs, and parent education programs. Unfortunately, the distribution of and access to these services and resources has historically been different among groups based on income and race or ethnicity (Courtney, Barth, Berrick, Brooks, Needell, & Park, 1994). Differential patterns of utilization and representation by ethnic minorities in the United States are not unique to child welfare. National data from the U.S. Bureau of the Census, the National Center for Juvenile Justice, the National Institute of Mental Health, the Law Enforcement Assistance Administration, and the Children's Defense Fund consistently reveal patterns of discrimination and differential treatment (Rivera-Martínez, 1992).

A review of the literature published over the past decade offers specific areas in which discrepancies occur in the child welfare experiences of ethnic minority children compared to Caucasian children. The most notable areas are in the substantiation of child maltreatment reports, placement outside the home and in less desirable placements, referral to the juvenile justice system for behavioral problems, referral to public sector social services rather than private sector agencies, and placement outside the home prior to receiving therapy, in-home services, or other support. In general, children of color were viewed as largely at a disadvantage in terms of system responsiveness, access to ancillary services, decisions about out-of-home placement, and achieving permanency (Barth, Courtney, Berrick, & Albert, 1994; Eckenrode, Powers, Davis, Munsch, & Bolger, 1988; Fein, Maluccio, & Kluger, 1990; Goerge, Wulczyn, & Harden, 1994; Hogan & Sui, 1988; McMurtry & Lie, 1992; Stehno, 1990; Tracey, Green, & Bremseth, 1993).

A number of criticisms have been raised about the above findings relevant to study methodology, differential definitions of abuse and neglect, differences in outcome measures, and failure to contextualize the outcomes in terms of geographic or regional differences (Barth et al., 1994; Goerge et al., 1994). As compelling as these criticisms are, differential treatment based on race or ethnicity in child welfare has deep historical roots and is worthy of further study since, according to the Child Welfare League of America, the number of children in the United States entering out-of-home care increased by 65 percent between 1984 and 1994, from 270,000 to 460,000, with over half the out-of-home placement population believed to be children of color (Curtis, Boyd, Liepold, & Petit, 1995; Tatara, 1993).

To say that there is a need to focus on discrepancies in child welfare service delivery according to race or ethnicity is not enough. Clearly, the challenge must be directed toward addressing the unique needs of the various ethnic groups who come in contact with the child welfare service system (Hogan & Sui, 1988; Stehno, 1990). For example, a review of the literature indicates that Latinos tend to vary greatly in their use of out-of-home care, to wait longer for permanency placement while in placement, and to be less likely to experience permanency placement when compared to Caucasian children (Goerge et al., 1994). The use of the term *Latino* is problematic since most child welfare studies fail to differentiate Latinos based on ancestry and instead give the impression that Latinos are a monolithic ethnic group. Typically, the generic term *Latino* refers to individuals of Mexican, Puerto Rican, Cuban, Dominican, and Central and South American ancestries. Combining Latinos and reporting their status in the aggregate fails to differentiate Latino children according to ancestry, language, geographic region, economic and immigrant status, generation, and other important sociodemographic differences. In many states as well as national reports, Latinos are included in a racial "other" category which combines Latinos with children of Native American, Asian, biracial, and unknown ancestry. This lack of clarity and relative diffusion poses a serious challenge to the child welfare system's ability to accurately account for Latino children in their care (Ortega, Guillean, & Gutierrez-Nagera, 1996).

Among the many other challenges facing the child welfare system of care is how to implement services taking into account the developmental needs of children. With the exception of a growing concern about the number of infants placed out of home, a specific focus on developmental age groups has failed to take shape in the child welfare literature. Adolescent child welfare, for example, has gained minimal attention in the literature despite the fact that 21 percent of child maltreatment victims in 1994 were between the ages of 13 and 18 years (Chaffin, Bonner, Worley, & Lawson, 1996; Gil, 1996; U.S. Department of Health and Human Services [DHHS], 1996). Much of what does exist presents sexual abuse, particularly against females, as a critical child welfare issue although it has been suggested that teenagers represent 25 to 45 percent of all physically abused children (Chaffin et al., 1996; Doueck, Ishisaka, Sweany, & Gilchrist, 1987). As Gil (1996, p. 75) asserts:

> The cognitive, physical, personality, sexual, and moral developmental tasks of childhood and adolescence are monumental at best. Youngsters need support, guidance, encouragement, and safety in order to make a successful transition to maturity. Without safety, consistency, fulfillment of dependency needs, and attainment of love and a sense of belonging, they will struggle to develop a positive sense of identity, attachment and ego strength. Child abuse greatly hinders the developmental process, and chronic child abuse causes serious concerns for adolescents.

For abused adolescents, developmental delays, impaired identities, problems in developing and maintaining appropriate social relationships, and anger and hostility are likely consequences of their abusive experiences. Because adolescents are misperceived as having adequate skills to protect themselves from maltreatment, their abuse often goes unnoticed, suggesting that the incidence of abuse is far greater than what the actual data convey. It must also be remembered that adolescent abuse does not necessarily emerge as parents struggle with their child's search for autonomy during this particular life stage; it could also be the result of a cumulative abusive process that began long before the onset of adolescence (Chaffin et al., 1996; Gil, 1996). In many ways adolescents can be compared to other disempowered groups to the extent that they lack experience, maturity, and resources and are economically vulnerable, helpless, and likely perceive themselves as having a decreased sense of control over outcomes in their lives (Gibson, 1993; Hegar, 1989; Parsons, 1989). Adolescent children of color, then, particularly in child welfare, are greatly disempowered in a system that already treats children of color in a manner considered oppressive and in some cases exploitive (Fox, 1984; Hogan & Sui, 1988).

Again, turning to Latinos, most of the research on Latino adolescents focuses on deviant behaviors and their social consequences. This chapter describes current knowledge about Latinos and child welfare and presents implications for Latino adolescents. The chapter is organized around the following topics: first, the child maltreatment context is discussed as it relates to Latino children in general; second, child welfare service utilization issues are discussed in terms of access, "career" patterns, and outcomes; third, gaps in current child welfare services are discussed; and finally, future directions are proposed for the delivery of effective child welfare services to Latino adolescents in the United States.

CHILD MALTREATMENT AND LATINOS

Across the United States, the number of child abuse and neglect reports received by child protective service agencies and referred for investigation rose steadily over the past decade, from 1,727,000 in 1984 to 2,890,234 children in 1993—a 68 percent increase, according to the National Council on Child Abuse and Neglect (DHHS, 1996). In 1993, 27 percent of the nation's reported child maltreatment victims were 3 years old or younger, 20 percent were 4 to 6 years of age, 17 percent of the victims were 7 to 9 years old, and 15 percent were between the ages of 10 and 12 years. Adolescents, between 13 and 18 years of age, accounted for 21 percent of child maltreatment victims.

In 1993 more than 87,000 Latino children of all ages were victims of child maltreatment, accounting for 9.4 percent of the national child maltreatment population. Most of the victim reports occurred in California and Texas, although it is important to keep in mind the limitations of administrative data related to differing definitions of abuse and neglect, errors and lags in reporting information, poor quality assurance with record keeping, and variation in the types of information that each state reports (Goerge et al., 1994). Florida, for example, does not consider "Hispanic" to be a race and therefore includes this population in "white—

not Hispanic" or "black—not Hispanic" racial categories. The law of other states such as Pennsylvania and New Hampshire do not require tracking children according to race or ethnicity. Still, the vast majority of states have a large "other" race/ethnic category which can reasonably be expected to include a significant number of children of Latino ancestry. So at a basic level, knowing precisely how many Latino children are maltreated is problematic, leaving an obvious gap in understanding national incidence rates.

Consistent themes thought to distinguish Latino families typically center around clear commitment to family interaction, maintenance of values consistent with the theme of interdependence, and flexibility when handling familial and extrafamilial stressors (Mirande, 1977; Szapocznik & Kurtines, 1989; Williams, 1990). The absence of these qualities is associated with child behavior problems, delinquency, gang involvement, and other consequences likely to lead to tension between parents and their adolescent children (Adler, Ovando, & Hocevar, 1984; Rio, Santisteban, & Szapocznik, 1991). Tension related to acculturation and maintenance of language and traditional culture have also been attributed to Latino family conflicts, although the relationship between exposure to drugs, alcohol, and domestic violence and child maltreatment remains a growing concern (Buriel, Calzada, & Vasquez, 1982; Rio et al., 1991). Granted, such a perspective tends to overlook the diverse realities between and among Latino families and should consider the ways in which family composition and family functioning are affected by social stratification shifts, fertility, changing gender role statuses, intermarriage, and cultural diffusion (Jiobu, 1988; Ortiz, 1995; Williams, 1990; Vega, 1995). The point is that current discussions of child maltreatment among Latinos extends beyond parent-child interactions and must recognize threats to familism related to shifts in family structure and functioning, tension relevant to economic well-being, and value conflicts associated with acculturation.

According to Hay and Jones (1994), an ecological developmental approach argues that to understand child maltreatment, certain structural factors of both community and society at large must be considered within various contexts of social interaction, along with understanding their impact over time (cf. Belsky, 1980; Bronfenbrenner, 1979; Garbarino, 1977). In this regard, poverty and unemployment, inaccessible and unaffordable health care, fragmented social services, limited resources, social isolation, neighborhood violence, and drug activity become recognized as significant risk factors, particularly in cases of physical abuse and neglect (Belsky, 1980; Gelles, 1983, 1992; Gil, 1970; Pelton, 1978; Steel & Pollack, 1968). The poorest of the poor and certain groups among the poor—single parents, young caregivers, and those with young children—are perceived as most susceptible to physical violence (Gelles, 1992; Jones & McCurdy, 1992).

Hay and Jones (1994) point out that the observed relationship between poverty and maltreatment may be a function of selection bias; poor families who actively seek supportive and supplemental social services are more likely to be involved with fairly intrusive agencies such as AFDC and are more likely to be viewed as abusers than are families who traditionally underutilize social services (Newberger, Reed, Danile, Hyde, & Kotelchuck, 1977; O'Toole, Turbett, & Nalpeka, 1983). Wealthier families, for example, are more likely to be insulated from social service discovery which greatly enhances the bias against poor help-seeking families. Poor families who traditionally underutilize public services such as Latinos are unaccounted for.

Clearly, an ecological developmental approach has interesting appeal for understanding just how vulnerable Latino children and adolescents are to maltreatment and perhaps how their needs are underserved. Data on maltreatment indicate a 2.5 percent increase in national incidents among Latinos from 1993 to 1994, which is undoubtedly higher in states where Latinos are more concentrated. In addition, the percentage of Latino children entering out-of-home placement in at least five states where Latinos are more concentrated increased from 12 percent to 18 percent over the past decade (Goerge et al., 1994). Coinciding with these trends is the recent announcement by the U.S. Bureau of the Census indicating that for the first time, the poverty rate for Latinos surpassed that of African Americans, making Latinos the poorest of the poor. During the past decade, the number of poor Latino residents rose 8 percent, and now represents 24 percent of the nation's poor population (*New York Times*, 1997). The proportion of Latino children and adolescents living in single-parent families increased from 25 percent to 34 percent (Solis, 1994). Currently, Latino children living in poverty are raised by a growing number of single mothers who are young themselves. Parents of Latino children remain under- and uneducated and in fact are proportionately less educated today when compared to non-Latinos than they were in the 1970s. For example, in 1994, 9 percent of Latinos over the age of 24 held college degrees compared to 24 percent of non-Latinos. In 1977, 5 percent of Latinos held college degrees compared to 11.6 percent of non-Latinos (*New York Times*, 1997).

Latino youth (12 to 15 years old) are about two and a half times as likely as Caucasians to be two or more grades behind in school, with poor English skills and a lack of academic support increasing the likelihood of grade repetition (Duany & Pittman, 1990; Delgado-Gaitan, 1988). In some areas of the country, the high school dropout rate for Latinos exceeds 80 percent, and that figure refers only to those students who actually show up on the doorsteps of high schools after advancing from middle or junior high school.

Beyond the constraints of living in poverty, Latino children and adolescents must also contend with issues associated with segregation, migration/immigration and acculturation (Vega, Zimmerman, Warheit, Jackson, Gil, & Sokol-Katz, 1994). The experience of a growing number of Latino adolescents is complicated by high rates of mortality (particularly among males), school dropout, substance abuse, sexually transmitted diseases, gang violence, and teen pregnancy (Mendoza, 1994). Depression and suicide attempts due to the accumulated effects of family burden, school problems, psychiatric and acculturation problems, and value conflicts further complicate the Latino adolescent experience (COSSMHO, 1996; Queralt, 1993; Roberts, 1994; Roberts & Sobham, 1992). Given these conditions, one would think that concern for the welfare of Latino children and adolescents would be greatly increasing, especially since the Latino population has grown at a rate seven times faster than the rate of non-Latinos over the past decade (Enchautegui, 1995). Since very little research has been conducted which focuses exclusively on Latinos, the ability for child welfare services to meet the potential demands of Latino children and families remains a relative unknown.

Latinos have traditionally underutilized formal human services, and in the case of child welfare, this lack of familiarity has definite consequences for the safety and well-being of Latino children. To date, very little is known about the role child welfare services play in the lives of Latino children, even at a time when child welfare services are delivered to a growing number of ethnic minority children (Curtis et al., 1995; Goerge et al., 1994; Ortega et al., 1996). The dramatic increase in the Latino child population, the fact that a large and growing number of Latino children live in poverty, national data indicating an increase in substantiated cases of child maltreatment among Latinos, and evidence that a greater number of Latino children are entering out-of-home care all underscore the urgency of closely examining the child welfare status of Latino children. Utilizing an ecological developmental approach for understanding child maltreatment, as well as understanding issues unique to growing up Latino in terms of segregation and marginalization, language differences, high rates of mobility, cultural barriers to accessing services, and acculturative stress, helps to further understand critical risk factors confronting Latino youth (Canino & Spurlock, 1994; Inclan & Herron, 1998; Ramírez, 1998; Zambrana, 1996).

CHILD WELFARE UTILIZATION

Knowledge about Latino adolescents in child welfare is obscure despite evidence indicating they account for about 15 percent of the adolescent foster care population in states where significant numbers of Latinos reside.[1] In fact, until recently no study was found from an extensive review of the literature to date that focused exclusively on Latino child maltreatment and the need for child welfare services. The only known study utilized a multimethodological approach which included both qualitative and quantitative methods. The final report, *Latinos and Child Welfare*/Latinos y el Bienestar del Niño: Voces de la Comunidad (Ortega et al., 1996) summarizes the results, some of which will be presented here as a way to begin to understand the relationship between Latinos and child welfare.

One aspect of the study involved surveying ninety Latino child welfare service providers located in six study states (California, Texas, Florida, New York, Illinois, and Michigan), where 75 percent of the nation's Latino population resides. These service providers were surveyed after being identified by the National Latino Child Welfare Advocacy Group.[2] Special care was taken to select service providers whose ancestry, educational attainment, commitment to the issues, access to relevant data, geographical location, and direct practice knowledge for working with Latino children facilitated the most accurate view of the Latino child welfare experience.[3]

The survey was designed to tap into perceptions of service providers about a variety of issues relevant to the need for and use of child welfare services by Latinos. Survey items included information requests about safety and security, protective service involvement, use of substitute care, permanency planning outcomes, and several other areas of interest. Thirty-eight service providers responded, resulting in a 42 percent response rate, thus limiting the conclusiveness of the findings. Since no significant differences were found in the data about to be presented, either between or among respondents in the study states, their results are presented in the aggregate.

Among the findings, over one-third of the Latino child population were believed to live in conditions that pose a serious threat to their safety and security. Of these children, respondents estimated that only about one-third would be reported to protective services, and only half of these children were believed to eventually receive services. Respondents believed that nonreporting (and nonreceiving) services were due to certain barriers or obstacles. As indicated in Table 12.1, barriers and obstacles included fears (e.g., of the child being removed, retaliation, authority, and that citizenship status would be questioned); services not available, accessible, or acceptable; lack of Spanish-speaking workers; and the use of family supports to buffer the need for agency-based services. Additional concerns were raised about a lack of culturally relevant services, and lack of trust in the service system.

Nearly all of the respondents believed that family or other informal sources of social support were called upon for help when the safety and security of a Latino child was in question. As Table 12.2 indicates, family/extended family were identified as the major sources of social support, followed by close friends, the church, and to a lesser extent, service agencies.

Respondents also believed that less than half of the children (45 percent) who relied on family or other types of support actually received the necessary help. Respondents raised this as a concern, suggesting that in many cases social support, primarily from the child's family, is assumed to be available to most Latino children, although respondents were concerned about the belief that many of these children actually received the social support necessary to maintain safe and secure conditions. Limited

Table 12.1 Types of Barriers/Obstacles to Reporting Latino Children to Protective Services (N = 38)

Percentage	Barriers/Obstacles
25	Fear (e.g., removal, retaliation, authority, status)
24	Services (unavailable, inaccessible, unacceptable)
16	Language (lack of Spanish-speaking staff, written materials)
15	Family support
12	Culture (e.g., congruence, competence, beliefs)
8	Other (e.g., trust)

Source: From Ortega et al. (1996). *Latinos and child welfare*/Latinos y el bienestar del niño: Voces de la comunidad, pp. 3–7.

Table 12.2 Types of Social Support Relied on to Maintain the Safety and Security of Latino Children

Percentage	Source of Support
60	Family/extended family
21	Friends/close friends
14	Church
5	Services/agencies

Source: From Ortega et al. (1996). *Latinos and child welfare*/Latinos y el bienestar del niño: Voces de la comunidad, pp. 3–7.

resources, diminished support networks due to migration or recency of immigration, as well as knowledge about and trust in social services interventions were some of the concerns raised as barriers to the family's ability to adequately care for their kin.

Referral to Child Welfare

In terms of types of child maltreatment most likely associated with the referral to child protective services, Table 12.3 summarizes survey responses. Table 12.3 compares the survey results to national maltreatment data. For Latinos, child neglect (defined as unattended/unsupervised, physical needs unmet, medical needs unmet, malnourishment, educational neglect, and uncertain return of parents) clearly ranked highest among referral reasons, followed by physical abuse. The survey results differ from national reports by suggesting a higher percentage of emotional abuse and child labor exploitation for Latino children and a lower percentage of sexual abuse.

When asked to indicate the primary referral sources to protective services, respondents listed school, followed by health care providers such as physicians and other medical staff, then child care facilities and neighbors. Other referral sources for Latinos included family, police, friends, religious leaders, and the child victim himself or herself. When compared to national reports, there appears to be some similarity in the results, although social services, family, and relatives play a more prominent role in the national data.

Table 12.3 Reasons Latino Children are Referred to Protective Services: Survey Results Compared to General National Reports of Child Maltreatment

Survey Percentage	National Percentage	Reason
57	55	Neglect
19	26	Physical abuse
10	14	Sexual abuse
10	5	Emotional abuse
4	—	Exploitation/child labor

Source: From Ortega et al. (1996). *Latinos and child welfare*/Latinos y el bienestar del niño: Voces de la comunidad, pp. 3–7.

Out-of-Home Placements

According to the respondents, an estimated 40 percent of all Latino children reported to protective services were removed from their homes and placed in substitute care. Initial placements, indicated in Table 12.4, were believed to be primarily into relative and nonrelative foster homes. Other placements that were mentioned included emergency shelter and group homes as well as residential and mental health facilities. These results support a concern expressed earlier about the importance of kinship care data.

Table 12.4 Initial Out-of-Home Placement Type for Latino Children

Percentage	Initial Placement
41	Relative foster home
35	Nonrelative foster home
13	Emergency shelter
7	Group home
3	Residential
2	Mental health facility

Source: From Ortega et al. (1996). *Latinos and child welfare*/Latinos y el bienestar del niño: Voces de la comunidad, pp. 3–7.

In terms of permanency planning, respondents estimated that almost half (48 percent) of the Latino children placed in substitute care are returned home within one year, while an estimated 28 percent of Latino children had parental rights terminated. Respondents believed that many termination of parental rights (TPR) situations are preventable with appropriate services. Reasons for TPR are listed in Table 12.5.

Regarding adoption, the majority of the respondents believed that Latino children are adopted at a rate below average when compared to Caucasian and African American children, and over half of the adoptions of Latino children are estimated to occur with non-Latino families.

Several areas of strength were identified by respondents when asked about their state's ability to meet the needs of their Latino child population. Both strengths and weaknesses focused on issues of awareness, availability, accessibility, and acceptability of services and the ability of these services to accommodate cultural and language differences. Most of the respondents believed that service monitoring was inadequate, which made it difficult to assess the effectiveness of child welfare services with Latino children and families. Prevention services were mentioned as available in all of the states surveyed, although respondents

Table 12.5 Reasons for Terminating Parental Rights (TPR) of Latino Parents

Percentage	TPR Reasons
22[a]	Abuse/neglect
18	Substance/alcohol abuse
16	Abandonment
16	Lack of capacity stability
14	Noncompliance/lack of interest
14	Other[b]

[a]Percentage distribution refers to physical abuse (12%), physical neglect (7%), and sexual abuse (3%).
[b]"Other" refers to parental health/mental health problems, voluntary relinquishment, lack of resources, involvement in criminal activities, incarceration, and death.
Source: From Ortega et al. (1996). *Latinos and child welfare*/Latinos y el bienestar del niño: Voces de la comunidad, pp. 3–7.

believed that only about a quarter of Latino families utilized prevention services.

VOCES DE LA COMUNIDAD

Another aspect of the Latinos and Child Welfare study was the use of focus group discussions within Latino communities in the study states. Community members who were experienced with raising a Latino child in their community were asked to talk about what it was like raising their children and about the role child welfare services played in their lives. From their discussions, it became immediately clear that Latino parents saw raising their children as a highly integrative process, and at times resisted focusing on one particular aspect of their child-raising experience. As one parent asked,

> How come you're only asking about child welfare? How come you're not asking about the welfare of the Latino child?

Participants almost unanimously expressed how stressful it was raising their children in hostile environments which they saw as constantly threatening family stability and community well-being. Gang violence in neighborhoods as well as violence and drug use in schools were presented as the most serious threats. Several parents agreed:

> Violence in the city and schools is what concerns me most. I also had to move my children to private school due to violence in their previous school.

Participants talked with a great deal of sadness about their feelings of social isolation and lack of community which prevented them from relying on each other for support in dealing with these problems. According to one mother,

> We don't even know who our neighbors are . . . we could be living right next to each other for a long time and not even know each other's names . . .

Consequently, children, especially in single-parent families, often found themselves left unprotected and vulnerable to a whole host of negative outside influences. As one tearful mother expressed,

> I've been affected by my being a single mother. Because I work, there are times when I've had to leave the children alone [at home] . . . the eldest one has been affected [negatively] by my absence.

Participants agreed on the need for a supportive community environment which linked schools, religious institutions, and other community resources. They shared in their discussions conflicting demands of wanting to raise their children in a safe and secure home located within a hostile environment while at the same having to work and being forced to leave their children alone and vulnerable. Many of the participants saw this as a major gap in community services and programs. They also saw the importance of educating parents about available services and programs.

Specific to child welfare, participants did not seem to rely on these services for support. Some participants knew about them but felt ignored and alienated when trying to access them. One parent summarized this sentiment:

> They begin to intimidate me. I get the runaround . . . I get lost in the system.

Others described language and cultural barriers and a lack of trust as major obstacles to seeking child welfare services. Still others simply did not know the meaning of child welfare services. Participants for the most part indicated that if efforts were made to address their concerns about the child welfare system's responsiveness to the needs of Latino families, they were likely to want to learn more about them.

Participants emphasized the importance of family when the safety and security of a child was in jeopardy. They described culturally relevant supports such as godparents (*compadres*) and fictive kin (*padrinos*) as integral to family preservation. When participants were asked to respond to a vignette illustrating physical abuse which resulted in a Latino child being placed in nonrelative substitute care, they acknowledged the importance of preserving a child's safety and security but were emphatic about needing to maintain the integrity of the family bond. In the event a child's safety and security were at risk in situations where relatives were unavailable, participants viewed out-of-home placement, albeit with much reluctance, as an option; however, they stressed the importance of preserving the Latino child's language and culture.

CURRENT GAPS

This discussion reveals serious gaps in understanding and addressing child welfare needs of Latino adolescents. The first issue to consider is that of counting and accountability. It is difficult to imagine how understanding the experiences of Latinos in child welfare can occur without accurate identification and tracking of Latino children during child welfare intervention. The literature presents example after example of differential treatment based on race and ethnicity, yet without accurate data very little can be discerned about the effectiveness of child welfare services in meeting the needs of Latino families and their children. Such an absence of knowledge has serious implications for the growing number of Latino children living in poverty, many of whom are believed to be at risk of maltreatment. Furthermore, some consideration must be given to the variation among Latino subgroups and the complexity involved in considering agendas unique to each group. Failure to do so further alienates child welfare services from Latino families and children.

Another gap focuses on the extent to which developmental issues are addressed once a child encounters child welfare services. Currently, there is a dearth of literature focusing on the extensiveness of adolescent abuse and on the victims' child welfare needs. Specific to Latinos, challenges to traditional child welfare services are likely to emerge due to the unique experiences of Latino adolescents. Most notably, Latino adolescents often carry with them the burdens of acculturative stress and related conflicts with parents; stress from poverty; exposure to violence, drugs, disease, and environmental hazards; high rates of mobility; and barriers to accessing resources and services due to language and cultural differences. Many Latino adolescents will experience segregation, social marginalization, discrimination, and oppression—all of which are manifested in high rates of depression, suicide, and social withdrawal. Currently there is no indication that child welfare services as a whole recognize these unique aspects of growing up Latino.

From a survey of service providers knowledgeable about Latino children and their child welfare experiences, a number of issues were raised. The absence of this knowledge has been a major gap in the child welfare literature since an exclusive focus on Latinos and child welfare is relatively nonexistent. From survey responses, concerns were raised about the extensiveness of maltreatment among Latino children. Service providers describe barriers to reporting and receiving services highlighted by numerous fears thought to emerge when contacting the child welfare agency, lack of available and accessible services, as well as the lack of services to accommodate language and cultural differences.

The importance of extended family (which includes fictive kin) was emphasized in survey responses with attention drawn to the limitations of fulfilling their roles due to scarce resources and supports for poor Latino families, particularly for recent immigrant and migrant families. Similar to national reports, neglect and physical abuse were identified as the primary forms of maltreatment against Latino children, with emotional abuse and child exploitation believed to be higher among Latinos and sexual abuse lower when compared to national data. Clearly more formal and extensive methods of discovery are necessary in order to develop a clear picture of why Latino children are entering child welfare. The fact that barriers and obstacles are perceived to exist suggests that Latino children are most likely to come to the attention of child welfare officials only when their situation is severely threatening, making recovery and reunification more difficult.

Foster care, both relative and nonrelative, was described as the most common type of out-of-home placement, with relative care relied on slightly more than nonrelative. While this is more consistent with the Latino family commitment to children, it should not overlook the conflicts likely to emerge particularly with a Latino adolescent. Lifestyle differences, peer associations, and developmental demands will most likely converge and clash with the stability offered by supportive kin. Without supportive services and resources, there is no reason to believe that kinship care under these circumstances will be any more successful than other nonrelative care. Likewise, in those instances where parental rights were terminated, it is suggested that many such outcomes could be prevented if appropriate support services were available and accessible to assist in the reunification process.

A number of concerns were raised about systemic issues that serve as obstacles to meeting the child welfare needs of Latino families. Community outreach, bilingual/bicultural service providers, and prevention programs designed specifically for Latino families were identified as essential for effective service delivery. Concerns, for the most part, extended beyond child welfare, calling attention to negative social influences embedded within communities and society at large which have a negative impact on Latino child and family well-being. Ignoring these influences is thought to have significant bearing on whether family functioning can be improved so that the Latino family can be preserved.

Latinos themselves are rarely actively engaged in the process of establishing policies, procedures, and practices to address their unique child welfare needs (Enchautegui, 1994). Allowing the opportunity for parents to speak about their experiences during focus groups illustrates one way to promote participation which, in the case of the Latinos and Child Welfare study, proved to be both illuminating and rewarding. Focus group participants, for example, emphasized the importance of acknowledging the needs of the whole child as opposed to their child welfare needs separately. Participants described a concern about their children's exposure to violence, drugs, and criminal activity in their neighborhoods and schools. There was consensus among participants that community was all but lost in their lives. Participants expressed a strong desire for services and programs that would support poor and working families, promote community development, and eliminate negative influences which threaten their well-being and the healthy development of their children.

Child welfare, rather than "family welfare," has historically led to individual-based policies and practices which consistently threaten Latino familistic values. These clashes have placed a long-standing wedge between social institutions and Latino family needs. Clearly, a focus on strengthening and preserving the Latino family must promote a validation of language and cultural differences beyond the need to develop a partnership in protecting and caring for Latino children. Grassroots Latino organizations, made up of knowledgeable and concerned indigenous individuals, have been underutilized in policy, practice, and research decisions. Their absence from the decision-making table represents another gap in understanding Latino child welfare needs and in promoting effective change.

FUTURE DIRECTIONS

The fact is that research is needed on child maltreatment among Latino adolescents which more closely examines both causes and types of Latino adolescent maltreatment. Furthermore, an effort must be made to track and monitor Latino adolescents upon entry into the child welfare system to assure that their developmental needs are addressed and goals of permanency are met expeditiously. Obviously such an effort requires a willingness on the part of federal, state, and local agencies to appropriate administrative and financial support (Thompson & Wilcox, 1995). It also requires a national commitment and plan for more systematic research with coordination and cooperation at the state and local levels.

The goal of family preservation cannot be seriously pursued without an appreciation of the Latino family experience. By necessity, this requires Latino involvement in planning, decision making, implementation, and monitoring of child welfare policies, programs, administrative procedures, and practices. The evidence is clear in indicating that the most successful programs designed to meet the needs of Latinos are those in which Latino participation is obvious, unique Latino cultural perspectives are accommodated, Latino family strengths are valued, and their perspective on interests and needs are validated (Shartrand, 1996).

There is no question that Latino families present a significant complexity of needs. Clearly the call is for diversity in methods and contexts of service delivery. Training and technical assistance must be offered to improve awareness of and sensitivity to language and cultural differences. Latinos are fairly heterogeneous in terms of racial and ethnic composition, level and extent of segregation, immigrant status, and language preference (Massey, Zambrana, & Bell, 1995). Generalizing services without recognizing differences among and between Latinos will add nothing to improving their current status or to understanding their child welfare needs. Such an effort, again, calls for active participation by the Latino community, particularly among grassroots organizations, since the call for child welfare extends beyond the responsibility of the child welfare system. Community participation and development in relation to Latino child and family well-being is the larger challenge. Included in this effort is the need to build linkages between and among the various programs, organizations, and agencies who have been charged with nurturing the healthy development of all children—school, child welfare, the courts, religious affiliations, community-based organizations, and so on (Duany & Pittman, 1990).

Current social trends and social problems confronting Latino adolescents suggest their state of crisis is real and not likely to subside. Latino teenagers experience economic, psychological, and social pressures with diminishing support and resources. A growing number will reside with single parents and more still will become parents themselves. Future directions must consider the unique challenges presented by Latino adolescents who come into contact with child welfare in particular, and social services in general. As Duany and Pittman (1990, p. 30) assert:

> The problems of Latino youths in this country cannot be ignored. Representing a significant portion of the population in the next century,

Latinos must be capable of participating fully in society to ensure this nation's long-term security. We cannot afford to sacrifice the Puerto Rican, Cuban American, Mexican American, Central and South American, and other Latino youths. The risk is too great—for Latino youths and for the country as a whole.

For a whole host of reasons, Latino adolescents must be instilled with validation and hope. In those cases where child welfare intervention is necessary, these goals are no less relevant or essential.

NOTES

[1] This estimate is based on data from Goerge et al. (1994).
[2] The National Latino Child Welfare Advocacy Group (NLCWAG) was initially formed as a consulting group for the W. K. Kellogg Foundation's Families for Kids Initiative. The group is comprised of eleven members, reflecting a rich mix of various Latino ancestries throughout the United States. NLCWAG members represent all levels of children's services administration, from executive directors to direct service providers, and are nationally recognized for their commitment to Latino children's issues.
[3] While this method may present a relatively subjective impression of child welfare use and needs, the knowledge of seasoned professionals justified the drawing of at least tentative conclusions.

REFERENCES

Adler, P., Ovando, C., & Hocevar, D. (1984). Familiar correlates of gang membership: An exploratory study of Mexican American youth. *Hispanic Journal of Behavioral Science, 6*, 65–76.

Barth, R. P., Courtney, M., Berrick, J., & Albert, V. (1994). *From child abuse to permanency planning: Child welfare services pathways and placements.* New York: Aldine DeGruyter.

Belsky, J. (1980). Child maltreatment: An ecological integration. *American Psychologist, 35*, 320–350.

Bronfenbrenner, U. (1979). *The ecology of human development: Experiments by nature and design.* Cambridge, MA: Harvard University Press.

Buriel, R., Calzado, S., & Vásquez, R. (1982). The relationship of traditional Mexican-American culture to the adjustment and delinquency among three generations of Mexican- American male adolescents. *Hispanic Journal of Behavioral Sciences, 1*, 45–55.

Canino, I. A., & Spurlock, J. (1994). *Culturally diverse children and adolescents: Assessment, diagnosis, and treatment*. New York: Guilford Press.

Chaffin, M., Bonner, B. L., Worley, K. B., & Lawson, L. (1996). Treating abused adolescents. In J. Briere, L. Berliner, J. A. Bulkley, C. Jenny, & T. Reid (Eds.), *The APSAC Handbook on Child Maltreatment* (pp. 119–139). Thousand Oaks, CA: Sage.

Courtney, M., Barth, R. P., Berrick, J. D., Brooks, D., Needell, B., & Park, L. (1994). Race and child welfare services: Past research and future directions. *Child Welfare, 75*, 99–137.

Curtis, P. A., Boyd, J. D., Liepold, M., & Petit, M. (1995). Child abuse and neglect: A look at the states. *Child Welfare League of America stats book*. Washington, DC: CWLA Press.

Delgado-Gaitán, C. (1988). Sociocultural adjustment to school and academic achievement. *Journal of Early Adolescence, 8*, 63–82.

Doueck, H., Ishisaka, A., Sweany, S., & Gilchrist, L. (1987). Adolescent maltreatment: Themes from the empirical literature. *Journal of Interpersonal Violence, 2*, 139–153.

Duany, L., & Pittman, K. (1990). *Latino youths at the crossroads*. Washington, DC: Children's Defense Fund.

Eckenrode, J., Powers, J., Davis, J., Munsch, J., & Bolger, N. (1988). Substantiation of child abuse and neglect reports. *Journal of Consulting and Clinical Psychology, 56*, 9–16.

Enchautegui, M. E. (1995). *Policy implications of Latino poverty*. Washington, DC: Urban Institute, Population Studies Center.

Fein, E., Maluccio, A. N., & Kluger, M. P. (1990). *No more partings: An examination of long term foster care*. Washington, DC: Child Welfare League of America.

Fox, J. (1984). Social work ethics and children: Protection vs. empowerment. *Children and Youth Services Review, 6*, 319–328.

Garbarino, J. (1977). The human ecology of child maltreatment: A conceptual model for research. *Journal of Marriage and the Family, 39*, 721–735.

Gelles, R. J. (1983). International perspective on child abuse and neglect. *Child Abuse and Neglect, 7*, 375–386.

Gelles, R. J. (1992). Poverty and violence toward children. *American Behavioral Scientist, 35*, 258–274.

Gibson, C. M. (1993, September). Empowerment theory and practice with adolescents of color in the child welfare system. *Families in Society: The Journal of Contemporary Human Services*, pp. 387–395.

Gil, D. G. (1970). *Violence against children: Physical abuse in the United States*. Cambridge, MA: Harvard University Press.

Gil, E. (1996). *Treating abused adolescents.* New York: Guilford Press.
Goerge, R. M., Wulczyn, F. H., & Harden, A. W. (1994). *Foster care dynamics 1983–1992: A report from the multistate foster care data archive.* Chicago: University of Chicago, Chapin Hall Center for Children.
Hay, T., & Jones, L. (1994). Societal interventions to prevent child abuse and neglect. *Child Welfare, 73,* 379–403.
Hegar, R. (1989). Empowerment-based practice with children. *Social Service Review, 63,* 372–383.
Hogan, P., & Sui, S. (1988). Minority children and the child welfare system: An historical perspective. *Social Work, 33,* 493–498.
Inclan, J. E., & Herron, D. G. (1998). Puerto Rican adolescents. In J. T. Gibbs, L. N. Huang, and Associates, *Children of color: Psychological interventions with minority youth* (pp. 240–263). San Francisco: Jossey-Bass.
Jiobu, R. (1988). *Ethnicity and assimilation.* Albany: State University of New York Press.
Jones, E. D., & McCurdy, K. (1992). The links between types of maltreatment and demographic characteristics of children. *Child Abuse and Neglect, 16,* 201–215.
Massey, D. S., Zambrana, R. E., & Bell, S. A. (1995). Contemporary issues in Latino families: Future directions for research, policy, and practice. In R. Zambrana (Ed.), *Understanding Latino families* (pp. 190–204). Thousand Oaks, CA: Sage.
McMurtry, S. L., & Lie, G. W. (1992). Differential exit rates of minority children in foster care. *Social Work Research and Abstracts, 28,* 42–48.
Mendoza, F. S. (1994). The health of Hispanic children. *The future of children: Critical health issues for children and youth, 4,* 43–72. Los Altos, CA: The David and Lucille Packard Foundation, Center for the Future of Children.
Mirande, A. (1977). The Chicano family: A re-analysis of conflicting views. *Journal of Marriage and the Family, 39,* 747–755.
National Coalition of Hispanic Health and Human Services Organizations [COSSMHO]. (1996). *Growing up Hispanic: Leadership report.* Washington, DC: Author.
Newberger, E., Reed, A., Danile, J. H., Hyde, J., & Kotelchuck, M. (1977). Pediatric social illness: Toward an etiological classification. *Pediatrics, 60,* 178–185.
New York Times. (1997, January 30). Hispanic households struggle as poorest of the poor in the U.S. (National Edition), pp. A1 and A12.
Ortega, R. M., Guillean, C., & Gutierrez-Nagera, L. (1996). *Latinos and child welfare/ Latinos y el beinestar del niño: Voces de la comunidad.* Ann Arbor: University of Michigan, School of Social Work.

Ortiz, V. (1995). The diversity of Latino families. In R. Zambrana (Ed.), *Understanding Latino families* (pp. 18–39). Thousand Oaks, CA: Sage.

O'Toole, R., Turbett, P., & Nalpeka, C. (1983). Theories, professional knowledge, and diagnosis of child abuse. In D. Finkelhor, R. J. Gelles, G. T. Hotaling, & M. A. Straus (Eds.), *The dark side of families: Current family violence research* (pp. 349–362). Beverly Hills, CA: Sage.

Parsons, R. (1989). Empowerment for role alternatives for low income minority girls: A group work approach. *Social Work with Groups, 11*(4), 34–49.

Pecora, P. J., Whittaker, J. K., Maluccio, A. N., Barth, R. P., & Plotnick, R. D. (1994). *The child welfare challenge: Policy, practice, and research.* New York: Aldine de Gruyter.

Pelton, L. H. (1978). Child abuse and neglect: The myth of classlessness. *American Journal of Orthopsychiatry, 48*, 608–617.

Queralt, M. (1993). Psychosocial risk factors associated with suicide in a small community sample of Latino adolescent attempters. *Social Work in Education, 15*, 91–103.

Ramírez, O. (1998). Mexican American children and adolescents. In J. T. Gibbs, L. N. Huang, and Associates, *Children of color: Psychological interventions with minority youth* (pp. 215–239). San Francisco: Jossey-Bass.

Río, A. T., Santisteban, D. A., & Szapocznik, J. (1991). Juvenile delinquency among Hispanics: The role of family in prevention and treatment. In M. Sotomayor (Ed.), *Empowering Latino families: A critical issue for the 90s* (pp. 191–214). Milwaukee, WI: Family Services America.

Rivera-Martínez, C. (1992). Hispanics and the social service system. In P. San Juan Cafferty & W. McCready (Eds.), *Hispanics in the United States: A new social agenda* (pp. 195–213). New Brunswick, NJ: Transaction.

Roberts, R. E. (1994). Research on the mental health of Mexican origin children and adolescents. In C. Telles & M. Karno (Eds.), *Latino mental health: Current research and policy perspectives* (pp. 17–39). Washington, DC: National Institute of Mental Health.

Roberts, R. E., & Sobham, M. (1992). Symptoms of depression in adolescence: A comparison of Anglo, African, and Hispanic Americans. *Journal of Youth and Adolescence, 21*, 639–651.

Shartrand, A. (1996). *Supporting Latino families: Lessons from exemplary programs* (Resumen en español). Volume I. Cambridge, MA: Harvard Family Research Project.

Solís, J. (1994). The status of Latino children and youth: Challenges and prospects. In R. Zambrana (Ed.), *Understanding Latino families* (pp. 62–81). Thousand Oaks, CA: Sage.

Steel, B. F., & Pollack, C. B. (1968). A psychiatric study of parents who abuse infants and small children. In R. E. Helfer & C. H. Kempe (Eds.), *The battered child* (pp. 89–133). Chicago: University of Chicago Press.

Stehno, S. M. (1990). The elusive continuum of child welfare services: Implications for minority children and youth. *Child Welfare, 69,* 551–562.

Szapocznik, J., & Kurtines, W. M. (1989). *Breakthroughs in family therapy with drug abusing and problem youth.* New York: Springer.

Tatara, T. (1993). *Characteristics of children in substitute care: A statistical summary of the VCIS National Child Welfare Data Base.* Washington, DC: American Public Welfare Association.

Thompson, R. A., & Wilcox, B. L. (1995). Child maltreatment research. *American Psychologist, 50,* 789–793.

Tracey, E. M., Green, R. K., & Bremseth, M. D. (1993). Meeting environmental needs of abused and neglected children: Implications from a statewide survey of supportive services. *Social Work Research and Abstracts, 29*(2), 21–26.

U.S. Department of Health and Human Services, National Center on Child Abuse and Neglect. (1996). *Child maltreatment 1994: Reports from the states to the National Center on Child Abuse and Neglect.* Washington, DC: U.S. Government Printing Office.

Vega, W. (1995). The study of Latino families: A point of departure. In R. Zambrana (Ed.), *Understanding Latino families* (pp. 3–17). Thousand Oaks, CA: Sage.

Vega, W. A., Zimmerman, R. S., Warheit, G. J., Jackson, D., Gil, A., & Sokol-Katz, J. (1994). The role of cultural factors in mental health problems of Hispanic adolescents. In C. Telles & M. Karno (Eds.), *Latino mental health: Current research and policy perspectives* (pp. 3–18). Washington, DC: National Institute of Mental Health.

Williams, N. (1990). *The Mexican American family: Tradition and change.* Dix Hill, NY: General Hall.

Zambrana, R. (Ed.) (1996). *Understanding Latino families.* Thousand Oaks, CA: Sage.

AFTERWORD
Pensamientos

MARTHA MONTERO-SIEBURTH
AND FRANCISCO A. VILLARRUEL

This volume reflects the beginning of a journey for the authors, for all who are concerned with Latino youth, and for the future of research on and with Latino youth and communities. As evidenced in this volume, both by what has been presented and by what has not, it should be evident that the magnitude of the issues confronting Latino youth are such that one volume cannot adequately or comprehensively provide an in-depth analysis.

As such, the authors are left with *pensamientos* (afterthoughts) as to future directions of research, policy, and programs for Latino youth. While the following list is by no means comprehensive or exhaustive, it reflects an array of issues that we believe future research endeavors should consider.

1. As Latinos stabilize communities, the need to understand their intergroup strengths and weaknesses will need to be closely examined in order to build coalitions between Latinos and among other ethnic groups.
2. The maintenance of a bicultural existence for Latinos will require in many cases making a choice for using Spanish as a medium of communication along with English, and negotiating between U.S.-dominant culture and Latino cultures. The choice of English only as opposed to English plus may have dire consequences for cognitive and cultural flexibility. Issues about acculturation and assimilation as opposed to the maintenance of Latino cultural values and beliefs should be a major focus of fu-

ture research endeavors. Moreover, this tension might impact the identity formation of youth from various Latino cultures.
3. With the aging of Latinos, reflecting upon the wisdom that can be derived from established Latino cultures and communities will be essential in the identification of models that promote positive and healthy development of various Latino communities and individuals. Identifying such models from one community to another will bear invaluable information that can guide future research. Within this framework specific attention should be placed upon the context in which these models exist, and the similarities or differences that result as a consequence of regional and cultural differences.
4. The issue of legal versus undocumented Latino immigrants needs to be addressed from a positive perspective. Recently, Mexico has passed dual citizenship status, allowing Mexicans to maintain Mexican citizenship along with a secondary country. The implications of this may range from the minimization of distinct barriers and psychological distances that were necessary to dual existence (i.e., the pattern of circular migration), to increased voter and political participation on the part of Mexican youth in the United States. Economic challenges may be confronted at the familial level as a consequence of paying taxes to two countries, which may minimize disposable income at the family unit level.
5. As the numbers of Latino youth increase, their need for educational opportunities will be greater. Responses, then, to various proposed policies (e.g., the anti-bilingual education Unz proposal in California, the Hopwood case in Texas which attacks affirmative action in higher education), which have been interpreted as anti-Latino and anti-immigrant, present daunting challenges. If these policies are passed, the educational equality and opportunity will be eroded. As a consequence, the institution of education in the United States, which is viewed as one of the principal means of socialization to facilitate the transition of youth to adulthood, will be essentially denied to Latino and immigrant youth.
6. Opportunities to develop leadership skills for Latino youth are essential if Latino communities and youth are to benefit from collective and group action. Latino leadership, while having many of the traits of mainstream leadership, differs by demands

from the community, negotiating skills, decision-making processes, cultural brokerage, customs, and language. Latino leadership in the United States requires a consistent "border crossing" between "cultural ways of knowing" and mainstream ideology. It is important to recognize nascent versus seasoned leaders within Latino communities and to develop the leadership skills of Latino youth to create collaborations among grassroots organizations. For Latino youth, this means that they must do "double duty," learning from both mainstream and Latino leaders. Only when conscious and purposeful training and quality mentorship opportunities are made available will the tensions between community demands and individual leadership be minimized.

7. With the induction of Latinas into the educational and economic pipeline, gender issues which have traditionally been defined within Latino cultures will need to be a focus of future research, program, and policy development. Latina feminism will need to be considered in light of the cultural changes and adaptations that Latinas are undergoing in various contexts (e.g., schools, higher education, health and legal professions). These new paradigms of gender understanding and participation will be premised upon developing cultural competencies that appropriately reflect differences in gender.

8. The consequences of generational integration pose a unique set of challenges to researchers and practitioners. Given that Latino cultures ascribe to collective familial and community cohesiveness, assimilation to different values and beliefs may result in an erosion of the cohesiveness of intergenerational interdependency. As Hayes-Bautista, Schink, and Chapa (1988) have noted, Latinos do not abandon their cultural mores as readily as do other immigrant communities. Rather, there is a "circular" abandonment and reinvestment in cultural mores. This "reinvestment," however, may result in an evolutionary set of mores that do not necessarily reflect cultural values across earlier generations. As such, the range of Hispanicity may actually become greater over time, and in turn result in different socialization patterns for Latino youth.

9. The impact of music and media may have a tremendous impact on Latino youth and their understanding of cultural mores. With the "crossover" to and increased marketing of music such as

gangsta-rap, Latino youth are being exposed to ideologies that are culturally incongruent. Moreover, the dearth of positive role models in print and visual media minimizes the opportunities of possibility for Latino youth. In other words, negative portrayals of Latinos may result in a sense of alienation, depreciation of self, and lessening of the values related to cultural identity.

10. Traditionally, Latino adolescents do not share the same experiences as mainstream adolescents of growing from childhood to an actual period of adolescence and, subsequently, adulthood. In fact, for many Latino youth, the passage of childhood to adulthood is fraught with responsibilities normally carried only by adults, for example, interpreting for parents, accompanying parents to doctor appointments, taking care of younger siblings, doing household chores, and negotiating language and community systems for their parents. Attention to stressors inherent with such obligations and responsibilities must be understood by mainstream professionals, and rather than be viewed as pejorative or negative, viewed within the cultural context of a period of life span development that is "different" from mainstream perspectives. The development of cultural competencies in this domain will result in a cultural alignment with Latino youth and their families which may result in development of programs and practices that build upon existing capacities. Thus, researchers should be sensitive that the progressions and stages of Latino youth development may not be identical to those of non-Latino cultures.

11. The concept of morality within Latino cultures has a different epigenesis. For example, for traditional Latinas the notion of *pudor* (keeping the dignity of one's body and spirit) still acts as a deterrent to promiscuity. In contrast, for more acculturated Latinas, who have grown up in a society that has less restrictive sexual norms, the notion of losing *pudor* becomes replaced with *libertinaje* (looseness or promiscuity). Hence, attention to stages of moral development for Latino and Latina youth may not adhere to the same moral development stages that mainstream researchers, such as Kohlberg and Gilligan, have advanced. Needed is research that will facilitate our understanding of Latino youth morality from their changing perspectives in response to the cultural contacts, conflicts, and contexts that exist across and between community institutions.

Pensamientos

The opportunities for positive and healthy development of Latino youth, as evidenced throughout this volume and in the aforementioned challenges, will require new paradigms and commitments of understanding. Not to invest in Latino youth, given the rapidly changing demographic landscape, the growing needs of this population, and the contributions which they can make to the general welfare, compromises the well-being of this nation. We cannot afford to divert our attention from the compelling questions raised within this volume and the need to sustain a just, moral, and ethical multicultural society. From a pragmatic perspective, the United States has benefited immensely from the contributions of Latino cultures, and undoubtedly will become stronger if a serious commitment and dedication to Latino youth issues is promulgated.

REFERENCES

Hayes-Bautista, D. E., Schink, W. O., & Chapa, J. (1988). *The burden of support: Young latinos in an aging society.* Stanford, CA: Stanford University Press.

Contributors

Odette Alarcón
Odette Alarcón is a Senior Research Scientist at the Center for Research on Women, Wellesley College, where she is Principal Investigator and Director of the Puerto Rican Child Health Study funded by the Maternal Child Health Bureau of the Department of Public Health and Co-Principal Investigator of the Puerto Rican Normative Adolescent Project funded by NICHD.
  Dr. Alarcón is also a practicing psychiatrist in the Boston area and a staff psychiatrist at Children's Hospital.

Nancy A. Busch-Rossnagel
Nancy A. Busch-Rossnagel is Professor and Chair of the Department of Psychology at Fordham University. She received her B.A. in psychology from Scripps College, her M.A. in human development and family studies from Wayne State University, and her Ph.D. in human development and family studies from the Pennsylvania State University. She has taught at Colorado State University and is an integral part of the team developing instrumentation for the assessment of mastery motivation in toddlers. She is co-editor of *Individuals as Producers of Their Development: A Life-Span Perspective* and her work has appeared in several book chapters and scholarly journals. She serves as a reviewer for the *Journal of Research on Adolescence* and is currently editor of the series *Research Monographs on Adolescence*. Her most recent work has focused on the development and socialization of Latino children. She is principal investigator of an NICHD grant on the normative development

of Puerto Rican and Dominican toddlers to develop culturally appropriate measures. The measures will be used in the future on a longitudinal study on socioemotional development. During the most recent SRCD conference, she organized and chaired a symposium bringing together other recipients of grants targeting minority populations. On that occasion, she also presented a paper on the parenting behaviors of Puerto Ricans and Dominicans. She is married and has two children.

Jaime Chahín
Dr. Jaime Chahin is Associate Vice President, Human Resources and University Affairs, at Southwest Texas State University.

Sumru Erkut
Sumru Erkut, Ph.D., is Associate Director of the Center for Research on Women at Wellesley College where her work focuses on adolescent development, racial and ethnic diversity, and equity in education and employment. She is one of the co-directors of a longitudinal research program on the health and growth of Puerto Rican youth and another project on middle school girls from diverse backgrounds. Dr. Erkut consults to corporations, educational institutions, and social service agencies on issues of gender equity and racial/ethnic diversity.

Cynthia García Coll
Cynthia García Coll is Professor of Education, Psychology and Pediatrics, Chair of the Education Department, and Director of the Center for the Study of Human Development at Brown University. She received her Ph.D. in developmental psychology from Harvard University in 1981. She has published over 70 articles and chapters on the sociocultural and biological influences on early childhood development and teenage pregnancy. She has also been on the editorial boards of many prestigious academic journals, including *Child Development, Development and Psychopathology,* and *Infant Behavior and Development.* She is currently a member of the MacArthur Foundation Network, "Successful Pathways Through Middle Childhood." She is a member of the Committee on Racial and Ethnic Issues for the Society for Research on Child Development (SRCD), which she chaired from 1991–1993. She currently serves on the SRCD Executive Committee. She has served as the SRCD representative to the National Head Start Conference Committee from 1994 to the present. García Coll has co-edited several books: *The Psychosocial Development of Puerto Rican Women; Puerto Rican Women and Children:*

Issues in Health, Growth and Development; and *Mothering Against the Odds: Diverse Voices of Contemporary Mothers.* She also was a co-editor of a special issue for the journal *Child Development* entitled "Children and Poverty." She is a Fellow of the American Psychological Association.

Rudy Hernández
Rudy Hernández was born in Detroit, Michigan, and received his Bachelor's degree in political science from Wayne State University. He has worked for several years as a youth advocate with Latino communities throughout the state of Michigan. Currently he works as an outreach specialist for Michigan State University, where he is a Ph.D. candidate in family sociology.

Bertha López
Bertha Marie López earned her undergraduate degree in sociology from Siena Heights College in 1969, a master's in social work from the University of Michigan in 1989, and has worked in the field of family therapy for the last 15 years. The last 10 years have been focused on the Hispanic population of Lenawee County, Michigan, and the migrants who come to this area. She served as Chair of the Southeastern Michigan Migrant Resource Council for five years, and has also been a member of the Michigan Department of Mental Health's Standing Committee on Multicultural Populations. She presently sits on the Board of the Midwest Migrant Health Information Office.

Martha Montero-Sieburth
Martha Montero-Sieburth received her Ed.D. in instructional development and administration from Boston University, and a postdoctoral fellowship in international education from Harvard University. She is currently an Associate Professor in the Graduate College of Education at the University of Massachusetts, Boston (UMB). Formerly she was Director of Educational Research at the Mauricio Gaston Institute, UMB. She taught at the Harvard Graduate School of Education as an Assistant and later an Associate Professor in the Division of Teaching, Curriculum, and Learning Environments from 1984–1991. Montero-Sieburth was the first and only full time Latina faculty member at HGSE during her tenure. She also became the first Latina faculty member at the UMB Graduate School of Education in 1996. Her interests are in the direct application of cultural anthropology and qualitative research to the development of instructional materials and curricula, quality teacher and

parent education, the restructuring of schools, and the development of cross-cultural understanding between communities of learners. She recently published *The Struggle for a New Paradigm: Qualitative Research in Latin America* with Gary Anderson and co-edited *Latinos in a Changing Society* with Edwin Melendez. She has conducted ethnographic research in rural and urban schools in Costa Rica, Honduras, and Guatemala with international research projects and is starting a public policy project with the Latino Parents Association in Jamaica Plain. For the past twenty-five years, Montero-Sieburth, a native of Mexico and Costa Rica, has been gathering cultural data on Mexican celebrations and rituals, as well as folk-healing practices.

Raimundo Mora
Raimundo Mora received his Ph.D. from New York University. He is an Assistant Professor at LaGuardia Community College of the City University of New York, and writes about language use in the classroom as well as second language academic literacy.

Lucila Nerenberg
Lucila Nerenberg, M.D., is Medical Consultant for Migrant Outreach Services, which involves intercultural and medical supervision of health care volunteers and treating migrant farmworkers on site. She is Director of Medical Education at Chelsea Arbor Treatment Center in Ann Arbor, Michigan, and has been a faculty member of the University of Michigan's Addiction Psychiatry Fellowship Program, a Clinical Instructor in Psychiatry, University of Michigan Medical School, and Adjunct Lecturer in Psychology, College of Literature, Science and the Arts, University of Michigan. Recent courses taught at the University of Michigan include Medicine, Culture and Creativity, Farmworker Outreach, and Multicuturalism and Medicine.

Robert M. Ortega
Robert M. Ortega received his Ph.D in social work and social psychology in 1991 from the University of Michigan. He is an Associate Professor in the School of Social Work at the University of Michigan. Professor Ortega's teaching and research interests are in the areas of relationship development, group work practice, treatment interventions and service utilization, particularly in the areas of mental health and child welfare. He has presented and written on these topics with a special focus on multiculturalism in research and practice. Ortega's current research interests

focus on Latinos, child welfare and mental health help-seeking behaviors. He has expertise in both qualitative and quantitative research methods. His research examines the underutilization of mental health and child welfare services by the rapidly-growing Latino population. His work has important implications for how social workers provide services to Latinos and how universities train social workers to address the unique needs of Latinos. He is a cofounder of the Latino Community Outreach Project which provides research, student training and evaluations of programs serving Latino communities throughout the state of Michigan. Professor Ortega has published in the areas of Latino mutual aid, multicultural issues in group work, child welfare permanency planning and family preservation. He serves as a consultant to several national research projects and organizations focusing on child welfare and adoption issues.

Daniel F. Perkins
Daniel F. Perkins, Ph.D., is an Assistant Professor in the Department of Family, Youth and Community Sciences at the University of Florida. He received his Ph.D. from Michigan State University in 1995.

Refugio I. Rochin
Refugio I. Rochin is Director of the Smithsonian Center for Latino Initiatives at the Smithsonian Institute, Washington, DC. Formerly he was Professor of Sociology and Agricultural Economics at Michigan State University and Professor Emeritus of the University of California, Davis, Chicana/o Studies and Agricultural Economics program.

Anna M. Santiago
Anna Maria Santiago is an Associate Research Scientist at the University of Michigan. Dr. Santiago received her Ph.D. in urban social institutions from the University of Wisconsin, Milwaukee, in 1984 and completed an NICHD/Rockefeller postdoctoral fellowship in demography and poverty and public policy at the University of Michigan in 1992. From 1991-93, she also was the recipient of a postdoctoral fellowship from the Program on the Urban Underclass of the Social Science Research Council. Her teaching and research interests include residential segregation and social mobility of Blacks, Mexicans, Puerto Ricans and Cubans; long-term poverty and welfare dependency in minority communities; the economic consequences of disability status for minority populations; and the dynamics of Latino family life. Her research has been published in journals

including *Social Problems, Urban Affairs Quarterly, Journal of Economics and Family Issues* and *The Gerontologist*.

Marcelo Siles
Marcelo Siles is a Senior Research Associate at the Institute for Public Policy and Social Research, Michigan State University.

Ricardo D. Stanton-Salazar
Professor Ricardo Stanton-Salazar completed his graduate studies at Stanford University in 1990. Subsequently, he commenced a new research project on the social networks of Mexican-origin adolescents in San Diego, California. He has been on the faculty of the Department of Sociology at the University of California, San Diego, since 1992. His main fields of interest are the sociology of education, youth culture, race and ethnic relations, and family studies. His current research deals with how various social forces in society affect the development of minority adolescent social networks and help-seeking behavior, and how these factors influence their receptivity to educational interventions. His ideas are most extensively presented in an article in the Spring 1997 issue of the *Harvard Educational Review*. With financial support from the Ford Foundation and the Institute of American Cultures at UCLA, Stanton-Salazar spent the 1997-98 academic year in residence at the Chicano Studies Research Center at UCLA, finishing a book on the social networks of Mexican-origin adolescents.

Linda R. Tropp
Linda R. Tropp is an advanced doctoral student in the social psychology program at the University of California, Santa Cruz. Her main research interests include prejudice and intergroup relations from the perspective of members of socially devalued groups, along with the conceptualization and measurement of group identification and other aspects of the self-concept.

Marina Valdez
Marina Valdez, M.S.W., received her master's degree in social work from the University of Michigan in 1996 and her bachelor's degree in human services from Siena Heights College in 1991. She has worked as a mental health outreach worker with the migrant community for six years. She was Coordinator of Substance Abuse Prevention Activities for the local Intermediate School District to offer prevention services to the migrant

population. She has also volunteered as a 4-H leader and has worked to increase the number of Latino youth in 4-H programs in Lenawee County through the Michigan State University Cooperative Extension Program. She served on the Foster Care Review Board of Michigan for three years.

Maribel Vargas
Maribel Vargas is a Research Associate in the Psychology Department at Fordham University in New York City. She is currently project manager for an NICHD grant on normative development in Puerto Rican and Dominican toddlers. She received her B.A. in psychology from the University of Puerto Rico and a master's in educational psychology from New York University. She completed her doctorate in applied developmental psychology at Fordham University. Her research interests are in the area of maternal (teaching) behaviors in Latino populations and normative behavioral development in Latino children and youth. Her publications include a chapter with N. A. Busch-Rossnagel, D. E. Knauf, and R. Planos, in D. Messer (Ed.)'s *Mastery Motivation in Early Childhood: Development, Measurement, and Social Processes,* and an article with Busch-Rossnagel and M. P. Fracasso in the *Hispanic Journal of Behavioral Sciences* on the reliability and validity of a Q-sort measure to assess attachment in Hispanic infants.

Heidie A. Vázquez-García
Heidie A. Vázquez-García, M.S., is a doctoral student in the clinical psychology graduate program at Pennsylvania State University. Her main research interests include acculturation processes in Latino adolescents, the influence of environmental factors on identity development in ethnic minority youth, and the development of interethnic and interracial relationships among ethnic/racial minority and majority adolescents.

Antonia M. Villarruel
Antonia M. Villarruel is an Assistant Professor in the School of Nursing at the University of Pennsylvania. She received her Ph.D. from the University of Michigan in 1993 and was a Postdoctoral Fellow there from 1993-1995. She is a Fellow of the American Academy of Nursing and was selected as a "Top 20" for *Who's Who of Latino Medicine* in 1996. Her current research projects include HIV risk reduction interventions for Puerto Rican youth, funded by a Minority Faculty Award from the University of Pennsylvania. Her publications include numerous journal articles and book chapters on Latino health issues.

Francisco A. Villarruel

Francisco A. Villarruel is an Associate Professor of Family and Child Ecology at Michigan State University. Villarruel has a master's degree in assisted computer learning and language and a doctorate in child and family studies. Awards include a W. K. Kellogg Foundation National Fellowship, an MSU/Lilly Foundation Teaching Fellowship, and an MSU Teacher-Scholar Award in 1996. Villarruel's research focuses on Latino youth and families in the United States.

Index

Abuse, 87
   adolescents, 311–312
   childhood, 100
   physical, 87, 90, 94
   sexual, 87, 90, 94
Academic achievement, 156–158
Accelerated program, xx
Americanization, 192, 247
Anglo-American culture, 113
Anglo-Saxon population, 109, 113
Anti-immigrant bashing, 15

Bell Curve, The (Hernstein & Murray), xxi
Best practice efforts, viii
Bilingual education programs, 148
Boricua, 1, 11, 22
Bracero program, 290
Browning of America, 2
Bureau of Labor Statistics, 46

Caribbean, 266
Case studies of students, parents, and teachers, 159–187
Center for Research on Education of Students Placed at Risk (CRESPAR), xx

Central Americans, 3, 65, 173, 191, 266
Chávez, César, 14
Chávez, Linda, 113
Chévere, 159
Chicano, 1, 10, 22, 85, 116, 122, 204, 225, 269
Child maltreatment, 312–316
Child poverty, 30
Child welfare services, 309–312
   out-of-home placements, 319–321
   referral, 318–319
   utilization, 316–321
Children's Defense Fund, 240, 245
Cold silent treatment, 181
Coleman, James, xix
Collectivism, 242–243
Colombia and Columbians, 160, 173, 192, 268
Comadre (godmother), 76, 171
Comer, James, xx
Compadre (godfather), 171
Comunidad, 13
Community Based Profile of Michigan Youth Study, 90
Community Funds of Knowledge, xii
Conceptual framework, viii

Condescension, 181
Confianza (trust), 14
Costa Rica and Costa Ricans, 162, 170, 192
Cuba, xiv, 85, 246
Cuban Americans, 3, 5, 64, 68, 73
Cultural capital, xix
Cultural context, xvii
Cultural deprivation, xix
Cultural deterministic viewpoint, 114–118
Curse words, 173

De Vos, George, xxiv, 157–158
De Vos and Suárez-Orozco
 notions of ego rigidification, 189
 spiral effects of affective dissonance, xxiv, 189
Differential treatment, xix
Dominicans and Dominican Americans, 11, 254, 266, 270, 273

Easy classes, 160
Ecological developmental approach, 313–314
Ecuadorians, 192
Education
 context, xvii
 culturally compatible programs, 156
 emancipatory education, 144
Educational context, xvii
Educational Opportunity Fund (EOF), 137
Effective programs for Migrant Youth, 302–304
 Midwest Migrant Health in Adrian, Michigan, 303
 Siena Heights College and Community Mental Health, 303
 Student with Action Farmworkers (SAF), 302
 The Cornell Migrant Program, 302

Viviremos/Se Pou Nou Viv/ Learn to Live, 302
English only, 14
Erickson, Frederick, xviii
ESL students' academic illiteracy, 143–144
Españoles, 4

Familia, 13, 23–24, 69
Familism, xxv, 69–70, 267, 280
Filipinos, 11
Fourteenth Amendment, 107
Frescos (fresh), 173
Friere, P., 144

General Accounting Office (1994), 142
Godparents, 76, 171
Guatemala and Guatemalans, 169, 180, 254

Heller, Celia, 114
Hispanic, 1, 4, 9, 10, 11, 12, 13, 64–65, 68, 119, 190
Hispanic Health and Nutrition Examination Survey (HHANES), xii, 64
Hispanic Policy Development Project, 149
Honduras and Hondurans, 169, 192
Human capital, 8, 53

Jefe (boss), 19
Johns, 143

Kamehameha Early Education Program, 156
Kluckhohn, Florence R., 113

Labor market conditions, 53
Latino adolescents
 academic achievement, 156–158, 188–189

Index

acculturation, 241, 247–250, 255, 268, 283
adaptation, 245–253
adaptive responses, 220, 221
age structure, 7–8
Americanization, 247
at-risk students, xvi, 142, 158–187, 240–241
bicultural survival skills, 256
burden of support, 7
case studies of students, 159–187
collectivist culture, 242–243
communalism, 219, 220
coping behavior, 211
discrimination, 241, 256
diversity, 245–253
dropouts, xvi, 142, 240
education, 18–19,156–158, 188–189, 241
families, 239, 241–245, 271–272, 280–281
gender roles, 239, 250–253
help-seeking orientations, 211–220
high-risk groups, 240–241
independence, 215, 216
institutional/subcultural influences, 215
intergenerational gap, 249
invisible status, xxi
marginal youth, 224, 228
migrant, 289–293
migration, 241, 245, 246
mistrust, 215, 216
network orientation, 215
overacculturation, 250
poverty and, 16
resourcefulness, 299–300
respeto (respect), xxv, 239, 254–256, 267–271, 280
school performance, 244
self-differentiation, 247
self-reliance, 218, 222
social and cultural origins, 213

socioeconomic status, 241
unemployment rates, 240
urban life and, 203
value systems and, 241, 281–282
See also Precollege Latino students, Migrant adolescents, National Longitudinal Survey of Youth (NLSY)
Latino cultural beliefs, 267
allocentrism, 267, 310–311
assets, xi, xii, xxiii, 84
collectivism, 242–243
familism, 267
machismo, xxv, 70, 267, 282
marianismo, 267
respeto (respect), xxv, 239, 254–256, 267–271, 280
simpatia (sympathy), 267
simpatico (nice/agreeable), 273
Latino dropout rates, xvi, 142
Latino ethnicity, xv
Hispanic, xv
Latino, xv
Latino families, xiv, 239, 266
Latino migrant families, 290
Latino National Political Survey (LNPS), xii
Latino origin, xi
Latino parenting, 265–283
Baumrind's model application, 275, 276
child and adolescent outcomes, 276
Euro-American parenting models, 266
parental power, 276
parenting qualities, 275
Latinos
Acquired Immunodeficiency Syndrome (AIDS) and, 20
case studies of students, parents, and teachers, 159–187
comunidad, 13
education, 19, 21–23
entrepreneurs, 20

Latinos (*continued*)
  family values, 13, 239
  female-headed households, 15, 18, 83
  foreign born, 15
  historic origins, 4–5
  Human Immunodeficiency Virus (HIV) and, 20
  immigrants, 14, 15
  labor force participants, 16
  media images, 155
  minority status, 7
  naturalized citizens, 15
  negative images, 155
  poverty rate, 15
  race and, 5–7
  socioeconomic indicators, 15
  Spanish language, 13
  unemployment, 83
  unity, 12–18
  U.S. born, 16, 158
  work ethic, 16–18
  working poor, 16–18
Levin, Henry, xx
Libertinaje (looseness or promiscuity), 336
Literacy acquisition continuum, 143

Machismo, xxv, 70, 267, 282
Marianismo, 70, 267
Marielitos, 5
Martinez, Zavala, 241
Mayans, 11
McDermott, Ray, xviii
Mehan, Hugh, xviii
Melting pot, 109, 248
Mestizo (mixed ancestry), 6, 10, 108
  generation, 108–109
  raza mestiza, 10
Mexicans, xiv, 5, 67, 89, 159, 173, 203, 225, 245, 250, 252, 254, 266, 268–269, 272, 278–280
Mexican Americans, 3, 64–66, 68–69, 73, 85, 107–126, 249, 273, 276
  achievement patterns, 123
  aspirations, 117–118, 120
  civil rights, 111, 115, 116
  cultural values, 113, 114
  deficit philosophy, 113, 114
  demographic analysis, 123
  deterministic perspective, 114
  economic and immigration patterns, 110–112
  education, 119, 122
  historical presence, 108–110
  identity formation, 116
  Mexican War, 109
  Mexican revolution, 110
  migrants and nonmigrants, 121–122
  parental involvement, 125
  pathological attributes, 107–126
  present-time orientation, 121
  status and aspirations of migrants and nonmigrants, 121
  stereotypical orientations, 107
  Texas Independence, 109
  Treaty of Guadalupe Hidalgo, 109, 110
Mexican American Study Project at UCLA, 114
Migrant adolescents, 289–293
  education, 291–293
  resourcefulness, 299–301
  school assessment and entry procedures, 292
Migrant health issues, 293–297
  mental health, 296–297
  occupational diseases, 296
  substance abuse, 296
Moll, Luis, xii
Monolingualism, 146
Myrdal, Gunnar, xix

National Center for Education Statistics, 240
National Center for Health Statistics (HCHS), 61, 64

Index   351

National Longitudinal Survey of
    Youth (NLSY), 43, 44, 74
National Survey of Family Growth
    (NSFG), 65, 68, 74
Nation at risk, xx
New Haven program, xx
Nicaragua and Nicaraguans, 160,
    169, 254
Non-Hispanic white youth, xi, 83
Non-Western (nonwhite) people, 218
North American Free Trade
    Agreement (NAFTA), 15
Nuyurican, 10

Orgullosas (prideful), 173

Parenting, 273
    Baumrind's model, 273–276
    child and adolescent outcomes,
        276–278
    Latino model, 275
Parsons, Talcott, 113
Patton, 175
Pensamientos (afterthoughts),
    333–337
Poverty, 31–35
    ironic, 41–43
    parental, 42
    persistent, 33
Precollege Latino students, 131–150,
    180
    at-risk, 155, 156, 158
    literacy, 149–150
    multicultural literacies, 131–150
    non-native Latino students, 131
    language use/ESL classes, 131,
        133–137, 140, 143, 145, 148
    regular students, 140
    social contexts/academic literacy
        132, 137–141
Problematization, xxii
Profiles of Student Life: Attitude and
    Behavior Questionnaire (ABQ),
    90, 91

Proposition, 15, 187
Pudor, 336
Puerto Rican, xiv, 67, 68, 85, 158,
    159, 163, 204, 250–251, 254,
    266, 272, 275
    family, 244, 246
    migration, 246
Puerto Ricans, 3, 64–65, 159, 173,
    191, 225, 245, 247, 267
Puerto Rico, 160, 161, 165, 166, 169,
    180, 190, 247, 251

Quality, xx
Quechuas, 11

Rand report on Latino education, 18
Raza (race), 1, 10, 115
Raza, La: Forgotten Americans
    (Sánchez, George), 115
Raza cósmica (cosmic race), xxvii
Respeto (respect), xxv, 239, 254–256,
    267–271, 280
Rodríguez, Clara, 155
Salvador, El, and Salvadorans, 159,
    160, 169, 180

Sexual activity, 83–102
    age, 90, 95, 97, 100, 101
    alcohol use, 90, 95, 97, 101
    attitudes, 70
    cumulative risk analysis, 96
    early sexual activity, 84–87
    engagement, 83, 102
    extrafamilial, 88
    gender role expectations, 70–71
    grade point average (GPA), 91, 95,
        97
    home alone, 92
    Latino adolescents, 83, 102
    logistic regression analyses, 96–97
    negative peer group pressure,
        91–92
    non-U.S. born, 63
    parental monitoring, 73, 87, 91, 100

Sexual activity (*continued*)
  physical abuse, 90, 94, 97, 100
  religion, 91, 95, 97
  risk factors, 63, 83–102
  school climate, 92, 95
  sexual intercourse average, 65
  suicide ideation, 91, 95, 97
  U.S. born, 63
  virgin v. nonvirgin status, 86
Sexual behaviors
  Acquired Immunodeficiency Syndrome (AIDS), 62
  adolescence, 61–77
  Alan Guttmacher Institute (AGI), 64, 74
  Belsky's model, 67
  biologic, social, and cultural factors, 66–71
  birth control, 73
  birth outcomes, 64
  Catholicism, 101
  cervical cancer, 61
  health care, 71
  health consequences of early sexual intercourse, 61–62
  heterosexual contact, 62–63
  Hispanic Health and Nutrition Examination Survey (HHANES), 64
  Human Immunodeficiency Virus (HIV), 62–63
  infertility, 62–63
  menstruation, 73
  National Center for Health Statistics (NCHS), 64, 65, 68
  National Council of La Raza (NCLR), 72
  preadolescence, 61–77
  pregnancy rates, 64
  preventive measures (pregnancy and STDs), 76

recommendations for research and practice, 74–77
sexual intercourse, 65, 73
sexually transmitted diseases (STDs), 62–63
Udry's model, 68–69
vulnerability, 71
Sizer, Ted, xx
Slavin, Robert
Snow, 143
South Americans, 3, 65, 191, 266
Spanish language, 13
Spener, 148
Stereotypes, 107
Suárez-Orozco, Marcelo, xxiv, 157–158, 190
Success, 188
  social construction, 189, 190
  students' definitions, 188–189
Swain, 145

Tejano, 10
Treaty of Guadalupe Hidalgo, 5, 109, 110

U.S. Constitution, 107

Value orientations, 113
Vasconselos, José, 10
Venezuelans, 192

Welfare dependency, 35–41, 54
  AFDC, 36–38, 43–51
  predicting, 47–51
  Women, Infants, Children (WIC), 55–56

Zapata, Emiliano, xxvii